# Summary of Contents

# Professional
# MTS and MSMQ
# with VB and ASP

**Alex Homer**
**David Sussman**

Wrox Press Ltd. ®

# Professional MTS and MSMQ with VB and ASP

**wrox**

Published by Wrox Press Ltd,
Arden House, 1102 Warwick Road, Acocks Green, Birmingham B27 6BH, UK.
Printed in Canada
7 8 9 TRI 00 99

ISBN 1-861001-46-0

## Trademark Acknowledgements

## Credits

**Authors**
Alex Homer
David Sussman

**Editors**
Jeremy Beacock
Jon Duckett

**Index**
Simon Gilks

**Cover**
Andrew Guillaume

**Technical Reviewers**
G. Andrew Duthie
Andy Enfield
Brian Francis
Rick Kingslan
Victor Mangasing
Krishnamurthy Srinivasan
Andrew Zack

**Design/Layout**
Frances Olesch

# About the Authors

## *Alex Homer*

Alex is a software consultant and developer, who lives and works in the idyllic rural surroundings of Derbyshire UK. His company, Stonebroom Software, specializes in office integration and Internet-related development, and produces a range of vertical application software. He has worked with Wrox Press on several projects.

## *David Sussman*

David Sussman is a developer, trainer and author currently living in Buckinghamshire. He seems to have found the perfect job where he can sit at home all day and then copy the contents of a help file and pretend he's just written it. One day soon he intends to acquire a more permanent home in a quiet rural village, stop working so hard, and get some form of social life.

I don't want this to sound like an Oscar speech but I want to thank some people. Everyone at Wrox, as this is the best job I've ever had. Especially Jeremy and Jon for correcting my appalling spelling and grammar. To Alex, who seemed to have written half of the book before I'd started coding . Also to Mum—I will find a place to live soon—honest.

But mostly to Jan - a few wise words express it all:

At thy side
Softly fly the golden hours
Ev'ry moment brings new rapture
Ev'ry care is lull'd to rest

# Table of Contents

# Introduction

Another year, another distributed application design methodology. Maybe this is what makes a programmer's life so exciting. If you've just finished building a Web site based around custom CGI applications, or a distributed database system with a Visual Basic interface, perhaps you ought to put this book back on the shelf before your stress levels go beyond critical.

Yes, Microsoft have decided it's 'all-change time' again, and have developed a new methodology for designing and building distributed applications. What's prompted this? Mainly it's the rapid rise in the influence of the Web–and the implementation of the associated protocols to existing networks, creating Intranets and Extranets. Once you take that big step outside the cozy confines of the office network lots of things just don't work, or at least don't work well. The new architecture, imaginatively named **Distributed interNet Applications** (DNA) Architecture, is designed to solve all of these problems.

## What Is This Book About?

This book is about DNA. However, DNA is a methodology, and you need to know more than just marketing-speak–you want the inside track on how it works, and (more importantly) how you can use it to build the distributed applications that your CEO is baying up a tree to get right now.

Implementing a DNA-based solution involves creating applications as separate tiers that can communicate between themselves. This itself is nothing new, but DNA provides standard protocols and pre-implemented interfaces which allow you to concentrate on building the logic into the system, without worrying about the plumbing that connects it all together.

And like plumbing in the more traditional sense, because they all use the same type and style of connector, the components in the tiers are often interchangeable between applications–and reusable in new applications. At last we are getting towards the object-oriented nirvana of computing that has been promised for so long, but stubbornly refused to appear in the real world.

# What Does This Book Cover?

This book not only covers the principles of DNA, but also shows how you implement each component in each tier, and how you get them to talk to each other and achieve the results you need. DNA in practice is based around a range of technologies that are now becoming available from Microsoft in final or near-final release forms. These are **Microsoft Transaction Server** (MTS), **Microsoft Message Queue Server** (MSMQ), and of course at the heart of it all **Microsoft NT Server** with **Internet Information Server** and **Active Server Pages**.

These technologies cover the server end of the process, and the plumbing used to communicate between the tiers of an application. Placed within these tiers are the logic components that implement business rules. At the client end is some type of interface that can interact with our application components, and turn the whole thing into a distributed application.

In the first two chapters of this book we look at the theory behind DNA, and see how the server end and the business rules components work. This provides you with a grounding in the individual elements that are involved in a distributed application. Then, in Chapter 3, we move on to look at the theory and practice of transactions within an application—and how we work with Microsoft Transaction Server.

Chapter 4 continues the construction of applications as a whole, showing how all the parts fit together. Our sample application implements a fictional retail car showroom system, where customers can browse lists of available vehicles and place an order with the vehicle manufacturer, who is located elsewhere.

In Chapters 5 to 7, we move on to consider the real-world scenario of less than 100% reliable Wide Area Networks (WANs), and how DNA copes with the concepts of delayed and remote transactions. This involves another new technology, Microsoft Message Queue Server.

In Chapter 8, we look at the security implications of the DNA master-plan, and see how we protect our applications from unwelcome visitors. Throughout the book, you'll see each of the techniques we discuss applied to our sample car showroom application.

Finally, in Chapter 9, we'll discuss going live on the Internet with your application.

# Who Is This Book For?

This book is designed for developers who are now building, or just starting to build, high performance and reliable web-based applications for a whole range of uses. It will also benefit those who want to learn more about the design and structure principles behind DNA as a whole.

DNA is very likely to become the cornerstone of Microsoft's Web and distributed application strategy in the coming months and years. Together with the new OLE-DB and ActiveX Data Objects (ADO) data access techniques, the whole package of tools and technologies is ready to be put to work. You just can't afford to be left behind.

# What You'll Need To Use This Book

This book assumes a working knowledge of basic web site construction techniques, HTML, Active Server Pages, and some Visual Basic. The aim is to provide you with concise and relevant reference material aimed directly at the subjects you want to learn about. So you won't find instructions on installing Windows NT, descriptions of what the HTML tags do, or VBScript and JavaScript syntax explanations.

To build applications like the one you'll see in this book yourself, you'll need to be running Microsoft **Internet Information Server 4** (IIS4) on either Windows NT or another supported platform—such as Personal Web Server running on Windows 9x. This automatically implements Active Server Pages version 2.0. IIS4 is available as part of the Windows NT4 Option Pack, or integrated with Windows NT5.

The Windows NT4 Option Pack and Windows NT5 include Microsoft's **Transaction Server** (MTS) and **Message Queue Server** (MSMQ), both of which are used in this book. MSMQ requires at least one Windows NT machine to be available, with SQL Server 6.5 or later installed and running. However, the remote machines that connect to MSMQ can be running Windows NT Workstation or Windows 9x.

Linking your machines, you will require a network that supports the TCP/IP or IPX protocols. We are using TCP/IP, which provides access across the Internet as well as a local network.

# Where you'll Find the Sample Code

Our prominent presence on the Web provides you with assistance and support as you use our books. Our Internet-related books (including this one) have a special site that provides examples, and allows you to download code to run on your own machine. This is at **http://rapid.wrox.co.uk**. You can also find a US based mirror of this site at **http://www.rapid.wrox.com**. Our main US-based site is at **http://www.wrox.com**, and it provides details of all our books. There is also a mirror site at **http://www.wrox.co.uk** that may be more responsive if you're accessing it from Europe.

# Conventions

We have used a number of different styles of text and layout in the book to help differentiate between the different kinds of information. Here are examples of the styles we use and an explanation of what they mean:

*Advice, hints, or background information comes in this type of font.*

---

**Important pieces of information come in boxes like this**

---

❑ **Important Words** are in a bold type font
❑ Words that appear on the screen in menus like the File or Window are in a similar font to the one that you see on screen
❑ Keys that you press on the keyboard, like *Ctrl* and *Enter*, are in italics
❑ Code has several fonts. If it's a word that we're talking about in the text, for example, when discussing the **For...Next** loop, it's in a bold font. If it's a block of code that you can type in as a program and run, then it's also in a gray box:

```
Set oCars = CreateObject("WCCCars.Cars")
    Set recCars = oCars.GetAll(RegistryRestore("Showroom", "Not Set"))
```

❑ Sometimes you'll see code in a mixture of styles, like this:

```
If IsMissing(ConnectionString) Then
        varConn = RegistryRestore("Showroom", "Not Set")
    Else
        varConn = ConnectionString
    End If
```

❑ The code with a white background is code we've already looked at and that we don't wish to examine further.

# Tell Us What You Think

We've worked hard on this book to make it useful. We've tried to understand what you're willing to exchange your hard-earned money for, and we've tried to make the book live up to your expectations.

Please let us know what you think about this book. Tell us what we did wrong, and what we did right. This isn't just marketing flannel: we really do huddle around the email to find out what you think. If you don't believe it, then send us a note. We'll answer, and we'll take whatever you say on board for future editions. The easiest way is to use email:

**feedback@wrox.com**

You can also find more details about Wrox Press on our web site. There, you'll find the code from our latest books, sneak previews of forthcoming titles, and information about the authors and editors. You can order Wrox titles directly from the site, or find out where your nearest local bookstore with Wrox titles is located.

## Customer Support

If you find a mistake, please have a look at the errata page for this book on our web site first.

If you can't find an answer there, tell us about the problem and we'll do everything we can to answer promptly!

Just send us an email to **support@wrox.com**.

# What Are Web Applications?

Microsoft is promoting their **Distributed interNet Applications** (DNA) architecture as a platform for developing fully distributed applications, but they haven't been having too much success at gaining wide recognition for it so far. Perhaps the problem is that it just sounds like marketing-speak. In fact DNA is not a solution in itself, but rather a methodology—and one that encompasses features which make it really useful, i.e.:

- ❑ DNA helps to design and build multi-tier client/server applications
- ❑ DNA provides client transparency
- ❑ DNA applications provide full transactional processing support
- ❑ DNA can be used to create applications that are fault tolerant
- ❑ in other words, DNA is ideal for distributed applications

In this chapter, we start by looking in more detail at what DNA is, where it came from, and why it can benefit us. We'll explain each of the features listed above, and see how we can take advantage of them in our own applications. You'll also briefly see the application around which this book is based, and which demonstrates how we can use the various components of DNA to create reliable and attractive Web and distributed applications.

So, this chapter covers:

- ❑ A look at what DNA actually is, and where it came from.
- ❑ What we need to consider when creating multi-tier applications.
- ❑ How a multi-tier approach using DNA makes design and development easier.
- ❑ An introduction to the application that we'll be building throughout this book.

To begin, then, what actually is DNA?

# What is DNA?

The first thing we need to do is get a discussion of the strange acronym that Microsoft has adopted for its new distributed application architecture out of the way. No, it has nothing to do with genetics, hybrids, and the meaning of life–and yes, it was probably chosen so that it sounds like it does. Maybe **DIA** doesn't have the same 'ring' to it as **DNA**. Ours is not to reason why; just to see if the **Distributed interNet Applications** really is as good as it's made out to be, and how we can use it in our applications.

❑ **DNA helps to design and build multi-tier client/server applications**

DNA provides a structured approach to creating applications whose components are clearly separated into distinct functional groups, with common communication protocols linking these groups. This provides the benefits of faster and less error-prone design and development, and interchangeability of components.

❑ **DNA provides client transparency**

No matter what the 'back end' of the application does, or how it does it, the front-end (or client) needs no knowledge of this. As long as it follows the DNA protocol and processing guidelines, the client can be almost anything–from a standard Web browser to a specially developed application written in almost any programming language.

❑ **DNA applications provide full transactional processing support**

In applications of any real level of complexity, multiple operations are performed at different levels of the application, and at different times. To guarantee integrity of the results, there needs to be control over each set of operations as a whole, as well as monitoring of every individual step. DNA, and the associated software plumbing components, can accomplish this almost transparently and seamlessly.

❑ **DNA can be used to create applications that are fault tolerant**

Even in today's world of reliable and high-availability communications, no network can ever be 100% guaranteed to give continuous and fast performance. A distributed application needs to be able to cope with network delays and software failures, while protecting data integrity and providing high availability and reliability.

❑ **DNA is ideal for distributed applications**

Once an application becomes distributed, i.e. divided into separate parts linked by a network, the problem of communication between the parts arises. In the past, developers have often had to create their own custom formats and techniques for passing information between each part of the application, leading to longer design and implementation periods, an increased number of bugs, and poor interoperability between different applications. By standardizing the communication protocols and interfaces, and by removing the need for the programmer to be concerned with the plumbing that connects each part, developer productivity and application reliability are (hopefully!) boosted.

Overall, the DNA methodology is really an umbrella term that covers many existing technologies to help us design and implement robust distributed applications. It visualizes this whole application as a series of tiers, with the client at the top and the data store at the bottom. The core of DNA is the use of **business objects** in a middle tier of the application, and this is supported by two new technologies: **Microsoft Transaction Server (MTS)**, which is a component manager offering full transaction support; and **Microsoft Message Queue Server (MSMQ)**, which provides the fault-tolerance required in a distributed application. Together with existing technologies, these make it simple to build into the DNA dream.

In DNA, business objects are implemented as software **components**. These components can be accessed by the client interface application or by another component, and can themselves call on other components, data stores, etc. Componentization of business rules brings many benefits, such as easier maintenance, encapsulation of the rules, protection of intellectual copyright, etc.

So, DNA is an approach to design that can speed up overall development time, while creating more reliable and fault tolerant applications that are easily distributable over a whole variety of networks. In this book, we're concentrating on the Internet, using TCP/IP as our protocol. However, as you'll see in later chapters, the components can just as easily be used with compiled applications specially written to follow the DNA principles.

Later in this chapter, we'll take a deeper look at DNA under the hood, and see what other benefits it offers to developers as well as those we are taking advantage of in our sample application.

# How Networks have Evolved

The next step is to understand the nature of the network that our applications must run on, and this will help you to see why DNA has developed along the routes it has. It will also help you to understand why DNA works the way it does, and the limitations that we face in the real world when we hand over our carefully crafted applications to the end user—and they promptly break them.

# Distributed Application Structure

The history of computing is littered with successful and not so successful networking architectures. Today we are seeing a new battle being fought, between the traditional networked PC and the new Network Computer (NC) architecture. Network operating systems themselves have also changed. Early Windows computers required add-on software to allow them to talk to each other, while the current Windows 95/98 and NT systems come complete with a whole range of integrated networking software.

However, going back even further (and this isn't going to be a history lesson), the foundations of modern computing were built on a networking system where all the processing power—and therefore the cost—was centralized on a server machine. The users had dumb terminals that communicated with the server, sending it simple instructions and getting back the results.

Over the years, with the fall in the cost of computing power, the processing started to migrate to the client end of the network, and in many situations the server became a simple file store. This is the networked environment that is so popular in many companies today. Users like this environment because response times tend to be quick, enabling them to have control over their machines and software, and they are a lot more independent from the central IT administrator.

Of course, the IT administrators are generally less keen on the idea, because it has been proven that this kind of distributed processing policy increases support costs and weakens company control over the applications and data formats that are used. This type of distribution also reduces the administrator's influence, although we would be the last to suggest that this kind of thing was important to any IT manager.

## *Distributed Client/Server Applications*

**Client/server** is a term that is often misunderstood when talking about networked applications. In its basic form, client/server is an approach that lets the processing tasks of an application be divided up so as to provide optimum efficiency. If there is oodles of spare power available on the client machine, it makes sense to do most of the processing there. However, if the company's requirements mean that only simple terminals are distributed across the enterprise, then the only place left to do the work is on the server–the client does no processing at all.

In reality, there's more to it than this of course. The processing itself can be divided up into different sub-tasks, such as the interface code, the business rules code, the database access code, and in between them the network operating system. This is generally referred to as an *n*-tier application. Good client/server application design depends on getting all the bits of the application onto the most efficient part of the system, in line with the requirements of security and availability.

As an example, a database access application falls naturally into four parts:

- ❑ The code for the interface that the user works with
- ❑ The business rules code that controls how the data is verified and manipulated
- ❑ The data access code, which is responsible for retrieving the requested data from the database, assembling it into the correct format, and storing the new data sent back from the client in the database
- ❑ The data store itself, which holds the information

If we are running a dumb terminal or **thin client** network, all but the interface code runs on the server (or more than one server–we may place the database and data access code on a separate machine from the server that does the business rules processing). This is very much the broad aim of the NC:

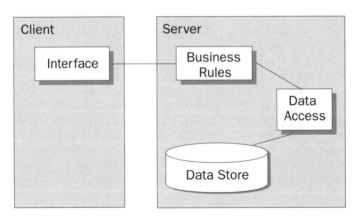

On the other hand, if we are running a **fat client** network, where the client has the power to carry out processing of the information, we would probably prefer to do a lot of the work there:

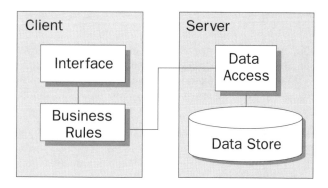

In this case, we do almost all the processing on the client, and just fetch data across the network from the server and return it when we're done with it.

## Distributed interNet Applications (DNA)

On the Internet, we have to adapt our traditional views of where the processing should take place. DNA provides a single solution to all our client/server problems. DNA provides a three-tier (or more) approach to application design, but in reality still follows the same broad pattern as existing client/server technologies. The difference is that it's designed with the Internet in mind, and can handle things that are traditionally difficult in this environment.

In particular it defines **business objects**, which carry out all the tasks of accessing back-end data and ensuring that transactions take place properly. In later chapters, we'll see how this comes about in terms of the code we write and the features of the operating system (such as Microsoft Transaction Server). For the meantime, what it means is that we should aim to create reusable objects that we can place on the server to carry out all the processing there—we're back almost to the dumb terminal network of the past:

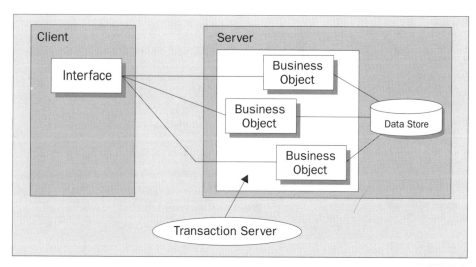

As you'll see later in this book, we often use business components on the client as well as the server. This introduces both advantages and disadvantages, and we'll be discussing this in more depth when we come to design and build some example applications.

### DNA Under the Hood

So far, our description and definition of DNA has been somewhat simplistic, aimed at showing how it applies when we come to build applications from components. In this section, we'll delve a little deeper to see what's under the hood. You don't need to know about this to use it, but familiarity with the architecture will make it easier to appreciate why it is so useful, and help you to make the most effective use of it.

# DNA Services

DNA centers around a set of **services** that are provided by Windows NT Server. These include both application and infrastructure services. The **infrastructure** services are provided by Windows NT Server itself, and consist of things like the Network service, the NT5 Active Directory service, the Remote File and Print service, the Security service and various other Component services that don't easily fall into one of these categories.

The **application** services are provided by components that are notionally separate from Windows NT, although integrated to work closely with it—such as:

| Application Services | Example |
|---|---|
| Database | Microsoft SQL Server |
| Java virtual machine | Microsoft JVM |
| Mail and collaboration service | Microsoft Exchange Server |
| Message queuing service | Microsoft Message Queue Server (MSMQ) |
| Scripting | Active Server Pages, Dynamic HTML, JScript, VBScript |
| Transaction service | Microsoft Transaction Server (MTS) |
| Universal data access | ADO, OLE-DB, ODBC, etc. |
| Web browser | Internet Explorer, or browser from other manufacturers. |
| Web server | Microsoft Internet Information Server (IIS) |

What DNA means is that each of these services provides a common and easily accessible interface through which other components and scripts can access them . There is no 'natural' language, and developers use whichever language best suits their particular requirements. And, because the interfaces are published and open, independent (non-Microsoft) suppliers can create components and services of their own which can 'plug into' NT Server.

## DNA and Scalability

The most important feature of DNA from our point of view is  scalability. This has long been a thorn in the side of Microsoft throughout the development of Windows NT. Their competitors use lack of scalability as the major argument against NT, but recent releases (including version 4.0) have proved able to handle huge numbers of users when the underlying hardware is up to the job.

Scalability is particularly important in a Web environment, where popular sites can attract thousands of visitors per day. It's a lot harder to plan capacity in this environment than on a local area network with a fixed number of users and a stable traffic pattern. To get round this, one of the new services supplied with Windows NT Server is the  Microsoft Transaction Server (MTS). As we'll see in later chapters, this can bring benefits to DNA-compliant applications in a number of different, and not always obvious, ways.

## The Other Benefits of DNA

Finally, the elements and services of Windows NT are designed to offer other special benefits:

- ❑ Lower cost of ownership through the Zero Administration for Windows (ZAW) initiative, where the Active Directory service controls how and when applications are installed on network clients, provides information about their use, and repairs them automatically if they get 'broken'.
- ❑ Transparent internal/external network connectivity, so that the Internet simply becomes an extension of the local network or  Intranet.
- ❑ A better 'disconnected' environment for mobile computer users, so that–for example–laptop users can connect when appropriate but still have all the necessary features available when they are not connected to the office network.
- ❑ Dynamic component utilization using a new technology called  **interception** that allows components to change their behavior dynamically as their environment changes.

These four features of DNA aren't particularly applicable to the aims of this book. We'll be concentrating on the networking and communication features of DNA, plus the overall application design model that it defines, and applying these to a Web-based distributed application.

# The Structure of DNA Applications

Microsoft publishes architecture diagrams that show the three level DNA  structure in its simplest terms. These usually label the three tiers as:

- ❑ User interface and navigation - the  **User Services** tier
- ❑ Business processes - the  **Business Services** tier
- ❑ Integrated storage - the  **Data Services** tier

We've seen these tiers described earlier, but notice the terminology used in the last one. One of the fundamental aims of DNA and associated technologies, as you'll see in the next section of this chapter, is concerned with access to data stores. While we generally think of these as databases , particularly relational databases such as SQL Server, Oracle, Sybase, etc., this is by no means the whole picture.

These days lots of useful information is stored in applications like email systems, spreadsheets, text documents, and—more recently—directory services. Microsoft talk about Universal Data Access, a series of drivers and interfaces designed to provide a way to get at all these kinds of data and more, such as specialist format files, geospacial position data, non-standard scientific data, etc.

## A Typical Web Data Access Application

The use of common communication protocols, and the availability of an array of services, are probably the two biggest advantages that DNA offers to the Web developer. For example, if we use the ActiveX Data Objects component to access a data store, we can do it using any scripting language supported by the component host. It doesn't matter whether the component is hosted by a Web browser, a custom application (written in Visual Basic, C++, Delphi, or any other suitable language), or the Web server itself.

For example, we can host components on the client and use them to communicate with the Web server directly. An example might be using an ActiveX control that displays streamed video or sound, or simply client-side Dynamic HTML scripting that updates the page content without any server interaction required:

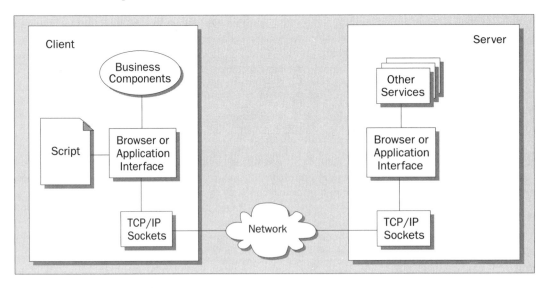

*Components hosted on the client.*

Alternatively we might host the components only on the server and send plain HTML to a browser, or send formatted data to an application that just displays it. The HTML or data could be created dynamically by a custom component or by an ASP script on the server:

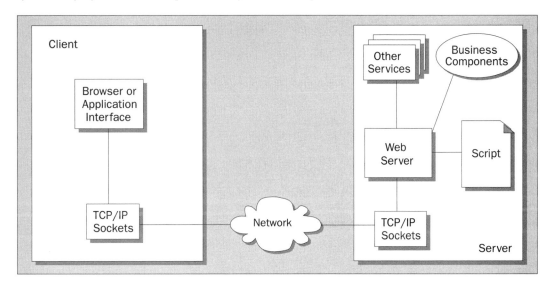

*Components hosted on the server*

And, of course, we could use a combination of the two approaches, by sharing the components between the client and server. This could be the case where we generate data dynamically on the server but process it again before displaying it on the client, for example.

The same applies to the services that DNA makes available to us. One standard protocol is TCP/IP, which we can use over almost any kind of network, including of course the Internet–which is based solely on TCP/IP. This means that, theoretically, the various components of our application can be distributed almost anywhere on the network so as to achieve the efficiency, reliability, and performance we require.

A typical three-tier data access application could look like the diagram on the next page, with all the services relevant to our sample application shown:

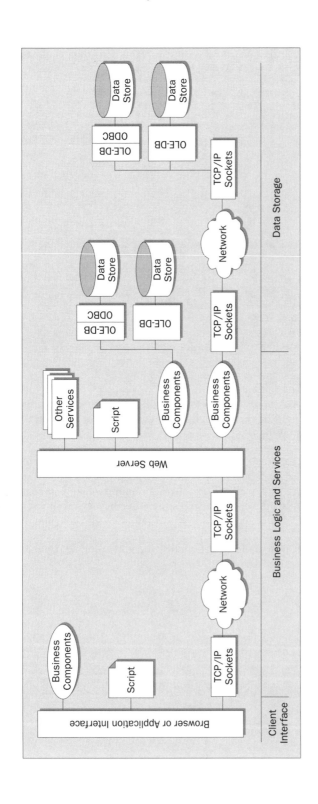

Here, the client and the Web server communicate over a standard network with TCP/IP and the HTTP Web protocol as the common format. At the same time, the Web server can talk to a back-end data store using TCP/IP as well. As you can see from this, changing the data source is simply a matter of changing the IP address and making sure that the correct OLE-DB drivers are set up.

*In Windows NT5 and the NT4 Option Pack, all database communication is done through an appropriate OLE-DB driver such as the one available for SQL Server. When you set up an ODBC data source, you are in fact using an OLE-DB driver that talks to the ODBC driver— which itself talks to the data source. New OLE-DB drivers are appearing all the time which will remove the need for an ODBC driver in many cases.*

### The Benefits of Componentization

What's more important in many situations, however, is how you modify and update the business logic in an application. This is one of the real strengths of the DNA plan. Business rules and application processing logic will usually be wrapped up inside components that run in the 'middle tier', which can be on either the client or the server. These components expose standard and custom interfaces that are used by the other components and services in the application.

This means, of course, that we can change the component internally and thereby change the way it implements the rules. We can even replace it with a whole new component, perhaps one written in a different language to get better performance. As long as the component's interfaces remain the same, the other services and components will continue to work with them just as before.

We'll be looking at components in depth in the next chapter, and there you'll see other ways in which componentization benefits our applications in the design, implementation and maintenance phases.

# Designing Web Applications

In the previous sections of this chapter, we've discovered some of the limitations that the Web places on our applications, and the way that DNA evolved as a design methodology to make developing Web applications easier. In this section of the chapter, we'll look in more detail at two particular areas that are encompassed by DNA– optimizing performance and data access strategies.

Most distributed applications are required to implement some form of data access. In our sample applications in this book, which revolve around a fictional retail car company, we must be able to access the showroom's local database to get information about the available vehicles, and to store an order. We also need to be able to access a remote database to place an order for the vehicle with the manufacturer.

# Optimizing for Network Performance

All this new architecture is fine, but if we all have Pentium-based computers on our desk, why should it be a problem to do more of the processing on the client? After all, most PCs connected to the Internet have plenty of power to spare. It's here that we need to consider the environment of the Web more thoroughly:

❑  The Internet is a cross-platform and vendor-neutral environment. Except within the confines of an Intranet, you have no control over which client application your users are viewing your pages with.

❑  Again with the exception of a corporate  Intranet or local network, the bandwidth available between the client and the server is a factor of 10, 100, or even 1000 times less than that we are used to.

❑  Network reliability is generally a lot lower than on a local area network. On top of this, the TCP/IP and HTTP protocols in current general use don't provide for a persistent connection that automatically identifies the client to the server.

❑  Finally, security issues mean that the application must be designed to limit anonymous user's access to data or business rules where they are sensitive or confidential.

The result is that the decision on how to spread the processing load  depends more on the nature of the network than on the actual hardware located at each end. While you can easily upgrade your office network by throwing money at it, this isn't an option for applications that must exist on, and perform across, the Internet.

## Controlling Network Traffic

To see how we make the most of limited network bandwidth, we have to understand how the client and server interact to create the results and present them to the user. The usual techniques for limiting bandwidth in your static pages, such as  minimizing graphic size and  color depth, still apply. As far as the data content is concerned, however, it really all comes down to the database access technology we decide to implement.

### Thin Client Data Retrieval

If we decide to place just the interface code on the client, in line with the thin client approach to network architecture, all we need to send to the client is a standard HTML page containing the results. OK, so we'll create the page dynamically on the server using some kind of scripting or executable program, but all the client sees is plain HTML. This keeps the network traffic down to the same level as an equivalent static page, but means that each time the user wants to see a different set of data, or change the way it's presented, they must submit another request to the server. Hence bandwidth requirements can increase dramatically as the application is used.

### Fat Client Data Retrieval

The alternative is to send the complete set of data to the client at the start of the application, and let the client manipulate it to their hearts content. Now we probably have a much larger initial download, but a lot fewer requests afterwards. This is the fat client approach we talked about earlier. This technique also means that we can effectively deliver the data and then forget about the client– remember that at present HTTP doesn't provide a connection that automatically identifies the user, so having to remember which page they had last time, and which one they need next, adds an extra layer of complexity.

There is, in fact, a third approach which blends the benefits of the two we've looked at here. You'll see more about this later in the chapter, after we've examined the first two alternatives in more detail.

# Choosing a Data Access Technology

In this section, we'll look at how we can choose which kind of database access technology is the most suitable for our applications. We've seen how there are two basic approaches to designing a data access application for the Web: the thin client approach, using just an interface on the client and doing all the work in the server, and fat client architectures such as the networked PC.

## Going Down the Thin Road

The thin client architecture is the one that is currently used almost exclusively on the Web at present for accessing server-side databases. If you've used the ISQL (or ISQLw) applications that are supplied with SQL Server, you'll have seen how this works in a traditional network environment. ISQL is a simple interface application that allows you to enter SQL statements and send them to a SQL Server.

Instead of requesting the entire contents of a table and extracting information on the client, you can provide a query that just returns the data you need. The query processing is done on the server, and only the results are sent back over the network to be displayed within ISQL. And because you can define an ODBC driver connection to a SQL Server database across the Internet, ISQL can be used to access a SQL Server database from a remote location, outside the confines of the office network.

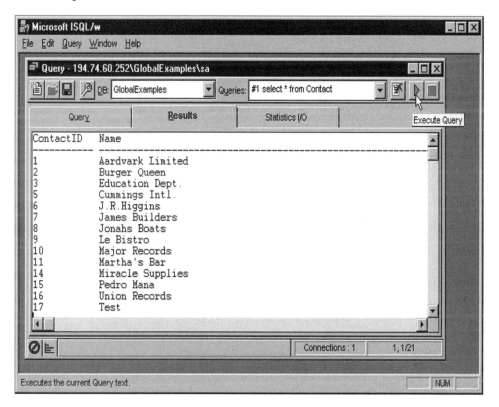

On the Web, we see the same technique in use. The browser requests a Web resource, often providing query information such as a SQL string or the name of a stored procedure. The results are extracted from a data store and assembled into an HTML page on the server, then sent back to the browser. If it's an application where you can update the information, the data will probably be displayed in HTML form controls:

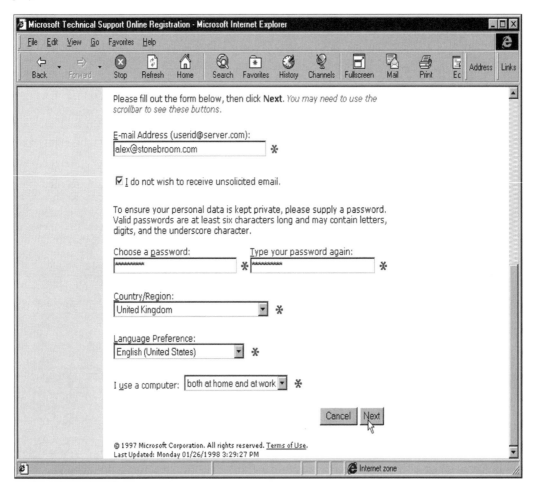

## Server-side Scripts and Applications

All this data retrieval, processing, and assembling of the results into a Web page is done on the server, by a script or some kind of executable program. Originally these would have been   Perl or maybe IDC scripts, or specially designed custom ISAPI applications that have access to the Web server. On Windows-based servers, however, many users are already switching to   **Active Server Pages** (ASP).

ASP is a highly flexible, extensible, and easy to master scripting environment that combines HTML and scripting code into the same page. By using appropriate   **Active Server Components**, in particular the **ActiveX Data Objects** component (ADO–the preferred data access technology for DNA), we can easily access any data store for which suitable ODBC or OLE-DB drivers are available. We can even create our own data access components that use the lower-level OLE-DB interface to access almost any other source of data, or provide extra functions that existing drivers or ADO don't support. Microsoft is currently working on a technology called **Universal Data Access** that will allow OLE-DB to automatically find ways to connect to all kinds of existing data stores.

However, ADO is not just a component, but a whole structured series of objects that provide a very powerful way to manipulate data using simple scripting techniques. ADO is at the heart of several Microsoft data access technologies, so you need to know about it for lots of reasons—not just to use Active Server Pages.

> *You can find out more about ASP in detail from our sister book* Professional Active Server Pages Programming, *ISBN 1-861001-26-6. There are also numerous articles and examples of ASP programs on the Microsoft* SiteBuilder *network* **(http://www.microsoft.com/workshop/server)**. *Also check out the* MSDN *site* **(http://premium.microsoft.com/msdn/library)** *for technical articles. Our Web site at http://rapid.wrox.co.uk includes links to many other non-Microsoft ASP-related sites such as the ASP Alliance (* **http://www.aspalliance.com**).

### The Downside of Active Server Pages

ASP can provide all the data manipulation features we need to provide a thin client environment over the Web. However, it suffers from one major problem—it requires a fast and reliable connection to get anywhere near the kind of interactivity users are accustomed to on their local network. For example, if they are working with a desktop database application like Microsoft Access, they will almost certainly expect to be able to scroll up and down through a set of records on a form or in a table. In general there should be no excessive delays while the records are fetched from the tables in the server's backend database.

In our ASP-based database running over the Web, however, each time users need to view more data, or change the way it's sorted or filtered, a new page must be generated on the server and transmitted over the network. None of the data is cached locally on the client. Even on a good day, when the Internet is performing well, delays of several seconds between each new page can be the norm.

## Taking the Fat Road

The alternative, as we've seen, is to abandon the thin client approach and store the complete recordset on the client. Now, the client can manipulate the data and the user gets instant updates on their screen. However, if they are only going to view a particular record, this method is inappropriate as well. If the dataset contains 5,000 records, a long wait for the whole lot to arrive is inevitable. If they only want to view or update one of the records, we're wasting bandwidth in a huge way.

But there are times when it is appropriate to send all the data to the client. If it's a small recordset, or if they will be doing a lot of work with it, it may be appropriate to send it all in one go and then let the client get on with it. Our server, and our share of Internet bandwidth, can then be used to supply data to another user without having to keep coming back to service this user again.

### Providing State Information

Up until recently, there has been no obvious way to build fat client database applications on the Web. The reasons include the fact that it's generally thought to be an inappropriate approach that hogs bandwidth and performs poorly, and because the connection between the client and server over HTTP is not persistent.

On a traditional network, using Microsoft Networking or Novell NetWare, the server knows which clients are logged in and connected all the time. This knowledge can be passed on to applications running on the server, so it can provide data caching and other services to that client as required. This is often referred to as **state** information.

*The proposed changes to the HTTP specifications will allow applications to implement state over the Web, but at present its use is not widespread. Active Server Pages also contain features that can provide state information automatically for a Web application.*

In the context of a desktop database application, the following diagram broadly demonstrates how the persistent connection between the client and server makes it possible to provide cached dynamic and updateable recordsets on the client:

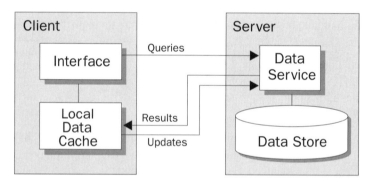

The client has suitable software installed to negotiate with the data service software component on the server on an ongoing basis, through a connection to a particular data store on the server. The server's data service software provides all or part of the results to the client where it is cached locally, and the interface can then display the relevant data. The client cache is automatically filled with the next set of records as required, and this happens in the background while the user is working with the data. The client software can also pass data updates back to the data service on the server, and instruct it to update the original data.

### Introducing Remote Data Services

In Internet Explorer 4, Microsoft have introduced a new technology called **Remote Data Services** (RDS). This aims to get around the problems we've discussed–the lack of state information, and Active Server Pages' requirements for regular repeated connections to the server and consequent delays in the presentation of data. RDS is currently implemented through client-side components, which can be used in any programming language that supports ActiveX controls.

In its simplest implementation, RDS allows a delimited text file containing the source data to be sent to the client in its entirety, and cached locally. The contents of the file can then be attached to

HTML elements and controls in a Web page ; and the user can view, sort, filter and generally manipulate the data with no further connection to the server being required. On a dial-up link, they can even drop the connection and continue to work with the data.

However, this is only a half-way solution. The second implementation of RDS is through a different ActiveX component on the client, inserted into a Web page, that creates a persistent connection with a data store on the server over the HTTP network link. It downloads data in blocks, rather than all in one go, and caches this locally. As the user pages through the data, the next block is fetched from the server in the background. When they want to scroll back, filter, or sort the data, there is no need to go across the network to fetch it all again.

On top of this, because RDS provides state synchronization between the server-based data and the client-side cached recordset, it's possible to update the data on the client and flush these changes back to the server in one batch—helping to reduce bandwidth requirements. It also means that changes made to the data on the server by other users can be reflected in the client-side cached recordset automatically.

As you can see, this is a huge improvement over the other techniques we've looked at. Remote Data Service works very much like the desktop database application we looked at in the previous section—providing fast response while minimizing network traffic.

### The Downside of Remote Data Services

But of course, there are downsides to even this technology. To use RDS, you have to meet a lot more environmental requirements than when using ASP. One point we mentioned earlier in the chapter is that (unless we are confining our application to an Intranet or local network) we have to build it in such a way as to be compatible with many different client systems. Using ASP, all the work is done on the server. The browser is even kind enough to identify itself when it requests data, so we can build appropriate pages and send back one which we know is suitable.

With RDS, we need to have an environment that is a lot more controlled. Currently only Windows NT4 (with the Option Pack) and NT5 provide the drivers that support it. Secondly, the only client-side control objects that can connect to RDS (at the time of writing) are ActiveX controls from Microsoft. These are supplied with Internet Explorer 4, and are automatically installed on the client. They won't work with other manufacturer's browsers, but the client object specification is open—so other manufacturers can build client-side objects that will work with RDS. Microsoft supply a Java-based control that allows some features of the technology to be used universally.

> You can find out more about programming with Remote Data Services from our sister book Professional IE4 Programming, ISBN 1-861000-70-7. Also look out for the forthcoming book Professional ASP and RDS Database Programming, ISBN 1-861001-64-9.

# Putting It All Together

Having looked at the theory of DNA and the different ways that our applications can access data, we're now ready to see how we actually use the technologies we've discussed—and build whole applications that follow this new methodology. In the following chapters, we'll examine each of the areas that DNA defines in turn, concentrating especially on the 'middle tier', where all the real processing work is done.

You'll recall from our list of features at the beginning of this chapter that DNA not only defines the overall design of the application's structure, but also the way that each layer and each component in that layer communicates with the other layers and components. As long as we design our components to meet the DNA guidelines, we can ignore the internal workings of the communication system.

What's important is the way the DNA concept makes us think about how we divide up our application, how we distribute it over the client and available servers, and how we implement reusable components in an efficient and reliable manner.

## So DNA Is Just Software Jigsaws?

You might even think of DNA as being like a jigsaw. Each piece slots into the rest so that, when complete, you have an application that appears to be a seamless whole—but underneath is a series of individual and reusable components. To connect components together we generally use Active Server Pages script running on the server. This is Microsoft's 'universal glue' that binds the whole thing together. It allows us to use existing objects as well a custom-designed ones, and mix and match to create fully working applications quickly and easily.

Want data access? Plug in an ADO component. Want to implement a secret business formula to provide results to users? Build a custom component using Visual Basic, C++, Java, or Delphi. Want to send messages to users? Go out and buy an email component. It as easy as that. Windows automatically looks after how each one talks to your ASP script, and how they communicate with each other.

That's not to say that we *have* to ignore what happens under the hood, however. Like all major Windows applications, DNA applications take advantage of Microsoft's **Component Object Model** (COM and the more recent COM+) technology to provide the low-level communication between software components. COM is a standard way of implementing interfaces that can be accessed directly in languages like C++ and Java. If there are functions available in the component that you want to use, but which are not exposed to ASP, you can access them in your chosen language instead. You can even wrap one or more existing components up in a new wrapper, and expose their functions in different ways.

But this is enough generality. What you want to do is get down to building applications of your own, and this is what we'll be doing in the remainder of this book. The chapters are based around the components of our sample application, and we'll finish off this chapter with a quick tour of this so that you are familiar with it.

# The Sample Applications

The main sample applications for this book implement systems based around a fictional car company. Customers can browse lists of available vehicles and place an order with the local showroom, which is then passed on to the vehicle manufacturer who is located elsewhere. It's called the Wrox Car Company, and you can try out the applications yourself either on our server at `http://rapid.wrox.co.uk/books/1460/`, or by downloading the sample files from the same address and installing them on your own machines. Instructions on setting it up are included in the download file.

The application itself is highly customized to demonstrate many of the ways that DNA and its associated technologies can be used. However, the principles of each technology are documented, and can be easily applied to your own applications.

# The Wrox Car Company

The fictional Wrox Car Company has a showroom where they display new cars for customers to browse and test drive. However, as in all car showrooms, they can't stock all the variations of model, engine size and color that are available—in fact not even the manufacturer has all combinations available from stock. Where the car is not available from showroom stock, an order is placed directly with the manufacturer. They will confirm the order and provide manufacturing progress and delivery details to the showroom.

We've created a range of interfaces for the Wrox Car Company application. The showroom has interfaces for placing orders and monitoring order confirmations constructed in both HTML, for use in a Web browser, and Visual Basic as an executable application. There's also a Visual Basic application for use in the head office, and a browser-based application for use on the Web to persuade people to order their new car from the comfort of their own home.

## The Car Showroom System

The showroom has a computer system that the salesmen can use to look up details of cars that are available, and check out the valid combinations of colors. For example, the most popular colors for the discreet sedan edition of the Wrox Mesij Q are silver and black. It's not available in pink , yellow or red like the high-performing Wrox Emtee S Sport or the popular soft-top Wrox Hardy S Coupe.

The showroom can also use the computer system to calculate the payments for a range of finance options, as well as storing details of customer's orders for future reference and handling of later inquiries about delivery. This is how the Visual Basic version of the interface looks, showing a list of available cars and providing simple facilities to calculate the finance terms:

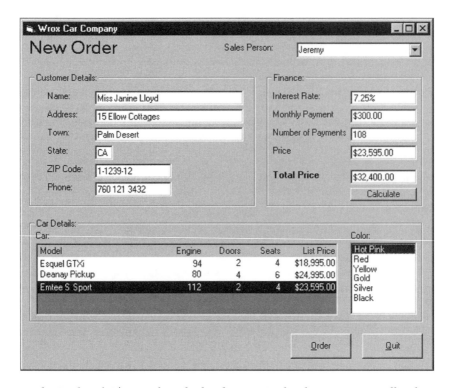

When an order is placed, it's stored on the local server in the showroom, as well as being sent to the manufacturer's head office. An order monitoring interface allows the showroom staff to check on the confirmation and anticipated delivery date of each vehicle:

## The Manufacturer's Head Office

The manufacturer's head office is the hub of all showrooms. It collects the orders, consolidates figures, supplies the vehicles, etc. Here, the staff have a different set of applications. The main application receives the order from the showroom and sends an acknowledgement back once the order has been placed. If it's out of stock, the anticipated delivery date can be entered once it is known:

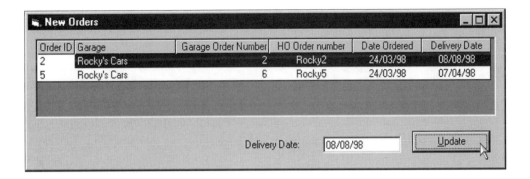

## The Public Web Application

Finally, we'll take advantage of the increasing acceptance of e-commerce on the Web by allowing prospective customers to view our cars on the Web, and place an order with the showroom directly. OK, so we're perhaps pushing frontiers here, but it may well become the accepted way to order your new car in the future. This is one of the pages from our public Web application, showing details of the Wrox Hardy S Coupe:

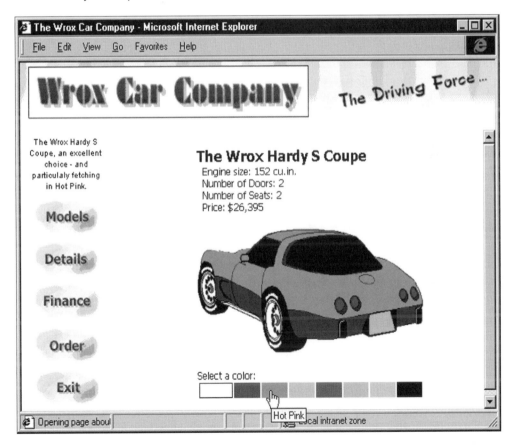

If a customer wants to know about finance options, a separate page can calculate the payments required. This page uses both client-side ActiveX controls and Remote Data Services to build up the quotation:

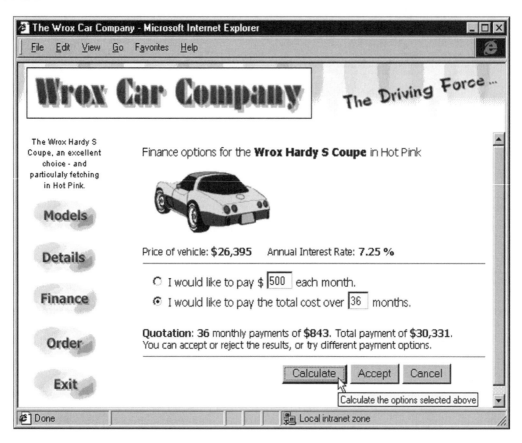

## Application Considerations

The application you've seen in use here is a relatively simple one, designed to provide you with a direct example of all the technologies involved in creating a DNA application—but without filling it with unnecessary clutter. You should be able to see that it raises a whole range of issues that we'll have to be able to deal with in a distributed application. For example:

❑ How do we implement the data stores on the local showroom server and the remote manufacturer's server?

❑ How do we implement the communication between the showroom and the manufacturer?

❑ When we come to use the application, what happens if the car is not in stock at the showroom?

❑ How do we ensure that data integrity is maintained when placing an order that has to go to two places (the local system and the manufacturer)?

❑ What happens if the car is not available from the manufacturer after we've accepted an order?

❑ What happens if we place an order while the network between us and the manufacturer is down?

❑ What happens when we want to query delivery dates and the network between us and the manufacturer is down?

❑ What happens if the network fails in between placing an order and receiving the acknowledgement?

There's probably a bunch more of interesting questions that you could come up with, such as what happens if someone is prepared to pay for a non-standard combination of features but that vehicle isn't listed as being available at all? After all someone, somewhere, must want to buy a Wrox Mesij Q Sedan in pink. We'll be addressing all these questions (except why people might want to buy a pink car) in the later chapters of this book.

# Summary

In this chapter we've examined what a Web application is, what it looks like under the hood, and the background to using Windows **Distributed interNet Applications**(DNA) to build these kinds of applications.

We found that the DNA methodology provided ways to use new and existing technologies to our advantage, for example:

❑ DNA helps us to design and build multi-tier client/server applications

❑ DNA provides client transparency

❑ DNA applications provide full transactional processing support

❑ DNA can be used to create applications that are fault tolerant

DNA itself is a way of visualizing the combination of new (and some not-so-new) concepts that make up a distributed application, including several new services. Some of these are designed to reduce the total cost of ownership of networked PCs, but others such as Microsoft Transaction Server (MTS) and Microsoft Message Queue Server (MSMQ) provide real benefits when building distributed applications. We'll be concentrating on these two services throughout the book, and seeing how they make the task of building robust, efficient, scalable and reliable distributed applications much easier.

Another area where DNA really interests us is the way it helps to conceptualize the division of the application into three distinct layers–the interface, the business rules, and the data storage layers. In this chapter we've seen how these ideas pan out in the real-world, and how they have developed both from earlier client/server techniques and the special needs of an Internet-based application.

The final part of DNA that provides a real advantage in designing Web applications is the standardized communication protocols and interfaces that it defines. This means that componentization of the business rules in the middle tier can speed design, implementation, and maintenance. This is the main topic of the next chapter, where we'll build some components for use in our sample application.

# Building and Using Components

In the previous chapter, we looked at the principles and concepts of the Microsoft **Distributed interNet Applications** architecture (DNA), and the way that it helps us to conceptualize the design and implementation of distributed applications as a series of separate tiers (or layers). The first tier is the user interface, which is generally a Web browser but could just as well be (as in this book) a custom application created with a language like C++, Java, Visual Basic or Delphi.

Set against this is the data storage tier, which holds data in a variety of formats, together with the appropriate drivers and data access objects that allow it to be accessed by our applications. However, as you'll have seen in the previous chapter, all the real programming work within a distributed application goes on in the middle tier. Here the **business rules** are implemented by a series of **components**.

So what is a component? What does it all mean? In this chapter we explain what exactly a component comprises, and where and how components can be used. We'll take an overview of components, and see how they can be implemented in a variety of ways.

So, in this chapter, we'll discover:

- ❑ What components are, and why they are so useful in our applications
- ❑ How we can create our own components, and the different ways this can be done
- ❑ How we use components as part of our applications on the client and the server

If you're wondering where the two headline topics for this book, Microsoft Transaction Server and Microsoft Message Queue Server, come into the picture—please be patient. Until you have a good understanding of the principles of componentization, you won't be able to take full advantage of these two technologies.

# What Are Components?

We've used the word **component**, and the phrase **business rules**, regularly in the previous chapter of this book, and it's time we delved a bit deeper into what they actually mean. Traditionally, applications have been written either as single executable files or as a group of files. Before Windows these files were often all part of a single application. In other words, each application came with all the code required to make it operate. This is often described as a **monolithic** application.

## Application Code As Components

In Windows and other modern graphical operating systems this kind of programming is no longer necessary, for several reasons. The most obvious is that the basic services required by all applications, such as creating screen windows, writing to the disk, and processing mouse and keyboard events, are built into the operating system. An excellent example is the standard Windows file **comdlg32.dll** that is installed in your **system** or **system32** directory. This provides the routines to create and process the File | Open, File | Save and several other dialogs used by all standard Windows applications. Using code component files like this allows applications to share commonly used code routines.

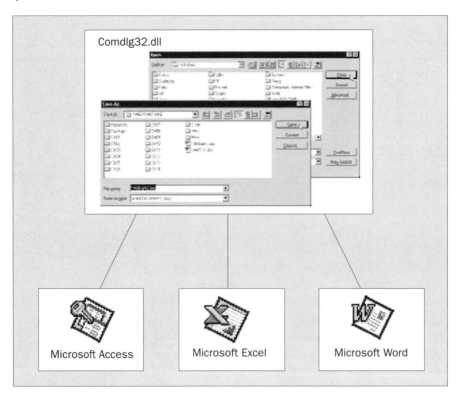

Applications can use these operating system routines rather than implementing their own versions. (In fact, in Windows NT, they often have no choice because only the built-in operating system routines have direct access to the hardware—so you have to take advantage of some pre-built operating system code even if you implement your own dialogs). This doesn't, however, mean that applications don't come with their own separate components and other files as well.

## Dynamic Link Library Components

We're all familiar with the way that many Windows applications scatter a heap of strangely named files all over the hard disk when you install them. These are generally **Dynamic Link Library** files (DLLs) or, sometimes, system-only executables (EXEs). They contain the separate code routines that the main executable file needs to function, but which are not part of the operating system.

How the code in a component like this is used varies. As you'll see later on, a component can implement a visible control, perform a business function, or just provide a library of hidden functions to applications that use it. The main system functions within Windows itself are implemented in a set of component files. Examples in Windows 95 are **krnl386.exe**, **gdi.exe**, and **user.exe**. These provide an **Application Programming Interface** (API) through which any application can perform standard system routines such as accessing disks, writing to the screen, and responding to the keyboard and mouse.

## ActiveX Control Components

A more relevant comparison is to the controls provided with Windows programming languages like Visual Basic and C++. These are often **OLE Control Extension** files (OCXs), although they can equally well be implemented as DLLs (internally the two are much the same—the distinction is really just in the file name). The term used to describe them is **ActiveX Controls** (OLE has now officially been retired as a name for controls, though it lives on in things like OLE-DB and in the realm of Compound Documents).

Many control components are also included with Internet Explorer and other applications. For example Microsoft Office and Visual Basic install a file named **mscal.ocx** on your system. This implements the Calendar control that can be inserted into your own applications:

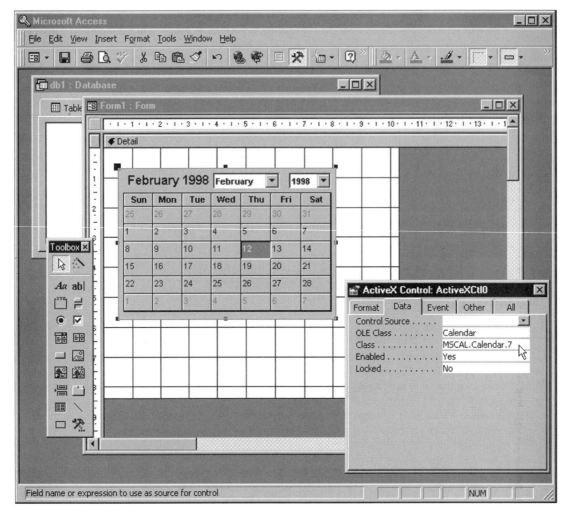

OCX files are often used to distribute components over the Internet. When you open a page in Internet Explorer that requires a control that isn't already available on your system, the browser goes out and fetches the component file from the URL defined in the page, and installs it if your browser security settings allow. You'll see more of how this is done later in the chapter. A range of ActiveX controls are available on the Web, from Microsoft's own Web site and from many hundreds of other sites. Check out the links on our Web site at **http://rapid.wrox.co.uk** for more details.

## How Windows Tracks Installed Components

Windows keeps track of which components are installed on your system using the Registry. This contains the **Class ID** (Class identifier) for each component, which uniquely identifies it. The Class ID is referred to in the registry as CLSID. The value is a globally unique identifier (GUID), which is generated automatically and is guaranteed to be unique for the component:

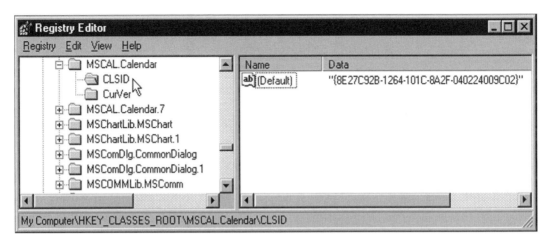

The Registry can also list the components 'the other way round': by Class ID, showing the name of the component, the file on disk that implements it, and other information required by Windows to initialize and use the component's routines:

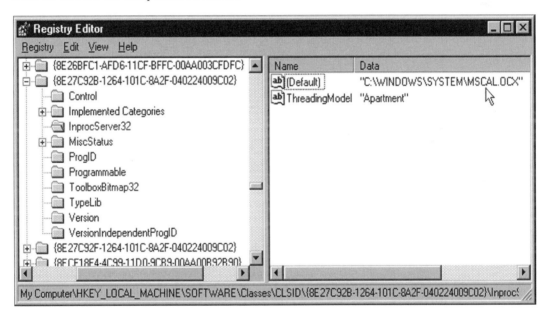

All this looks horrendously complicated, and may put you off starting to create your own components. However, the programming environments we use look after much of this complexity automatically, as you'll see when we come to build our own components later in this chapter.

## Business Logic Components in DNA

All of the components we've looked at so far are either parts of executable applications or controls that provide extra features to existing applications. However, we've also talked about implementing the 'logic' required by our applications–the **business rules**–as components. In fact, this isn't that different to the way that application code in function library DLLs is already used. What really differs is the way that the components expose their functions to the outside world. We'll look at three aspects of business rules components in this section:

- ❑ What are business rules?
- ❑ How rules can be implemented in components.
- ❑ How the component talks to the outside world.

## What Are Business Rules?

Many components, such as the Calendar control we saw earlier, are designed to add functionality to applications. They often have their own visible user interface, and remain active for long periods while the user interacts with them. When we talk about business rules, however, we're discussing a totally different concept of how the component is used.

All applications perform specific functions regularly, and have to comply with a set of constraints. For example, a data management application would need to have routines that fetched data from the data store, perhaps selecting data that matches particular criteria. It would probably also need ways of updating the data in a specific way, and controlling the changes that are returned to the data store. In terms of constraints, the application may be required to limit some functions to certain users, and some values of the data to within certain parameters.

As a different example, you can imagine that our sample Wrox Car Co application will require some particular business rules to be implemented. It must have a way of finding out whether a vehicle is in stock, what colors are available, and what the monthly payments would be. It must also have routines that can validate and store order details on both the local showroom and the remote head office databases.

All these are business rules. It's important to note that they are not limited to just applying *rules* in the ordinary sense of the word. In fact, a better description is business *functions*, or business *logic*. Our components will carry out a range of functions , so as to achieve the results required by our application.

## How Components Provide Business Rules

Once we think about the tasks we need to achieve as functions, it's not hard to see how we can encapsulate them into components. After all, in some ways, programmers have been doing this for years. We make our code easier to write, understand and debug by separating sections of it out into separate subroutines and functions (depending on the language in use). We can call these routines from elsewhere in our code at any time, and pass them any parameter values required.

In essence, this is how a component provides business rules and functions in DNA. For example, if we want to know how many payments a customer needs to make on a car, when they tell us how much they can afford per month and we know the standard rate of interest on credit payments, we can create a code function to do the work for us—this sample is Visual Basic code:

```
Function GetNumberPayments(CostOfCar, InterestRate, MonthlyAmount)
    '... code here to calculate the results, then return
    '... the result at the 'value' of the function
    GetNumberPayments = CalculatedResult
End Function
```

Every time our application needs to calculate the number of payments we can call this function, supplying the appropriate values for the parameters:

```
...
NumberMonths = GetNumberPayments(12000, 1.25, 180)
...
```

Instead of including this code directly in with the rest of our application we can create a component that includes the function, and then install it on our system, and call it using the appropriate syntax–you'll see more about this later on:

```
Dim FinanceObject As New WCCFinance.PaymentTerms 'the component
NumberMonths = FinanceObject.GetNumberPayments(12000, 1.25, 180)
...
```

Now that our function is in a separate component, we can use it over and over again in different applications. It also becomes a 'black box', in that other programmers don't have to know how it works–they only need to know the component name (so that they can  initialize it), and how to interface with it (i.e. the syntax of the **GetNumberPayments** function).

If we later decide to implement the component in a different language, or change the way the calculation is done, all the programs that use it will automatically use the new version. Neither users nor other programmers need be concerned what happens inside our black box. Of course, there is one limitation to this. If we change the actual interface (or even the object's class name or class identifier), programs that use it will almost definitely fail to work properly. To see why, we'll take an overview of how components communicate with each other.

### How Components Expose Their Interface

DNA takes advantage of the standard way that all the elements involved in building applications can talk to each other. Any part of an application can use the services provided by any component. As this isn't a COM programming book, we'll just cover the basics here to help you understand how it works in outline. The great thing with DNA, of course, is that you don't  *need* to know all the 'under the hood' details. However, as with all programming issues, it is very useful to have at least a basic grasp of what's going on.

Microsoft's **Component Object Model** (COM) definition (and the forthcoming COM+ definition which adds extra features that reduce the amount of work required to build components) provide a standard way for any code component to expose details about its interface to the outside world. This is achieved through a set of standard functions that the component must implement internally. By calling these functions, another component or application gets all the details it needs about the functions that the first component contains, and how to use them.

This interface description is often provided as a **type library**–a file that provides information to other components and application  setup programs on the interface(s) that this component implements. However, the interface details can be read directly from a component by all kinds of other applications. For instance Visual Basic and Visual C++ can get details of all the properties, methods, and events that the component supports and display them in the built-in  Object Browser. And, as you'll see later in this chapter, this feature helps us to create applications or components more easily than using traditional API declarations. Instead of having to look up the syntax of each function in the documentation, the programming environment recovers this information from the component automatically.

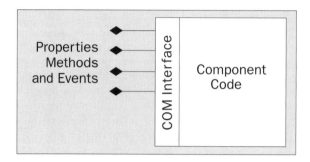

### The Component Interface Contract

Most books about components refer to the interface as a **contract** between the component and the outside world. While we are free to change the implementation of the functions inside a component (by changing the internal code), we have to maintain a consistent interface to avoid breaking applications that use it. If we change the interface by removing a function, or by changing the number or type of its arguments, applications that use this function will fail.

There are ways to get round this. We can add optional parameters to an existing function, so that new applications can take advantage of these parameters while older ones use default values set inside the function code. Alternatively, we can implement a new function with a different name that carries out the new task, and leave the existing one in place for older applications to use.

COM components can also support more than one interface, though we rarely go to these kinds of lengths with business rules components in our applications. It's more useful for maintaining backwards compatibility between different versions of commercial components, or in mission-critical environments.

### Class IDs and Class Names

One final point to be aware of is the way that components are recognized by the system. Earlier in this chapter, we saw how the Registry holds a class name and a class ID for each installed component. The class name is usually a combination of the component name and the internal class name, separated by a period, such as **ADODB.Connection**. You'll see more of where this comes from later in the chapter.

The class ID is generated by special routines in the compiler when the component is packaged into a DLL or OCX, and it is stored within the component package. In Visual C++, you use the GUID generator, either as an applet in your **devstudio\Vc\Bin** directory or as the GUID Generator component available from the Component Gallery. These **GUID**s (**globally unique identifiers**) are long number strings that are guaranteed to be unique—two components will never share the same one.

However, a problem arises when you recompile a component (maybe after changing its contents). If the compiler allocates a new class ID to a component, applications that use it won't recognize it. In some places, such as a Web page `<OBJECT>` tag, the class ID is specified directly in the page. In ASP and compiled languages it's usual to specify the class *name*, but this is no help because the class name entry in the Registry simply points to a matching class ID entry, which itself contains the details needed to instantiate the component. In both cases, the application will try to use the old component instead of the new one.

We can get around this problem in one of two ways. Some compilers allow us to declare **Binary Compatibility** when creating the component package, and specify an existing component that the new one will be compatible with. This causes the new component to have the same class ID as the existing one. As a by-product, the programming environment will warn us if we make any changes to the interface (i.e. the property, method and event declarations) that will result in incompatibility.

The second solution is to simply **unregister** the existing component and **register** the new one. This updates the entries in the Registry. As you'll see later on, the Windows program `regsvr32.exe` can be used with COM components to carry out both of these tasks. We don't have to poke around in the Registry by hand—if we did, it's unlikely that DNA programming would have got beyond the drawing board!

# The Benefits of Using Components

Now that we've explored the nature of components you can see why they are an integral part of the DNA strategy, and how they can help us to build complex yet reliable applications quickly and more easily. Throughout an application's life cycle, components provide many advantages.

During the **Design** phase:

- ❑ **Abstraction** - the entire application can be designed as a series of 'black boxes' at the highest level, then expanded downwards with ever increasing complexity.
- ❑ **Delegation** - you can define the component's interface and the end results you need it to provide, then leave details of how it will be implemented to others.

During the **Implementation** phase:

- ❑ **Reduced cost** - the compartmentalization of rules and functions saves time and money. Often the number of bugs is reduced, and concurrent development of separate components by individual teams is possible.
- ❑ **Availability** - rather than creating all the components yourself, you can buy in suitable components from outside suppliers. For example, few people implement their grid controls, preferring to use the pre-built Microsoft or third-party controls instead.
- ❑ **Component reuse** - because many applications in your business have similar tasks to achieve, and work on similar data structures, many components will be reusable in other projects in the future. Once built and tested, they become part of a library of components that make new applications even quicker and cheaper to build.

During the **Run-time** phase:

❑ **Encapsulation** - because only the interface of a component is visible, programmers and users cannot see how it works. In the case of programmers, this prevents them from accessing and reusing components in ways that are dependent on the internal construction. If they did, their applications could fail if the internal workings changed. Using only the published interface is a good way of protecting against this. For users, it is good way to hide any 'secret' content, formulae, or business rules that are private—or to which restricted access is required.

❑ **Performance** - components that have a lot of intensive processing to do can be built using languages and methods most suited to the system or environment they are used in. In extreme cases you can even create critical components directly in optimized assembler code. As long as the component has a COM interface wrapped around it, it can be used within the DNA architecture.

❑ **Scalability** - when applications have to support a large number of users, it makes sense to provide components that can handle several requests simultaneously, and deploy them in an environment that caches them after use ready for the next request. We'll be looking at these issues later in this chapter, and again in the next chapter where we meet Microsoft Transaction Server.

During the **Maintenance** phase:

❑ **Stability** - because of the compartmentalized approach to the design, finding errors while the application is in 'real world' use is easier. They allow you to pinpoint bugs and troubleshoot problems within a more restricted scope. There is also reduced risk of maintenance changes to one part of the application resulting in errors elsewhere. In fact, it's easy to swap a 'bad' component for a new one without affecting the rest of the application.

❑ **Upgradability** - when the application's environment changes, such as when new hardware is installed or data stores move or change, it's easy to update the components that are affected by the changes without disturbing the rest of the application.

❑ **Extensibility** - As the business needs change, the rules and functions exposed by the components can be changed quickly and easily to reflect this, and new ones can be added. There's no problem with adding new functions to a component's interface as long as the existing ones continue to be available unchanged.

# Creating Your Own Components

Now that we've explored the theory of components we can start learning how to build them. In this section we'll look at some examples of the way components can be built, and create a very simple example. This will be a component that we'll develop further later on in the chapter, for use in our Wrox Car Co sample application.

# What Language Do I Use?

Because DNA defines standard ways for Windows components to communicate with the outside world via a universally agreed COM (or COM+) interface definition, you can create components in any language that can provide this type of interface. (There are also software wrappers becoming available that will allow COM communication to take place in other operating systems, such as

Unix). This is a major strength of DNA, because it means that the choice of language is based on real-world constraints rather than software imposed ones. You can select the language that best suits the combination of your own experience and the task in hand. We'll take a brief look at some of the available options .

## Creating Components with Visual Basic

For experienced Visual Basic programmers, this is the obvious choice for building components. It is also useful for prototyping and testing new ideas and concepts quickly, even if you intend to implement them finally in another language later on. The Visual Basic 5 environment contains a range of Wizards that will build the skeletons for several different types of component for you, leaving you to simply add the actual business rules code afterwards.

On top of this, there are tools and Wizards that will look after compiling the code to a DLL or OCX, adding the COM wrapper, creating the interface definition and type library, and registering the component with the system so that it's ready to use. (Of course, if you are running your development environment on a different machine from the eventual home of the component, you will still need to register it there when you implement the application). They will even create sample code to show how you use the component in your applications.

One disadvantage with Visual Basic is the need to provide the VB runtime libraries and other DLLs with your component when it is installed on another machine. While the Wizards can do all the work, it does mean that the distribution files can be quite large. They can also compress the files into cabinet (CAB) files–useful if you are creating components for downloading and automated installation over the Internet–and even arrange to automatically download any other files that the end user requires direct from Microsoft's own Web site.

## Creating Components with C++

One regularly voiced argument against using Visual Basic is its speed of execution. In general this only becomes a problem when there is a lot of work being done by the VB code itself. However in most cases, the VB component will use other services, such as ADO, to do all the work underneath– and code execution speed is not then a major issue. However, there are some things that you can't do in Visual Basic (or that are very cumbersome) and in these cases a more efficient and lower-level language like C++ is a better option.

C++ allows the programmer to get closer to the hardware than VB, and benefits from a tighter integration with the system as a whole. It's particularly useful if you are implementing a component that has a visual user interface, where the increased execution speed is a real advantage. Other than this, you may prefer to use C++ if you are experienced in the language anyway.

To build COM-enabled components in C++ you can do it the hard way by writing all of the interface code yourself to match the standard definitions, or use the ActiveX Template Library (ATL) to automate much of the process. With ATL, you work with the Interface Definition Language (IDL) to create your interface, then use the Wizards that are included with C++ to package up your component ready for distribution. Like Visual Basic, you may need to distribute other files with your component, particularly if you are targeting a range of Windows operating systems.

### Creating Components with Java and J++

Java alone does not provide the ability to create COM-enabled components, but with certain additions it can be achieved. Microsoft's Java-based programming environment, J++, provides features that let you create components and them wrap them up with a COM interface to allow them to be used within the DNA environment–a technology called Java Beans. Again, Wizards are included that automate some of the process for you.

### Creating Components in Other Languages

Other non-Microsoft COM-enabled programming languages can be used to create components that will work with DNA. The most obvious of these is  Borland's Delphi 3.0, which looks and feels much like Visual Basic, but offers execution speed and efficiency approaching that of C++. It too includes Wizards that help to create, compile and package up your code into a component. You may also find other languages that can create components, such as  SmallTalk, PowerBuilder, or even MicroFOCUS COBOL.

### Creating Components with HTML

One new and surprising way of creating COM-enabled components is by using HTML and scripting code (VBScript or JavaScript/JScript). Internet Explorer 4 includes a component that can be used to wrap up an HTML page in a COM wrapper at runtime. The script code in the page can be used to define an interface that looks to the outside world just like any other COM component–which is, of course, the whole purpose of the architecture. This is called a  **scriptlet**, and we'll look at an example of this in the next chapter.

# Designing Your Component

Unlike a single-user application, where it's often possible to design 'on the hoof' (i.e. experiment, build and adapt as you go along), building business object components really requires some forward planning and 'proper' design work. The simple reason is that, if we are going to achieve the benefits we examined earlier in the chapter, we have to plan both the requirements and the interface of the component so as to fit into the environment where it will function. Otherwise, we may well end up with a component that does the job in hand, but is not reusable or easy to update over time.

There are many methodologies, old and new, for designing applications. Particularly in monolithic applications, this is a vital step if the end product is to be delivered  on-time, on-budget, and with a full feature set. While DNA promotes architecture and concept, methodologies like the Microsoft Solutions Framework (MSF) and other more traditional tools are more concerned with things like the vision and scope of the final product, the functional requirements, and the stages of implementation.

> *We're not attempting any kind of in-depth coverage of these issues in this book. Instead, we'll take a simplified look at the general considerations for implementing components. If you are building enterprise-level applications, you will almost certainly take the time to create a fully functional requirements plan for the individual elements.*

## *Determining The Features Required*

It's generally important to ensure that you have an overall plan of your application, at a high level, before you start designing components. That said, there are often business functions that are common to many applications, and will be regularly reused. Only you can define what these are for your business, but examples could be one that retrieves a price for a product given it's part number, or one which updates a customer's address details.

The important point is to think 'reusable' at this stage. Make each component's functions as small and universal as is practical, for example, have one function that accepts a table and field names as criteria parameters, rather than several which work the same way but use different hard-wired criteria.

You can also combine several functions into one component, but do so judiciously. If one function is regularly used while the other five in the same component are used only rarely , you are wasting memory and resources initializing a larger component than necessary. It's better to group them by usage than by business area, so that only the commonly used ones are active most of the time. When using Microsoft Transaction Server, you'll probably want to use single-function components most of the time unless the usage patterns are very closely related. It's really a balancing act between the number of components that you need to instatiate, and the amount of resources consumed by the parts of the component that are not in use.

## *Designing the Interface*

Having decided which functions each component will implement, tabulate out a meaningful set of component and class names and specify the parameters required for each one. This is really an extension of the previous step, but produces a working plan for the implementation.

Often, the parameters required for functions in the component are specified as **properties** of the component. Earlier in the chapter, we described the interface of a **GetNumberPayments** function that accepts arguments. This is a **method** of the component:

```
Function GetNumberPayments(CostOfCar, InterestRate, MonthlyAmount)
```

Instead, we can provide the arguments as properties (but see note below), which are set to the appropriate values before the method is called. The method then takes no arguments. The code that uses the method in this case would look like this:

```
...
Dim FinanceObject As New WCCFinance.PaymentTerms
FinanceObject.CostOfCar = 12000
FinanceObject.InterestRate = 1.25
FinanceObject.MonthlyAmount = 180
NumberMonths = FinanceObject.GetNumberPayments()
...
```

This has benefits, in that we can use code in the component to check the values for each parameter as they are set by the calling code. We'll use this technique in a sample component later in this chapter.

> Note that using properties to store values within a component has some quite severe disadvantages when it comes to using the component in Microsoft Transaction Server. We'll look at the issues involved in detail in the next chapter.

There are several accepted ways of describing a component's interface, but the main things you must do are to decide on a final list of properties, methods, and events that each will provide. A couple of common styles of interface diagram are shown here—the one on the right uses the Microsoft visual programming tools graphics:

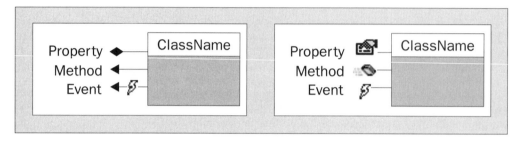

## *Other Component Design Issues*

While the choice of language that you use to create a component is reasonably open, there are other considerations that come into play. These include the intended host of the component, the internal threading model of the component, and the way it is packaged and installed on the target system. You'll see more details of these issues as you work through the remainder of this chapter and the rest of the book.

### *Host Implementation*

Business components are generally targeted at only a single host, probably Internet Information Server for use in Active Server Pages, as an ActiveX control for use in a Web browser, or a programming language like Visual Basic, C++, etc. If we are aiming for a programming language that supplies a visual development environment, such as Visual Basic or Microsoft Visual C++, we might wish to include extra features such as Property Pages, etc. We may also have to consider supplying license files and type library files to programmers who want to use our component. These issues are outside the scope of this book, but you may like to bear them in mind and investigate further if they are appropriate to your situation.

> *For more information on licensing terms and procedures check out the Help files supplied with your programming environment.*

If we are building a component that is designed to be used both on a browser and in ASP on the server, we also have to consider the requirements of each one more carefully. As an example, the current version of ADO (1.5 at the time of writing) is supplied in two different packages, depending on where it will be installed.

Internet Explorer 4 on Windows 95 installs the file **msdac0.dll**, which implements several client-side data-binding features for use with Remote Data Services. However, under the covers, it provides an implementation of the ActiveX Data Objects (ADO) library, and allows us to work with standard objects like **recordset** on the client.

In Windows NT, a file named **msado15.dll** implements the same ADO library for use within Active Server Pages on the server. Because the requirements of the client and server are different (IE4 requires automatic data binding whereas ASP creates recordsets directly), the components have to be different. But by providing the same ADO interface they allow the programmer to apply the same knowledge and techniques at either end of the network connection–the code they use is almost identical.

### Component Threading Models

Because we generally expect our applications to have more than one concurrent user, we have to be aware that the components we use will be in continual demand by different users at the same time. The programming languages we use offer various ways of setting the **threading model** for a component, which effectively controls how the component handles multiple users.

Single threaded components can only process one user at a time, and other processes that require the component's services have to wait until the first has completed (i.e. they are *serialized*). In a multi-user environment, a new instance has to be created for each user process that accesses it. This is generally unacceptable, especially where we are using Microsoft Transaction Server (MTS) to manage the creation and caching of components. We'll examine this topic in the next chapter.

Multi-threaded components allow more than one users' process to access the component simultaneously. On multiple processor machines, this can provide a real performance boost. A single instance of the component can process multiple users' requests at the same time, allowing components which provide methods with long execution times to process other requests while the long method call is running.

Apartment threaded components are a half-way solution, and are the kind usually created by Visual Basic. They support multiple processing by creating separate instances of objects within the component on demand. Generally, we'll be using this threading model in components we create for use with MTS.

> *You can force Visual Basic to create multi-threaded components as long as you don't require a user interface. This is the situation with business components that will be running on the server, where message boxes and other distractions are potentially disastrous!*

### Component Distribution

Finally, we need to consider how we will deliver the components to the appropriate place within our application. If we are working on an enclosed network, such as a corporate Intranet, we can ensure that each client has the same operating system, browser, and installed components and services.

If we are working with anonymous clients over the Internet, however, we have no control over the system they are using. In this case, we may choose to provide the components that need to run on the client as CAB files, which are downloaded from our server as required.

Now that we've looked briefly at the principles behind creating controls, we'll go ahead and build one in Visual Basic to see just how easy it is.

# A Finance Component in Visual Basic

Our first VB component will be simple. Ultimately, we'll be developing it further to use in our sample Wrox Car Co application. For the meantime we'll briefly step through the process of implementing it using Visual Basic–we're using version 5 from Visual Studio 97 Enterprise Edition here.

## Building A Component in Visual Basic

The first step is to select the correct project type. VB5 provides three kinds of ActiveX projects: the ActiveX EXE, ActiveX DLL, and ActiveX Control (OCX). For components that will be used with Microsoft Transaction Server we have to compile them as DLLs, so this is the option we choose:

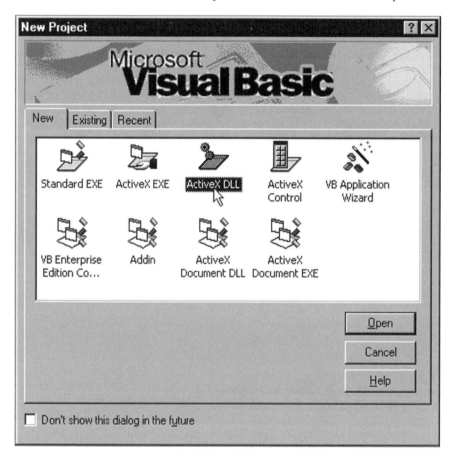

VB creates the files required for the component automatically. These are the **.vbp** project file (Project1) and the **.cls** Class Module (Class1). Our next step is to give them the appropriate names. An ActiveX component can contain more than one class, but ours will use just one. In the Project window, we change the name of the project to WCCFinance, and the Class Module to PaymentTerms. This will provide a complete class name for the compiled component of **WCCFinance.PaymentTerms**:

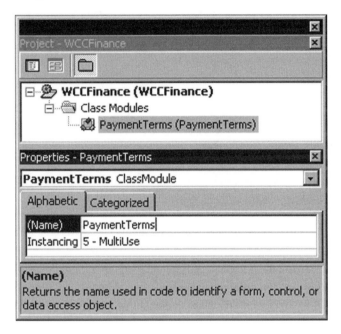

Next, we set the project options. In the Project | WCCFinance Properties dialog we select Unattended Execution because we want to be able to run this component on the server. Unattended execution means that the component is supposed to run without user interaction, and therefore it stores any functions that would normally require user input—such as a message box for an error message— to an event log. We should also enter a description for the component here, as this is the text which will appear once the component is registered. If you are building multiple components then it is a good idea to give them all a similar start to the description so they will all appear together in the references. All ours will start with Wrox Car Co:

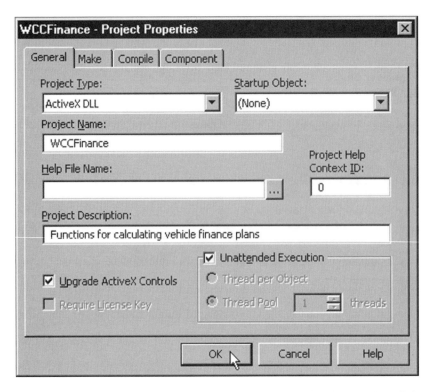

The next stage is to create the code for the component. This includes the interface definitions for the properties and methods we want it to provide. While it is easy enough to do by hand, we can use the VB Class Builder Utility to speed up the process. If it's not already visible on the Add-Ins menu, select Add-In Manager and put a tick next to it in the list of installed Add-ins (you might have to run setup again if you didn't install it with VB5):

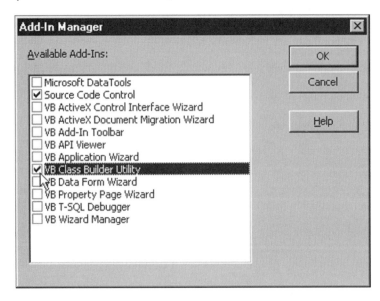

Once you've got Class Builder open, you can see the component in the left-hand window, and the classes it contains—in our case just the PaymentTerms class:

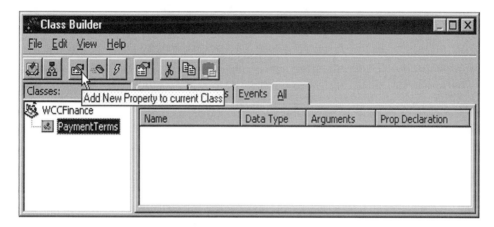

*Class Builder may warn you that it didn't create the class and can't find any members. This isn't important because we haven't added any yet.*

Clicking the Add New Property button opens a window where we can specify the details of a property to be added to our class. In the screenshot below it's the TotalPrice property.
We're specifying that the property has a data type of Currency, and that it is Public, i.e available outside the component:

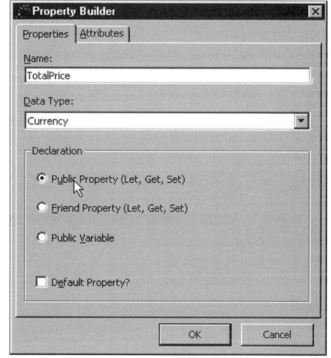

*The Friend option is used to create properties that are shared between classes but are not available outside the component, and the Public Variable option creates a variable that can be accessed directly from outside the component. You'll see more about the difference between a Public Variable and a Public Property in a while, when we look at what Class Builder has done.*

It's also worthwhile opening the Attributes page in this dialog and entering a brief description of the property. This will be visible in tools that read the interface details of the component, such as the VB Object Browser. Click OK to add the new property, and repeat the process to add the other two properties as well: MonthlyPayment which is also of data type Currency, and InterestRate which is of data type Single.

Then click the Add New Method button on the toolbar of Class Builder to open the Method Builder window shown below. This is where we create the function that will act as our GetNumberPayments method. We select the return value data type of Integer:

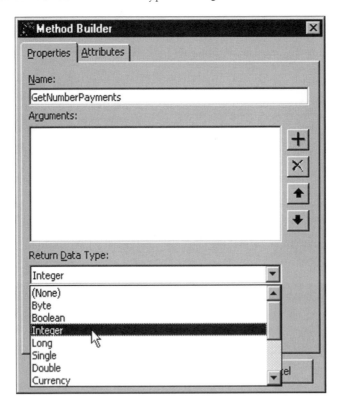

If you click on the All tab, Class Builder now shows the interface that our component will expose to the outside world:

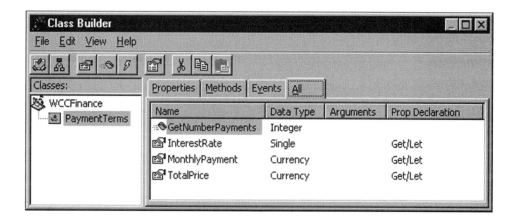

## What the Class Builder Has Done

This is all that's required to build a component. If we compiled it now, we'd have a fully DNA-compatible COM object that we could use in our applications. The only problem is that it doesn't actually do anything yet. We need to add the code that carries out the tasks or business rules we designed the component to accomplish.

Once you've chosen File|Update Project, the Class Builder utility will create a page full of code. This defines the interface for the component. At the top, after the **Option Explicit** line, are the local 'member' variables that will hold the values of the three properties internally while our component is running. These are not visible outside the component:

```
Option Explicit

'local variable(s) to hold property value(s)
Private mvarTotalPrice      As Currency
Private mvarInterestRate    As Single
Private mvarMonthlyPayment  As Currency
...
```

Next, the code contains the definition of the single method we specified. This is simply a **Public Function**, just as we would use in 'normal' VB application code:

```
...
Public Function GetNumberPayments() As Integer
End Function
...
```

Next come three pairs of routines, one pair for each property we defined, which expose the property to the outside world. The **Public** keyword indicates this, and the special terminology **Property Let** and **Property Get** indicates that they define the routines that code outside the component will use to set (**Let**) and retrieve (**Get**) the property value at runtime:

```
...
Public Property Let MonthlyPayment(ByVal vData As Currency)
```

```
        mvarMonthlyPayment = vData
    End Property

    Public Property Get MonthlyPayment() As Currency
        MonthlyPayment = mvarMonthlyPayment
    End Property
    ...
    'same for InterestRate and TotalPrice
    ...
```

When other code sets the value of a property, it runs the **Property Let** routine and supplies the value as the parameter **vData**—notice that the Class Builder has set the correct data type. The value that's supplied is assigned to the local 'member' variable. Likewise, the **Property Get** routine (which acts like a function) runs when another program tries to retrieve the property value. The code assigns the value of the local 'member' variable to the return value of the function, and hence returns it to the application that called it.

### Public Properties vs Public Variables

This is where **Public Properties** are different to **Public Variables**. We change the value of a property by calling the appropriate **Public Property Let** routine. If we had instructed Class Builder to create our **MonthlyPayment** as a Public Variable we would have ended up with a declaration for it of:

```
    Public MonthlyPayment As Currency
```

In this case any user (or other component) could change the value directly instead of having to call the **Public Property Let** routine. We'll see why this is important next.

### Read and Write Properties

Providing both the **Property Let** and **Property Get** routines for a property in a class makes that property **read/write**. In our component we want the properties to be **write-only**, so we can delete all the **Property Get** routines from our code. If we wanted a property to be **read-only** we would delete the **Property Let** routine instead.

We can also limit the values that can be placed in properties, a process known as **validation**. In our case, we want to ensure that only values above zero are applied to the properties. In the case of the **InterestRate**, we'll also limit it to being below 100—these are the modifications we made to the class builder's code:

```
    Public Property Let MonthlyPayment(ByVal vData As Currency)
        If vData > 0 Then
            mvarMonthlyPayment = vData
        End If
    End Property

    Public Property Let InterestRate(ByVal vData As Single)
        If vData >= 0 And vData < 100 Then
            mvarInterestRate = vData
        End If
    End Property
```

```
Public Property Let TotalPrice(ByVal vData As Currency)
    If vData > 0 Then
        mvarTotalPrice = vData
    End If
End Property
```

*Of course, we should really return an error to the calling application if a non-legal value is applied to the property, rather than just ignoring it. Here, we're trying to keep things simple. In Chapter 4 we'll see how to provide error feedback to the calling application, when we look at the Order components.*

You can see from this section why using properties is a better plan that using Public Variables. Through validation, we limit the values that the user can set the property to. If it was a Public Variable they could set it to any value they liked.

### Adding the Business Rules Code

The final part of the code we need to enter is that which calculates the result of the **GetNumberPayments** method. We just have to add this to the **Public Function** that the Class Builder created for us:

```
Public Function GetNumberPayments() As Integer

    Dim sngInterestMultiplier    As Single
    Dim curRemainderDue          As Currency
    Dim curFirstMonthInterest    As Currency
    Dim intNumberMonths          As Integer

    On Error GoTo GetNumberPayments_Error

    ' return zero if cannot calculate result
    intNumberMonths = 0

    ' see if payment is enough to cover interest
    curFirstMonthInterest = mvarTotalPrice * mvarInterestRate / 100

    If curFirstMonthInterest < mvarMonthlyPayment Then
      sngInterestMultiplier = 1 + (mvarInterestRate / 100)
      curRemainderDue = mvarTotalPrice

      Do While curRemainderDue > 0
        curRemainderDue = curRemainderDue * sngInterestMultiplier
        curRemainderDue = curRemainderDue - mvarMonthlyPayment
        intNumberMonths = intNumberMonths + 1
      Loop

    End If

    GetNumberPayments = intNumberMonths

GetNumberPayments_Exit:
    Exit Function

GetNumberPayments_Error:
```

```
        GetNumberPayments = 0   'zero indicates an error
        Resume GetNumberPayments_Exit

    End Function
```

This code is simple enough. After checking that the monthly payment amount is greater than the first month's interest (if it wasn't, the debt would rise, not fall, over time), it loops through adding the monthly interest and then subtracting the payment until the remaining debt is zero. Note that this a rather simple model of how interest is calculated; some creditors, especially credit card providers, calculate interest on the basis of a daily interest figure which makes the calculation significantly more complex.

### Compiling the WCCFinance Component

Our component is complete and ready to be compiled into a DLL. Selecting  Make WCCFinance.dll from the File menu brings up a File | Save As dialog where we specify the location for the DLL. This dialog also has an Options button, where we can add some useful information into the DLL, such as specifying the version number and the text for the description, copyright information, etc.:

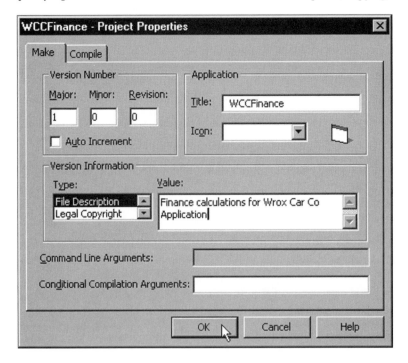

Once the DLL has been compiled, it is automatically registered on the local machine ready for use. If you peek into the Registry (run **regedit** from the Start | Run menu), you'll see the two entries there for your new component. Under the main  HKEY_CLASSES_ROOT key is the Class Name entry that shows the CLSID class ID value of our new component:

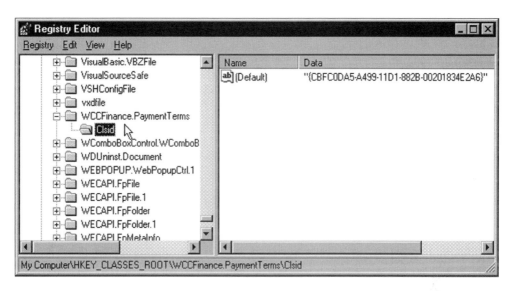

This class ID appears under the HKEY_LOCAL_MACHINE\SOFTWARE\Classes key, it contains the details about where our DLL is on the disk, and other information that Windows needs to instantiate it:

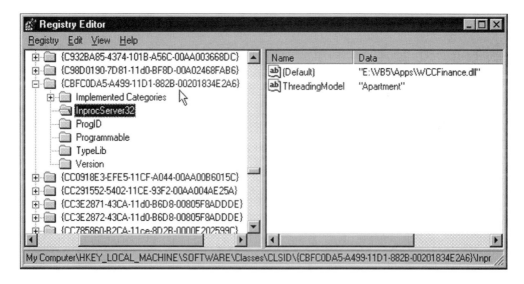

*You may like to make a note of the class ID for* **your** *component so that you can use it later on in a Web page. It won't (of course) be the same as the one allocated to our component in the screenshots above, or in the code you'll see later in this chapter. An easy way is to double-click the 'Default' entry for the CLSID key (see the screenshot above), copy the value into NotePad, and save it as a text file. Remember that it's wise to back up your Registry before working with it, even if you aren't planning to make any changes to it.*

### Setting Component Version Compatibility

Before we leave the creation of the component, open the Project | Properties window again and go to the Component page. Here we can specify the compatibility type. If we select Project Compatibility or Binary Compatibility, VB will warn us when we make changes that will cause the component to be incompatible with previous versions, i.e. if we remove a method or property, or change it's interface definition in other ways. Selecting Project Compatibility also forces the type library file to be updated each time the component is compiled:

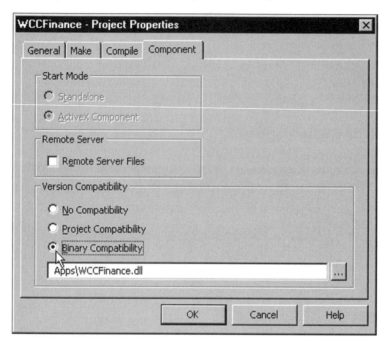

Once we select Project or Binary Compatibility, VB makes sure that new builds of the component have the same class ID and interface identifiers as earlier ones. This means that we won't have to un-register and re-register the control each time we compile it again. To be able to use compatibility we have to have already compiled the component at least once.

# Using Components In Applications

Having built a simple component, we'll explore some of the ways we can use it in our applications. We'll show you this simple component running within a normal Visual Basic application, on a Web page using scripting, and on the server through Active Server Pages.

# Using the Component in Visual Basic

If you have any doubt that the simple steps in the previous section of the chapter have created a fully COM-enabled component, let's see what it looks like in Visual Basic first. Before we can see the component in the VB development environment, we have to add a reference to it.

## Adding a Reference to the Component

Start a new standard Executable (EXE) project, open the Project | References dialog, click Browse and find the **WCCFinance.dll** you just created on your disk. Once selected it appears in the list. Notice that it uses the description we entered for our DLL project when we created it:

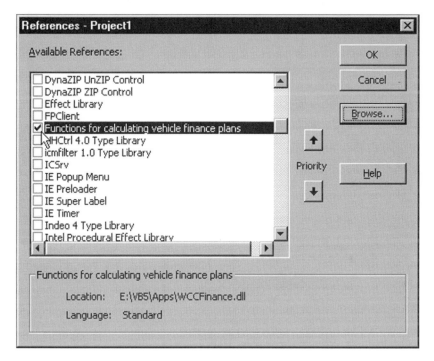

Now we can open Object Browser from the View menu and select the WCCFinance component from the list of referenced libraries. The properties, together with their descriptions and data types, are visible. Our new component appears just like any other COM component, including the 'help' text we added to the Attributes tab in the Class Builder when creating the methods and properties:

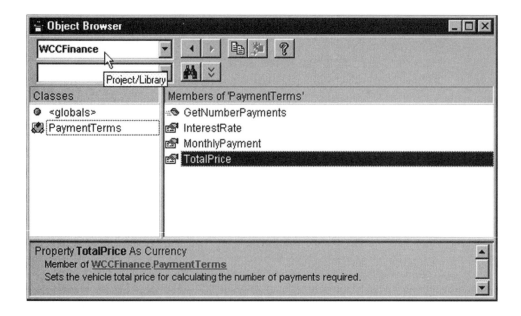

## Working With The Component

To try out the component, we can just add a button to the blank form in our open application project. Then, in the code window, we enter the code that will create an instance of the component, set the relevant properties, and call the **GetNumberPayments** method.

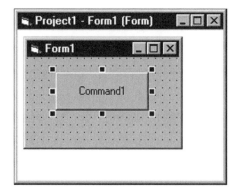

As you type the code, see how VB automatically uses the object's type library to provide a list of options—as it does with the integral VB objects. For example, it includes   WCCFinance in the list of objects when you enter the **Dim FinanceObject As New** line:

Pressing the space bar then offers a list of the classes within the object. In this case there's just the PaymentTerms class. And, as you use the new object variable, VB provides a list of its **members** (the properties and methods that form its interface):

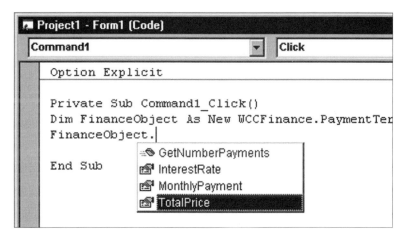

Once the code is complete, as shown in the next screenshot, clicking the button on the form provides a confirmation that our component is working perfectly:

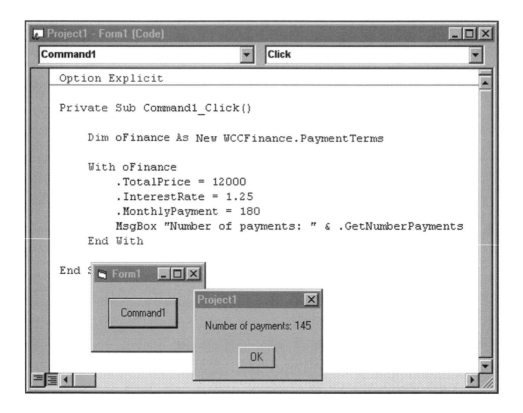

### Creating an Instance of the Component

In the example code, we used the line:

```
Dim FinanceObject As New WCCFinance.PaymentTerms
```

to create a new instance of the **WCCFinance** component. When we use the component within a DNA application, we don't generally use this technique because we'll expect MTS to provide instances of components that are already running. Instead we'll use the **CreateObject** function to return a reference to the object:

```
Set FinanceObject = CreateObject("WCCFinance.PaymentTerms")
```

# Using the Component in a Web Page

To see the component used in a Web page, we can create a simple HTML page on the machine where the component is stored and registered, and activate the component with some client-side script code. We'll include both the VBScript and JavaScript code in our sample page.

## Creating the HTML Page

To instantiate a component in the browser we use an **<OBJECT>** tag, and specify the class ID of the component—this is why we suggested you make a note of it. If you don't know the class ID, you can search through the HKEY_CLASSES_ROOT key using the Registry editor **regedit.exe**. Here's the first part of the page:

```
<HTML>
<HEAD><TITLE>Testing the WCCFinance Component</TITLE></HEAD>
<BODY>

<!-- the finance control, change classid to suit your control -->
<OBJECT ID="FinanceObject"
   CLASSID="CLSID:CBFC0DA5-A499-11D1-882B-00201834E2A6">
</OBJECT>
...
```

We also need three text boxes to enter the values for the component's properties:

```
...
Total Price ($):
<INPUT TYPE="TEXT" ID="txtTotalPrice" NAME="txtTotalPrice"><BR>
Interest Rate (%):
<INPUT TYPE="TEXT" ID="txtInterestRate" NAME="txtInterestRate"><BR>
Monthly Payment ($):
<INPUT TYPE="TEXT" ID="txtMonthlyPayment" NAME="txtMonthlyPayment"><P>
...
```

Next come the two buttons that will run the script code, one each for JavaScript and VBScript:

```
...
<INPUT TYPE="BUTTON" VALUE="Calculate using JavaScript"
      ONCLICK="calculateResultsJS()"><P>
<INPUT TYPE="BUTTON" VALUE="Calculate using VBScript"
      ONCLICK="calculateResultsVB()">
...
```

### The Client-side Script Code

Finally, the page contains two script routines that are executed when the appropriate button is clicked. The contents are fundamentally the same as in the VB application example we used earlier. They set the properties using the values from the text boxes on the page, call the **GetNumberPayments** method, and display the result in an **alert** dialog:

```
...
<SCRIPT LANGUAGE="VBScript">
Sub calculateResultsVB()
   Set objFinance = document.all("FinanceObject")
   objFinance.TotalPrice = document.all.txtTotalPrice.Value
   objFinance.InterestRate = document.all.txtInterestRate.Value
   objFinance.MonthlyPayment = document.all.txtMonthlyPayment.Value
   alert "Number of Payments: " & objFinance.GetNumberPayments
End Sub
```

```
</SCRIPT>
<SCRIPT LANGUAGE="JavaScript">
function calculateResultsJS()
{
  var objFinance = document.all['FinanceObject'];
  objFinance.TotalPrice = document.all['txtTotalPrice'].value;
  objFinance.InterestRate = document.all['txtInterestRate'].value;
  objFinance.MonthlyPayment = document.all['txtMonthlyPayment'].value;
  alert("Number of Payments: " + objFinance.GetNumberPayments())
}
</SCRIPT>

</BODY>
</HTML>
```

Here's the result when the JavaScript code is run—the VBScript code produces the same result:

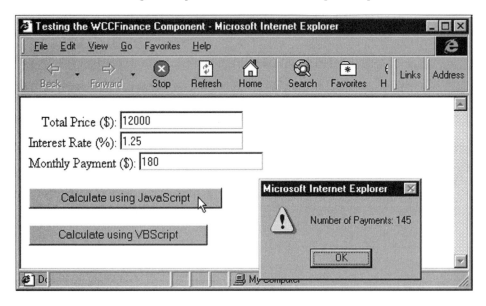

*When you first click the button, you may receive a warning that the page contains an ActiveX control that is not marked as 'Safe for Scripting'. We can mark controls as safe for scripting using the Visual Basic Setup Wizard, and if you are targeting the component at the client-side (i.e. for use in a browser) you should do this when you package up the control. For more information about Setup Wizard search the VB5 Books Online for setup.*

# Using the Component with ASP

To use the component on the server, in this example, we will physically place it there. While it's possible to use components that reside on a remote machine via **DCOM** (Distributed COM), this is outside the scope of this chapter.

## Installing Components On Other Machines

So, the first step is to move (or copy) the **WCCFinance.dll** file to the server's disk. It's not important where it goes—you can use a directory under **Program Files** or **Winnt/System32**, or a new directory elsewhere that will hold your completed application. A recommended practice for components used with ASP, is to create a folder called **components** in the **INetPub** folder for all components used with IIS. Alternately, you can set up a **components** folder for each application on your server.

If the component requires support files, such as the VB runtime files needed by our component, you can run the VB Setup Wizard (from your Start menu) to create a complete installation program that will also register the component on the other machine. This is a handy way to set up the server the first time you develop a component in a different language. It also provides an Uninstall option that will remove the component and all its associated files and Registry entries.

After you've installed the component once, and need to upgrade it, you soon find that packaging it up as a full set of Setup files, running the Uninstall, and then installing it all again is time consuming. It's easier to just copy the DLL to the server each time. Providing you've set the Binary Compatibility option so that it has the same class ID and interface ID (as discussed earlier), you don't need to re-register it.

### Coping With Component Caching

Once a component has been instantiated on the server, having been used in (for example) ASP, it will be cached in memory. You have to stop and restart the server to release the component, so that the new one can be copied over the top of it.

In IIS4, if the component is placed in a virtual directory and set to run 'out of process' (see below), you can unload components using the Web server manager in the MMC. Alternatively you can stop and restart the WWW service to release components. However, you may still find with some components that you have to reboot the machine, although in theory this should rarely be necessary.

### Registering Components Manually

If a replacement component does not have the same class ID as the one it is replacing, you have to un-register the old one and then register the new one. The Uninstall and Install programs will do this if that's the way you decide to work, but you can easily do it manually instead, with the **regsvr32** program.

To unregister a component, change to the component's directory in a Command window and enter: **regsvr32.exe -u** *<filename>*, for example:

```
regsvr32.exe -u WCCFinance.dll
```

To register the new component, omit the **-u** parameter and enter **regsvr32.exe** *<filename>*, for example:

```
regsvr32.exe WCCFinance.dll
```

In each case a dialog appears with a 'Success' message (or 'Failed' if you get it wrong).

### Running Components in Separate Address Space

In the Management Console for Internet Information Server 4 (IIS4) and above, you can use the Properties dialog of a directory within your Web site to force components to run in a separate address space from the Web server itself—i.e. **out-of-process** with respect to IIS. This means that if the program fails (i.e. crashes), it won't bring down that Web server as well—as it could do if it was running in the same address space.

However, this technique can slow down execution because calls to the component from ASP have to cross the address space boundaries, usually referred to as **far addressing** or **cross-process marshalling**. If the component shares the Web server's address space that is, if it is running **in-process**, it can be referenced with a relative address, which is much quicker.

Mind you, the difference will probably not be perceptible except on very busy sites, where the ASP script makes many references to the component. You may decide to use a separate address space while testing a component, then switch back to shared address space afterwards as performance limitations start to occur.

## Creating the Active Server Pages Files

To use our component in ASP, we first need to have a page that submits the values required for the calculation to the Web server. This is our simple example , adapted from the client-side page we used earlier. We place the HTML controls on a **<FORM>**, whose **ACTION** is the name of the ASP page that will calculate the results (we could have used a single page that submitted the information to itself, but separate pages make it easier to follow the code). We also need a **SUBMIT** button, and we can remove the other two buttons along with the client-side script sections:

```
<HTML>
<HEAD><TITLE>Testing the WCCFinance Component</TITLE></HEAD>
<BODY>

<FORM ACTION="finance.asp" METHOD="POST">
Total Price ($): <INPUT TYPE="TEXT" NAME="txtTotalPrice"><BR>
Interest Rate (%): <INPUT TYPE="TEXT" NAME="txtInterestRate"><BR>
Monthly Payment ($): <INPUT TYPE="TEXT" NAME="txtMonthlyPayment"><P>
<INPUT TYPE="SUBMIT" VALUE="Submit to ASP script">
</FORM>

</BODY>
</HTML>
```

The ASP file that will process the request from the HTML page is simple enough, and is placed in the same directory on the server as the HTML page that references it. We also use similar code in it to that which we used client-side, but now the values come from the **Request.Form** collection and not directly from the controls' **value** properties. This time, we'll also check that we get a legal result, something we haven't been doing in earlier examples:

```
<%@ LANGUAGE="VBSCRIPT" %>

<HTML>
<HEAD><TITLE>Results from the WCCFinance Component</TITLE></HEAD>
<BODY>
```

```
<%
Set objFinance = Server.CreateObject("WCCFinance.PaymentTerms")
objFinance.TotalPrice = Request.Form("txtTotalPrice")
objFinance.InterestRate = Request.Form("txtInterestRate")
objFinance.MonthlyPayment = Request.Form("txtMonthlyPayment")
intResult = objFinance.GetNumberPayments

If intResult > 0 Then %>

A total price of <B>$<% = Request.Form("txtTotalPrice")%></B> at a
monthly interest rate of <B><% = Request.Form("txtInterestRate")%>%</B>,
and paying <B>$<% = Request.Form("txtMonthlyPayment")%></B>
per month, will require <B><% = intResult %></B> payments.

<% Else %>

Sorry, a monthly payment of
<B>$<% = Request.Form("txtMonthlyPayment")%></B>
is not sufficient to pay off a loan of
<B>$<% = Request.Form("txtTotalPrice")%></B> at an interest rate of
<B><% = Request.Form("txtInterestRate")%>%</B>

<% End If %>

<P><A HREF="finance_useasp.htm">Continue</A>
</BODY>
</HTML>
```

The ASP code gets the result into **intResult**, and checks if it's greater than zero. Either way, we can drop suitable values into the text of the returned page using the ASP placeholder code:

```
<% = Request.Form("txtTotalPrice")%>
```

Here's the result, showing both the HTML that submits the values and the output from the ASP page that calculates the results:

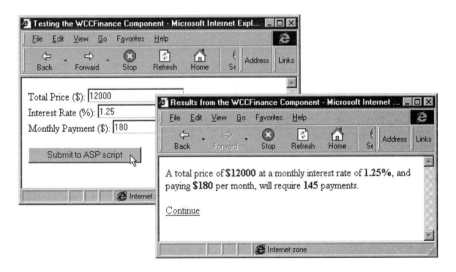

# Scriptlets As Business Object Components

In an earlier section, we mentioned that you can create components using HTML, in a new technique that is currently only supported by Internet Explorer 4. These kinds of components are called **scriptlets**. We'll look very briefly here at the technique, and you'll see more in later chapters.

## A Simple HTML Scriptlet Using RDS

**Remote Data Services** (RDS) allow us to connect HTML controls on the client to an **ActiveX Data Control** object (ADC). We'll be looking at RDS in more depth later in the book, and the object of this section is simply to show you how we can use scriptlets to create COM-compatible components that use HTML.

Here's the first part of a scriptlet page that uses RDS. The data control is defined in an **<OBJECT>** tag in the **<HEAD>** section of the page. It is bound to an invisible text box control using the control's **DATASRC** and **DATAFLD** attributes:

```
<html>
<head>
<title>RDS Scriptlet Example</title>

<object id="adco" height=1 width=1
  classid="clsid:BD96C556-65A3-11D0-983A-00C04FC29E33">
</object>

</head>
<body>

<input type=text id=txtBound datasrc=#adco datafld=Color
       STYLE="visibility:hidden">
...
```

### The Scriptlet Interface

The next section of the page defines the interface of the scriptlet, in a very similar way to that which we've seen in Visual Basic. We have a member variable **mResult**, and a function name **public_get_dataList()** which provides a read-only property named **dataList**. This function simply returns the value of the member variable **mResult** to the calling code:

```
...
<script language="vbscript">

Dim mResult                  'member variable for result
mResult = "Initializing"     'default value for property

Function public_get_dataList()
  public_get_dataList = mResult
End Function
...
```

### The RDS Script Code

The final section of code defines a global variable that will refer to the data control object, and sets the properties so that RDS will fetch the results from the source database. There's also an event-handler subroutine that runs when the data has arrived. It loops through the data control's recordset and creates a comma-delimited string of the values in all of the records:

```
...
Dim myadc                                'global reference to ADC object
Set myadc = document.all("adco")
myadc.Server = "http://yourserver"       'change to your server name
myadc.Connect = "YourSystemDSN"          'system DSN for Colors table
myadc.SQL = "SELECT Color FROM tblColor ORDER BY Color"

Sub adco_ondatasetcomplete()
  If window.event.reason = 0 Then        'data arrived OK and complete
    myadc.recordset.moveFirst
    While not myadc.recordset.EOF
      If strResult <> "" Then strResult = strResult & ", "
      strResult = strResult & myadc.recordset.fields("Color")
      myadc.recordset.moveNext
    Wend
    mResult = strResult
  Else
    mResult = "Error while reading from database"
  End if
End Sub

</script>

</body>
</html>
```

### Using the RDS Scriptlet

We can embed this fully working scriptlet into an HTML page, and use the **dataList** property it exposes to get a listing of available colors from the **Colors** table in our database. Here's the complete source of the page:

```
<html>
<head>
<title>RDS Scriptlet Example</title></head>
<style> BODY {font-family:Tahoma; font-size:12pt} </style>
<body>

<!-- declare the component -->
<object id="ColorList" width=0 height=0 style="visibility:hidden"
  type="text/x-scriptlet"
  data="datalist.htm">    'the URL of the scriptlet page
</object>
Click the cars for a list <BR>of available colors:
<!-- image to click to display list of results -->
<img src="cars.gif" align="middle" language="VBScript"
```

```
onclick="MsgBox 'Colors Available:' & Chr(13) & ColorList.dataList, _
  vbInformation, 'Color List'"
>

</body>
</html>
```

It uses an **<OBJECT>** tag to embed the scriptlet page **datalist.htm** into this page, and makes it invisible with the **style="visibility:hidden"** attribute. When we click on the image of the two cars, the code in the image element's **onclick** attribute displays the value of the **dataList** property in a message box:

Under the hood, Internet Explorer 4 is using a special component that is installed with the browser to wrap up the HTML page into a COM-enabled object. This is the whole principle of scriptlets, and provides a superbly easy way to accomplish one-off tasks, prototype applications, and general experimentation.

### Visible Interface Scriptlets

Our example was a hidden scriptlet, because it simply carried out a business function and returned the result via its COM interface. No visible interface was required. However, there's no reason why the HTML page that makes up the scriptlet should not have its own interface if required. This technique may provide some useful ways of adding extra functionality to your application client. You'll see how we used it in our sample application later on in this book.

## A Scriptlet Created By ASP

The previous example used a scriptlet created from standard HTML and text. We can also use ASP to create dynamic scriptlets, just as we can use it to create dynamic HTML pages. As an example, here we've changed the **datalist.htm** page to **datalist.asp** by using some simple ASP code to open the **Color** table in our database and build up the comma-delimited string of colors in the variable **strResult**:

```
<html>
<head><title>ASP Scriptlet Example</title></head>
<body>

<%
On Error Resume Next
Dim oRs          'the reference to the recordset
Dim strResult    'the string of colors we're creating
Set oRs = Server.CreateObject("ADODB.Recordset")
oRs.Open "tblColor", "DSN=YourDSN;UID=uid;Password=pw;", , , 2  'table
oRs.MoveFirst
Do While Not oRS.EOF
   If strResult <> "" Then strResult = strResult & ", "
   strResult = strResult & oRS.fields("Color")
   oRS.MoveNext
Loop
oRs.Close
Set oRs = Nothing
If Err.Number <> 0 Then strResult = "Error while reading from database"
%>
...
```

The remainder of the page contains client-side script code that will be executed on the browser:

```
...
<script language="vbscript">

  Dim mResult 'member variable for result
  mResult = "<% = strResult %>"

  Function public_get_dataList()
    public_get_dataList = mResult
  End Function
</script>

</body>
</html>
```

Remember that code between the **<%** and **%>** delimiters is ASP, and is executed on the server. When the page is sent to the client, the ASP code is not itself sent: instead, the client-side code appears just as is in the ASP page—with one exception. The placeholder **<% = strResult %>** is replaced with the value of the **strResult** variable that was created by the ASP script. So what the client actually receives is:

```
...
Dim mResult 'member variable for result
mResult = "black, blue, pink, red"
...
```

To use the ASP scriptlet, in place of the RDS one in our previous example, we just have to change the **DATA** attribute of the **<OBJECT>** tag that inserts the scriptlet into the page:

```
<!-- declare the component -->
<object id="ColorList" width=0 height=0 style="visibility:hidden"
  type="text/x-scriptlet"
    data="datalist.asp">  'the URL of the scriptlet page
</object>
```

When the HTML page that uses this scriptlet queries the **dataList** property, the value returned will be the string containing the list of colors. In other words, the results—as far as the user and the application itself are concerned—are exactly the same. We've changed the whole way that the business function is implemented in the component, from client-side data binding to server-side ADO data access, yet no changes are required to the application itself (except of course, in this case, to change the file name of the scriptlet in the **DATA** attribute).

*At the time of writing, Microsoft were also developing an associated technology called **Remote Scripting**. This will provide a new way for code in a Web page on the client to call methods and set properties of components running on the server. However, in its early stages, the techniques, syntax, and operation were changing with each update and it's likely that the final results will be very different from the early previews that were available. For this reason, we won't be covering remote scripting in this book.*

# Summary

In this chapter, we've tackled the core DNA subject of **components**. This isn't designed to be a complete primer to building components, but a day-trip through the concepts and possibilities—so that you can appreciate what they are, why we use them, and how you can create your own quite easily in a variety of ways.

DNA defines a structure for distributed applications that takes advantage of all the benefits that components provide, i.e.:

- ❑ **Abstraction** and **delegation** during the application design phase.
- ❑ **Reduced cost**, **better availability** and **component reuse** during the application implementation phase.
- ❑ **Encapsulation,** better **performance** and **scalability** during the run-time life of the application.
- ❑ **Increased stability**, **upgradability** and **extensibility** during the application's maintenance phases.

We've also looked at some of the techniques for creating components, discovering that the wide choice of programming languages and the excellent tools that are available make the task approachable for all programmers, irrespective of their particular skill sector.

Finally, we stepped through the process of building a simple component in Visual Basic, and a couple of scriptlets that use RDS and ASP. We saw how these components can encapsulate a simple business function, and how they can be used in a variety of ways—both on the client and on the server.

In the next chapter, we move on to look at the first headline topic of this book in detail—**Microsoft Transaction Server**. You'll see the kinds of problems that we have to handle in multi-user and distributed applications, and how MTS assists us. Now that you have a broad understanding of components and their use, you'll be able to see the benefits MTS brings more clearly.

*For more detailed information about creating your own components, and associated issues, look out for other books from our range:*

### Components:

*Beginning ATL COM, ISBN 1-861000-11-1*

*Professional VB5 Business Objects, ISBN 1-861000-43-X*

*Instant Scriptlets, ISBN 1-861001-38-X*

### Remote Data Services:

*Professional IE4 Programming, ISBN 1-861000-70-7*

### Active Server Pages:

*Professional Active Server Pages 2, ISBN 1-861001-26-6*

*Professional ASP and RDS Database Programming, ISBN 1-861001-64-9*

### ActiveX Data Objects:

*Professional Active Server Pages 2, ISBN 1-861001-27-4*

*You'll find a list of links to associated Web sites and on-line resources on our own Web site at* **http://rapid.wrox.co.uk/**

# Introducing Transaction Server

Now that we've examined the core concepts of DNA and seen the kinds of components that we can use within its architecture, we can move on to look at where **Microsoft Transaction Server** (MTS) comes into the picture. Unfortunately, Microsoft momentarily lost their legendary knack of giving their products really useful and meaningful names when they christened this little baby. Yes, MTS does have something to do with 'transactions', but in fact it does many other useful things as well.

In this chapter we'll start off by looking at what MTS is, and why it's suddenly become one of the hottest new technologies around at the moment. We'll also discuss what transactions are, and you'll see why the name Transaction Server is a misnomer for this exciting new technology.

Then, once we've got to grips with the theory of MTS, we'll move on to look at how we use it in our applications. We'll show you just how easy it is to take advantage of its services with existing components, and we'll also be adding MTS integration to the simple **WCCFinance** component we developed in the previous chapter.

So, in this chapter, you'll see:

- ❑ What Microsoft Transaction Server is, and what it can do.
- ❑ What transactions are, and how MTS makes them more powerful and easier to use.
- ❑ What levels of transaction support are available now, and will be in the future.
- ❑ How we build new components and adapt existing ones for use with MTS.
- ❑ How we install components into MTS, and use them in applications.

To start with, let's look at the background and basic principles of MTS.

# What is Transaction Server?

MTS is an integral part of Windows NT, and is installed by default as part of the operating system in NT5. It is a **service** in much the same way as Internet Information Server or the File and Print services that we now take for granted. In other words, it is part of the system that is available in the background whenever one of our applications requires it.

Control and configuration of MTS is via either a snap-in to the Microsoft Management Console, or through the HTML administration pages that are included with MTS. This is very similar to the interface provided for Internet Information Server 4, and gives an integrated management function that is useful when building and setting up distributed applications.

> *At the time of writing, MTS was available as an add-on to Windows NT4 in the form of the* **NT4 Option Pack**, *or as part of the Windows NT4* **Enterprise Edition**. *The Option Pack can be installed over the top of Windows NT4, requiring Service Pack 3 and Internet Explorer 4.01. Both are included in the Option Pack and are installed automatically.*

# What Does Transaction Server Do?

To understand what MTS is and what it does, we need to first make one very important point clear. This software should really have been named Microsoft **Component** Server, not Microsoft Transaction Server. MTS is all about managing the way applications use components, and *not* just about managing transactions. Yes, transactions are a big part of many applications we write and MTS can help to manage these—but MTS also provides a very useful service for applications that don't use transactions at all.

We're already tossing about words like 'transactions'—which are short on real meaning at the moment. To be able to define MTS accurately, we first need to understand what goes on inside it in the most basic way. That's what we'll do in this section, and you won't see anything more about transactions until later in the chapter.

We'll start by looking at the way we traditionally use components within our applications. This will help you to understand how and why MTS can make the whole process more efficient.

## Using Components Without MTS

When we use a component in an ASP page, for example, we have to create it before we can use it. The sequence of events is:

- ❑ Instantiate the component to create an instance of it
- ❑ Initialize the component instance, so that it is ready for use
- ❑ Use the component instance within our page
- ❑ Destroy the component instance after use

For example, in the previous chapter, we created and used an instance of the **WCCFinance** component like this:

```
...
Set objFinance = Server.CreateObject("WCCFinance.PaymentTerms")
objFinance.TotalPrice = Request.Form("txtTotalPrice")
objFinance.InterestRate = Request.Form("txtInterestRate")
objFinance.MonthlyPayment = Request.Form("txtMonthlyPayment")
intResult = objFinance.GetNumberPayments
'rest of page
...
```

### The Problem - Holding Component Instances

Although we didn't destroy the component explicitly in our page, it is implicitly destroyed as soon as the last reference to it is lost—i.e. when our page finishes executing, the results have been sent to the client, and the ASP code is removed from memory. Because we held the reference until our page was complete, the component was retained in memory. Even while it's not being used, it is taking up resources on the server.

In a multi-user environment, where there are high demands on server resources, it makes sense to destroy each instance of a component as quickly as possible. We could have improved the behavior of our page by adding a line that destroys it directly after the call to the method that provides the result:

```
Set objFinance = Server.CreateObject("WCCFinance.PaymentTerms")
objFinance.TotalPrice = Request.Form("txtTotalPrice")
objFinance.InterestRate = Request.Form("txtInterestRate")
objFinance.MonthlyPayment = Request.Form("txtMonthlyPayment")
intResult = objFinance.GetNumberPayments

Set objFinance = Nothing

'rest of page
```

However, if we decide that we need to use the component again later in the page, we will then have to create a new instance. We'll also have to set all the properties again, because the new instance will contain the default values. In this case we often tend to hang on to our object instead of explicitly destroying it, because it is far slower and much less efficient to keep recreating it.

It's also possible to hold on to component instances throughout the life of an application or user session in ASP, by defining it in **global.asa**. This is fine if the component is used very regularly, but forces it to stay in memory for the life of the application or session.

### Holding Database Connections

While holding on to component instances is bad enough, there is an even worse scenario. Most applications require access to a data store of some kind, usually a database such as Oracle, SQL Server, Sybase, etc. To provide database access in a component, we generally create a connection to the appropriate database through an OLE-DB or ODBC driver.

Database connections are expensive things to hang onto. There are a limited number available in any system, and they also take time and server resources both to create and maintain. Holding onto one in your ASP page is fine until you get a lot of users. At this point the database driver will begin to refuse connections, or the server will run out of resources. On the other hand, creating them over and over again slows the application down. Take, for instance, this pseudo code:

```
get a database connection

read some records
process some user-input values
process the record values
store the updated records
read some more records
calculate values for new records
create and store the new records

close and free the database connection
```

All the time this code is executing it holds onto the database connection, preventing other pages from using it. What we should really be doing is:

```
get a database connection

read some records

close and free the database connection

process some user-input values
process the record values

get a database connection

store the updated records
read some more records

close and free the database connection

calculate values for new records

get a database connection

create and store the new records

close and free the database connection
```

Now, the connection is available to other users while we are doing some other processing in our code. The problem is that the page will perform far more slowly. To help in this situation, many database drivers implement connection pooling to minimize the delays.

### Database Connection Pooling

Rather than having to create a new database connection each time a user requests one, many database (or data store) drivers, such as the ODBC 3.0 or later drivers for SQL Server, provide **connection pooling**. After a connection has been created, used by an application, and then freed when the application has finished with it, the driver holds the connection in memory in a pool.

When another application requests a connection the driver software searches the pool of available unused connections and, if it finds one that matches the requirements, supplies this instead of creating a new one. This provides much faster response. However, applications still have to acquire, use, and then free the connections, and this is still a time-consuming business.

*Note that connection pooling is not enabled by default in IIS 3, as it is in IIS4. In IIS 3 it can be enabled via a Registry setting—check out the IIS documentation for more details.*

## Providing Persistent Context for Components

MTS gets round the problems of component creation and destruction by providing a pool of component instances in much the same way as the data store drivers can provide a pool of available connections. However, it does this in a much more intelligent and comprehensive way.

MTS can provide a component to an application on demand, and allow other applications to use the component when the first one is just hanging on to the component instance, but not actually *using* it. It does this by fooling the application into thinking it still holds a reference to the component, when in fact MTS has spirited it away while the application wasn't looking and given it to someone else.

If the application suddenly wants to use the component that it thinks it's holding a reference to, MTS rushes around the pool of available instance and steals one from another application. Only if there are no available instances does it create a new one, and hand it over to the first application.

This rather risky-sounding technique is called **persistent context**, and it works because MTS provides a substitute 'dummy' context to the application, which thinks this is a real component. What it's actually got, of course, is just an empty shell...

### How MTS Provides Persistent Context

To see how MTS provides persistent context, take a look at this following series of events. Imagine we have three clients that at some point require access to a component that is on the server, which already provides instances to clients. In the following diagram (stage one) only clients **A** and **B** are using instances of the component. Client **C** has not yet created an instance of the component:

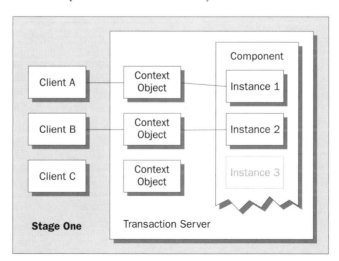

What's happened is that MTS has intercepted the calls from **A** and **B** that create the component instances (in our code earlier this was **CreateObject**), and instead created virtual **context objects** and returned references to these, rather than references to the component instances themselves. By reading the interface of the component it can (as we saw in the previous chapter) tell what functions the component provides, and thereby impersonate this interface within the context object.

> *A **context object** is not actually a physical object in itself. In COM terms, MTS creates a context and class factory wrapper for the component, and links this to a class factory object. However, the way it is actually implemented internally is not important here.*

Now (at stage two), client **A** has finished using the component, but has held on to the reference to it—in other words it hasn't destroyed it by setting the object variable it received when it created the instance to **Nothing**. What it's actually holding on to, of course, is the context object and not the component. MTS reclaims the component instance and returns it to the pool of available instances. At the same time, client **C** has requested an instance of the component, so MTS creates the context object for client **C** and links it to the instance of the component that it just took away from client **A**:

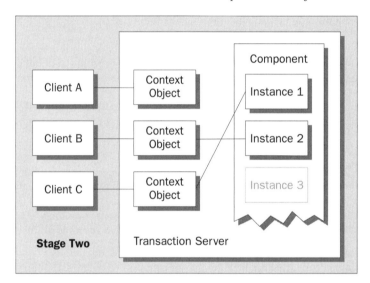

But, in stage three, client **A** wants to use the component again, maybe by calling another method within it. Unfortunately client **C** is still using it, but client **B** has temporarily finished with its instance of the component so MTS can grab this one and pass it to client **A**—by pointing **A**'s context object to this instance. Notice that client **A** will use this component instance without being able to tell that it is a different instance to the one it used last time:

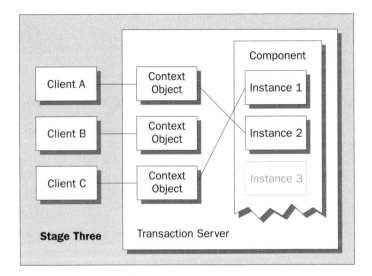

So, MTS can provide a seamless context for each client application for the life of the page or application process. The clients don't realize that the objects they are referencing are being constantly shuffled around behind the scenes. Like a good magic show, it's all smoke and mirrors.

### State and the Component Context

The big question is, of course, how does MTS know when an application has finished using a component instance? Obviously when the application tries to destroy the object either explicitly (with **Set** *objectvariable* **= Nothing**) or implicitly, when the page or process is complete, MTS knows that the object can be returned to the pool and the application's context object is then destroyed. But this is only half the story.

We looked at how an application may hold on to an instance of a component right through its lifetime. However, it may not actually be using the component all the time, and this is just the point where MTS needs to be able to reclaim the object and let other applications or processes use it. This is done by a couple of special lines of code added to the component.

When a component has finished a task, it calls the **SetComplete** or **SetAbort** methods of its context object, which effectively tell MTS that the component has finished the task and that it no longer requires its internal **state** to be maintained–i.e. all the data it was holding has either been returned to the client or stored permanently on disk. At this point MTS knows that it can reclaim the component and use it again elsewhere. When the original application comes back to use the component again, MTS can provide a fresh copy of it with default values for all the properties, etc.

This last point is vitally important to bear in mind. MTS can only reuse a component when the client application no longer expects the **state** to be the same as before. In other words, property settings and other information stored inside the component will probably *not* be the same as the last time it used the component. The application must reset any values that it needs by, for example, setting all the properties again.

> It's important to realize that it is the design of a component that dictates whether it requires its internal state to be maintained in order to function properly. Essentially, an object (in the traditional sense of the word) is a collection of data and methods that act upon the data. Most traditional client/server components follow a stateful paradigm, in which an object retains its data and methods in memory. Such components are created early and kept around for the entire duration of processing–and only released when the process completes.

### Component Caching and Pooling

Originally it was suggested that MTS would provide pooling of component instances, as hinted at in the section above. In fact in the current release–and probably for the foreseeable future–this is not actually the case. The `CanBePooled` method that MTS implements for each installed component has no effect at present.

> *The non-implementation of object pooling arises because all components currently used in MTS run under the Apartment threading model. However, if you mark the objects as Both threaded (only C++ or J++ support this, and not VB) then these object will be able to be pooled when (and if) MTS does support this feature in the future.*

MTS will cache the component itself, but it destroys instances of it when they are freed by the application that uses them; in other words when the application ends (or the ASP page is complete), or when the application or ASP code releases it's reference to the component explicitly. This may, for example, be the result of executing the line `Set` *objectvariable* `= Nothing`.

However, MTS can efficiently create new instances of the component on demand from the cached object, so the lack of component instance pooling is not generally a disadvantage. In the cached state, a component is said to be **deactivated**. By default MTS maintains a component object in this state for three minutes after the last time it was referenced by an application, though this delay can be changed. The process of caching components like this is often referred to as **Just-In-Time** (JIT) **Activation**.

# What Are Transactions?

Right, now that we know what MTS is capable of, it's time to see how it got its 'transaction' name. In this section of the chapter, we'll discuss what is meant by **transactions**, and then see how MTS changes the traditional ways that transactions are implemented in DNA.

The word **transaction** conjures up visions of banks and accounting systems, and most books use these kind of examples to overview what a transaction actually is. Here at Wrox, we're more laid back than that–we'll talk about ice-cream instead.

## *The Happy Ice-cream Seller*

There you are lying on a beach enjoying the sun, and you could kill for an ice-cream. You go up to the ice-cream stand and give the assistant some cash. They give you an ice-cream and your change. Yes, this is a transaction. You're both happy because you both get what you want—the seller makes a few cents profit and you get your popsicle.

Of course, if you hand over your money and get no ice-cream, you're not going to be too pleased. Likewise, if you take the ice-cream and run off without paying, the seller will feel less than happy with the deal. For it to work out, both actions have to take place. This is the basic principle of transactions, and where we get on to the technical stuff.

### *ACID Transactions*

For a transaction that involves more than a single action to succeed, all the parties involved in it must be satisfied with the result. This generally means that all the actions have to have taken place successfully—although in some cases, as you'll see when we come to look at Message Queue Server in later chapters, a promise that the action will take place is enough. The official definition of a robust transaction is the **ACID** test (pun intended). ACID stands for **Atomic, Consistent, Isolated** and **Durable**.

❑ A transaction meets the requirement of being **Atomic** if it must execute completely or not at all. In other words the actions that make up the transaction must either all complete successfully, or none be executed at all.

❑ To be classed as **Consistent,** a transaction must leave its environment and any data that it processes in a state that does not endanger integrity. In other words the sum of all the actions that make up the transaction must not break any rules laid down for the environment. In most practical cases this affects databases, and means that data integrity must be assured and the contents of the database be left in a state that is consistent with the data schema.

❑ A transaction meets the requirement of being **Isolated** if the sum effect of all the actions within a transaction give the same overall result as running these same actions one at a time serially (i.e. one after the other) would. This is because the system may actually run several actions within a single transaction concurrently, such as launching a stored procedure on one database, then going on to update another while the first is still executing. If the results are different in this situation the transaction is not **Isolated**.

❑ Finally, to be classed as **Durable**, all the actions within the transaction must have stored their results on some kind of permanent or durable device before they report success. This ensures that system software or application faults will not result in lost data after a transaction has completed and the user thinks the process was successful. Normally 'permanent' or 'durable' storage will be the hard disk, which should have logs files and other recovery features to prevent loss of data if this should, itself, fail.

## *Database Transactions*

Much of what we've talked about here is already implemented within modern database systems. For example SQL Server offers transactional processing, where the code can instruct SQL Server to start a transaction, edit, add and update data within the database; then tell SQL Server that all the work is complete and it that can **commit** the transaction.

While a transaction is in progress, SQL Server keeps note of all the changes to the data that are made by this process. Only when the transaction is committed does it make them permanent in the database. The application, in the meantime, can check for errors as it makes each change to the data. If one or more fails, it can **abort** the transaction rather than committing it. SQL Server then effectively 'rolls back', or undoes, all the changes made since the transaction started.

This ensures that the database is left in the same state as before. In our earlier example, it means that if we run away without paying the ice-cream seller, he will get his ice-cream back. Likewise, we will get our money back if the ice-cream seller can't supply our ice lolly. In a more real-world example, you can see how this would apply in the Wrox Car Co application. One of the components it uses accesses both local and remote databases to place an order. If the local action succeeds but the remote action fails, head office will not know about the order—and so there's no car for the customer. We've effectively taken the money and run away.

Most other databases implement this kind of system, using different syntax and methods. What's important here is that once we start to use MTS, we will avoid using *any* kind of explicit database transactions directly. For example, it's no longer necessary to create stored procedures in SQL Server that use the **BEGIN TRANSACTION** statement. MTS looks after them all for us automatically—the reason why the 'transaction' part appears in its name.

# Transactions Within MTS

MTS evolved as a **Transaction Processing** (TP) system to provide on Windows NT the same kinds of features as available in CICS®, Tuxedo®, etc. on other platforms. These are purely designed for creating stable transactional environments for data sources—predominantly relational databases like IBM's DB/2, Oracle, Informix and Sybase. Microsoft Transaction Server already offers support for SQL Server and Oracle, and will be extended to cover the other mainstream database systems in the future.

## *Distributed Transactions*

The first thing to consider is why we might want to extend transactions to MTS, instead of using the traditional database-implemented transactions we discussed earlier. The most obvious is that transactions within a database system can only encompass that database, although they can—of course—span different tables within it.

In the real world, we often need to carry out transacted operations that span different databases, which may be on different servers and even at different sites. Think back to the Wrox Car Co application where, as you saw earlier, we need to update both a local database on the showroom server and a remote database at the head office. Both updates must fall within the same transaction to make any sense. MTS can do this for us (almost) automatically.

### Resource Managers and the DTC

When MTS (or SQL Server) is installed, a separate service is added to Windows NT called the **Distributed Transaction Coordinator** (DTC). This runs as a service under Windows NT, and is used to coordinate transactions that span separate data stores or resources. To work, it requires each data store to implement its own proprietary **Resource Manager** (RM). SQL Server and most major databases already include these, though at present not all are compatible with the Windows NT DTC. They are generally part of the driver software—perhaps OLE-DB but more often ODBC at the moment.

The common protocol for communication between the DTC and the resource managers is **XA**, developed by the X/Open group. MTS supports this, and also its own protocol called **OLE Transactions** (currently only available for SQL Server). Notice, however, that we talk about 'data stores' rather than databases–one of the aims of Microsoft's **Universal Data Access** initiative is to provide seamless access to all kinds of data. OLE-DB drivers are becoming available for of Microsoft's own applications, such as the Active Directory Service and Exchange message stores.

To understand how a distributed transaction works, look at the following diagram. When a component requests access to a data store, the data store driver (usually OLE-DB or ODBC) checks with the appropriate MTS context object to see if a transaction is required. If it is, it informs the DTC, and then contacts the resource manager for the data store and tells it to start a transaction within that data store–in other words it automatically starts an integral 'database' transaction for this operation. Then the component (in this case via ADO) can work with the data on this device through the driver software; adding, updating and deleting records as required:

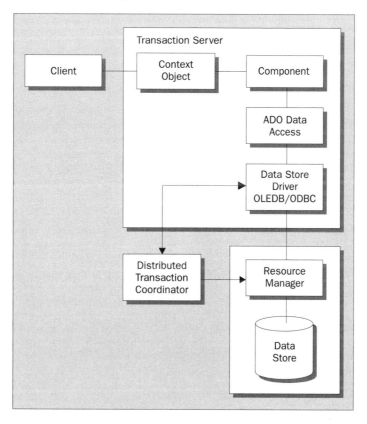

In the simplest case, where the component only accesses this data store and no other, it can call the **SetComplete** (or **SetAbort**) method once all the actions on the data are complete. This tells the DTC that the transaction is complete, and (under XA protocol) it instructs the driver software to commit or abort the transaction as appropriate. If the system is using OLE Transactions, the DTC can communicate directly with the resource manager to commit or abort the transaction instead of getting the driver to do it.

Now consider the case where we have two data stores to update within one transaction. In this case, the DTC and driver software start the database transaction in the first data store via the resource manager, as before. Then, once the component opens a connection to the second data store, the DTC and driver software contact this resource manager and tell it to start a new internal transaction for the updates that follow. Now both data stores are holding open transactions with the updates:

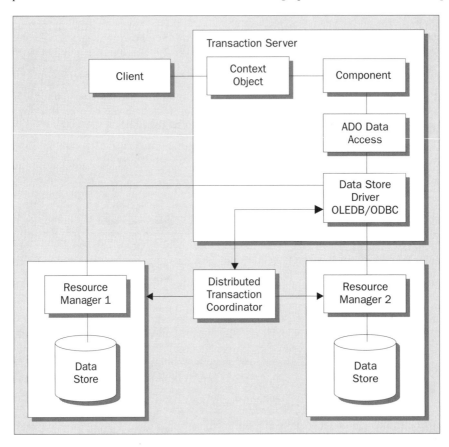

Once the component calls the **SetComplete** or **SetAbort** method, the DTC contacts both resource managers (via the driver software if XA is being used) and instructs them to commit or abort their current transaction. In this way, the transaction within MTS has been expanded to include the remote data stores as well. Either all the updates on all the data stores will succeed, or all will be rolled back.

## Controlling MTS Transactions Explicitly

When a client application references a component in MTS, the resulting context object provides information to MTS, the client, and other software such as the data source driver and the DTC. This information includes the 'transaction' setting for the component, which depends on the properties set when it was installed in MTS, and also on the code in the application—such as an ASP page that uses the component.

As well as calling the **SetComplete** and **SetAbort** methods, a component can exert control over how transactions work. For example, it can call the **DisableCommit** method, in order to prevent the DTC allowing a **SetComplete** or **SetAbort** method to commit open data store transactions on all resource managers until further notice. When it's ready to commit or abort the transaction, it can call the **EnableCommit** method.

### Creating Objects Within Transactions

Often, as it executes, a component needs to create instances of other objects with which to work. For example, an order handling component may need to create instances of a 'customer' object to get information about the customer that is placing the order. In VB, there are two main ways to create an instance of another object, **New** and **CreateObject**. MTS adds another method, **CreateInstance**. We'll look at the differences in the next section, where we examine all the methods that MTS provides in more detail.

# Using Components With MTS

Having seen in outline what MTS does, we'll now look in more detail at how we adapt components to work within it, and then how we adapt our applications to use the components once they are installed there. Later in this section we'll convert our simple **WCCFinance** component to take advantage of MTS. First, however, we'll examine the theory of designing, building and using components with MTS in more depth.

# Component Design Principles For MTS

We don't actually have to do anything to a component to use it in MTS, other than install it in a Package—as you'll see in a while. The component will benefit from the fact that MTS will run it in its own memory space separate from the Web server, and MTS will also control activation and deactivate to make it available to applications more quickly.

However, to feel the real benefits of MTS, we need to adapt our components and applications by adding MTS-specific code to them. This is easy enough to do, and generally involves only a few lines. There are some rules that we need to follow if we are to get the best performance from MTS, and there are also two different MTS interface objects that we can work with.

## Getting the Best Performance From MTS

The three main points to remember when you create applications or components for use in MTS are:

❑ **Acquire a pointer or reference to any components that you will use as early as possible**. In other words, create the object and store the reference to it throughout the life of the application, or until you are sure that it will not be required again. In Visual Basic, this means using the **CreateObject** statement (the **New** keyword should not be used to create instances of components that reside in MTS, as you'll see shortly). Because all you are holding is a reference to a context object, and not an instance of a real component, this is low on resource use. As you saw earlier, existing instances of the component will be dynamically shared between the applications or components that require it.

❑ **Acquire any data store (i.e. database) connections that you need as late as possible**, and free them as soon as you have finished with them and as often as possible in between. In most cases, data connections are pooled so that all applications can share them. This works best if applications only hold on to a connection for the minimum period possible. Also try and use the same connection information (such as username and password) where possible, because connections with different values for these cannot be shared, and this means that there is less chance of them being reused from the pool. We'll be looking at usernames and passwords in detail in Chapter 7.

❑ **Call the `SetComplete` method inside a component or application as often as possible** to allow MTS to recover the component instance and use it with another application. The component *reference* you are holding on to remains valid, but the component *instance* is not held in memory waiting to be used.

## Using MTS Interface Objects In A Component

There are two main COM interface objects available in MTS that we can code to, and between them they allow us to control how our applications and components behave within the MTS environment.

### The ObjectContext Interface Object

The most useful interface that the MTS provides for our components is that of the context object allocated to our application for this component. Every context object exposes the COM interface **`IObjectContext`**. There is a global MTS method **`GetObjectContext()`** that returns a reference (or interface pointer) to the context object. In a Visual Basic component, we normally use this as follows:

```
Dim objOContext As ObjectContext
Set objOContext = GetObjectContext()
```

Then we can use the methods of the context object to:

❑ Commit or abort the current transaction
❑ Enable and disable the current transaction from being committed
❑ Check out the security clearance of users of the component

We'll be looking at the whole subject of security in Chapter 8. For the meantime, we'll concentrate on how we use the other methods within our components. The **`SetComplete`** and **`SetAbort`** methods, as we've seen, are used to indicate to MTS whether our component is happy with the outcome of its operations. For example:

```
objOContext.SetComplete
```

tells MTS that we have completed all the operations that we intended to, and we are happy that everything went well. As far as this component is concerned, the complete transaction can be committed. If something went wrong, however, we call:

```
objOContext.SetAbort
```

This tells MTS that we aren't happy with the outcome of the operations we performed, and that it is to abort the entire transaction and roll back all the changes made by all the other components within this transaction.

If we are embarking on a series of operations, which at certain points could leave data in an indeterminate state, we can tell MTS that the current transaction is not to be committed under any circumstances until we're ready. To do this, we use:

```
objOContext.DisableCommit
```

Then, when we're ready we can call:

```
objOContext.EnableCommit
```

to indicate that MTS can commit the transaction, but should not release and reuse this object (if we called **SetComplete**, MTS would destroy our object instance).

Whether the transaction is committed will depend, of course, on whether all the components within the transaction (including ours) have signaled that they are also happy to commit.

### Creating Component Instances

The context object also provides the **CreateInstance** method, which we can use to create dependent instances of other objects, for use by our component. This doesn't stop us using the **New** or **CreateObject** methods, but it's important to understand the effects of each one as far as MTS is concerned.

The **New** keyword in VB is used to create a new instance of a class as an object, for use within the current application. When used in a component within MTS, it creates a **Private** instance of an object that MTS knows nothing about. It won't have its own context object, and won't be included within the current transaction. In other words, it has to look after itself with no help from MTS.

The **CreateObject** method is almost exactly the opposite. When used in a component running within MTS, this creates a new instance of an object that MTS will treat as separate from the current component instance—and it will get its own context object. However, this will not contain any information from the context of the component that created the new instance, so it will run outside the current transaction.

The **CreateInstance** method of the context object provides a solution to these two problems. It creates a new instance of the referenced component and provides it with a new context object. However, it also copies the transaction information from the context of the object that created it into the new context—thus making it part of the current transaction:

```
objOContext.CreateInstance("MyClasses.Customer")
```

### The ObjectControl Interface Object

The second COM interface, named **IObjectControl**, is that of the component class factory, as stored in MTS when the component is installed. This is useful for carrying out tasks during activation and deactivation of the component. In Visual Basic, we implement this interface within our component using the **Implements** keyword:

```
Implements ObjectControl
```

Our **ObjectControl** interface must provide three methods, **Activate**, **Deactivate** and **CanBePooled**. Together they provide a way for us to control how our object interacts with MTS. The **Activate** method is called when an instance of our component is created—either for the first time, or (if it has been deactivated after use) from the cached object pool. The **Deactivate** method is called just before it is returned to the cache after use. The **CanBePooled** method is used to tell MTS whether the component instance can be pooled or not; remember, though, that instance pooling is not currently supported—only a limited form of component caching is implemented at present.

Whether we implement it is entirely optional, but if we do need to carry out any processing when the component is activated or deactivated, we have to implement it so that MTS will provide the **Activate** and **Deactivate** events.

To see how we can use the **ObjectControl** interface, look at the following code. It acquires a reference to the context object as soon as the component instance is activated, and tells MTS that it will be OK to pool this instance if Microsoft ever gets round to implementing support for it:

```
Implements ObjectControl

Private objOContext     'global variable to hold the object context

Private Function ObjectControl_Activate()
  'get the object context as soon as instance is activated
  Set objOContext = GetObjectContext()
End Function

Private Function ObjectControl_Deactivate()
  'release the object context
  Set objOContext = Nothing
End Function

Private Function ObjectControl_CanBePooled()
  ObjectControl_CanBePooled = True
End Function
```

Of course, we can do any other initialization and clean-up we need to in the **Activate** and **Deactivate** methods. If the object needs to maintain state for any reason (though it generally shouldn't) we can save and reload values here. We can also use them to create and destroy instances of any other objects we need to use:

```
Implements ObjectControl
Private objOContext     'global variable to hold the object context

Private objCustomer     'global variable to hold customer object
```

```
Private Function ObjectControl_Activate()
    'get the object context as soon as instance is activated
    Set objOContext = GetObjectContext()

    Set objCustomer = objOContext.CreateInstance("MyClasses.Customer")
    objCustomer.LoadValues   'custom routine to load state from disk

End Function

Private Function ObjectControl_Deactivate()
    'release the object context

    objCustomer.SaveValues   'custom routine to save state to disk
    Set objCustomer = Nothing

    Set objOContext = Nothing
End Function
```

## Starting a Transaction

The example component we've been using so far, and which we'll continue to use in this chapter, is a stand-alone server component. It doesn't require a transaction, because only this component is used in the application. We're really only using MTS to get the benefit of its component instance management features. However, this isn't usually the case—we'll often have two or more components in use and these need to be part of a transaction.

### Component Transaction Support Options

MTS allocates a Transaction Support property to each component installed within it. This property has four possible settings, and defines how the component will behave within MTS when activated. The options are:

| | |
|---|---|
| Requires a transaction | The component will run within an existing transaction if one already exists. If not, MTS will start a new one. |
| Requires a new transaction | MTS will start a new transaction each time an instance of the component is activated. |
| Supports transactions | The component will run within an existing transaction if one exists. If not, it will run without a transaction. |
| Does not support transactions | The component will always run outside any existing transactions. |

So, we could set the Transaction Support property for one component (let's call it **A**) to 'Requires a new transaction' and the other (**B**) to 'Requires a transaction' (or even 'Supports transactions'). The only thing now is that we would have to be sure to always instantiate them in the right order. If we instantiate **A** *after* **B**, it won't be part of the same transaction as **B**— it will create a new transaction of its own. And if we had set **B** to just 'Supports transactions', we wouldn't get a transaction for this one at all unless the application had already started a transaction for a different component.

On top of this, we also reduce the opportunities for reusing components if we have to run them in a particular order. We can't use two components that have the 'Requires a new transaction' setting inside one transaction. What we need to do in this case is set all the components that actually carry out specific tasks to 'Requires a transaction' or 'Supports transactions', so that we can freely use them together in any combination.

### Using A Parent Component To Control A Transaction

The usual way to get round the problem of the Transaction Setting property is to have a 'parent' component that creates instances of the other components and manages them. In the case of the Wrox Car Co application, which you'll be seeing a lot more of in the following chapter, placing an order involves two components. One handles local database updates, and the other handles remote database updates:

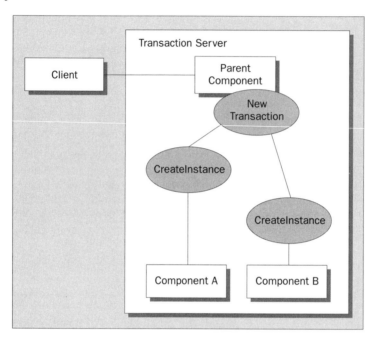

The parent component is responsible for initiating a transaction that includes the other two components. For this reason, the parent component has its Transaction Setting property set to 'Requires a new transaction' while the other two components, which do the real work, have their Transaction Setting properties set to 'Requires a transaction'.

### SetComplete And SetAbort In A Parent Component

The 'parent' component is part of the same transaction as any components that it creates using the **CreateInstance** method of the **ObjectContext** object. (Remember that this is not the case with **New** or **CreateObject**.) Therefore, both 'parent' and 'child' components can control the outcome of the transaction using the **SetAbort** and **SetComplete** methods, in just the same way.

This isn't usual, however, because the components that do the work should indicate success or failure to MTS by calling **SetComplete** or **SetAbort** as appropriate. The parent component would *only* use these methods if it has to cancel the transaction on command for some reason. However, it can use the **DisableCommit** and **EnableCommit** methods to control when MTS can make the transaction changes permanent, as we saw earlier. This might be useful in a situation where the data could be in an inconsistent state during certain parts of the process.

### Nested Transactions

We've seen how MTS automatically enlists components into an existing transaction when they are created with the **CreateInstance** method of the parent's **ObjectContext** object. However, this only works if the component either supports transactions or requires a transaction. If it requires a *new* transaction, it cannot be enlisted into an existing one.

In this case, MTS starts a new nested transaction for this component and any other components it enlists (unless they too require a new transaction). It is then up to this component to indicate to MTS whether it wants to commit or abort the original transaction (by calling **SetComplete** or **SetAbort**) based on the results of the nested transaction.

For example, the following diagram shows four components **A**, **B**, **C** and **D**, together with their transaction support property. **RT** means that this component requires a (existing) transaction or supports transactions, while **RNT** means that the component requires a *new* transaction:

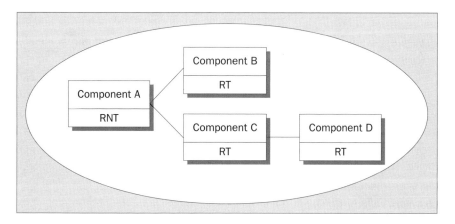

In this case a single automatic transaction encompasses all the components, and will only complete if all four components agree to commit. However, if component **C** was marked as requiring a new transaction, as in the next diagram, a nested transaction is created. Now component **C** can still commit the transaction (by calling **SetComplete**) even if component **D** failed—if this was appropriate.

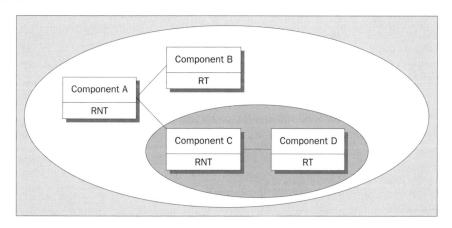

### Using ASP To Start A Transaction

We generally think of components as being compiled DLLs created in languages like C++, J++, Delphi or Visual Basic. However, Active Server Pages scripts can also be considered as server-side components, and ASP is an ideal tool for initiating and controlling a transaction within MTS. We can take advantage of the **ObjectContext** interface in Active Server Pages just as we can in other components.

In **Active Server Pages** (under IIS 4) we use a different technique to reference the MTS context object. We add a line to the start of the ASP page that indicates how we want to use components within MTS in this page:

```
<%@ Transaction = value %>
```

Here *value* can be:

| | |
|---|---|
| **Required** | Indicates that MTS should either use the current transaction for this page, or start a new transaction if one is not already available. |
| **Requires_New** | Indicates that MTS should start a new transaction even if there is an existing one. |
| **Supported** | Indicates that MTS should use the current transaction if one exists, but not start a new one. |
| **Not_Supported** | Indicates that this page is not to be included in a transaction. |

These values are, of course, similar to the Transaction Property settings we listed earlier for compiled components.

> *Note that ASP only allows one* **@** *' line in a page. If you already use this to set the default script language for the page, you can add the* **Transaction** *statement to the same line:*
>
> ```
> <%@ Language = VBScript Transaction = Required %>
> ```

### Using The ObjectContext Events in ASP

MTS also provides our ASP scripts with **events**. This gives us an easy way to discover the outcome of a single component's execution, or the result of a multi-component transaction. Remember that components can initiate processes that occur concurrently as part of a complete transaction. So, simply calling the methods of each component within a transaction may not provide confirmation that they all completed properly unless you design the components specifically to do this.

All we have to do is create an event handler for the **OnTransactionCommit()** and **OnTransactionAbort()** events that MTS provides:

```
Sub OnTransactionCommit()
    'code for when transaction completed OK
End
```

```
Sub OnTransactionAbort()
    'code for when transaction failed
End
```

We'll see how these can be used when we adapt and use the **WCCFinance** sample component in MTS in the next section of this chapter.

# Adapting Our Simple Finance Component

The context object that MTS provides for each component instance has the two methods we've mentioned already, **SetComplete** and **SetAbort**. In this part of the chapter we'll see how we can use these within the simple **WCCFinance** component that we created in the previous chapter. Then we'll install the component into Transaction Server and get our first glimpse of MTS in action.

## Modifying The Component Code

As we suggested earlier, the effort required to change a component so that it can take advantage of MTS varies from 'none at all' to 'loads of work'. It really comes down to whether or not the component was originally designed to maintain **state** (which isn't what we really want). Our sample component has only a single method, and three write-only properties. Generally, using properties in a component creates state, because the code that uses it will usually expect the values to remain the same after they've been set. This isn't, as we've seen, always the case within MTS.

So it's better to use methods in your components that accept **parameters**, and provide the values for the parameters when you call the method each time. That way, the component can become stateless, and operate more efficiently within MTS. However, we're going to live with properties in this example. You'll see how we use parameters instead of properties in subsequent components of the Wrox Car Co application.

### Changes To The Component Interface

One particular point to remember is the one we mentioned earlier about changing the interface of your component as you adapt it for use with MTS. To get the best performance you should call the **SetComplete** or **SetAbort** methods as often as possible within the component. However, each time suppose that one of these method calls is made, MTS assumes that the component's state (internal values) can be disposed of. Therefore, simply adding either of these calls to a component's methods will change the way the component behaves.

For example, suppose that our application sets some property values inside the component and then calls a method in that component, which contains **SetComplete** or **SetAbort**. Then MTS will reclaim the component instance and the property values are lost. If our application then comes back to the component again–through the context object that it thinks is a real component–and reads one of these values, it will get the wrong result. In this case, the application is treating the object as if it were still holding its state, whereas the **SetComplete** and **SetAbort** methods tell MTS that it is stateless at that point.

So even though we haven't changed any of the names or parameters of the component's members, or the way they work under the hood, we *have* changed the interface definition. Calling a method in it, or reading the value of a property, could well produce a different (and unexpected) result. To get round this, you may want to change the interface definition more obviously–by changing the names of the members for example. In C++ or other languages that permit it, you may prefer to implement a separate interface instead.

### Referencing MTS In The VB Design Environment

Before we start to work with MTS components in VB, it's useful to add a reference to the MTS interfaces type library to VB. In this way it can provide information about the properties, methods and events supported by each object–including pop-up syntax assistance.

In the Project | References dialog click Browse and locate the file **mtxas.dll** (probably in the **Program Files\Mts** folder on your server). If you are developing on a separate machine (always a good idea) you can copy the DLL into a folder on your local machine and select it there instead. This adds the Microsoft Transaction Server Type Library entry to the References dialog:

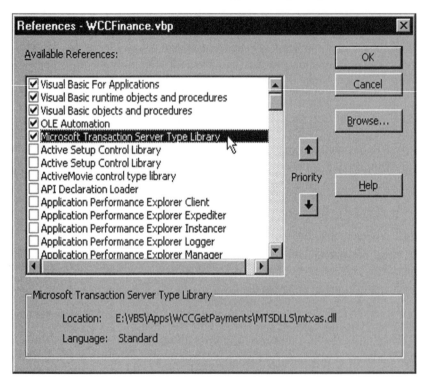

Once referenced within VB, we can then use the Object Browser to examine the members of the MTS interface objects as we work. Be sure to select the library MTxAS in the upper-left combo box:

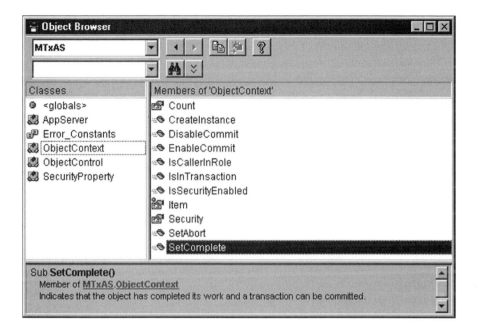

### Adding the MTS Code To The WCCFinance Component

The changes we need to make to our code are minimal, and only affect the `GetNumberPayments` method. We're not implementing the `ObjectControl` interface, because we have no procesing requirements for `Activate` or `Deactivate`. Instead, we get a reference to the context object as we enter the method. Here are the changes to the code:

```
Public Function GetNumberPayments() As Integer

    'get reference to the context object
    Dim objOContext As ObjectContext
    Set objOContext = GetObjectContext()

    'rest of function code goes here
    ...
```

The next part of the original code calculated the number of payments, and placed the result in the variable `intNumberMonths`. If the monthly payment was insufficient to pay the interest and reduce the balance, it set `intNumberMonths` to zero. The function also returned zero if there was an error. We'll do the same in the new version, but before we end execution of the method code we'll call either `SetComplete` or `SetAbort` as appropriate:

```
    ...
    GetNumberPayments = intNumberMonths

    'complete or abort the MTS context
    If intNumberMonths > 0 Then
        objOContext.SetComplete
    Else
        objOContext.SetAbort
```

```
End If
   Exit Function
   ...
```

To complete the method code we add a call to **SetAbort** in the error handler, so that an error will prevent a transaction from taking place:

```
   ...
GNP_Error:
   GetNumberPayments = 0   'indicates an error
   objOContext.SetAbort      'abort the MTS context
   Exit Function
End Function
```

And that's it. We just recompile the component and copy it to the server. You will have to stop and restart the server before you can replace an existing component if you installed the sample from the previous chapter.

## Installing Components Into MTS

Once the component is on the server and properly registered we can add it to MTS. The process is referred to as **installing** it in MTS because it permanently changes the way the component is referenced within Windows (until you delete it from MTS again).

### Microsoft Management Console and MTS

The main administration for MTS is the **Transaction Server Explorer**. In Windows NT Server this is a snap-in to the **Microsoft Management Console** (MMC), while in Windows 95 it is a separate executable file. MMC provides a one-stop-shop for working with several services at once, such as Internet Information Server and Index Server as well as MTS. If you don't see the Microsoft Transaction Server entry in MMC after installing MTS, you can add it using the Console menu.

The following screen shot shows Transaction Server Explorer in the MMC, together with some of the default components that are installed from the NT4 Option Pack. Notice that there is an entry for each computer, because MMC can be configured to administer remote servers as well as the local one. For each computer there is a set of **packages** that are installed within MTS on that machine. A package can contain one or more components, and is simply a way of setting up and managing them all together. Each package has a set of **roles**. Roles are part of the security mechanism implemented within MTS, and we'll be looking at this in more detail in Chapter 8:

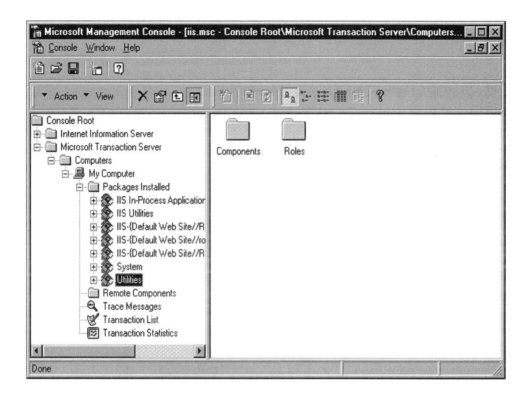

### Creating A New Package For WCCFinance

Creating a new package is as easy as right-clicking the Packages Installed entry and selecting New then Component. The Package Wizard opens, with a choice of two ways of creating a package:

*Like most other tasks that you can perform with the MMC, you also can do this from the drop-
down list marked Action. In Windows 95, Transaction Server Explorer does not support
right-click menus so the standard menu bar is used instead.*

We want a new, empty package rather than a pre-built one (components and their packages can be
exported, and then installed as pre-built packages package on other machines). The next screen (not
shown) just allows us to enter a name for the package. In the third screen, we set up the identity for
the package, i.e. the user account that it uses to access other services on the machine. We'll use the
default of the current user:

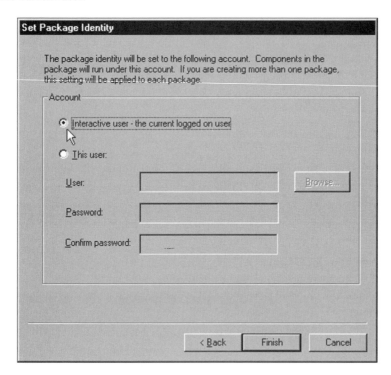

*While we are running the components from a Web browser with anonymous access, the current
user will be IIS. However there are often situations where this is not the case, and so selecting
Interactive User is the best plan unless you can be sure that you can validate the user
directly. You'll find a detailed discussion of users and identities in Chapter 8.*

Finally, clicking Finish creates the new package, which we named WCCFinanceTest, and we're
ready to add our component to it.

### Installing the WCCFinance Component

To add our component to the new empty package we right-click the Components entry and select
New | Component (or use the Action menu):

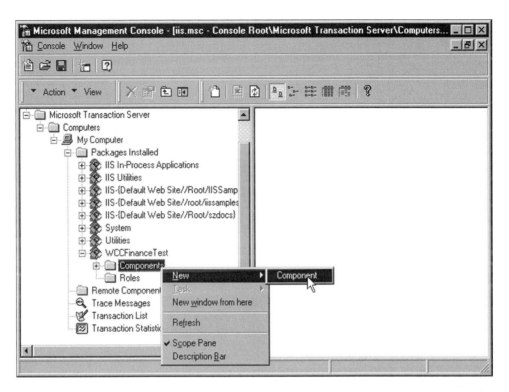

This starts the Component Wizard, and the first screen allows us to install a new (unregistered) component or import a previously registered one. We've already registered our **WCCFinance** component, so we choose the second option:

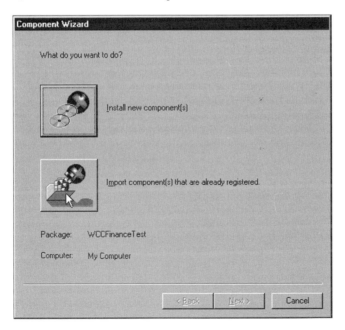

*Importing previously registered components has the minor disadvantages in that you can't set the properties for any individual interfaces within that component. In this case you should un-register it and install it as a new component.*

Clicking Next means coffee-time unless you have a fast machine. The Wizard trawls through the Registry building a list of available components. If you turn on the Details checkbox, you can get useful details about the components that are available. In the screen shot, we've found our **WCCFinance** component in the list:

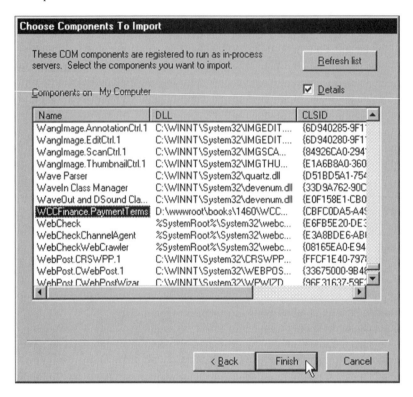

*When you install a component in MTS, the registry entries for it are changed. MTS swaps its own class ID for your component's class ID, so that references to the component are redirected to MTS with a parameter added that identifies which package and component was referenced. For this reason, you won't find any components that are **already** installed in MTS in the list.*

Selecting the component from the list and clicking Finish places it in the current package:

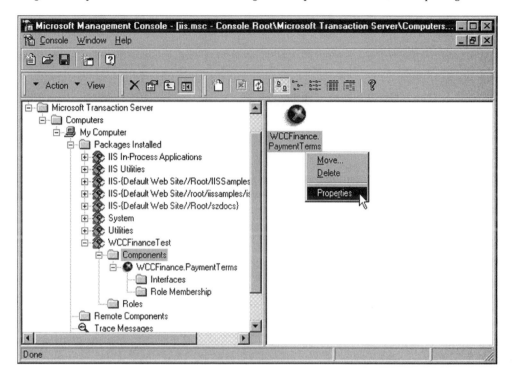

*You can also install components by dragging them from Explorer into the right-hand pane of MMC when the appropriate package's* **Components** *entry is selected.*

The final step is to set the MTS properties for the component, by right-clicking it and selecting Properties. The General tab provides useful information about the component, and allows us to enter a description for it:

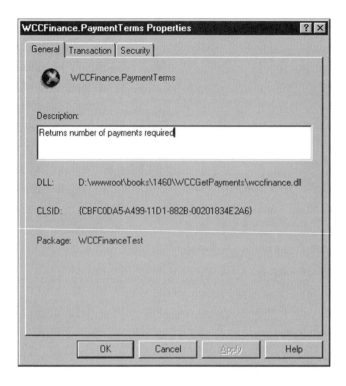

However, the most important property is the Transaction Support entry. We need 'Supports transactions' for our component:

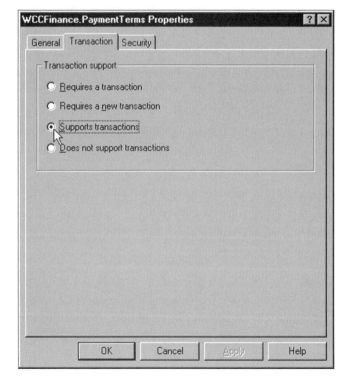

*We discussed the options available earlier in the chapter. If a component has been designed to be used either within a multi-component transaction or by itself, we'll usually choose 'Supports transactions'. However, if it is designed to be the parent of several components, and it always initiates a transaction, we would probably choose ' Requires a new transaction'.*

### Viewing Activated Component Information

The MTS snap-in for Microsoft Management Console provides some other useful extras. One is the ability to switch to Status View. This shows information about the number of cached and activated objects in use at any one time:

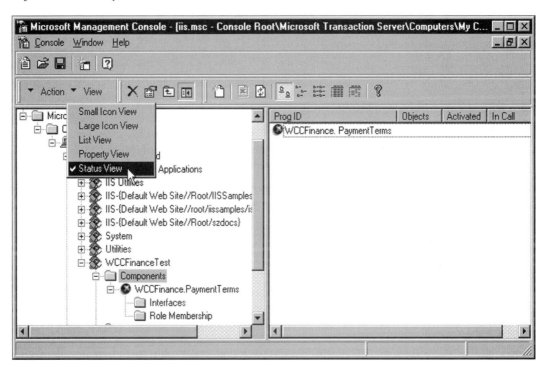

### Stopping and Starting the DTC

In a previous section of this chapter we talked about the way that Windows Distributed Transaction Coordinator (DTC) controls data store transactions. The DTC, like many other parts of our application's environment, is a service that can be started and stopped. This can be done from within MMC by right-clicking the appropriate Computers entry:

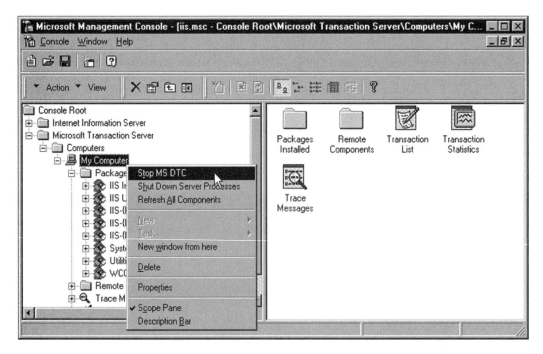

If your applications use the DTC, you should arrange for it to be started automatically each time Windows starts up. This can be done in the Services applet available from Control Panel, or from within the Server Manager program. The monitor screen of the My Computer icon changes color to reflect the state of the DTC–dark green shows that it is not running, yellow shows that it is starting to run, and light green indicates that it is running.

### Remote MTS Components

So far we've only discussed components that are installed on the server and referenced directly by applications that are also running there. However, COM allows an application to use a component that is stored on a remote machine. This means, for example, that we can place the component on the server inside MTS, but create and work with an instance of it remotely from an application running on the client–including client-side scripting in a browser. This is **Distributed COM** (DCOM) at work.

DCOM uses **proxy** and **stub** objects to provide transport remote activation and invocation. The proxy object is loaded on the client, and the stub is loaded in the process of the component. MTS makes it easy to create install routines that will set up components to be used in this way.

Remote components are useful in MTS where the performance or other issues dictate that a component should be installed on a remote machine, but still take part in a transaction with other components on the local machine. For example, a component that processes large sets of data but returns no result (other than indicating the result via **SetComplete** or **SetAbort**) might provide better performance if it was installed on the same machine as the data store. However, performance considerations must include the fact that invoking a method on a remote object is an order of magnitude slower than invoking a method on a local object.

DCOM allows servers running MTS to share their local components. In MMC you add the remote computer to the Computers folder by right-clicking on it and selecting New | Computer, or by using the Action menu. You can let MTS list all networked machines, and select the one you want to use:

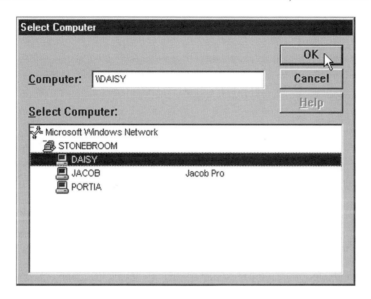

In the MMC entry for the source (local) machine, right-click the package you want to export and enter a name for the `.pak` file that MTS will create. This file can then be installed on the remote machine:

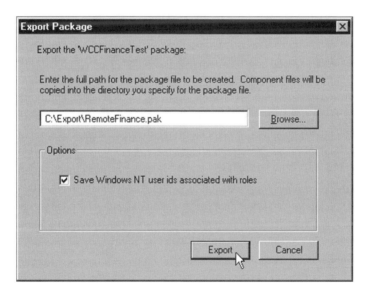

Then, within the MMC, select the remote machine (remember MMC can administer remote servers as well as the local one). Alternatively you can move to the remote machine and open the MMC there. To install the package, right-click the Remote Packages folder and select the machine, package, and components that you want to install. MTS doesn't copy the component itself, just the files required to access it via DCOM over the network.

*Microsoft's currently evolving **Remote Scripting** technology also allows a client-side script to interact with objects via a server-side ASP page. We aren't covering Remote Scripting in this book, as the technology is too young to be of real value yet. However, it will provide extra opportunities to use MTS components as it matures and stabilizes.*

## Why Packages?

Rather than install all our components as separate items in MTS, we must, as you've seen, create packages and install them within a package. It's a similar concept to storing disk files in separate sub-directories, rather than all in the root directory of your disk.

Each package should contain a set of components that between them perform related tasks within an application. Packages allow us to encapsulate components for installation as a group either locally or remotely. They also provide a way to allocate properties and security permissions to all the components within a package in one go, in the same way that we can allocate security permissions to users within a group in Windows NT. In a later chapter of this book, we'll look at the security properties in more detail. For the time being, we'll look at the other features that packages provide.

### Setting The Activation Timeout

When we discussed how MTS deactivates and caches components after use, we said that the default was to hold the component in memory for three minutes. This behavior can be changed in the Activation page of the Properties dialog for each package separately:

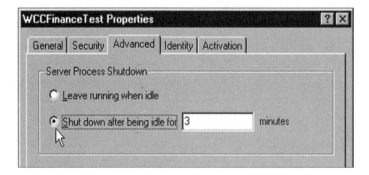

The setting you choose depends on the way the components in that package will be used—in general the default gives reasonable performance under average conditions. The shut down delay is the time-out period in minutes (between 0 and 1440) before the component will be removed from memory after use.

*In Transaction Server Explorer there are also two permission-related check boxes:* Disable
Deletion, *which prevents users from deleting the package from the Explorer without first
clearing the box; and* Disable Changes, *which prevents changes to the package's attributes
and contained components unless the check box is clear. In the MMC,  these features are handled
by Windows' own native security features.*

### Setting The Activation Location

The Activation page of the Properties dialog controls where the component instances will be created
and executed. In general, you will execute them in the MTS environment–in other words in a
'dedicated server process'. If you want to execute them within the memory space of the 'creator'
process, you can choose this option. It provides higher performance if there are multiple calls from
the creator application to the component, but means that a failure of the component can crash the
creator process as well.

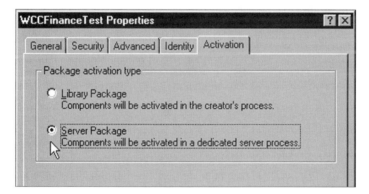

If you are using roles to control access permissions to your components, you should always choose
the default Server Package option. In general, we will use this setting for all our components.

## Modifying The ASP Code

Our component is now nestling warm and safe inside MTS, and we can start to use it in an
application. We're only going to show you one example here, using an updated version of the Active
Server Pages file that we used in the previous chapter with the  un-transacted component.

So, what do we need to do that's different? In the component, we added code that will call the MTS
**SetComplete** method if everything goes OK in the  calculation, and **SetAbort** if not. However this
will only happen if the component is running under a transaction. Because we set its  Transaction
Support property to 'Supports transactions', it will use an existing one, but it will not start a new
one if there isn't one running already.

This means that if we want to benefit from the transactional features of our component we have to
start a transaction running before we activate it. Of course, we could have set the  Transaction
Support property to 'Requires a transaction' but that would mean that we could never run it without
one.

In fact, as you saw earlier in the chapter when we looked at ways of starting a transaction, we can effectively override the Transaction Support property setting in our ASP script using the **Transaction** statement at the head of the page. This only affects the current page, and hence the instances of components that we create within the page. Once we start a transaction, all the instances of the components we create will join in this transaction unless they have a Transaction Support property of 'Requires a new transaction' or 'Does not supports transactions'.

So we just have to add the statement **Transaction = Required** to the head of our ASP page to make sure that a transaction is running for this component instance–here we've added it to the existing **LANGUAGE** statement:

```
<%@ LANGUAGE = VBScript Transaction = Required %>
...
```

### Creating The Component Instance

Now we can create our component instance, and set the properties as we did in the example of the previous chapter. As soon as we access the component for the first time, i.e. to set the **TotalPrice** property, MTS creates a context object and activates and holds onto the component for us. It won't be deactivated until **SetComplete** or **SetAbort** is called within the component's code, so we can continue setting the property values with no fear of it disappearing.

The final line of this section of code calls the **GetNumberPayments** method of our component:

```
...
<%
Set objFinance = Server.CreateObject("WCCFinance.PaymentTerms")
objFinance.TotalPrice = Request.Form("txtTotalPrice")
objFinance.InterestRate = Request.Form("txtInterestRate")
objFinance.MonthlyPayment = Request.Form("txtMonthlyPayment")
intResult = objFinance.GetNumberPayments
%>
...
```

### Into The Black Hole

Because we are using a transaction, we don't know what's going on now until MTS tells us. Although we can guess that when our method call returns the task will be complete, we can't always guarantee this in a more general case. We really only know that it will happen here because we're using a single component that we built ourselves–so we know how it works.

In the real world, we may not know what's going on in the component, and of course there could well be several different ones used in the page anyway. It's a bit like tossing the values into a black hole then waiting to see if anything comes out. The upshot of all this is that the only thing we can reliably do here is tell the user that something's happening:

```
...
<BODY>
Your inquiry is being processed, please wait...<P>
...
```

### Responding To The MTS Transaction Events

Thankfully you have a good deal more chance of something coming back from your component than you do with a black hole (even of you have only limited experience of creating components yourself). This is what we're depending on, but we need to know when MTS actually does return the result. We do this by handling the two MTS context object events **OnTransactionCommit** and **OnTransactionAbort**:

```
...
<%
Sub OnTransactionCommit()
   strResult = "<P>A total price of <B>$" & Request.Form("txtTotalPrice") _
            & "</B> at a monthly interest rate of <B>" _
            & Request.Form("txtInterestRate") & "%</B>, and paying <B>$" _
            & Request.Form("txtMonthlyPayment") & "</B> per month, " _
            & "will require <B>" & intResult & "</B> payments.</P>"
   Response.Write strResult
End Sub

Sub OnTransactionAbort()
   strResult = "<P>Sorry, the calculation could not be completed. " _
            & "Either the monthly payment amount you entered " _
            & "is not sufficient to pay off the loan, " _
            & "or another error occurred.</P>"
   Response.Write strResult
End Sub
%>

</BODY>
</HTML>
```

And here's the result. Isn't it wonderful when a plan comes together like this?

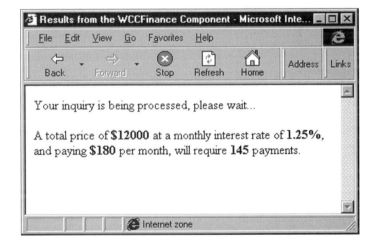

*Note that aborting a transaction does not rollback changes to any ASP session-level variables. The **OnTransactionAbort** event handler should be used to reset the session variables if this is appropriate in your application.*

# Summary

In this chapter we've introduced you to Microsoft Transaction Server, and used a simple component and ASP script to demonstrate it in action. At first, MTS seems a complex concept to grasp, but much of it operates transparently behind the scenes. We will, however, uncover some more of the details in later chapters.

MTS is a service running under Windows NT Server that caches, allocates, activates and deactivates instances of components that are used by your applications. This can improve response times and maximize resource availability, providing superior performance to distributed applications—particularly when they are built along the DNA guidelines. In this respect, it is comparable to what are often referred to as **Object Request Broker** (ORB) services available on other platforms.

But MTS can do more than this. It provides the services of a **Transaction Processor** as well, allowing components to be linked into transactions that must all succeed or all be rolled back. This feature makes building reliable and robust data management applications much simpler, especially in distributed applications where the data may reside on several different and remote servers.

So, in this chapter, we've seen:

❑   What Microsoft Transaction Server is, and what it can do.

❑   What transactions are, and how MTS makes them more powerful and easier to use.

❑   What levels of transaction support are available now, and will be in the future.

❑   How we build new components and adapt existing ones for use with MTS.

❑   How we install components into MTS, and use them in applications.

We move on in the next chapter to resume the story of the Wrox Car Co sample application. We'll adapt the components you saw in the previous chapter to use transactions, and look at how we go about designing and building an application that uses them.

# Building the Application

So far we have spent a lot of time laying foundations and looking at the theory of components and transactions. We've seen that components are simply class modules compiled into a COM object (ActiveX DLL). We've also seen that it is easy to add transaction support to a component, so that we can safely buy our ice cream without the seller running off with our money before giving us our Super Triple Scoop Choc 'n' Chip Combo.

The previous chapters have shown all of this with the **WCCFinance** object, but now we need to look at some more complex components to see these techniques in more detail.

In this chapter we are going to look at:

- ❑ The architecture of the Wrox Car Co database
- ❑ The Cars component
- ❑ The Showroom Ordering component
- ❑ The Head Office Ordering component
- ❑ A combined Ordering component
- ❑ Using the components

Within the construction of these components we will show how they are created, how transactions are supported, and how we can use the components in building our application. Since one of the ideas behind DNA is client transparency, we will build an application as both a Visual Basic project and a Web based project.

# The Wrox Car Co Database

The Wrox Car Co has a head office in Chicago and showrooms all over the country. The head office has a database with a list of cars and colors, and customer orders. Each showroom has a similar database, allowing them to keep track of their own orders. Let's have a look at these in a little more detail, starting with the Head Office database.

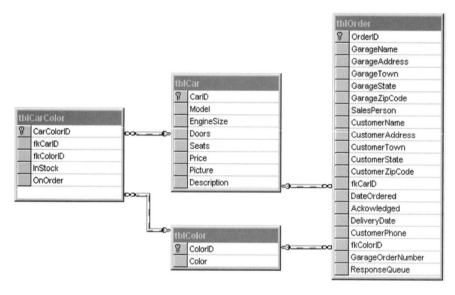

As you can see, this is a fairly simple database. There is a table for the cars, a table for the colors, and a table showing the car color combinations that are available. The order table combines everything about a particular order for a car, including the Garage (or showroom) details. The diagram is from Visual InterDev which doesn't show the relationships as easily as it could, so here they are in a more detailed form:

| From | To | Type |
|------|------|------|
| tblCar.ID | TblCarColor.fkCarID | One to Many |
| tblColor.ID | TblCarColor.fkColorID | One to Many |
| tblCar.ID | TblOrder.fkCarID | One to Many |
| tblColor.ID | TblOrder.fkColorID | One to Many |

The showroom database is not much different:

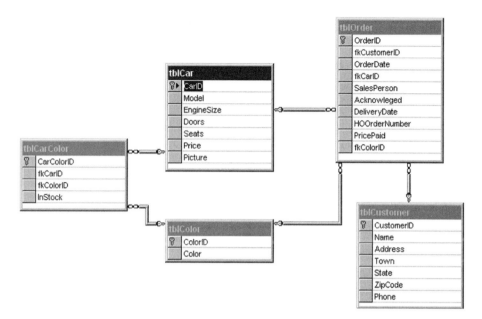

You can see that this differs in the order side, where customer details are split out from the order. We've deliberately kept it simple, but in reality the showroom order table might also be used for other items ordered, such as spare parts, etc. The relationships are shown below:

| From | To | Type |
|------|-----|------|
| tblCar.ID | tblCarColor.fkCarID | One to Many |
| tblColor.ID | tblCarColor.fkColorID | One to Many |
| tblCar.ID | tblOrder.fkCarID | One to Many |
| tblColor.ID | tblOrder.fkColorID | One to Many |
| tblCustomer.ID | tblOrder.fkCustomerID | One to Many |

Notice that we have an **InStock** column in the showroom database. This is not used in this example, but allows the showroom to keep a stock of its own cars, from which orders can be supplied. The business rules would then allow the showroom to order the car from head office if none were available locally.

A more detailed description of the columns for each table is shown in Appendix A. You can also download the SQL Scripts used to create the database from the Wrox web site. Installation instructions are included with this download, as well as in Appendix A.

# Business Rules

The business rules for this database are fairly simple–after all, buying a car is only a little more complex than buying an ice cream!

1. You can assume that the showroom database will always contain an up-to-date list of cars and colors. We won't be looking how this is updated here.

2. When an order is confirmed it must be placed in both the showroom database and the head office database. This ensures that head office can dispatch the correct car to the showroom.

When the order is created at the head office, the number of cars in stock must be reduced by 1. The number in stock is held in the **tblCarColor** table.

3. If there are not enough cars in stock at head office to fulfill the order, the order is cancelled.

4. When the order is confirmed by head office, the delivery date and head office order number must be placed into the showroom database.

From these rules you can see that we need three main actions:

1. Create a showroom order.

2. Create a head office order.

3. Update a showroom order.

So what we will do is build two ordering components, one for the showroom and one for head office. Now it could be argued that since the above actions are concerned with ordering, we ought to just build one component. There is nothing wrong with doing that, but we've decided to have two components for two main reasons. Firstly, we've assumed that the showrooms might enhance their local databases to incorporate additional ordering requirements, and therefore they might want to update their own components, perhaps to build in the allocation of commissions to the sales people. Having the showroom ordering in a separate component allows the showroom to update its functionality without affecting the head office component. Secondly, it will illustrate more clearly the point where we have a transaction spanning multiple components. So we end up with our two components interacting like this:

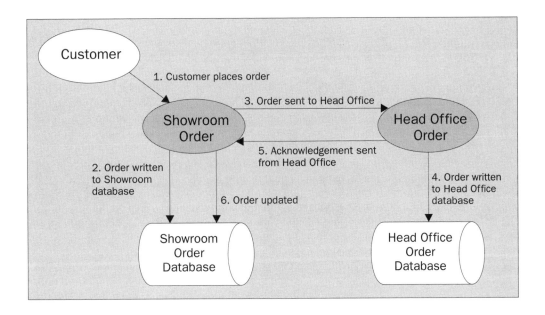

# Building the Components

We won't be looking at the finance component again until we need to use it, so we will concentrate on the new components:

- ❏ **WCCCars**, which is only concerned with retrieving car details from the showroom database. It will get a list of available cars, as well as the colors they are available in, returning a recordset of details to the client. This happens in the Order Placement Application, which we'll be seeing later.

- ❏ **WCCShowroomOrder**, which will add the customer order to the local showroom database (step 2) and also update the local showroom database, once the order has been confirmed by head office (step 6).

- ❏ **WCCHeadOfficeOrder**, which adds the order to the head office order database (step 4), and returns the delivery date (step 5).

- ❏ **WCCOrder**, which acts as a wrapper for the two order objects. You'll see when, and why, this is required when we start using the components. This is steps 2 and 3.

We are going to look at these in turn, and then at the end of the chapter we'll implement them.

You've seen the Class Builder in action before, so we won't be showing you that again. You can either use the builder to create these components or just type the code in manually. Remember that if you type it in yourself you need to add the code to a Class Module, as the Class Builder does this automatically for you.

# General Routines

As with most applications, we have a common routine that we need to look at before delving into the components. An important aspect of software design is configurability–how easy it is to reconfigure the component when things change. For example, databases get moved from machine to machine, renamed, and so on. The code, of course, must continue to run, so it must be easy to reconfigure the program so that those components don't have to be recompiled and redistributed.

In companies this is less of a problem than it is for us, the authors, since we are supplying components that will be used on many different machines. So what's the big issue? Let's have a look at an ADO connection string:

```
driver={SQL Server}; server=Tigger; UID=sa; PWD=; database=WroxCarCo
```

The items which are likely to change from implementation to implementation are:

- ❑ The **driver**: Possibly. We developed this under SQL Server, but there's no reason why it has to stay there. It could equally be moved to another database.
- ❑ The **server**: Almost certainly, unless your server is also called **Tigger**.
- ❑ The **UID** and **PWD**: More than likely. In a company you are more likely to have assigned names and passwords.
- ❑ The **database**: Probably not, although there is no reason why the name should be **WroxCarCo**.

So, when you install these components you're going to want to change at least one of the driver details, and possibly more. The best way to make an application configurable is the registry. To help with this, there is a small setup routine that asks for all of this information and stores it in the registry (this is discussed in more detail in Appendix A). We can then have a common routine that reads the values from the registry. This routine is not a component, but simply a BAS file that we include in each component. Let's look at the code now.

The first section of the code just holds the key name and section, and then there's a default constant for values not found.

```
' registry information
Private Const APP_NAME        As String = "Wrox Press"
Private Const APP_SECTION     As String = "Wrox Car Co"
Private Const NOT_FOUND       As String = "<Not Found>"
```

The first function just saves a value to the registry. Nothing complex there. It accepts a Key name and a Value.

```
Public Sub RegistrySave(ByVal sKey As String, ByVal sValue As String)
    SaveSetting APP_NAME, APP_SECTION, sKey, sValue
End Sub
```

The second function is also pretty simple. Its job is to read a value from the registry, and accepts the Key name to read, as well as a default value to return if the key isn't found.

```
Public Function RegistryRestore(ByVal sKey As String, _
                                ByVal sDefault As String) As String

    Dim sValue       As String

    sValue = GetSetting(APP_NAME, APP_SECTION, sKey, NOT_FOUND)

    If sValue = NOT_FOUND Then
        ' not found, so return default
        sValue = sDefault
    End If

    RegistryRestore = sValue

End Function
```

That's all there is to this module. It just encapsulates the standard Visual Basic registry function and supplys some default values for our application. The components will be using the **RegistryRestore** function to read the ADO connection string.

# The WCCCars Component

As our primary business is selling cars, we need to be able to get the car details from somewhere. Each showroom has its own database of cars and colors, as dictated by head office.

You've already seen what's stored in the car tables, so what we need is a way to get the list of cars and what colors those cars are available in.

The interface is very simple, with just two methods. **GetAll** will return a list of all of the car details and **ColorsByCar** will return just the colors for a particular car. There are no properties because we've already identified that MTS components are best served if all of the information they require is passed into the method calls as parameters.

The first method, **GetAll**, is responsible for returning a recordset of all the available color combinations for cars. It doesn't return all colors and all cars, but only those colors that are available for the cars:

```
Public Function GetAll(Optional ConnectionString As Variant) As
ADODB.Recordset

    Dim recCars             As New ADODB.Recordset
    Dim varConn             As Variant

    ' set the connection
    If IsMissing(ConnectionString) Then
        varConn = RegistryRestore("Showroom", "Not Set")
    Else
        varConn = ConnectionString
    End If
```

```
' go and get the cars
recCars.Open "usp_cars", varConn, adOpenStatic, adLockReadOnly, _
    adCmdStoredProc
Set GetAll = recCars
recCars.Close
Set recCars = Nothing

End Function
```

As you can see this really is very simple. Firstly, it checks to see if the **ConnectionString** has been supplied, and uses the value from the **Showroom** registry key. If not, it uses the connection string that will have been stored in the registry when you ran the setup program. Then it calls a stored procedure, **usp_cars**, to extract all of the car details from the **tblCars** table, and returns the recordset. Notice that we are using ADO recordsets here, and we are saying that we want a static, read only recordset. This makes sense as we are only retrieving information. Using **asCmdStoredProc** tells the **Open** method that the underlying object, where we are getting the data from, is a stored procedure.

The stored procedure is very simple:

```
Create Procedure usp_Cars
As
    SELECT    *
    FROM      tblCar
    ORDER BY  Price
```

To use ADO recordsets you will need to add a reference to the object library - from the Project menu pick References and then select Microsoft ActiveX Data Objects Library (at the time of writing 1.5 was the current version):

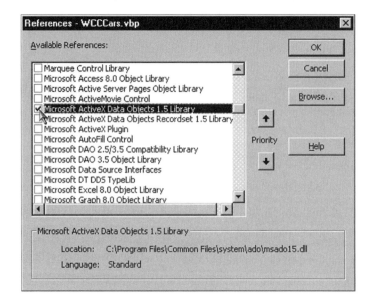

*ADO was briefly mentioned in the previous chapter, and is the latest and best way to access data stores. It's very similar to both DAO and RDO (in fact it's a superset), but its object model is much easier to deal with, making it smaller and faster. We'll be using ADO as the data access method in this book.*

The second method is only slightly more complex, as its purpose is to return a recordset of the colors for a particular car.

```
Public Function ColorsByCar(CarID As Long, _
                    Optional ConnectionString As Variant) As
ADODB.Recordset

    Dim cmdColors           As New ADODB.Command
    Dim varConn             As Variant

    ' Set the connection
    If IsMissing(ConnectionString) Then
        varConn = RegistryRestore("Showroom", "Not Set")
    Else
        varConn = ConnectionString
    End If

    ' go and get the colors
    With cmdColors
        .ActiveConnection = varConn
        .CommandType = adCmdStoredProc
        .CommandText = "usp_ColorsByCar"
        .Parameters.Append .CreateParameter("@CarID", adInteger, _
                                    adParamInput, 8, CarID)
        Set ColorsByCar = .Execute
    End With

    Set cmdColors = Nothing

End Function
```

This accepts the ID of a car, and then calls another stored procedure, **usp_ColorsByCar**, passing in the car ID. Once again it takes an optional **ConnectionString**, and since all of the components use this, we'll stop describing it now. Let's take a look in more detail at how this works.

Firstly, we define an ADO **Command** object:

```
Dim cmdColors               As New ADODB.Command
```

Now we have the command, we can tell it which data store connection to use, the type of command (a stored procedure again), and the stored procedure name:

```
With cmdColors
        .ActiveConnection = mvarConnection
        .CommandType = adCmdStoredProc
        .CommandText = "usp_ColorsByCar"
```

Since we are passing some information into the stored procedure, we create a **Parameter** object and append it to the **Parameters** collection.

```
        .Parameters.Append .CreateParameter("@CarID", adInteger, _
            adParamInput, 8, CarID)
      Set ColorsByCar = .Execute
    End With
```

The **Parameters** collection is how we pass information to and from stored procedures, and works in a similar way to the DAO Parameters collection. The parameter details must match those in the stored procedure. Here **@CarID** is the name of the parameter, it is an Integer, it has an input parameter of length 8, and has the value supplied by **CarID**. You'll see another way of using the **Parameters** collection when we look at the showroom order component. So you can see how this information matches, the stored procedure is show below:

```
    Create Procedure usp_ColorsByCar
                @CarID          integer
    As
        SELECT      tblColor.*
        FROM        tblCarColor, tblColor
        WHERE       tblCarColor.fkColorID = tblColor.ColorID
        AND         tblCarColor.fkCarID = @CarID
        ORDER BY    tblColor.Color
```

As you can see, this joins the car and color tables together, and returns the colors for the **CarID** passed in as a parameter.

The last thing we do is set the component details, in the same way as we did for the Finance object:

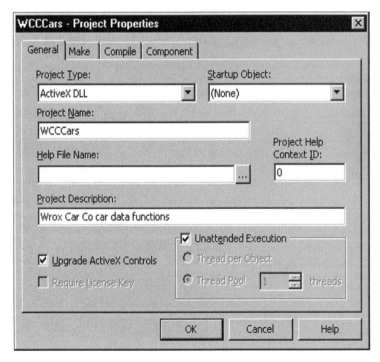

We've also set the Class name to Cars and set its Instancing property to MultiUse. You also want to set the Version Compatibility options on the Component page of this dialog. Set it to No Compatibility the first time you compile the component, and then once the DLL is built, set it to Binary Compatibility and enter the DLL name. This will ensure that if you recompile your component you won't have to re-register it.

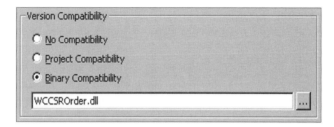

> **Binary Compatibility is extremely important when developing components. When you register a component it is given a unique ID, and if you have binary compatibility then this ID remains the same. If you choose one of the other compatibility modes, then the ID will change if you change your component, and you'll have to re-register your component.**

We can use the component in a similar way to the Finance component. For example, from ASP Script, we can get a list of the cars like this:

```
Dim objCars
Dim recCars
Dim recColors

Set objCars = Server.CreateObject ("WCCCars.Cars")
Set recCars = objCars.GetAll

Set recColors = objCars.ColorsByCar 3
```

You'll see more about how this component is used a little later in the chapter.

You may have noticed that there are no transaction statements in this component. What we've got is a component that just reads data from the database, and doesn't update it. There's no reason why we shouldn't put this type of component into MTS and let it manage the component, even though there are no transactions. MTS will still manage the dispensing of the component to clients and the management of its resources. Now this could be declared as a point of contention amongst programmers, since we've all been told to use **SetAbort** or **SetComplete**. In fact, MTS will release the component when the last client releases the object, but it could be argued that even if not using transactions it's better to explicitly tell MTS when to release the component, and free up any resources. So, although it's not been done here, it's probably good practice to do so.

# The WCCShowroomOrder Object

As the **ShowroomOrder** component is responsible for placing the order details into the showroom order table, it needs to take the details of the customer, the car and color they would like, and process the order. Since this only has two methods, the interface is very simple:

As with the other components there are no properties, and two methods. **Create** will create the new order, and **UpdateHODetails** will update the details with the head office order number and delivery date, once the order has been confirmed by head office.

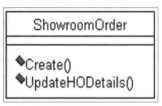

Let's have a look at the component in detail, starting with the **Create** method call.

## The Create Method

Well start by looking at the actual method, and then look at the stored procedure it uses.

```
Public Function Create(ByVal CarID As Variant, ByVal ColorID As Variant, _
    ByVal SalesPerson As Variant, PricePaid As Currency, _
    ByVal CustomerName As Variant, ByVal CustomerAddress As Variant, _
    ByVal CustomerTown As Variant, ByVal CustomerState As Variant, _
    ByVal CustomerZipCode As Variant, ByVal CustomerPhone As Variant, _
    ByRef OrderID As Variant, Optional ConnectionString As Variant) _
        As Boolean
```

You'll notice that there are a lot of parameters to this call, but that's because we aren't using properties. Since the component will just create the order within a single transaction it won't be able to retain the properties, so it's more sensible to have them as parameters to the method call. The first two are the ID numbers of the car and its color. Then we have the name of the sales person and the actual price paid—this is included because it may differ from the list price. Next are the customer details—name, address, etc. Then we have **OrderID**—notice that this is passed by reference, as it will hold the order number, which we will pass back to the caller of the method. Lastly we have the connection string. You'll also notice that they are mostly **Variant** data types—this allows the component to work even if null data is passed into it.

The first thing to do in the component is set the error handling. Because this component will be part of a transaction, we will need to be able to trap errors and abort the transaction.

```
On Error GoTo Create_Err
```

Now we can go ahead and define the object we are going to use, and get the transaction context.

```
Dim objCommand          As New ADODB.Command    ' Command to execute
Dim objContext          As ObjectContext        ' MTS Object context

' get the MTS object context for transaction
Set objContext = GetObjectContext
```

Next we set the connection string and the stored procedure used to add the order details:

```
With objCommand
    ' set the command type
    If IsMissing(ConnectionString) Then
        .ActiveConnection = RegistryRestore("Showroom", "Not Set")
    Else
        .ActiveConnection = ConnectionString
    End If
    .CommandType = adCmdStoredProc
    .CommandText = "usp_OrderInsert"
```

As with the previous component, the stored procedure has parameters, so these will need to be filled in. In **WCCars** we **Append**ed the parameter to the Parameters collection. We use a different technique here–the **Refresh** method, which will cause ADO to contact SQL Server and ask it for the parameter details. This is a perfectly acceptable technique as long as you realise that it involves a trip to the SQL Server. Under normal circumstances we would probably have used the **Append** method as before (and as we do elsewhere), but it has been included here just to show the technique.

```
.Parameters.Refresh
```

Now that the Parameters collection is full we can set the values:

```
.Parameters("@CarID").Value = CarID
.Parameters("@ColorID").Value = ColorID
.Parameters("@SalesPerson").Value = SalesPerson & ""
.Parameters("@PricePaid").Value = PricePaid
.Parameters("@Name").Value = CustomerName & ""
.Parameters("@Address").Value = CustomerAddress & ""
.Parameters("@Town").Value = CustomerTown & ""
.Parameters("@State").Value = Left$(CustomerState & "", 2)
.Parameters("@ZipCode").Value = CustomerZipCode & ""
.Parameters("@Phone").Value = CustomerPhone & ""
```

Notice that an empty string is being added to the string values, just to protect against null values being passed into the parameter. Once all of the values are stored we can execute the command.

```
.Execute
```

And finally, extract the order number. Remember that **OrderID** will be an output parameter of the method call. You'll see that **@OrderNumber** is defined in the stored procedure as an OUTPUT parameter.

```
            OrderID = .Parameters("@OrderNumber")
        End With
```

Since everything was OK we can tell MTS that the statement completed correctly, and we can clean up the object references and exit.

```
        Create = True

        ' tell MTS it's ok
        objContext.SetComplete

Create_Exit:
    ' clean up and exit
    If Not objCommand Is Nothing Then
        Set objCommand = Nothing
    End If
    If Not objContext Is Nothing Then
        Set objContext = Nothing
    End If
    Exit Function
```

Obviously, if an error occurred we need to tell MTS to abort the transaction, and we raise an error.

```
Create_Err:
    Create = False
    OrderID = -1

    ' tell MTS it's not ok
    objContext.SetAbort

    Err.Raise Err.Number, "WCCSROrder.Create", Err.Description
    Resume Create_Exit

End Function
```

The nature of Visual Basic's error handling allows you to have a single error routine at the top level, and then any subroutines that generate errors will back-track to the defined error routine. This doesn't work in MTS components, so we have to ensure that transactions are committed or aborted in the component.

That's it for the component, let's have a look at that stored procedure now:

```
CREATE PROCEDURE usp_OrderInsert    @CarID          integer,
                                    @ColorID        integer,
                                    @SalesPerson    varchar(20),
                                    @PricePaid      numeric,
                                    @Name           varchar(50),
                                    @Address        varchar(50),
                                    @Town           varchar(50),
                                    @State          varchar(2),
                                    @ZipCode        varchar(15),
                                    @Phone          varchar(15),
                                    @OrderNumber    int OUTPUT
```

```
AS
BEGIN
    DECLARE @CID        integer

    -- Insert the customer
    EXEC @CID = usp_CustomerInsert @Name, @Address, @Town,
              @State, @ZipCode, @Phone

    -- Now insert the actual order
    INSERT INTO tblOrder (fkCarID, fkColorID, fkCustomerID,
            SalesPerson, PricePaid, OrderDate)
    VALUES (@CarID, @ColorID, @CID, @SalesPerson, @PricePaid, GETDATE())

    -- return order id
    SELECT @OrderNumber = @@IDENTITY
END
```

You can see that the declaration of the parameters matches those in the **Parameters** collection of the **Command** object. The first thing to do in here is obtain the ID number of the customer, by calling **usp_CustomerInsert**. We won't look at that stored procedure here, but it checks the customer table first to see if the customer exists, and if so returns the ID number, otherwise it inserts the new customer details and returns the ID number. Once the customer ID is available we can then insert the order details into the order table. Notice that the last parameter, **@OrderNumber**, is an output parameter, which is used to return the order number.

## The UpdateHODetails Method

In this method we need to update the local showroom order with the order number from head office and the delivery date. Once again everything is passed into the method call as parameters.

With this method we are only updating two columns: the order number as returned from head office, and the date the car is due to be delivered. We pass in the showroom order number to identify which order to update.

```
Public Function UpdateHODetails(ByVal OrderID As Variant, _
    ByVal HOOrderNumber As Variant, ByVal DeliveryDate As Variant, _
    Optional ConnectionString As Variant) As Boolean
```

Again, we set up error handling, the variables we'll use, and the transaction context we want MTS to use.

```
On Error GoTo UpdateHODetails_Err

Dim objCommand        As New ADODB.Command    ' Command to execute
Dim objContext        As ObjectContext        ' MTS Object context

' get the MTS object context for transaction
Set objContext = GetObjectContext
```

And once more we set the connection and the stored procedure we will use. We also use **Refresh** to get the parameters, fill them with the supplied values, and run the command.

```
With objCommand
    ' set the command type
    If IsMissing(ConnectionString) Then
        .ActiveConnection = RegistryRestore("Showroom", "Not Set")
    Else
        .ActiveConnection = ConnectionString
    End If
    .CommandType = adCmdStoredProc
    .CommandText = "usp_OrderUpdate"

    ' go and get the parameters.
    .Parameters.Refresh

    ' now set the parameters
    .Parameters("@OrderID").Value = OrderID
    .Parameters("@HOOrderNumber").Value = HOOrderNumber
    .Parameters("@DeliveryDate").Value = DeliveryDate

    ' and now run the command
    .Execute
End With

UpdateHODetails = True
' tell MTS it's ok
objContext.SetComplete
```

The error handling is the same as the previous method, where we abort the transaction if an error occurred.

```
UpdateHODetails_Exit:
    ' clean up and exit
    If Not objCommand Is Nothing Then
        Set objCommand = Nothing
    End If
    If Not objContext Is Nothing Then
        Set objContext = Nothing
    End If
    Exit Function

UpdateHODetails_Err:
    UpdateHODetails = False

    ' tell MTS it's not ok
    objContext.SetAbort

    Err.Raise Err.Number, "WCCSROrder.UpdateHODetails", Err.Description
    Resume UpdateHODetails_Exit

End Function
```

So you can see that the style of these components is very similar, as is the stored procedure.

```
CREATE PROCEDURE usp_OrderUpdate
       @OrderID          int,
       @HOOrderNumber    varchar(10),
       @DeliveryDate     datetime
AS
    UPDATE   tblOrder
    SET      HOOrderNumber = @HOOrderNumber,
             DeliveryDate = @DeliveryDate
    WHERE    OrderID = @OrderID
```

That's it for this component. All we need to do now is set the name, description, and version compatibility properties, and compile it.

# The WCCHeadOfficeOrder Object

The head office ordering component is very similar, but does have one slight difference, to show you how to overcome a restriction with running components under MTS - that of handling errors in components. In a component you can use **Err.Raise** to raise errors, and trap these on the client. This is necessary if your components don't have any visual interface with which to show the error - in this case they just raise an error and let the client routine display it. This doesn't work with components that are managed by MTS, as MTS doesn't pass this error information back to the client - it returns its own error details, not the ones raised by the component. This means that you cannot raise an error in a component and have the error details returned to client, which rules out a trick that some SQL Programmer's use.

The SQL **RAISERROR** statement in a stored procedure was often used to return a user-defined error back to the calling routine. Very often this was done as a callback mechanism, perhaps to notify the client when some long running procedure was finished. The calling code, perhaps a Visual Basic component, could then trap the user-defined error and act on it accordingly, often passing it back to the components caller. So it was used as a server to client communication mechanism. Obviously with MTS handling the error codes this isn't possible, so we've a slightly modified form. Let's see what this component does and why we've coded it this way.

The Head Office Ordering component runs on the showroom machine, alongside the other components, but it accesses a remote SQL Server database—the head office one. This is used to place the order in the head office database, and decrement the number of cars in stock. We've also created a business rule so that, if there are not enough cars in stock, then the order cannot be processed. In real life this would probably just delay the delivery date, but we wanted to show you how to manage the forced termination of a stored procedure. Because this is different from the other components we'll look at the stored procedures first, starting with **usp_OrderInsert**, which actually inserts the order.

As with our other order insert stored procedure in the showroom order client, this accepts all of the order information as a list of parameters. Notice that the last two parameters are output parameters—these are the order number and delivery date to be passed back to the client.

```
CREATE PROCEDURE usp_OrderInsert
              @GarageName          varchar(50),
              @GarageAddress       varchar(50),
              @GarageTown          varchar(20),
              @GarageState         varchar(2),
```

```
              @GarageZipCode        varchar(15),
              @GarageOrderNumber    int,
              @SalesPerson          varchar(20),
              @CustomerName         varchar(20),
              @CustomerAddress      varchar(50),
              @CustomerTown         varchar(20),
              @CustomerState        varchar(2),
              @CustomerZipCode      varchar(15),
              @CustomerPhone        varchar(15),
              @CarID                int,
              @ColorID              int,
              @OrderNumber          varchar(10)    OUTPUT,
              @DeliveryDate         datetime       OUTPUT
```

Within the procedure we declare two variables and set one of them to the current date.

```
AS
BEGIN
     DECLARE @InStock      integer      -- number in stock
     DECLARE @Today        datetime     -- today's date

     SELECT @Today = GETDATE()
```

Now we can go ahead and insert the order details into the order table:

```
-- add order to order table
INSERT INTO tblOrder (GarageName, GarageAddress, GarageTown,
                      GarageState, GarageZipCode, GarageOrderNumber,
                      SalesPerson,
                      CustomerName, CustomerAddress, CustomerTown,
                      CustomerState, CustomerZipCode, CustomerPhone,
                      fkCarID, DateOrdered, fkColorID)
VALUES (@GarageName, @GarageAddress, @GarageTown,
        @GarageState, @GarageZipCode, @GarageOrderNumber,
        @SalesPerson,
        @CustomerName, @CustomerAddress, @CustomerTown,
        @CustomerState, @CustomerZipCode, @CustomerPhone,
        @CarID, @Today, @ColorID)
```

Once the order details have been inserted we run another stored procedure to decrement the stock number by one. This returns the new number of cars in stock:

```
EXEC @InStock = usp_StockDecrement @CarID, @ColorID
```

Finally, we create the order number. This is a combination of the first five characters of the showroom name and the actual order number. We also set the delivery date–for simplicity we are assuming it takes 14 days to deliver. And lastly, we return the number of cars in stock:

```
SELECT @OrderNumber = SUBSTRING (@GarageName, 1, 5) +
                      CONVERT(varchar(5), @@IDENTITY)
```

```
    SELECT @DeliveryDate = DATEADD(day, 14, @Today)

        RETURN @InStock
    END
```

That seems simple enough so let's look at **usp_StockDecrement**. This is where we'll be generating the error.

The first thing is to find out the number of cars in stock.

```
CREATE PROCEDURE usp_StockDecrement
        @CarID          int,
        @ColorID        int
AS
    DECLARE @InStock    integer

    SELECT  @InStock = InStock
    FROM    tblCarColor
    WHERE   fkCarID = @CarID
    AND     fkColorID = @ColorID
```

Now we can see if we've sold out of this particular model. If we have, we use **RAISERROR** to abandon the procedure, returning **50001** as the error number.

```
IF @InStock < 1
    BEGIN
        -- not in stock therefore raise error
        RAISERROR (50001, 16, -1, @CarID)
        RETURN 50001
    END
```

If there are enough in stock we can just decrement the number by one and return the new number in stock.

```
    ELSE
    BEGIN
        -- in stock so decrement stock count
        UPDATE  tblCarColor
        SET     InStock = InStock - 1
        WHERE   fkCarID = @CarID
        AND     fkColorID = @ColorID
    END

    RETURN @InStock - 1
```

It's actually fairly simple code. If you haven't come across **RAISERROR** before, it takes four arguments. The first is the ID of the message to raise—this is a custom message we created when we built the database (you can also use a message string here, but we actually want a number returned). The second is the severity of the error, and the third is the SQL state. The last argument is inserted into the message. To learn more about this you should refer to the SQL Server help files or SQL Server Books Online.

Before we explain the reason for using this method, let's look at the component and see how it's handled there.

The WCCHeadOfficeOrder component has a simpler interface than the others, with just one method call.

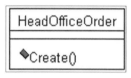

You'll probably be able to guess that this has a lot of parameters.

```
Public Function Create(ByVal GarageName As String, _
        ByVal GarageAddress As String, ByVal GarageTown As String, _
        ByVal GarageState As String, ByVal GarageZipCode As String, _
        ByVal GarageOrderNumber As Long, ByVal SalesPerson As String, _
        ByVal CustomerName As String, ByVal CustomerAddress As String, _
        ByVal CustomerTown As String, ByVal CustomerState As String, _
        ByVal CustomerZipCode As String, ByVal CustomerPhone As String, _
        ByVal CarID As Long, ByVal ColorID As Long, _
        ByRef OrderNumber As Variant, _
        ByRef DeliveryDate As Variant, _
        ByRef ReturnValue As Variant, _
        Optional ConnectionString As Variant) As Boolean
```

The only difference is the extra **ReturnValue** parameter, which we'll use to return error information back to the caller.

The first part of the code is the same as the others, setting the MTS context and the command details.

```
On Error GoTo Update_Err

Dim comC        As New ADODB.Command      ' Command to execute
Dim objContext  As ObjectContext          ' MTS Object context

' get the MTS object context for transaction
Set objContext = GetObjectContext

With comC
    ' set the command type
    If IsMissing(ConnectionString) Then
        .ActiveConnection = RegistryRestore("HeadOffice", "Not Set")
    Else
        .ActiveConnection = ConnectionString
    End If
    .CommandType = adCmdStoredProc
    .CommandText = "usp_OrderInsert"
```

Now come the command parameters. Notice that we are not using **Refresh** here. This is because the SQL Server is remote and it would be an unnecessary delay to get this information. Using **Refresh**, however, is a good idea whilst developing the component, as ADO can be a little fussy about the data types for parameters. You'll notice that **@DeliveryDate** is defined as **adDBTimeStamp** despite the fact that it's not a timestamp field, just a normal **datetime** field. This is because a Visual Basic date includes the time, and ADO has three types for dates and times— **adDBDate**, **adDBTime**, and **adDBTimestamp**. So you have to use the latter one for your date since it includes the time.

```
With .Parameters
    .Append comC.CreateParameter("@GarageName", adVarChar, _
                             adParamInput, 50, GarageName)
    .Append comC.CreateParameter("@GarageAddress", adVarChar, _
                             adParamInput, 50, GarageAddress)
    .Append comC.CreateParameter("@GarageTown", adVarChar, _
                             adParamInput, 20, GarageTown)
    .Append comC.CreateParameter("@GarageState", adVarChar, _
                             adParamInput, 2, GarageState)
    .Append comC.CreateParameter("@GarageZipCode", adVarChar, _
                             adParamInput, 15, GarageZipCode)
    .Append comC.CreateParameter("@GarageOrderNumber", adInteger, _
                             adParamInput, 8, GarageOrderNumber)
    .Append comC.CreateParameter("@SalesPerson", adVarChar, _
                             adParamInput, 20, SalesPerson + "")
    .Append comC.CreateParameter("@CustomerName", adVarChar, _
                             adParamInput, 20, CustomerName + "")
    .Append comC.CreateParameter("@CustomerAddress", adVarChar, _
                             adParamInput, 50, CustomerAddress + "")
    .Append comC.CreateParameter("@CustomerTown", adVarChar, _
                             adParamInput, 20, CustomerTown + "")
    .Append comC.CreateParameter("@CustomerState", adVarChar, _
                             adParamInput, 2, CustomerState + "")
    .Append comC.CreateParameter("@CustomerZipCode", adVarChar, _
                             adParamInput, 15, CustomerZipCode + "")
    .Append comC.CreateParameter("@CustomerPhone", adVarChar, _
                             adParamInput, 15, CustomerPhone + "")
    .Append comC.CreateParameter("@CarID", adInteger, _
                             adParamInput, 8, CarID)
    .Append comC.CreateParameter("@ColorID", adInteger, _
                             adParamInput, 8, ColorID)
    .Append comC.CreateParameter("@OrderNumber", adVarChar, _
                             adParamOutput, 10)
    .Append comC.CreateParameter("@DeliveryDate", adDBTimeStamp, _
                             adParamOutput, 8)
End With
```

Now we can execute the procedure and extract the output parameters.

```
    ' and now run the command
    .Execute

    ' get output parameters
    OrderNumber = .Parameters("@OrderNumber")
    DeliveryDate = .Parameters("@DeliveryDate")
End With
```

And assuming everything has worked we can tidy up and exit with a sensible return value:

```
        Create = True
        ReturnValue = -1

        ' tell MTS it's ok
        objContext.SetComplete

Update_Exit:
        ' clean up and exit
        If Not comC Is Nothing Then
            Set comC = Nothing
        End If
        If Not objContext Is Nothing Then
            Set objContext = Nothing
        End If
        Exit Function
```

However, if there was an error, we not only want to abort the transaction, but also pass some error information back to the client. Remember that the stored procedure generates an error if there are not enough cars in stock to meet the order. So we check the error returned from SQL Server and if it's 50001 then we don't raise an error, we set the return value accordingly. We do, however, still abort the transaction.

```
Update_Err:
    Create = False

    If comC.ActiveConnection.Errors(0).NativeError = 50001 Then
        ReturnValue = 50001
    Else
        Err.Raise Err.Number, "WWCCHOOrder.Create", Err.Description
    End If

    ' tell MTS it's not ok
    objContext.SetAbort
        Resume Update_Exit

End Function
```

So this is how we can pass error information back from an MTS controlled component. MTS will handle the transactions as normal, but because we haven't actually raised an error, the method call finished normally. We could also have returned error information from the stored procedure as the return value, instead of raising errors, but we wanted to show how the **RAISERROR** technique could be used. If you are building new components it's probably best to return error information as a return parameter, as using **RAISERROR** causes SQL Server to do slightly more work.

The component properties should be set as for the previous components, and the component then compiled.

# Putting it all together

Now that the main components have been created they need to be added to Microsoft Transaction Server. We've created a new package in MTS called WroxCarCo, and we'll add the components to that. If you've got the finance component in the test package you can either leave it where it is, or move it into the new package. You can do this by clicking the right mouse button on the component and selecting Move from the menu (or by selecting the component and then selecting Move from the Action menu), and then picking the WroxCarCo package from the dialog.

When you've added the components, you need to set the transaction capabilities for the new components. Remember that the Cars component doesn't support transactions, so you can leave this as it is, but the two order components will require transactions. So what you should end up with is this:

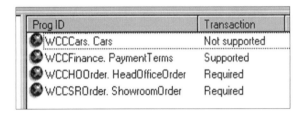

Now that you have the components in MTS you can use them to build a fully transacted application. However, here we come to a little problem, which is how to build the application. Do we build it in Visual Basic or as a Web based application? Well, we can do either, because the components will work just as well from both. Which you choose depends on your needs, and the skills of your developers, but when creating applications that use transacted components you must understand how they will be used.

The previous chapter talked about using a parent component to initiate the transaction, and that's exactly what you need to consider. When using ASP to instantiate your components you can simply use the **TRANSACTION=Requires_New** to start a new transaction, so ASP acts as the parent:

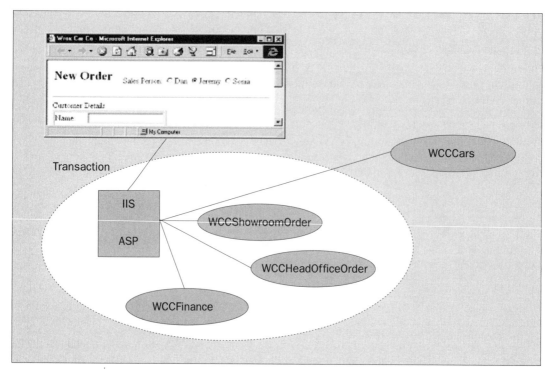

The problem when building a Visual Basic interface is how to start the transaction, and the solution is quite simple—just create another component to do it.

## The WCCOrder Object

You have to create a new component for this because the interface will only call the existing components. It has no knowledge of where they are stored or how they are managed, and that's how it should be. The components can be used directly from Visual Basic, but the only way to start a transaction is to set the Requires New option on the component. However, this will not give the desired effect since each component would now run in its own transaction, and we want both components to run in a single transaction. So we need to create a new component whose job is to instantiate the other components, and we set its transaction property to **Requires New**. This means that the new component will start the new transaction, and the two existing components will run within this transaction. Let's see how this is done.

The first thing to do is a set a reference to the two components we are going to call:

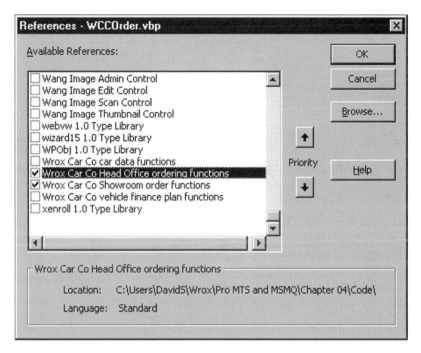

These are set using exactly the same method as that used to set the MTS and ADO library references. Your Location will probably differ depending upon where your DLL is. Now we can look at the code.

Notice that the parameters combine all of the parameters from both of the order components. We are also passing in two connection strings this time, one for the showroom database and one for the head office database.

```
Public Function Create(ByVal GarageName As String, _
        ByVal GarageAddress As String, ByVal GarageTown As String, _
        ByVal GarageState As String, ByVal GarageZipCode As String, _
        ByVal SalesPerson As String, ByVal PricePaid As Currency, _
        ByVal CustomerName As String, ByVal CustomerAddress As String, _
        ByVal CustomerTown As String, ByVal CustomerState As String, _
        ByVal CustomerZipCode As String, ByVal CustomerPhone As String, _
        ByVal CarID As Long, ByVal ColorID As Long, _
        ByRef OrderNumber As Variant, ByRef DeliveryDate As Variant, _
        ByRef ReturnValue As Variant, _
        Optional HOConnectionString As Variant, _
        Optional SRConnectionString As Variant) As Boolean


    On Error GoTo Create_Error
```

Now we need some variables. The first two will hold the order objects for the other components.

```
Dim objHOOrder       As HeadOfficeOrder   ' Head office order
Dim objSROrder       As ShowroomOrder     ' Showroom order
Dim objContext       As ObjectContext     ' MTS object context
Dim strSROrderID     As String            ' showroom id
Dim strRV            As String            ' return value
```

We can then set the MTS context as normal.

```
Set objContext = GetObjectContext
```

Now we have to instantiate the two objects. Previously when instantiating MTS objects you have used **CreateObject**, but when you want to instantiate an object and have it share the current context, you use **CreateInstance**. Notice that we are using the current context to do this, so the new objects will be part of the current MTS transaction.

```
Set objHOOrder = objContext.CreateInstance("WCCHOOrder.HeadOfficeOrder")
Set objSROrder = objContext.CreateInstance("WCCSROrder.ShowroomOrder")
```

Now we can create the order in the local database.

```
If IsMissing(SRConnectionString) Then
    SRConnectionString = RegistryRestore("Showroom", "Not Set")
End If
objSROrder.Create CarID, ColorID, SalesPerson, PricePaid, _
                CustomerName, CustomerAddress, CustomerTown, _
                CustomerState, CustomerZipCode, CustomerPhone, _
                strSROrderID, SRConnectionString
```

And now the head office order.

```
If IsMissing(HOConnectionString) Then
    HOConnectionString = RegistryRestore("HeadOffice", "Not Set")
End If
objHOOrder.Create GarageName, GarageAddress, GarageTown, _
                GarageState, GarageZipCode, strSROrderID, _
                SalesPerson, CustomerName, CustomerAddress, _
                CustomerTown, CustomerState, CustomerZipCode, _
                CustomerPhone, CarID, ColorID, _
                OrderNumber, DeliveryDate, _
                strRV, _
                HOConnectionString
```

The two orders have now been created, so we need to check the return value from the creation of the order in head office. Remember that we were passing back a value if there were not enough cars in stock. In this case we set the return value to indicate why. We don't need to do a **SetAbort** to abort the transaction here because the head office component will have done that for us. **SetAbort** and **SetComplete** work like a voting system, with each component voting towards the Committing or Rolling Back of the transaction. When all votes have been tallied, if it is a unanimous Complete, then the transaction is committed, otherwise it is aborted.

```
    ' if we've raised our own error (not enough in stock) just
    ' set return value and exit - component will have aborted transaction
    If strRV = 50001 Then
        ReturnValue = 50001
```

If the return value was not our forced error, then we can go ahead and update the showroom order with the details from head office, and tell MTS that everything is OK.

```
    Else
        ' update the showroom order with the head office details
        objSROrder.UpdateHODetails strSROrderID, OrderNumber, _
                                    DeliveryDate, SRConnectionString

        ' all done, so tell MTS to commit the transaction
        objContext.SetComplete

        ReturnValue = -1
    End If
```

The error handling section consists, as you would expect, of cleaning up the object variables and raising an error if necessary.

```
Create_Exit:
    ' clean up and exit
    If Not objContext Is Nothing Then
        Set objContext = Nothing
    End If
    If Not objHOOrder Is Nothing Then
        Set objHOOrder = Nothing
    End If
    If Not objSROrder Is Nothing Then
        Set objSROrder = Nothing
    End If
    Exit Function

Create_Error:
    ' tell MTS to abort the transaction
    objContext.SetAbort

    Err.Raise Err.Number, "WCCOrder.Create", Err.Description
    Resume Create_Exit

End Function
```

Once the properties have been set, and the component compiled, it can be added to MTS. The Transaction property should then be set to **Requires New** to make sure that any other components that the component calls are bundled within the same transaction.

So that's how we use a Visual Basic component to do the same job as the ASP page to start a transaction.

Now, let's move on to look at creating a whole application using transacted components.

# Visual Basic

The Visual Basic application is the one that will be used within the showroom.

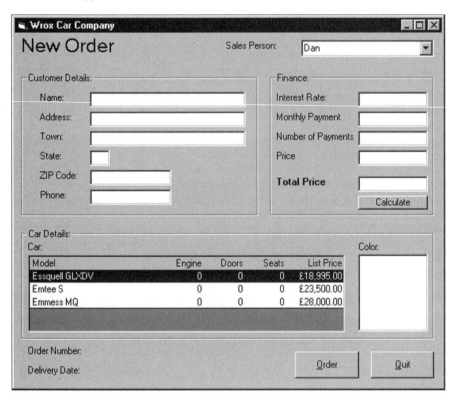

We won't take you through all of the controls on the form, or even the properties of them, as you can download the Visual Basic project from the Wrox Web site (details in Appendix A). What we will concentrate on is the use of the components. The first thing we need to do is make sure that we have references to the correct components.

Notice that we are not including the showroom or head office ordering components here. Remember that the Order component calls these, so we don't need to include them here. We do, however, need the Finance and Cars components.

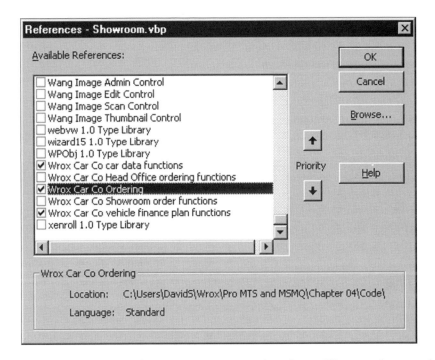

The first thing to do when the application is run, is get a list of cars. We created a procedure to do this.

Firstly, you'll note that we set an object variable for the Cars component, as well as a recordset to hold the car details.

```
Dim oCars        As WCCCars.Cars

Dim recCars      As ADODB.Recordset
Dim strCar       As String
```

Now we can instantiate the object. Remember, we have to use **CreateObject** to ensure that MTS has control over this object instance. Once created, we set a recordset variable to the return value of the **GetAll** method, and then we open the recordset.

```
Set oCars = CreateObject("WCCCars.Cars")
Set recCars = oCars.GetAll(RegistryRestore("Showroom", "Not Set"))
recCars.Open
```

That's all there is to it—the component has been created and its method called. We now have a recordset of the car details, so we can build up a string with these and add it to the grid.

```
While Not recCars.EOF
strCar = recCars("Model") & _
    vbTab & recCars("EngineSize") & _
    vbTab & recCars("Doors") & _
    vbTab & recCars("Seats") & _
```

```
                vbTab & Format(recCars("Price"), "currency") & _
                vbTab & recCars("CarID") & _
                vbTab & recCars("Picture")
            grdCars.AddItem strCar
            recCars.MoveNext
        Wend
```

Once the grid is full, the recordset is closed, and the component deactivated by setting its object variable to nothing.

```
        recCars.Close
        Set recCars = Nothing
        Set oCars = Nothing

    End Sub
```

Easy, huh? OK, so now we have a list of cars, but what about when someone clicks on a car? We still need a list of colors that are available for that car.

Once again we create a variable to store the component's instance and a recordset for the colors.

```
    Private Sub grdCars_Click()

        Dim oCars           As WCCCars.Cars
        Dim recColors       As New ADODB.Recordset
```

Then we instantiate the object and call the **ColorsByCar** method to get the colors for the selected car. **GridCellContents** is a function that returns the value of a particular column—in this case we get the ID of the car from column 5.

```
        Set oCars = CreateObject("WCCCars.Cars")
        Set recColors = oCars.ColorsByCar(GridCellContents(5), _
                    RegistryRestore("Showroom", "Not Set"))
```

We can now populate the list box of colors from the returned recordset.

```
        lstColor.Clear

        While Not recColors.EOF
            lstColor.AddItem recColors("Color")
            lstColor.ItemData(lstColor.NewIndex) = recColors("ColorID")
            recColors.MoveNext
        Wend
```

And finally, we can set the price of the car (ready for the Finance component) and deactivate the component.

```
        txtPrice = GridCellContents(4)
        recColors.Close
        Set recColors = Nothing
```

```
        Set oCars = Nothing

    End Sub
```

OK, so now we have the cars and colors, what about placing our order?

Once again, we create an object variable to hold the instance. We also have a few variables to hold the return values from the component.

```
    Private Sub cmdOrder_Click()

        On Error GoTo cmdOrder_Error

        Dim oOrder          As WCCOrder.Order
        Dim sHOOrderID      As String
        Dim sDeliveryDate   As String
        Dim sRV             As Variant
```

Now we can create the component and call the **Create** method to create the order. The **mstr** variables are just constants defined to hold the garage details—in real life these would probably be stored in an initialization file, or the registry.

```
        Set oOrder = CreateObject("WCCOrder.Order")
        oOrder.Create mstrGarageName, mstrGarageAddress, _
                    mstrGarageTown, mstrGarageState, _
                    mstrGarageZipCode, _
                    cboSales, txtPrice, _
                    txtName, txtAddress, _
                    txtTown, txtState, _
                    txtZipCode, txtPhone, _
                    GridCellContents(5), _
                    lstColor.ItemData(lstColor.ListIndex), _
                    sHOOrderID, sDeliveryDate, _
                    sRV, _
                    RegistryRestore("HeadOffice", "Not Set"), _
                    RegistryRestore("Showroom", "Not Set")
```

Once we return from the component we can check to see if our error was raised. If it was, then we know that not enough cars were in stock so we can tell the customer.

```
        If sRV = 50001 Then
            lblOrderNumber = ""
            lblDeliveryDate = ""
            lblOrderConfirmed = "Not enough in stock"
```

If everything was OK, we can show the order number from head office and the date that the car will be delivered.

```
        Else
            lblOrderNumber = sHOOrderID
            lblDeliveryDate = Format(sDeliveryDate, "Short Date")
```

```
            lblOrderConfirmed = "Order Confirmed"
        End If
```

And lastly, some error handling, just in case a real error occurred.

```
cmdOrder_Exit:
    ' close up and we are done
    If Not oOrder Is Nothing Then
        Set oOrder = Nothing
    End If

    Exit Sub

cmdOrder_Error:
    Err.Raise Err.Number, Err.Source, Err.Description
    lblOrderNumber = ""
    lblDeliveryDate = ""
    Resume cmdOrder_Exit
    Resume

End Sub
```

That's it. You can see that, once the component has been created, its use is extremely simple. It is just like performing a normal function call, except that the function is stored elsewhere. So now when we place an order, we'll get the details displayed on the screen.

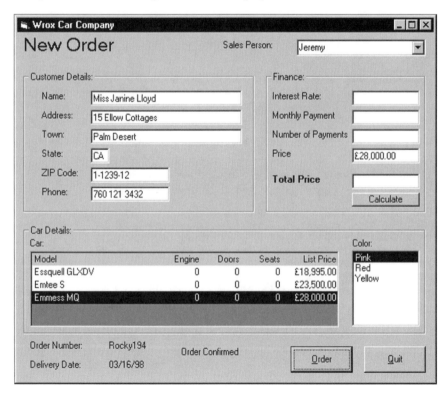

Notice that Janine is one of those rare people who actually want to own a pink car. You see we still haven't solved that question!

The previous diagram shows that the order has been accepted correctly. You can confirm this by looking at the order tables in the two databases.

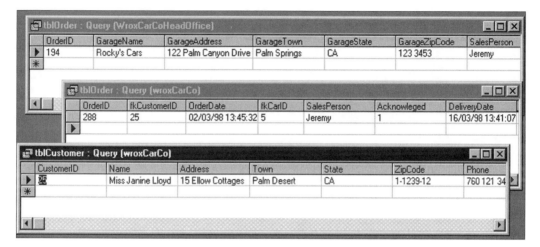

However, if you place an order for a car which has sold out (after all, Wrox cars are extremely popular), then no data will be in the tables. For example, the Esquell GLXDV in Black has sold out. If you try ordering this car, instead of being told the order is confirmed, you will be told there are not enough in stock. Despite the fact that the details have been written to the showroom order table (both the order and customer details), no record of this will exist because the transaction has been rolled back. MTS handled this transparently.

# Web

Building an interface for the Web is slightly different. In the future the Wrox Car Co might offer an ordering service over the Web, but for now it will just emulate the existing Visual Basic application.

We've already seen that a web application will work differently, because the order page will call an ASP page, which in turn will call the components—the ASP page is acting as our parent component. So, let's look at this ASP page.

Firstly, we start by identifying that this page requires a new transaction.

```
<%@ LANGUAGE=VBScript TRANSACTION=Requires_New %>
```

We then include the garage settings file and the data store.

```
<!-- #INCLUDE FILE="WCCGarage.inc" -->
<!-- #INCLUDE FILE="DataStore.inc" -->

<HTML>
<BODY>
```

`WCCGarage.inc` contains the following:

```
<%
' Wrox Car Co settings

' Garage details
sGarageName          = "Rocky's Cars"
sGarageAddress       = "122 Palm Canyon Drive"
sGarageTown          = "Palm Springs"
sGarageState         = "CA"
sGarageZipCode       = "123 4567"
%>
```

This just contains the details of the garage showroom. These can then easily be changed if the application is moved to another garage.

`DataStore.inc` contains:

```
<%
' Data store connection strings
' Auto generated by Setup.exe

sHeadOffice = "driver={SQL Server}; server=Tigger; UID=sa; PWD=; _ "
        & "database=WroxCarCoHeadOffice"
sShowroom = "driver={SQL Server}; server=Piglet; UID=sa; PWD=; _ "
        & "database=WroxCarCo"

%>
```

These are the ADO connection strings, as generated by the setup routine. This is the same routine that writes these values to the registry. We need to have an include file because we can't read from the registry in asp. Appendix A details how this setup routine creates these files.

Now comes the script to process the order. Firstly we extract the order details from the Form.

```
<SCRIPT LANGUAGE=VBScript RUNAT=Server>

    ' get the user details
    sSalesPerson    = Request.Form("SalesPerson")
    cPrice          = Request.Form("Price")
    sName           = Request.Form("Name")
    sAddress        = Request.Form("Address")
    sTown           = Request.Form("Town")
    sState          = Request.Form("State")
    sZipCode        = Request.Form("ZipCode")
    sPhone          = Request.Form("Phone")
    lCarID          = Request.Form("CarID")
    lColorID        = Request.Form("ColorID")
```

Now we can create the order in the showroom database. You can see that the code is almost exactly the same as the Visual Basic application.

```
set oOrder = Server.CreateObject("WCCSROrder.ShowroomOrder")
oOrder.Create lCarID, lColorID, _
              sSalesPerson, ccur(cPrice), _
              sName, sAddress, _
              sTown, sState, _
              sZipCode, sPhone, _
              sOrderID, _
              sShowroom
```

Once the showroom order is created, we can create one for the head office.

```
set oHOOrder = Server.CreateObject("WCCHOOrder.HeadOfficeOrder")
oHOOrder.Create sGarageName, sGarageAddress, _
                sGarageTown, sGarageState, _
                sGarageZipCode, sOrderID, _
                sSalesPerson, _
                sName, sAddress, _
                sTown, sState, _
                sZipCode, sPhone, _
                lCarID, lColorID, _
                sHOOrderID, sDeliveryDate, _
                sRV, _
                sHeadOffice
```

And if the forced error is not returned we can update the delivery date and order number:

```
if sRV <> 50001 then
    oOrder.UpdateHODetails sOrderID, sHOOrderID, sDeliveryDate
end if
```

Then, we deallocate the objects.

```
Set oOrder = Nothing
Set oHOOrder = Nothing
```

Lastly, because the ASP page has a way to tell if the transaction was committed or aborted, we can display some information. If it was successful we can display the order number and delivery date.

```
Sub OnTransactionCommit()

    Response.Clear
    Response.Write "<P>Order Accepted"
    Response.Write "<BR>Order Number:    " & sHOOrderID
    Response.Write "<BR>Delivery Date:   " & sDeliveryDate

End Sub
```

And, if unsuccessful, we can say why.

```
Sub OnTransactionAbort()

    Response.Clear
    If sRV = 50001 Then
        Response.Write "Not enough in stock - order not placed"
    Else
        Response.Write "<P>Unknown Error: Order not placed"
    End If

End Sub

</SCRIPT>
</BODY>
</HTML>
```

So you can quite clearly see how this ASP page resembles the **WCCOrder** component, with responsibility for gluing the components together. In fact, there's no reason why we have to do this, since we already have a component available for use that does this gluing, and we could just use this component instead.

```
Set oOrder = CreateObject("WCCOrder.Order")
oOrder.Create mstrGarageName, mstrGarageAddress, _
              mstrGarageTown, mstrGarageState, _
              mstrGarageZipCode, _
              cboSales, txtPrice, _
              txtName, txtAddress, _
              txtTown, txtState, _
              txtZipCode, txtPhone, _
              GridCellContents(5), _
              lstColor.ItemData(lstColor.ListIndex), _
              sHOOrderID, sDeliveryDate, _
              sRV, _
              mstrHeadOffice, mstrShowroom
```

This saves a bit of ASP work, and encapsulates the business logic more efficiently. If you do this, however, you might want to consider whether or not you want the ASP page to start the transaction, since **WCCOrder** is going to start one anyway. This would mean that the ASP transaction is redundant. However, if you do remove the transaction, you no longer get the callback ability of **onTransactionCommit** and **onTransactionAbort**.

So that's how we actually perform the ordering from within ASP, but what about the visible portion of the application? Again, we are using an ASP page:

We won't look at the top two sections, since they are straight HTML, although we will discuss the finance object in a little while. Firstly we'll look at the code for the car details, and how we get these into the page.

Initially, we define a **FIELDSET**, to put a nice border around the area. (Note that since we are using **FIELDSET** and, later, RDS, so it's clear that the client must be IE4. See Appendix A for further details.)

```
<FIELDSET ID=fldCar STYLE="position:absolute; width:390; height:145;
top:260">
<LEGEND>Car Details:</LEGEND>
```

Then we start a table and put the headings in. We also make sure that the BODY has an event to respond to the user selecting a car—we'll need this to display the colors.

```
<TABLE BORDER=0>
    <THEAD BGCOLOR=Gray>
        <TD WIDTH=175>Model</TD>
        <TD>Engine</TD>
        <TD>Doors</TD>
```

```
        <TD>Seats</TD>
          <TD ALIGN=RIGHT WIDTH=75>Price</TD>
      </THEAD>
      <TBODY onClick=lstCars_onClick()>
```

Next comes the ASP script to build the table. Firstly, we create two objects—one to hold the recordset of cars and the other for our **WCCCars** component.

```
<%
     Set recCars = Server.CreateObject("ADODB.Recordset")
     Set objCars = Server.CreateObject("WCCCars.Cars")
```

Now we call the **GetAll** method, just as we did in the Visual Basic application, and open the recordset it returns.

```
     Set recCars = objCars.GetAll()
     recCars.Open
```

The recordset contains all of the details of the cars, so we can loop through this building up the HTML table.

```
     While Not recCars.EOF
         strID = recCars("CarID")
         strRow = ""
```

We give each row a unique name—in this case, **Car** followed by the car ID, for example, Car1. This allows us to uniquely identify the rows, because DHTML events are triggered at the deepest level, that is, for each cell. When the user selects a car we want to highlight the whole row.

```
     strRow = strRow & "<TR ID=Car" & strID & ">"
```

For each cell in the table, we show the appropriate column from the recordset of cars. We give each cell an **ID** corresponding to the ID of the car, except for the price column, as we need to identify that distinctly too, so for this we simply put **"Price"** in front of it.

```
     strRow = strRow & "<TD ID=" & strID & ">" & _
                             recCars("Model") & "</TD>"
     strRow = strRow & "<TD ID=" & strID & " ALIGN=CENTER>" & _
                             recCars("EngineSize") & "</TD>"
     strRow = strRow & "<TD ID=" & strID & " ALIGN=CENTER>" & _
                             recCars("Doors") & "</TD>"
     strRow = strRow & "<TD ID=" & strID & " ALIGN=CENTER>" & _
                             recCars("Seats") & "</TD>"
     strRow = strRow & "<TD ID=Price" & strID & " ALIGN=RIGHT WIDTH=75>" & _
                             FormatCurrency(recCars("Price"), 0) & "</TD>"

     strRow = strRow & "</TR>"
```

Once the row is built we can write it to the Response object, to stream it into the HTML page, and move to the next row.

```
        Response.Write strRow
        recCars.MoveNext
    Wend
```

Finally, we release our objects and end the table.

```
    Set recCars = Nothing
    Set objCars = Nothing

%>

</TBODY>
</TABLE>
</FIELDSET>
```

So, we end up with a table with ID tags like this (assuming the car IDs are 1 to 5).

| RowID | Model | Engine | Doors | Seats | Price |
|-------|-------|--------|-------|-------|-------|
| Car1  | 1     | 1      | 1     | 1     | Price1 |
| Car2  | 2     | 2      | 2     | 2     | Price2 |
| Car3  | 3     | 3      | 3     | 3     | Price3 |
| Car4  | 4     | 4      | 4     | 4     | Price4 |
| Car5  | 5     | 5      | 5     | 5     | Price5 |

Now we have a table that will react when we click on a row on the client. Remember what happened in the Visual Basic application–it called the **ColorsByCar** method of **WCCCars** to retrieve the colors for that car. That was easy for that application to do, but in the Internet world we don't want to make a round trip to the server every time we need to see the colors; a better solution is to have the colors available locally. We could have done this with the Visual Basic application too, but we wanted to show you that, now you are programming in a different arena, you might have to think slightly differently. So let's see how this is handled at the client.

We begin with the loading of the document:

```
Function Window_onLoad()
    ' create a client side recordset of all of the colors
    ' by using the server side ADF

    sServer = "http://<%=Request.ServerVariables("SERVER_NAME")%>"
<%
    QUOT=Chr(34)
    Response.Write "sShowroom=" & QUOT & sShowroom & QUOT
%>
    strSQL = "usp_AllColorsForAllCars"
    Set ADF = ADS.CreateObject ("RDSServer.DataFactory", sServer)
```

```
    Set recColors = ADF.Query(sShowroom, strSQL)

    strCarID = "CarID"
    strLastCarID = "CarID"

End Function
```

This looks pretty complex, but it's fairly easy to follow, as long as you remember that everything between **<%** and **%>** is run on the server. So, as the page is run on the server, **sServer** is filled in with the name of the web server, from the **ServerVariables** collection in ASP. The second server side script section gets the ADO connection string. Remember that we had an include file that defined **sShowroom**. This is fine for server side script, but what if we want to use that connection string in client side script? The trick here is just to create the code as we process the file on the server. All we do is write out the code that sets a variable to the connection string. When this code appears at the client it looks like this:

```
Function Window_onLoad()
    ' create a client side recordset of all of the colors
    ' by using the server side ADF

    sServer = "http://Piglet"
    sShowroom = "driver={SQL Server}; server=Piglet; UID=sa; PWD=; " _
        & "database=WroxCarCo"

    strSQL = "usp_AllColorsForAllCars"
    Set ADF = ADS.CreateObject ("RDSServer.DataFactory", sServer)
    Set recColors = ADF.Query(sShowroom, strSQL)

    strCarID = "CarID"
    strLastCarID = "CarID"

End Function
```

Now, onto the ADF and ADS stuff. This is something you might not have seen before, as it's part of Remote Data Services. It's a set of services that allow clients to manipulate sets of data independently of the server. **ADS** is an ActiveX object that has been embedded on the page by using an **OBJECT** tag, and provides us with a connection back to the server so we can get recordsets. The **DataFactory** is a server-based component that accepts requests from the client and processes them on the server. In this case, we are running a **Query**, passing in a stored procedure, and the **DataFactory** will then return a standard recordset. This differs slightly from the previous color recordsets because it contains a list of all colors for all cars. That way we have all of the data we need, and don't have to return to the server again, as it is cached locally. The data it returns is in the form shown below–the real one is larger than shown here– and we've cut the list down to make it easier to see.

| fkCarID | ColorID | Color |
|---------|---------|-----------|
| 1 | 1 | White |
| 1 | 2 | Gainsboro |
| 1 | 3 | Red |

| fkCarID | ColorID | Color |
|---------|---------|-----------|
| 2 | 1 | White |
| 2 | 3 | Red |
| 2 | 4 | Hot Pink |
| 3 | 1 | White |
| 3 | 2 | Gainsboro |

The recordset is declared globally so we can use it in other procedures, and speaking of other procedures, how about what happens when we click on a car?

Firstly, we set a pointer to the object that caused the event to trigger—this will be one of the cells in the Cars table:

```
Function lstCars_onClick()

    Set oCar = Window.Event.srcElement
```

Now we need to check to see if it was the price column. Remember that each cell in the same row will have an **ID** that matches the ID of the car but in the form Price **ID**. So we just check to see whether we are on the price column, and, if so, extract the real ID number. We then build a string that will match the **ID** of the row, by adding **"Car"** to the real ID number.

```
If Left(oCar.ID, 5) = "Price" Then
    strRealID = Right(oCar.ID, Len(oCar.ID) - 5)
Else
    strRealID = oCar.ID
End If
strCarID = "Car" & strRealID
```

Now we know which row we are dealing with, we can highlight it. We use **strLastRow** to point to the last row selected so that we can take the highlight off it.

```
Document.All(strLastCarID).Style.BackgroundColor = "White"
Document.All(strCarID).Style.BackgroundColor = Document.BGColor
```

Then we call the ShowColors routine to show the list of colors—we'll look at that in a moment.

```
ShowColors (strRealID)
```

Now we can set the **CarID** field to contain the real ID of the car and the **Price** field to contain the price—note that this is why we needed to identify the price column separately, so that we could extract the price. The **CarID** field is hidden because it doesn't need to be shown, but it will be passed to the ASP page that we saw earlier to process the order.

```
Document.All("CarID").InnerText = strCarID
```

```
Document.All("Price").InnerText = _
                    Document.All("Price" & strRealID).InnerText
```

All that's left to do is set the last car selected to be the current one, and clear the last   color selected, as we have a new list of colors.

```
strLastCarID = strCarID
strLastColor = ""

End Function
```

Let's look at the **ShowColors** routine now. This will need to build a table of the   colors for the selected car.

We start by creating a table, giving it an event, and moving to the first row in the   recordset.

```
Function ShowColors (lngCarID)

    strColors = "<TABLE ID=lstColors onClick=lstColors_onClick()>"
    recColors.MoveFirst
    While Not recColors.EOF
```

Now we check to see if the car ID in the   recordset is the same as the one passed into the procedure–that's the one the user clicked on. If it is, we can continue to build up the HTML table, adding the **ColorID** as the ID for the row.

```
        If CInt(recColors("fkCarID")) = CInt(lngCarID) Then
            strColors = strColors & _
                "<TR ID=Color" & recColors("ColorID") & ">" & _
                "<TD ID=" & recColors("ColorID") & ">" & _
                recColors("Color") & _
                "</TD></TR>"
        End If
        recColors.MoveNext
    Wend

    strColors = strColors & "</TABLE>"
```

Once the table is fully built we can set the   **OuterHTML** property of the table to the new HTML string we've just created. That gives us a table full of the new   colors.

```
    Document.All("lstColors").OuterHTML = strColors

End Function
```

Remember that this   recordset is stored locally. At no time during the above procedure will the client return to the server for more data.

So now that we have the list of colors, what happens when we click on a color? In fact, the process is actually much the same as for the cars. Here we only have one column, so we just need to keep a track of the previous selection to un-highlight it. The **ColorID** field is then filled with the ID of the color selected.

```
Function lstColors_onClick()

    Set oColor = Window.Event.srcElement

    lngColorID = oColor.ID
    strColor = "Color" & lngColorID

    Document.All(strLastColor).Style.BackgroundColor = "White"
    Document.All(strColor).Style.BackgroundColor = Document.BGColor

    strLastColor = strColor

    Document.All("ColorID").InnerText = lngColorID

End Function
```

# Custom Business Objects

One of the things you may have noticed is that we have talked a great deal about business objects and component reuse, but we used a stored procedure directly in this piece of code:

```
Function Window_onLoad()

    strServer = "http://piglet"
    strConn = "driver={SQL Server};server=PIGLET;database=WroxCarCo"
    strSQL = "usp_AllColorsForAllCars"

    Set ADF = ADS.CreateObject ("RDSServer.DataFactory", strServer)
    Set recColors = ADF.Query(strConn, strSQL)

End Function
```

Doesn't that seem to ignore all of the ideas we've been pushing? To a certain degree yes, but there are only four ways to get a recordset to the client:

❑ Use an RDS Data Control. This is a pre-built an embedded object that automatically calls the **DataFactory**. You'll see this method used in Chapter 6.

❑ Manually call the **DataFactory**, as above.

❑ Use Remote Scripting. This is still a fairly new technology and is outside the scope of the book, but would allow client side script to call server side script.

❑ Create a custom business object. This would take the place of the **DataFactory**.

If the last option is what we should really be aiming at, why didn't we do it? There are two reasons. The first is that we wanted to show another method of getting data to the client. Using the **DataFactory** is perfectly valid, even though the user can see the name of the stored procedure—after all, the contents of the stored procedure are still hidden, and we are still preserving the data. However, the user can still see the data store details, so perhaps it isn't the best solution.

So let's examine the approach of using a custom business object. For this example, we will assume that the business object is called **WCCWebCars.Cars**, and that it has a method called **AllColorsForAllCars**, which returns a standard recordset. We could now change the **Window_onLoad** routine to this:

```
Sub Window_onLoad()

    strServer = "http://piglet"
    Set oADS = CreateObject("RDS.DataSpace")
    Set objCars = oADS.CreateObject ("WCCWebCars.Cars", strShowroom)
    Set recColors = objCars.AllColorsForAllCars ()

End Sub
```

The **DataSpace** is an RDS object that acts as a proxy between the web page and the server. We need this because we can't directly instantiate an object on the server, so the DataSpace does this for us:

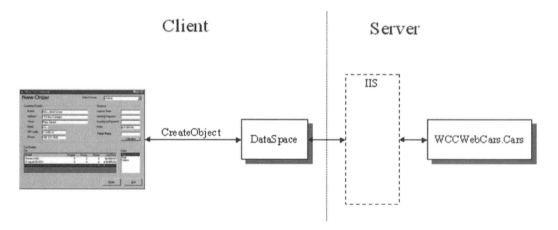

So all we do is create the **DataSpace** object, tell it to create our custom business object, and then execute the method of the object. So if it's that simple why didn't we do that? In fact you probably won't be surprised to learn that it's not quite that simple—there's a few other steps you have to make.

Firstly, you have to register the business object with RDS. This protects your IIS security, only allowing it to run valid business objects. To do this you'll need to modify the Advanced Data Control entries in the registry. The key is shown below:

```
HKEY_LOCAL_MACHINE\System\CurrentControlSet\Services\W3SVC\Parameters\ADCL
```

You need to select **ADCLaunch**, add a new key and add the **ProgID** of your business object as the key name:

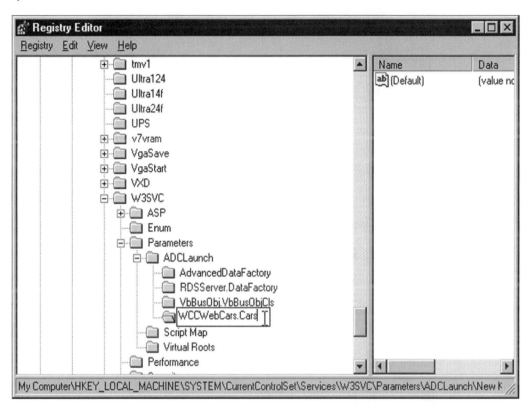

You only need the name here, and can leave the value blank.

Once you've told ADC that the business object can be created, you need to mark the object as Safe for Scripting. This ensures that it won't be rejected as an unsafe control by the web browser. The simplest way to do this is to use the Visual Basic 5 Application Setup Wizard. Make sure you select the Internet Download Setup option when selecting the project.

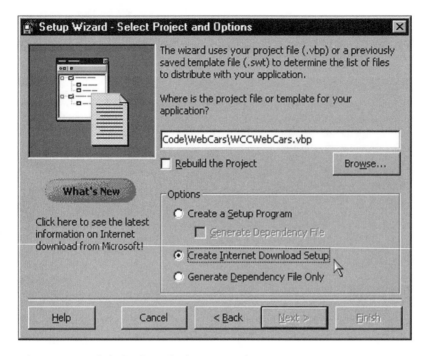

Then make sure you click the Secu rity button on the next screen:

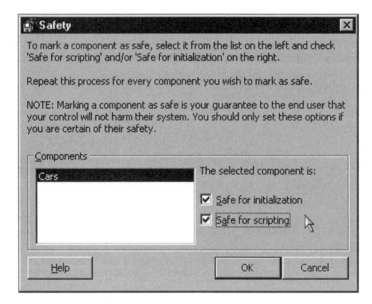

This allows you to mark the control as safe for use in web  browsers.

When you have finished the  setup wizard you have a  **.cab** file and a  **.htm** file, and you can load the
**htm** file to correctly register the component, adding two new keys to the registry to mark the
component safe.

The end result of this is that we want the following keys added to the registry:

```
[HKEY_CLASSES_ROOT\SOFTWARE\Classes\CLSID\<GUID>\Implemented
Categories\{7DD95801-9882-11CF-9FA9-00AA006C42C4}]
[HKEY_CLASSES_ROOT\SOFTWARE\Classes\CLSID\<GUID>\Implemented
Categories\{7DD95802-9882-11CF-9FA9-00AA006C42C4}]
```

Where **<GUID>** is the GUID of your business object.

If you've already created your component and installed it in MTS, then you won't be able to use the Visual Basic Setup Wizard, because the control will already be registered. So the easiest thing to do in this case is create a file with a **.reg** extension and copy the above two lines into it. Then have a look at the component properties in MTS Explorer and copy the GUID from there into the above file, replacing **<GUID>**. You can then double-click on the **.reg** file to add these keys to the registry. You can also add the keys manually if you wish.

Although this process isn't very complex, it is quite time consuming, especially if you have a large number of business objects. This is the very reason we chose to use the **DataFactory** to get our recordset of colors back to the client web page. This will only be run once, when the page is loaded, and we took the view that letting the users view the stored procedure name was acceptable. When you create components and web pages though, you should consider both methods before starting development.

# Finance Component

You will notice that we haven't talked again about the Finance component. Let's think about what it does for a moment. It takes a few details and then calculates a number. Seems obvious, but remember that this component is handled by MTS, running on the server, and the web application is running on the client. So what we would be doing every time we pressed the Calculate button would be invoking a round trip to the server. Not only is that bad practice, but the user is soon going to get fed up with waiting for a response.

So there are two solutions to this problem:

❑   Remove the component from MTS and embed it into the HTML page with the **OBJECT** tag, so it is downloaded when the page loads and is run on the client machine.

❑   Rewrite the component. We mentioned earlier that in reality the database would probably store a list of payment methods and plans. This could generate a recordset of all of the data in a similar way to fetching the colors, and could then be manipulated at the client side by use of RDS.

Which is the best solution? Well either really, depending upon your client base. If your users are wary of downloading ActiveX controls that run in their web pages then the second solution is best for you. In this example though, we've included it as an object:

```
<OBJECT ID="FinanceObject"
  CLASSID="CLSID:CBFC0DA5-A499-11D1-882B-00201834E2A6"
  CODEBASE="WCCFinance.cab#version=1,0,0,0"
```

```
        STYLE="position:absolute; height:1; width:1; visibility:hidden">
    </OBJECT>
```

We've created a CAB file using the Visual Basic setup wizard, and placed the cab file in the same directory as the asp pages. In the asp file, we can refer to this component in the following manner:

```
Function btnCalculate_onClick()

    On Error Resume Next

    Set objFinance = document.all("FinanceObject")

    ' check the component is installed
    If Not IsObject(objFinance) Then
        strMesg = "This calculation requires an ActiveX control " _
            & "that has not been installed. You must reload the " _
            & "page and allow the of the control from our server " _
            & "to take place by selecting 'Low Security' in your " _
            & "'Internet Options' settings."
        Msgbox strMesg, vbInformation, "Finance Control Error"
        Exit Function
    End If

    ' now calculate the finance
    objFinance.InterestRate = Document.All("InterestRate").InnerText
    objFinance.MonthlyPayment = Document.All("InterestRate").InnerText
    objFinance.TotalPrice = Document.All("Price").InnerText
    Document.All("NoOfPayments") = objFinance.GetNumberPayments()

    Set objFinance = Nothing

End Function
```

# Summary

This was a very practical chapter and there's been a large amount of code shown, but you can see that writing a DNA based application is just common sense. Much of the success of an application can come with the way it is designed, and this becomes more important when you start to develop with components.

What we've specifically looked at in this chapter has been how to use database access in components and how to link the components together. We've seen that once created they can be used from either Visual Basic (or VBA) or Script code. This is the important middle tier, leaving you free to develop the visual portion of the application in whatever tool you desire.

Now that we have a working application, we have to consider what happens if the head office database becomes unavailable. This is where message queuing comes in to practice, and is the subject of the next chapter.

# 5

# Introducing Message Queuing

So far in this book we've looked at Microsoft's latest application design methodology, the **Distributed interNet Applications** (DNA) architecture, how it uses components to implement the business rules and functions, and how these components can be integrated with **Microsoft Transaction Server** (MTS) to produce robust and reliable distributed applications. It's now time to explore the second headline technology from the title of the book, **Microsoft Message Queue Server** (MSMQ).

MSMQ, like MTS, is part of the Windows NT4 Option Pack and an integral part of Windows NT5. It fills the final gap in a distributed application, something that we intimated may be of concern way back in Chapter 1 when looking at what our Wrox Car Co application was designed to do. The question we asked at the time was: 'What happens if the head office database, or the network that connects our showroom to it, is out of action?' In this chapter, you'll see the answer.

Before we go into details, however, we'll take an overview of the whole topic of message queuing. You won't be surprised to know that it isn't a Microsoft invention, but has been a core part of distributed applications on other platforms for quite some time. We'll be covering:

- ❑ What message queuing is, and why it's so useful in a distributed application
- ❑ How Microsoft's message queuing technology, MSMQ, works, and what it can do
- ❑ Some simple examples of message queuing using the built-in MSMQ tools
- ❑ The ways that we can add message queuing to our applications

We won't be adding the final message queuing features to our sample Wrox Car Co application in this chapter—we'll do this in Chapter 6 when we come to finalize the application and the two different client interfaces.

# What Is Message Queuing?

Like Transaction Server, Microsoft has christened the technology that we'll be looking at in this chapter with what might seem to be a somewhat misleading name. As you'll see in this section, the stuff we are actually queuing is application-independent **data**, rather than **messages** in the more conventional sense of the word.

However, message queuing is an established term in the market, and Microsoft rightly want their share of this market. One of the best-known message queuing applications is the MQ (Message Queue) Series from IBM, and this could possibly have influenced Microsoft's choice of name for their competitor–Message Queue Server.

But none of this answers the real question: what is message queuing and why do we need it? To answer this, we'll consider two obvious problems that arise when we build distributed applications. These are generic problems that concern all types of distributed application–not just those created to conform to Windows DNA architecture.

# Integrating With The Real World

While we all tend to build example or test-bed applications that revolve around a particular operating system and methodology, such as our Wrox Car Co sample application, the real world often dictates that our applications must be integrated into an existing system; often one that uses legacy components and 'foreign' data stores.

## Integration With Existing Systems

For example, it's unlikely that your financial director would agree to shift the whole company's payroll system onto, say, Windows NT and SQL Server just so that you can add a new interface to it. Likewise, your applications or components may need to interface with data processing components that run on a different operating system, perhaps on another server across the other side of the continent.

Coping with 'foreign' data sources is not such a major headache, providing that a suitable OLE-DB or ODBC driver is available for us to connect to it from a Windows platform. As you saw in previous chapters, we can talk to almost any data source this way, and (together with MTS) easily implement distributed transactions.

But this technique has one big drawback. Usually, we'll be implementing business rules that carry out the data access operations in a controlled and pre-defined way, rather than just hitting the data store directly. These objects will often be running on the foreign server's operating system, and this means that we may have to rewrite the business rules components in order to run them on our own system. If we can't do this, or if we don't want to, we're into the second problem situation. How does our Windows-based application communicate with (say) a component written in COBOL and running on a mainframe system?

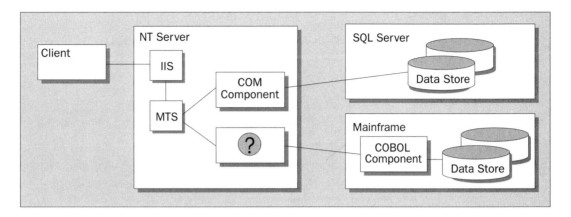

While there are other ways that it can be achieved, message queuing provides one of the simplest solutions for communication between disparate systems in this kind of environment.

## Coping With Real-World Networks

Message queuing also provides another major benefit in a distributed application. For some time it's been rumored that computer networks are not 100% reliable. OK, so you might get 99% availability on your office LAN–but that argument doesn't hold much water when a customer is complaining that you charged them for a product, but the update to the warehouse shipments database in Mexico failed to get processed.

One of the benefits of using a transacted application, as in our example with MTS, is that you can be sure that this situation doesn't arise. If the remote database can't be updated then the transaction aborts and the customer is not charged for the goods. Your application tells the order clerk that this is the case, and they can do something about it.

### The Downside Of Transacted Applications

While using transactions to provide an all-or-nothing process is great, it has a major downside. Your application can't commit any of the operations involved in the transaction until all of them have completed successfully. And of course, if your application steps outside the   cozy confines of your fast and 'reliable' LAN, it's likely to meet problems such as the latency–or even non-availability–of the connection to the remote system. If that connection is via the Internet, the situation is probably going to be even worse.

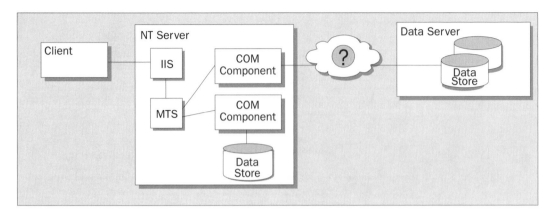

To get round this, and provide a responsive and reliable interface for our applications, we really want some way of coping with the non-availability or slow response of a remote system. We came across this when we built our **Wrox Car Co** application in previous chapters. It needs to update a remote database at head office with the order. So what do we do if the phone company just dug through our cables when installing next door's new line? Do we tell the customer that they can't buy a car today? Again, message queuing can provide a solution.

# What Message Queuing Offers

Message Queuing offers two main advantages to a distributed application:

❑ **Communication between disparate systems and components.**
❑ **Connectionless communication with guaranteed delivery.**

We'll look at each of these features in turn, and see how we can take advantage of them in our applications.

## Disparate System Communication

When we build an application under the DNA methodology, the interface, components and data store drivers will usually be talking to each other using COM and DCOM. If we need to communicate with a component or a system that doesn't support COM, we have a problem. Of course, this also applies the other way round. Message queuing provides a way for applications that run on a different operating system, or that live in a non-compatible environment, to talk to our applications.

It does this by providing a platform-independent system of storing and forwarding messages that can be interpreted by a different application. Rather than communicating directly through operating system and inter-process calls, both applications agree on a standard format for the data so that both can interpret it. It's like the situation where you meet someone from Spain who doesn't speak English and you can't speak Spanish, but you both speak another language—say Russian. By agreeing on this as the standard for your conversation, the only limitations are your grasp of the intermediate language.

## *Connectionless Communication*

Even when two systems natively speak the same language, such as COM or DCOM in the Windows case, direct and continuous communication is not always possible. Take, for example, a traveling salesperson who goes round the country collecting orders, using the interface to your application on their mobile computer. For most of the day they won't be connected to the office network, and so their orders have to be stored locally and then transmitted to the invoicing office as a batch.

However, you'll want to be sure that these orders all get processed, and that none are duplicated. This means that it's a good idea to implement transactions that encompass the taking of the order and its processing within the office. To be able to do this, you need to have a way for the mobile application to store the orders, and tell the interface (i.e. the salesperson and the customer) that the transaction succeeded. Otherwise, it would be impossible to place an order–the transaction would be aborted because the 'office end' of the process would not indicate success.

Normally, the 'other half' of the transaction can take place only when the mobile computer is connected to the office network. However, message queuing allows this to occur by standing in for the office half of the transaction. It accepts the instructions and tells MTS that the process completed OK, and that it can commit the transaction. Once connected to the office system, it passes on the instructions to the other half of the application for it to process. Effectively, it's making a promise to the mobile application that the process will complete successfully, and that it can get on with the next one.

# What Is Message Queue Server?

Having seen what message queuing means in a general sense, we'll move on to look at how it is implemented in **Microsoft Message Queue Server** (MSMQ). To understand how MSMQ works, there are a couple of important points that you have to be clear about:

❑ Message Queuing is *nothing* to do with managing email, and the messages it uses are *not* email messages.

❑ The easiest way to appreciate how MSMQ works is to compare it with email.

So, providing you promise not to forget point one, we'll continue along the lines of point two.

# What Message Queue Server Does

The basic principles of MSMQ are remarkable simple. When you want to pass a message on to another application, you just create it, wrap it up in a special package, and dump it into a message queue. The receiving application can interrogate the message queue and retrieve any waiting messages whenever it likes. Until it does, the message sits in the queue waiting.

## *Connectionless Messaging*

This is, of course, how email works. A user sends their email message to their own mail server, where it is stored and then forwarded to the appropriate mail server for the recipient to collect. Of course, the sender and recipient may be using the same mail server, so the message is simply stored in the recipient's mailbox there. If they aren't connected to their mail server when the message arrives (perhaps they use a dial-up account rather than a permanent connection) it waits in their mailbox until they do connect and retrieve their mail. This is **store-and-forward** messaging, and it provides the kind of connectionless messaging environment we need in our distributed applications.

## Guaranteed Once-Only Delivery

Email servers also provide extra features to make the delivery of email more reliable, and MSMQ implements the same kind of core features. For example, a message is only flagged as received by the recipient once they signal to the mail server that the message arrived intact. Until then it is marked as undelivered, so a network failure while it is being delivered will leave it as 'new mail' on the mail server ready to be collected again. Once it's been safely delivered and acknowledged, it is marked as such. The mail server will only send it as new mail once, and will keep trying to deliver it until it is successful (or generate a return message to indicate an error if it can't be delivered after a preset time).

## Prioritization and Routing

On most systems, email messages can optionally be marked as 'urgent', and these will be delivered first by the mail server—either directly to the recipient, or to the recipient's mail server. It's also possible to configure the mail server to route messages depending on rules. And of course, out on the Internet, dynamic routing is the norm anyway. Packets can take different routes to their destination depending on network traffic and availability. MSMQ can provide all these kinds of features as well.

## Message and System Security

Users have to identify themselves to the mail server before both sending and receiving messages. They can also encrypt and digitally sign messages to prevent unauthorized interception and tampering with the content. Again, MSMQ provides these kinds of features to the messages and data it transmits between applications.

## Disparate System Integration

Finally, email is often a platform-independent communication method. Users can send text email and attached files to recipients that use different email software, and which can run on different platforms and in different environments. MSMQ message data is stored in a format that both sender and recipient agree on, and so it doesn't matter what the recipient's environment looks like—it can convert the data into whatever format it likes after receipt.

### Supported Platforms

MSMQ only directly supports Windows NT (Server and Workstation) and Windows 9x. However, because the data format is standardized, other platforms can use it to communicate with Windows applications, and with each other. A company called **Level 8 Systems** manufactures a range of components that can access proprietary message queues on other systems, such as IBM MVS, MQ, CICS, OS/2, and AS/400 platforms; Sun Solaris, HP-UNIX, and AIX UNIX.

The SDK (Software Development Kit) supplied with MSMQ also allows you to build applications and components that can integrate with MSMQ in other environments.

*For more information on the Level 8 Systems products see their web page at*
`http://www.level8.com/`. *Microsoft also provide their own MSMQ pages at*
`http://www.microsoft.com/msmq/`.

# How Message Queue Server Works

MSMQ runs as a **service** under Windows, and exposes a set of objects that client applications and components can use to create messages and queues. It also handles delivery of the messages to the appropriate queue. It also provides methods that can find and search through message queues, and retrieve messages from queues. This is the basic functionality required to work with message queuing.

The MSMQ objects also provide methods for encrypting messages, acknowledging their receipt, and securing the queues. Finally, there are tools and samples available that allow you to set up, test, monitor and administer the service as a whole. We'll be using some of these tools later in this chapter. First, however, we'll look at the architecture and structure of MSMQ.

## The MSMQ Architecture

MSMQ depends on a hierarchical structure of servers and clients. At the root is the **Primary Enterprise Controller**, which stores details of the queue locations and the other servers and clients that have access to the queues and messages. When you first install MSMQ you have to provide a location and name for the **enterprise** as a whole. Normally you will have only one enterprise that contains all the systems that you wish to communicate with, although it is possible to pass messages between enterprises.

The Enterprise Controller supplies information about the entire enterprise to all other systems when they need to locate or work with a queue, and is responsible for the routing of messages between queues. MSMQ also defines the concepts of sites and connected networks. Within the enterprise are **sites**, which consist of machines that have generally fast and reliable links between them. Often sites are defined by physical boundaries, such as all the machines within one building. The links that connect each site can also have 'costs' defined for each one, which provide information that MSMQ uses to efficiently route messages between sites. We'll come back to this aspect later.

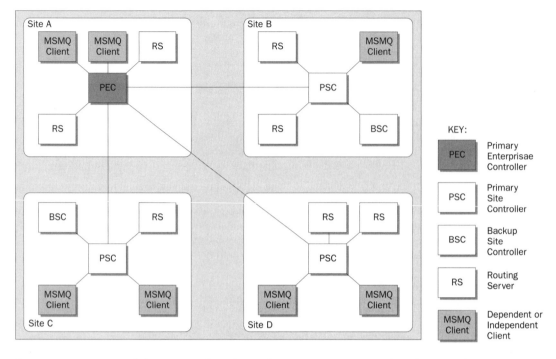

A **connected network** defines a set of machines that can communicate directly using the same protocol (either IPX or IP). A connected network may mirror a site, but doesn't have to. It's also possible to connect machines using **Remote Access Services** (RAS) to pass messages between them, providing they are not using the NetBEUI protocol.

### The Enterprise Controller And Other Servers

Once an **Enterprise Controller** is available, other servers and clients can connect to it. An MSMQ server can only run on Windows NT Server. You can also install MSMQ as a Primary Site Controller, a Backup Site Controller, or a Routing Server. If you need to communicate with machines that run different operating systems, you can also set up an MSMQ Server as a **Connector Server**, where it acts as a bridge between native and foreign queues. The Primary Enterprise Controller also provides the services of a Primary Site Controller for the site it's located in, and a Routing Server within that site.

**Site Controllers** hold read-only copies of the parts of the enterprise information store that relate to their own site, and each site can contain both a Primary and a Backup Site Controller. All other MSMQ Servers are Routing Servers, which can provide intermediate queuing of messages as well as routing them to their final destination. You must have a Primary Enterprise Controller installed and available before you can install any other MSMQ Servers. Primary and Backup Site Controllers also provide the services of a Routing Server.

**Routing Servers** don't hold any site information, and are used only to route messages between queues. They allow computers using different protocols to communicate, and can send messages between other MSMQ Servers and MSMQ Clients.

The MSMQ Administrator's Guide (installed with MSMQ and available from the MSMQ section of the Start menu) provides a full description of each type of Server, as well as valuable information on how you should partition a large enterprise in order to maximize performance.

### Dependent and Independent Clients

MSMQ Clients can be installed on Windows NT or Windows 9x, and require a Primary Enterprise Controller to be available when they are installed. **Dependent Clients** can only communicate with MSMQ synchronously (i.e. they have to wait for communication to complete when accessing the message queue) while **Independent Clients** can communicate asynchronously.

What this means in essence is that a Dependent Client can only send and receive messages while it is connected to, and can access, its site controller. This is because they use DCOM to access the functions of the MSMQ Server to which they connect, and have no facilities to create queues or store information locally.

In order to provide connectionless (or **disconnected**) messaging, an Independent Client–which can store messages in a local queue and synchronize them when a connection becomes available–must be used. This connection can be made through the LAN in the normal way, using IP or IPX protocols, or through RAS to a remote MSMQ Server.

An Independent Client can even move from one site to another, and it is automatically configured by MSMQ to allow messages to be sent from it while it is connected to the new site. However, it cannot receive messages while connected to the new site unless it has previously specified details of the new site, while still connected to its original site and before moving to the new one. You can think of it as having to tell your local post office to redirect your mail while you're away.

### How The Messages Are Stored

In its simplest form, a message queue is just a bucket for holding messages that are in transit or waiting for collection. In MSMQ, they can be implemented as either disk-based ( **recoverable**) or RAM-based (**express**) queues. Using memory to hold the queue provides high performance, but, for a robust application the queue needs to be stored on disk. In mission-critical applications, this will be protected by backups, and possibly fault-tolerant disk systems, to allow reliable recovery in the event of a failure.

The messages themselves are stored in native format–as text and/or binary data–and as separate disk files in the case of disk-based queues. This gives maximum performance. If you implemented MSMQ through the Windows NT4 Option Pack, you'll also need to have Microsoft SQL Server available. However, this is only used to store details of where each queue is located–and *not* the contents of the messages. In NT5, the details of the queue locations are stored in the Active Directory Service, and SQL Server is not required.

Queues can be specified as **public** or **private** queues, and MSMQ also provides special queues that act as the journal, dead letter, transactional dead letter, administration, system, and report queues. It's also possible to specify the maximum size of a queue, or the total size limit for all queues on a machine.

## How The Messages Are Routed

The diagram we used earlier to show the topology of an MSMQ enterprise included connections between the various computers that indicated the hierarchy, with the Primary Enterprise Controller at the root. However, in most networks, there are multiple communication paths between computers, both within a site and between sites. This is also the case with the Internet, where packets can be routed in many different ways to reach the same destination.

Obviously it makes sense to use the 'cheapest' route between two machines. However 'cheapest' is not always 'shortest', so there has to be some way of defining the suitability of a route for messages so that they can be delivered with the maximum efficiency and speed, and the least cost. MSMQ does this by allowing administrators to allocate a **cost** to each route between computers. For machines within the same site there is generally no cost, because they are connected by a fast and reliable network—probably Ethernet at 10 MB/s or more. Between sites, however, it may be a 28.8 KB/s modem over normal telephone lines. Site link costs can be set to any number between zero (no cost) and 999,999 (highest cost).

The following diagram shows the original connections we defined in the previous diagram, but adds some new connections in darker lines. You can see that, despite there being a direct connection between them, the cheapest way to get a message from **Site C** to **Site B** is via **Site A**. For example, this route could be via a leased line, while the direct route is a dial-up Internet link.

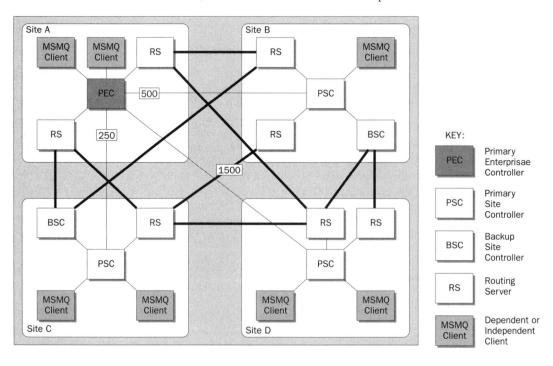

### The Message Queue Object

Before you can send a message you need to have a queue available, either an existing one or one you create specifically. This is one area where message queuing differs from traditional email. When you send email, you address it to one or more individual recipients. Even email to a named group of people, such as a mailing list, is only delivered to one place—where it is replicated and delivered to all the appropriate recipients. When you receive mail, you can only access your own mailbox, or those declared as being public on the mail server.

In MSMQ, your application can search for and access any public queue, and write, read and remove the messages there. To prevent unauthorized access, queues can be assigned permissions in a similar way to files and directories on a disk. We'll be looking at these aspects in more detail in a later chapter of this book.

The physical location of each queue can also be specified. It can be on the Primary Enterprise Controller, another MSMQ Server, or an Independent Client—either at the sender's or the recipient's end of the network, or somewhere in between. Queues cannot be created on Dependent Clients, which themselves demand a permanent connection to the enterprise.

### The Message Object

MSMQ messages are implemented by creating an instance of a **MSMQMessage** object, and setting its properties. Once the message is complete it is sent to the appropriate queue where it resides either until another application collects it, or until it expires. The conditions for expiry and the time-out period can be set when the message is being created.

One of the major advantages of message queuing in MSMQ is that an acknowledgment from the recipient can be requested. The sender simply specifies the queue that is to be used for the reply, and MSMQ looks after all the details. Recipients can also reply with custom acknowledgments if required.

### About Transactional Messaging

In Chapter 3 we looked at the concept of a **Distributed Transaction Coordinator** (DTC). This is a software component which ensures that a transactional process completes, and it is controlled by the transaction server—in our case MTS. MSMQ contains its own DTC, allowing compliant applications to send messages under transactional control.

By setting a flag on the message, and sending it to a queue that is defined to support transactions, the DTC can provide full support for a transacted process. If the message is delivered correctly, MSMQ will allow the transaction to succeed. If not, the transaction will be aborted, along with all the other processes that were part of it. Alternatively, if another component within the transaction causes it to abort, the DTC ensures that any messages relevant to the transaction are removed from the queue without being sent. MSMQ can thereby guarantee both delivery of a message, and that it has been delivered exactly once. It can also guarantee that multiple messages arrive in the correct order.

The standard Microsoft DTC also supports MSMQ messaging, using a two-phase commit mechanism. In other words, an acknowledgment message from the recipient is used by MSMQ to provide evidence of success. This method is known as a **coordinated transaction**, and is usually slower and less efficient than the native MSMQ technique.

*Transactional messaging is not supported on Windows 95 with Independent Clients. However, Windows 95 Dependent Clients can use the MS DTC Proxy, which is installed along with the Dependent Client software, to achieve transactional messaging.*

So MSMQ can provide several useful services to our distributed application, including translation between different operating environments, disconnected messaging for network links that are slow or not always available, and support for transactions via Microsoft Transaction Server.

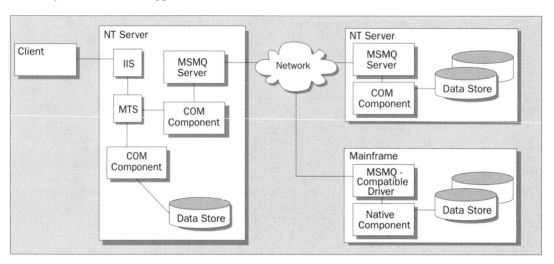

# The MSMQ Tools And Samples

MSMQ comes with a series of sample applications and tools, together with the main administrative tool Message Queue Explorer. The samples include an application named  Distributed Draw that allows two people to draw on a window and see the other person's drawings at the same time—the drawing instructions are sent from one machine to the other using MSMQ.

We're going to look at a less exciting, but potentially more useful tool in this chapter. Before we do so, however, there's no better way to get familiar with MSMQ than by having a quick play with Message Queue Explorer. This is our first step.

## Using MSMQ Explorer

Although it seemed likely that the MSMQ Administrator would become just a snap-in to the Microsoft Management Console (MMC), this hasn't happened yet. Instead a similar but independent application called Message Queue Explorer is provided. This shows the MSMQ enterprise as a tree in the left-hand pane, and the right-hand pane displays information about the currently selected item in the tree:

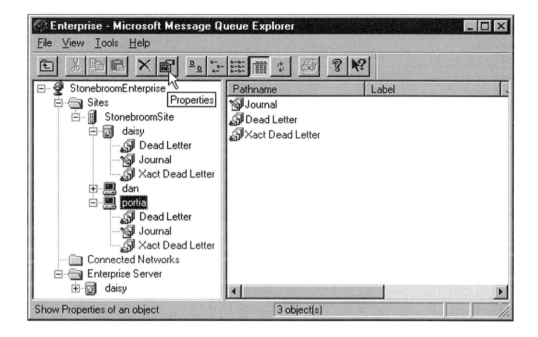

### Display Columns and Properties

MQ Explorer is more configurable than the MMC. By selecting Columns from the View menu, you can specify the columns that will appear in the right-hand window, and their ordering, for each type of item that you might select in the left-hand window:

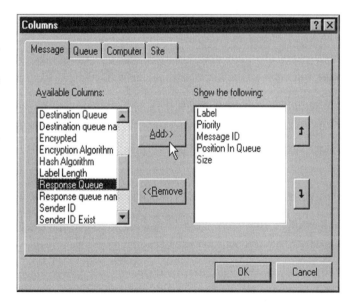

By selecting a computer in the left-hand pane and clicking the **Properties** toolbar button (or right-clicking and selecting **Properties** from the short-cut menu in the usual way) you get useful information about that computer. Here, we're setting the **quota limits**, which control the maximum size of all the messages and journals stored on this machine. If the machine is an Independent Client (as ours is here) you can also use this dialog to change the site that it 'belongs' to—the parent site. As we mentioned earlier, you have to do this before moving to a new site if you want to be able to receive messages whilst connected to that site:

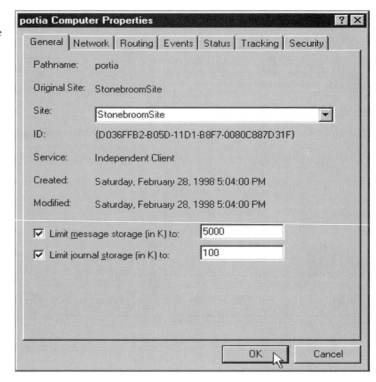

## Sending Test Messages

The **Send Test Messages** option on the **Tools** menu of MQ Explorer can be used to send test messages to confirm that the installation is working properly. This opens a dialog where you can select an existing queue or create a new one:

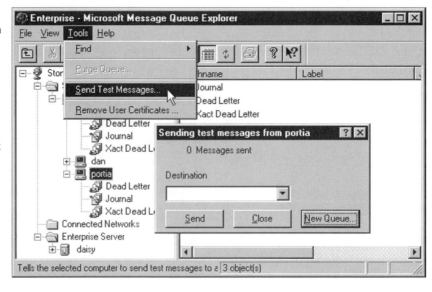

In our case, we're creating a new queue named test queue on a remote machine named daisy:

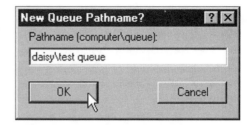

Now, clicking the Send button sends one message each time to that queue. You can see that the queue is displayed in MQ Explorer in the next screen shot, and the messages are visible:

We can also use MQ Explorer to view the private queues on the machines, and to create new queues that will accept transactional messages. Recall that transactional messaging requires this special type of queue to be available:

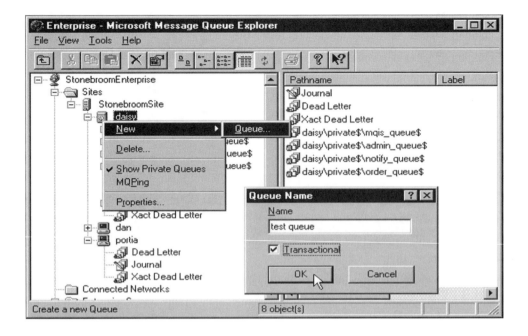

### If It Doesn't Seem To Work

Finally, if nothing seems to be working you can use a special form of 'ping' called MQPing to see if remote machines are responding. In the following screen shot you can see from the small arrows added to the computer icons (they're actually green in MSMQ Explorer) that daisy and portia are responding, but dan seems to be asleep. In fact this is because that computer is not currently running.

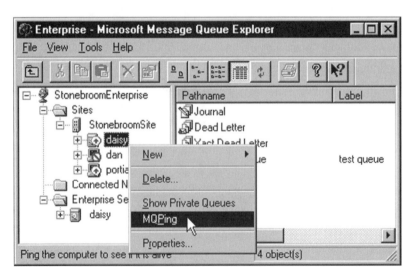

## *Using The MQ API Test Sample*

While MQ Explorer can create simple test messages, you get more idea of the possibilities by using the MQ API Test tool. This is available from the Start menu, unless you chose not to install the samples during setup. As you can see from the next screenshot, the interface is less than intuitive– with just a series of buttons that allow you to perform the standard actions available in MSMQ. The letters on the buttons stand for, respectively, **Cr**eate Queue, **D**elete Queue, **O**pen Queue, **Cl**ose Queue, **S**end Message, **R**etrieve Message, **L**ocate Queue. These options are also available from the Api menu.

### *Locating And Opening A Queue*

Rather than creating a new queue this time, we'll locate an existing one. Here we've clicked the L button to locate the queue named test queue that we created in MQ Explorer in the previous section of this chapter. If you didn't create this queue you'll need to do so first if you want to follow through this example:

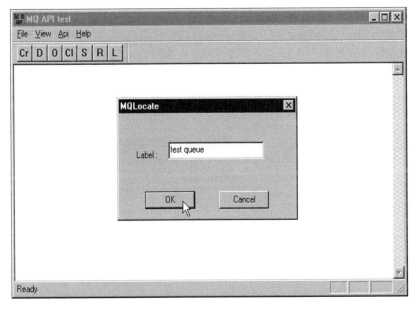

As you can see in the main window in the screenshot on the next page, MSMQ returned the full path and name of the one matching queue, and that it's not currently open in our application:

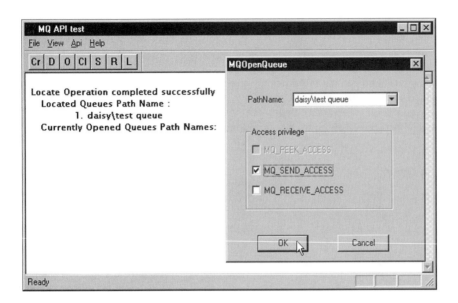

Next we open the queue, by clicking the O (Open) button, and specify that we want SEND access, as shown in this screen shot.

### Sending A Message And Closing the Queue

Providing we get confirmation in the main window that the queue opened successfully, we can send a message. This is done by clicking the S button to open the MQSendMessage dialog:

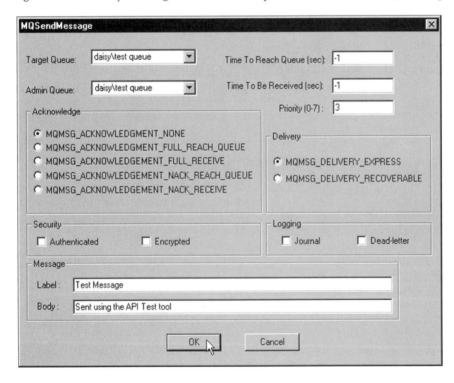

We've left most of the settings at their defaults, and just entered the Label and Body of the message we want to send. The values -1 for the Time To Reach Queue and Time To Be Received settings indicate that there is no timeout, or expiry, for the message. You'll meet these and the rest of the options later in this chapter, where we'll discuss the possible values and their meanings in more detail. In the main window of the screen shot below, you can see that the message was sent successfully. So now we can close the queue by clicking the Cl (Close) button:

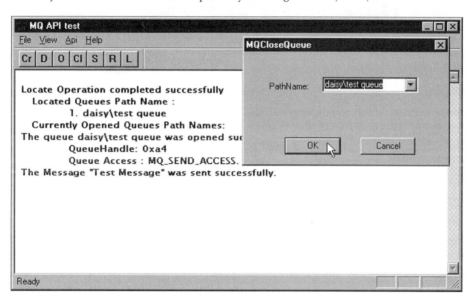

### Retrieving A Message

To retrieve the message, we need to open the queue for read access by clicking the O (Open) button again. In the next screen shot you can see that we're selecting the RECEIVE access option this time:

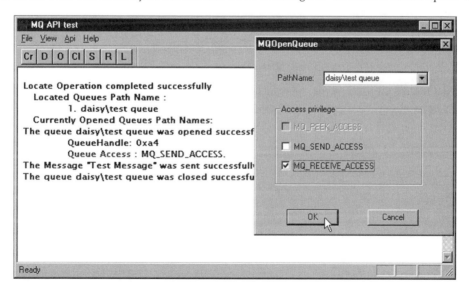

Again, the main window indicates that the queue was opened OK, and so we can click the R (Retrieve) button to receive the topmost message in the queue—the one we just sent. We've left the values for the Timeout (the time to wait for the message to be retrieved before giving up) and the Body Length (the maximum number of characters to retrieve from the message body) set to the MQ API Test application's defaults:

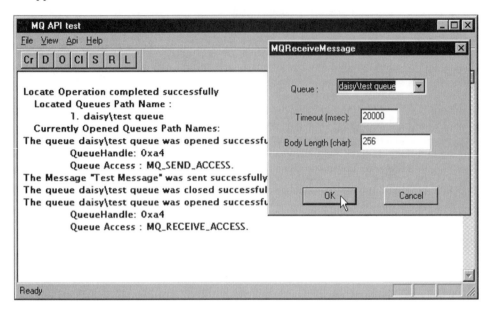

The contents of the received message are displayed in the main window. You can then tidy up by using the Cl button to close the queue again, and the D button to delete it.

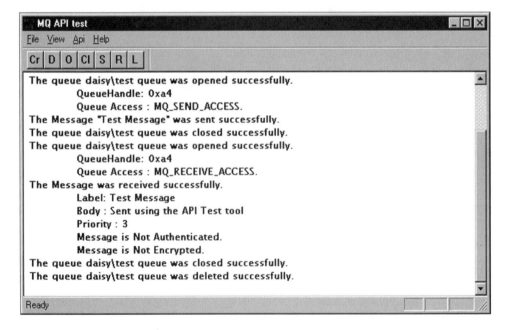

Even though we sent and received the message on the same machine, we used a message queue located on another, *remote*, MSMQ Server–which could easily have been on the other side of the continent (OK, so ours was only on the other side of the office). Of course, we could just as easily have accessed this remote queue from that machine, or any other MSMQ Server within our enterprise.

# Working With Message Queue Server

Now that you have a good idea of how MSMQ works, we'll move on and look at how we interact with it from our applications and components. MSMQ supports two programming approaches, the MSMQ API (Application Programming Interface) and a set of ActiveX (COM) objects that act as wrappers for the API functions.

It's probably obvious that the previous example used the API method, through a sample tool written in C++ and supplied with MSMQ. This technique is fine for languages that can use API functions, and offers the best performance. However, programming with the ActiveX objects is generally easier, and, as the actual amount of code that we use is minimal, performance is not generally an issue. Besides, some languages cannot support API function calling, the most obvious of which are the scripting languages available for use in Active Server Pages.

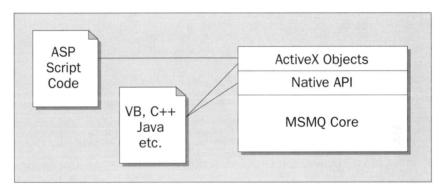

We'll be exploring the ActiveX objects in the remainder of this book, as this approach is open to all the usual Windows DNA programming languages.

## The MSMQ ActiveX Objects

The ActiveX programming interface for MSMQ consists of a series of ten objects. The five objects we're mainly interested in are:

❑ **MSMQQuery** is the main 'containing' object for MSMQ, and is used to query the enterprise to obtain sets of queues.

❑ **MSMQQueueInfos** is a set, or list, of queues that have previously been created. Although it looks like a VB collection, it's handled in a different way.

❑ **MSMQQueueInfo** is a single queue object within a set of queues, and is used to work with the queue's properties and methods.

❑ **MSMQQueue** objects represent the individual *open* instances of a queue, because a queue can be opened by more than one application at a time. It is also used to work with the queue's properties and methods.

❑ **MSMQMessage** is the message object used to create and send messages, and refer to received messages.

You can think of the relationship as being like that shown in the diagram here. However, you don't have to create instances of all the objects each time—if you just want to create a new queue you can instantiate an **MSMQQueueInfo** object directly.

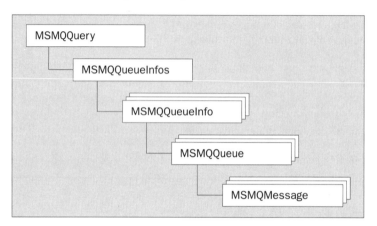

> Note that these are the class names within the DLLs that implement the objects. If you are creating object instances using Active Server Pages you need to prefix each with the registered name of the DLL. The objects become MSMQ.MSMQQuery, MSMQ.MSMQQueueInfos, MSMQ.MSMQQueueInfo, MSMQ.MSMQQueue and MSMQ.MSMQMessage. You'll soon get fed up typing 'MSMQ'.

The other MSMQ ActiveX objects are:

❑ **MSMQApplication** is used to obtain the ID of a computer running an MSMQ-based application, given its name.

❑ **MSMQEvent** is used to provide event handling, so that the arrival of messages or message errors can be detected when the system is running asynchronously. This saves our receiving code from having to keep looking for messages in a queue, and provides a more efficient application. You'll see this technique used in the next chapter.

❑ **MSMQTransactionDispenser** represents the MSMQ built-in transaction dispenser, and can be used to obtain a reference to a transaction running under it.

❑ **MSMQCoordinatedTransactionDispenser** represents the external MS DTC transaction dispenser, and can be used to obtain a reference to a transaction running under it.

❑ **MSMQTransaction** represents the transaction returned by one of the two previous objects. It provides methods to commit or abort a transaction.

*A full list of all the properties, methods and events of the MSMQ objects is in Apeendix D, at the end of this book. We'll be covering the ones you use most often here.*

Generally, there are four kinds of tasks that we'll regularly want to carry out with MSMQ:

- ❑ **Creating, refreshing and deleting a queue.**
- ❑ **Locating and opening an existing queue.**
- ❑ **Sending a message to a queue.**
- ❑ **Receiving a message from a queue.**

We'll look at each of these topics in turn now.

## Creating, Refreshing And Deleting Queues

To create a new queue, we simply use the **Create** method of the **MSMQQueueInfo** object:

*MSMQQueueInfoObject***.Create([***transactional***][,***open_to_all***])**

To make the queue a transactional one, the first (optional) parameter is set to **True**, the default is **False**. Setting the second (optional) parameter to **True** means that the messages in the queue and its journal can be read by any other application. The default is **False**—readable only by the owner of the queue.

### The MSMQQueueInfo Object Properties

Before we can create the queue we have to set the **PathName** property of the **MSMQQueueInfo** object—which defines where the queue will be located, and its name. Queue names must be unique on each machine, but there can be different queues with the same name on different machines. We can also set the **BasePriority** property to set the priority of all messages for the queue, unless explicitly over-ridden (see the section on sending messages for more details). The **PrivLevel** property can be used to control the privacy and encryption setting of the queue (discussed in more detail in Chapter 8). The **Quota** property can be set to control the maximum size in KB of the queue, and we can add a comment to the queue with the **Label** property. If we don't set the **Label** property explicitly, the queue name in the **PathName** property is used.

The following is the minimal **Visual Basic** code to create a queue named **FinanceQueue** on the local machine:

```
Dim objQueueInfo As New MSMQQueueInfo
objQueueInfo.PathName = ".\FinanceQueue"
objQueueInfo.Create
```

To create a queue on a remote machine, we just specify the machine name:

```
Dim objQueueInfo As New MSMQQueueInfo
objQueueInfo.PathName = "portia\FinanceQueue"
objQueueInfo.Create
```

In **Active Server Pages**, we can't use the **New** method to create an instance of an object. Instead, we use the ASP **Server.CreateObject** method, and specify the full registered class name:

```
<%
Set objQueueInfo = Server.CreateObject("MSMQ.MSMQQueueInfo")

objQueueInfo.PathName = ".\FinanceQueue"
objQueueInfo.Create
%>
```

*Also note that Active Server Pages (like VBScript and JavaScript) does not recognize the MSMQ named constants that you'll meet in subsequent examples. Instead, you have to use the actual constant values in your code.*

## Creating Private Queues

Queues that we create using a combination of the machine name and the queue name are **public queues**, and are registered in the MSMQ enterprise information store so that other applications can find and use them. We can also create **private queues**, on the local machine only, which are not registered with the enterprise and so are not available to other applications. This code creates a private queue named **FinancePrivate**:

```
Dim objQueueInfo As New MSMQQueueInfo

objQueueInfo.PathName = "PRIVATE$\FinancePrivate"

objQueueInfo.Create
```

## Using the FormatName Property

The **MSMQQueueInfo** object also provides a **FormatName** property, which MSMQ actually uses to create the queue. Normally, we don't specify a value for this property unless we want to define the queue in a special way, and the queue is created by MSMQ using machine defaults combined with the **PathName** we provide. One example of a special situation is when we use an Independent Client to provide disconnected messaging. To be able to open a queue while not connected to the appropriate MSMQ Site Controller we can use the **DIRECT** format:

```
objQueueInfo.FormatName = "DIRECT=Protocol:MachineAddress\QueueName"
```

This also allows us to create a queue by specifying an Internet URL or IP address, for example:

```
objQueueInfo.FormatName = "DIRECT=TCP:194.73.51.228\FinanceQueue"
```

*See the MSMQ Documentation for a full discussion of the other ways to use **FormatName**.*

## Updating, Refreshing and Deleting Queues

Some properties of a queue can be changed after it has been created, by changing them in the relevant **MSMQQueueInfo** object and then calling its **Update** method:

```
objQueueInfo.Label = "New label text"
objQueueInfo.Update
```

Other applications using the queue can then get the current settings of the queue's properties into their **MSQMQueueInfo** object using the **Refresh** method:

```
objQueueInfo.Refresh          'in a different application
```

To delete a queue, we simply call the **MSMQQueueInfo** object's **Delete** method. None of these methods require any parameters:

```
objQueueInfo.Delete
```

## Locating And Opening An Existing Queue

To locate an existing queue involves four steps:

- ❑ Create a **MSMQQuery** object to reference MSMQ itself.
- ❑ Use the **MSMQQuery** object to return a **MSMQQueueInfos** object.
- ❑ Search the **MSMQQueueInfos** list of queues to find the one we want.
- ❑ Assign this queue to a **MSMQQueueInfo** object.

### Getting A List Of Queues

To return a list of queues we use the **MSMQQuery** object's **LookupQueue** method:

```
Set MSMQQueueInfosObject = MSMQQueryObject.LookupQueue
                          ([QueueGuid][,ServiceGuid][,Label]
                          [,CreateTime][,ModifiedTime]
                          [,RelServiceGuid][,RelLabel]
                           [,RelCreateTime][,RelModifiedTime])
```

By specifying one or more of the parameters, we can force the list to only contain queues we're interested in. The five parameters that define aspects of the queues are:

*QueueGuid* - the string identifier of the queue.
*ServiceGuid* - a string indicating the type of service provided by the queue.
*Label* - the label of the queue as a string.
*CreateTime* - the date and time that the queue was created.
*ModifiedTime* - the date and time that the queue properties were last set or modified.

```
Dim objQuery As New MSMQQuery        'a reference to MSMQ itself
Dim objQueueSet As MSMQQueueInfos   'to hold the list of queues
'look for all queues named FinanceQueue
Set objQueueSet = objQuery.LookupQueue(Label:="FinanceQueue")
...
```

It's also possible to specify a relationship between the value provided in one of the five parameters above and the actual values of that property in queues that will match. This is done by setting the appropriate *Relxxx* relationship parameters to **REL_EQ** (equal), **REL_NEQ** (not equal), **REL_LT** (less than), **REL_GT** (greater than), **REL_LE** (less than or equal), **REL_GE** (greater than or equal) and **REL_NOP** (ignore this value):

```
Dim objQuery As New MSMQQuery
Dim objQueueSet As MSMQQueueInfos
'look for all queues created on or after 10/5/98
```

```
Set objQueueSet = objQuery.LookupQueue(CreateTime:="10/5/98", _
                                       RelCreateTime:=REL_GE)
```

```
...
```

In Visual Basic it's usual to use **named arguments** (or named parameters) with this method, as shown above. However, VBScript and JScript, as used in Active Sever Pages, do not support named arguments. Instead we supply empty parameters up to and including the parameter we require, for example:

```
<%
Set objQuery = Server.CreateObject("MSMQ.MSMQQuery")    'in ASP
Dim objQueueSet
Dim objQueueInfo
'look for all queues named FinanceQueue
Set objQueueSet = objQuery.LookupQueue(, , "FinanceQueue")
...
%>
```

*In ASP, the values for the relationship parameters are REL_EQ=1, REL_NEQ=2 REL_LT=3, REL_GT=4, REL_LE=5, REL_GE=6 and REL_NOP=0.*

### Searching the Queue List

Once we've got a list of queues in a **MSMQQueueInfos** object, we can search through it for the **MSMQQueueInfo** queue object that we want, or see that none matched the criteria we used in the **LookupQueue** method. The **MSMQQueueInfos** object is not a true VB-style collection. To loop through it we have to use the **Reset** and **Next** methods. When we get to the end of the list, an empty **MSMQQueueInfo** object is returned by the **Next** method:

```
...
Dim objQueueInfo As MSMQQueueInfo    'to hold an individual queue
objQueueSet.Reset
Set objQueueInfo = objQueueSet.Next
While Not objQueueInfo Is Nothing
    MsgBox "Found queue:" & objQueueInfo.PathName
    Set objQueueInfo = objQueueSet.Next 'assign queue to QueueInfo object
Wend
```

The result is that we now have a **MSMQQueueInfo** object that references the queue we want to use, and we can get on and open it.

### Opening a Queue

To open a queue once we've created or located it, we use the **Open** method of the **MSMQQueueInfo** object. This returns a **MSMQQueue** object:

```
Set MSMQQueueObject = MSMQQueueInfoObject.Open(accessmode, sharemode)
```

The first parameter defines how the application will use the queue. The options are:

| MQ_PEEK_ACCESS (32) | Messages can be examined but cannot be removed from the queue. |
|---|---|
| MQ_SEND_ACCESS (2) | Messages can only be sent to the queue. |
| MQ_RECEIVE_ACCESS (1) | Messages can be examined (peeked) or retrieved (removed) from the queue. |

The second parameter defines who can access the queue. The options are:

| MQ_DENY_NONE (0) | must be used if *accessmode* is **MQ_PEEK_ACCESS** or**MQ_SEND_ACCESS**. It allows any application to access the queue. |
|---|---|
| MQ_DENY_RECEIVE_SHARE (1) | can only be used when *accessmode* is **MQ_RECEIVE_ACCESS**. It allows only this application to retrieve messages from the queue. If another application has already opened the queue in this mode an error occurs. |

To open the **FinanceQueue** queue, assuming we know where it is, we can use:

```
Dim objQueueInfo As New MSMQQueueInfo
Dim objQueue As MSMQQueue
'set the name of the queue to open
objQueueInfo.PathName = "portia\FinanceQueue"
Set objQueue = objQueueInfo.Open(MQ_SEND_ACCESS, MQ_DENY_NONE)
If objQueue.IsOpen Then
  'OK to send a message
End If
```

Likewise, to open a queue for receiving messages, we change the parameters for the **Open** method:

```
...
objQueueInfo.PathName = "portia\FinanceQueue"
Set objQueue = objQueueInfo.Open(MQ_RECEIVE_ACCESS, MQ_DENY_NONE)
If objQueue.IsOpen Then
  'OK to receive a message
End If
```

In Active Server Pages we have to use the actual constant values in our code, and the **Server.CreateObject** method:

```
<%
Set objQueueInfo = Server.CreateObject("MSMQ.MSMQQueueInfo")
Dim objQueue
'set the name of the queue to open
objQueueInfo.PathName = "portia\FinanceQueue"
Set objQueue = objQueueInfo.Open(2, 0) 'send and deny_none
If objQueue.IsOpen Then
   'OK to send a message
End If
%>
```

*Remember, the* **MSMQQueueInfo** *object is a reference to the queue itself, while each* **MSMQQueue** *object is a reference to an individual* **open** *instance of that queue. Several applications can have the same queue open simultaneously.*

### 'Quick And Dirty' Queue Creation and Opening

If a queue with the same machine name and path as the one we are creating already exists, an error occurs. If we only want to use a queue that may already exist, or if not needs to be created, an easy way is to add an **On Error Resume Next** line to the code before the call to the **Create** method. Then, if the queue already exists, the code will continue and open it ready for use. This saves having to use the **LookupQueue** method first:

```
Dim objQueueInfo As New MSMQQueueInfo
Dim objQueue As MSMQQueue
objQueueInfo.PathName = ".\FinanceQueue"
On Error Resume Next
objQueueInfo.Create
Set objQueue = objQueueInfo.Open(MQ_SEND_ACCESS, MQ_DENY_NONE)
...
```

## Sending A Message

To send a message we use the **Send** method of the message itself, the **MSMQMessage** object, rather than a method of a particular queue. This allows us to send the message to any queue we like, as long as it is of the appropriate type (i.e. transactional or encrypted if the message requires this type of queue):

*MSMQMessageObject*.**Send(***DestinationQueue,* **[***Transaction***])**

The required *DestinationQueue* parameter is a reference to the queue object to which the message is to be sent, as returned from a call to the **MSMQQueueInfo** object's **Open** method. It can also be a **MSMQQueue** object's **Handle** property, which is a long integer queue identifier that is available when the queue is opened.

The optional *Transaction* parameter indicates if the sending of the message is part of a transaction. The default is **MQ_MTS_TRANSACTION** (**1** - part of any existing transaction), and other values are **MQ_XA_TRANSACTION** (**2** - part of an XA-compliant external transaction) and **MQ_NO_TRANSACTION** (**0** - not involved in a transaction). This parameter can also be a reference to an existing transaction which the send action is to join.

## The MSMQMessage Object Properties

The **MSMQMessage** object has almost thirty properties. Some of these are the same as the properties we met for the **MSMQQueueInfo** object, and allow us to explicitly change the values for this message from the defaults specified by the queue. Some of the more useful ones are listed and described below:

The **Label** and **Body** properties are used to define the content of the message. The **Label** is a string of up to 250 characters. It appears in MQ Explorer, and can be used to identify messages. The **Body** property holds the real content of the message. It can be a **String** variable, an **Array** of **Byte** variables, any numeric, **Currency** or **Date** variable, or a persistent ActiveX object. Persistent ActiveX objects are files that can be serialized, and which support the **IPersist** interface. Examples are Microsoft Word and Excel document files.

The **Delivery** property controls how the message is handled and delivered by MSMQ. The two possible values are:

| | |
|---|---|
| **MQMSG_DELIVERY_EXPRESS (0)** | Default; indicates that the message is held in memory on each machine it passes through, and on the destination machine until it can be delivered (it may be cached to disk temporarily if the machine runs short of memory). This method is faster than **recoverable** delivery, but less robust as messages can be lost in a machine failure or shut down. |
| **MQMSG_DELIVERY_RECOVERABLE (1)** | Indicates that, on every machine along the message route, the message is stored locally in a backup file on disk until it has been safely delivered to the next machine or to the destination queue. This guarantees delivery even in the case of a machine crash. |

The **MaxTimeToReachQueue** and **MaxTimeToReceive** properties are used to specify timeouts (or expiry periods) in seconds for the message to either to reach the destination queue, or to be retrieved from that queue. The default for both is **INFINITE (-1)** if not specified.

The **Priority** property can be set to values from **0** (lowest priority) to **7** (highest priority) to specify the urgency of the message. The default if not specified is **3**. Messages with the highest priority are transmitted from one machine to the next, and to the destination queue, first.

> **Because messages are usually retrieved from the queue in the order that they arrive, this can affect the way an application works. If you are using mixed priority messages you need to make sure that the receiving application can identify each message if this is appropriate, so that it acts on them in the correct order and in the correct way.**

The **Ack** property specifies what action MSMQ should take with the message if it can't be delivered. The usual values are:

| | |
|---|---|
| **MQMSG_ACKNOWLEDGMENT_ NONE** (**0**) | The default, indicates that no acknowledgment should be returned. |
| **MQMSG_ACKNOWLEDGMENT_ FULL_REACH_QUEUE** (**5**) | Indicates that a positive or negative acknowledgment will be returned depending on whether the message reaches the destination queue. |
| **MQMSG_ACKNOWLEDGMENT_ NACK_REACH_QUEUE** (**4**) | Similar to the above, but only sends back negative acknowledgements. If all goes well no acknowledgement is returned. |
| **MQMSG_ACKNOWLEDGMENT_ FULL_RECEIVE** (**14**) | Indicates that a positive or negative acknowledgment will be returned depending on whether the message is retrieved from the destination queue before it times out or expires). |
| **MQMSG_ACKNOWLEDGMENT_ NACK_RECEIVE** (**12**) | Similar to the above, but only sends back negative acknowledgements. If all goes well no acknowledgement is returned. |

The **AdminQueueInfo** property is set to a reference to a queue where the delivery acknowledgements are to be sent.

The **ResponseQueueInfo** property is a reference to a **MSMQQueueInfo** queue object where the receiving application should send responses. This allows the response queue to be specified dynamically by the sender, and change as and when required.

The **Journal** property can be set to **MQMSG_JOURNAL** (**2**) for a message, which indicates that a copy should be sent to the Journal queue that is attached to this queue. Setting the **Journal** property to **MQMSG_DEADLETTER** (**1**) indicates that undeliverable messages should be returned to the local machine's Dead Letter queue or Xact Dead Letter queue (for transactional messages).

Using most of these properties, the following example shows how a message can be created and sent to the queue **objQueue** we opened earlier:

```
...
If objQueue.IsOpen Then
   'OK to send a message
   Dim objMessage As New MSMQMessage
   objMessage.Label = "Finance Test Message"
   objMessage.Body = "This is a test message for the Finance application"
   objMessage.Delivery = MQMSG_DELIVERY_RECOVERABLE
   objMessage.MaxTimeToReachQueue = 30
   objMessage.MaxTimeToReceive = INFINITE
   objMessage.Priority = 5
   objMessage.Ack = MQMSG_ACKNOWLEDGMENT_NONE
   objMessage.Journal = MQMSG_DEADLETTER
   'create a queue for response messages and get a reference to it
   Dim objReturnInfo As MSMQQueueInfo
   objReturnInfo.PathName = ".\ReturnQueue"
   objReturnInfo.Create
   objMessage.ResponseQueueInfo = objReturnInfo
   objMessage.Send objQueue
End If
```

### Closing the Queue

Once we're finished with a queue after sending messages to it, we can close it by calling the **MSMQQueue** object's **Close** method:

```
objQueue.Close
```

# Receiving A Message

To receive the top message from a queue, we use the **Receive** method of the **MSMQQueue** object that references the *open* queue from which we want the message to come. The message is removed from the queue, which must have been opened with the access mode **MQ_RECEIVE_ACCESS** (**1**):

```
Set MSMQMessageObject = MSMQQueueObject.Receive
                    ([Transaction][,UpdateDestinationInfo]
                    [,IgnoreBody][,Timeout])
```

The optional parameters define how the message will be received. The *Transaction* parameter indicates if the receive is part of a transaction. The default is **MQ_MTS_TRANSACTION** (**1** - part of any existing transaction), and other values are **MQ_XA_TRANSACTION** (**2** - part of an XA-compliant external transaction) and **MQ_NO_TRANSACTION** (**0** - not involved in a transaction). This parameter can also be a reference to an existing transaction which the receive action is to join.

The *UpdateDestinationInfo* parameter defines whether the other (remote) **MSMQQueueInfo** objects will be updated to indicate that a message has been removed from the queue. This can slow down the system considerably, and the default is **False**.

The *IgnoreBody* parameter can be set to **True** if we don't want to retrieve the body of the message from the queue. The default is **False**.

Finally, the *Timeout* parameter is used to define the number of milliseconds until the receive action times out. The default is **INFINITE** (**-1**), and if this is not changed the **Receive** method will stop application execution if the queue is empty. It's usual to use named arguments (in Visual Basic) with the **Receive** method, and you should always specify a value for this argument.

```
...
If objQueue.IsOpen Then
   'OK to receive a message
   Set objMessage = objQueue.Receive(ReceiveTimeout:=1000)
   MsgBox objMessage.Label
End If
```

Note that the code above will wait for the **RecieveTimeout** period (one second) for a message to arrive if there isn't already one in the queue. The application will be stalled at this point until either a message arrives and is retrieved, or the timeout period passes. If you fail to set the timeout, the default value of **-1** (infinite) means that the application will stall indefinitely until a message arrives.

### Asynchronous Message Retrieval

As you may have noticed from the previous discussion of the **Receive** method, there is a minor problem. How do we know if a message has arrived? If we try to receive a message from an empty queue, we will stall the application. One of the core concepts of MSMQ is that it guarantees delivery of messages over slow and unreliable networks, or from disconnected clients. To save our receiving application from having to sit in a loop calling the **Receive** method continually, we use the events that MSMQ exposes through its **MSMQEvent** object. Our code can react to an event that is raised when a message arrives, rather than keep looking for a message. This technique is called **asynchronous** message retrieval.

To keep the discussion of the MSMQ methods simple here, we're ignoring asynchronous message receipt for the time being. You'll see how it is implemented in the next chapter, as it's a core part of the way our main Wrox Car Co sample application works.

### Peeking At Messages

Providing a queue has been opened with an access mode of **MQ_PEEK_ACCESS** or **MQ_RECEIVE_ACCESS**, we can examine messages without removing them from the queue.

```
Set MSMQMessageObject = MSMQQueueObject.Peek
                ([Timeout] [,UpdateDestinationInfo] [,IgnoreBody])
```

The parameter meanings are the same as with the **Receive** method shown above. As well as peeking at the topmost message in the queue, we can search through the queue using the **PeekCurrent** and **PeekNext** methods. The **Reset** and/or **PeekCurrent** method must be called first to initialize the position to the top of the queue, and each call to **PeekNext** moves an implied cursor down the queue. If the queue has been opened for **MQ_RECEIVE_ACCESS** while peeking, we can call the **ReceiveCurrent** method to retrieve the current message from the queue.

### Closing the Queue

Once we're finished with a queue, after reading from it, we can close it by calling the **MSMQQueue** object's **Close** method:

```
objQueue.Close
```

# Adding Code to Components

Although we've by no means covered all the objects, properties, methods and events available in MSMQ in the previous section, we now have enough information to start using MSMQ in our own applications. In the next chapter, you'll see how we implemented MSMQ in our Wrox Car Co sample application. In the meantime, to give you a gentle introduction, we'll add some MSMQ features to the Finance component that we started creating way back in Chapter 2.

## A Finance Component With Messaging

In Chapter 2 we created a component named **WCCFinance.PaymentTerms**, which could be used to calculate the number of payments required to clear a loan at a fixed monthly interest rate. In today's world of close scrutiny on financial institutions, it's usual to be required to keep records of all credit advice you give to customers. To comply with this, we want our component to be able to log all the calculations it does.

### Logging Credit Calculations

Of course the easy place to log them is in a text file on the local machine. However, it makes more sense for our head office to log all quotations from all the company's branches. To do this we have to find a way of sending each calculation off to head office. We could do it in daily batches, but MSMQ seems to offer the opportunity to do it in (almost) real time. We can create a message for each calculation and send it off to head office via MSMQ.

Using MSMQ has another advantage. If we were accessing the head office database using an OLE-DB or ODBC driver directly, our component would be stalled while waiting for the operation to complete–especially if the network was running slowly that day. And if the network   was down altogether, we wouldn't be able to do any calculations at all.

### The User Interface

The user interface doesn't change from the earlier examples. It just submits the values to an ASP script. To do so, it uses a **<FORM>** with three HTML text boxes and a **SUBMIT** button. Here's the **<FORM>** code again:

```
<FORM ACTION="financeMQ.asp" METHOD="POST">
Total Price ($):
<INPUT TYPE="TEXT" NAME="txtTotalPrice"><BR>
Interest Rate (%):
<INPUT TYPE="TEXT" NAME="txtInterestRate"><BR>
Monthly Payment ($):
<INPUT TYPE="TEXT" NAME="txtMonthlyPayment"><P>
<INPUT TYPE="SUBMIT" VALUE="Submit to ASP script">
</FORM>
```

And here's what it looks like in the browser:

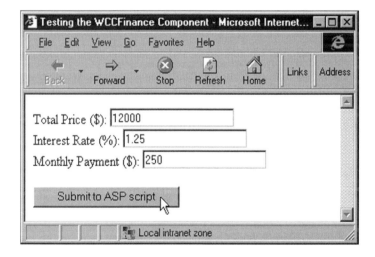

### The Active Server Pages File

The page that processes the values sent from the browser is the main business rules component for our application. It calls the **PaymentTerms** component to carry out the calculation, and returns the results by writing them into the HTML page that it creates and sends back to the browser. The initial section of this code is the same as we used in Chapter 2:

```
<%@ LANGUAGE="VBSCRIPT" %>

<HTML>
<HEAD>
<TITLE>Results from the WCCFinance Component</TITLE>
</HEAD>
<BODY>

<%
Set objFinance = Server.CreateObject("WCCFinance.PaymentTerms")
objFinance.TotalPrice = Request.Form("txtTotalPrice")
objFinance.InterestRate = Request.Form("txtInterestRate")
objFinance.MonthlyPayment = Request.Form("txtMonthlyPayment")
intResult = objFinance.GetNumberPayments
Set objFinance = Nothing

If intResult > 0 Then %>

A total price of <B>$<% = Request.Form("txtTotalPrice")%></B>
at a monthly interest rate of <B><% =
Request.Form("txtInterestRate")%>%</B>,
and paying <B>$<% = Request.Form("txtMonthlyPayment")%></B>
per month, will require <B><% = intResult %></B> payments.<P>

<% Else %>

Sorry, a monthly payment of
<B>$<% = Request.Form("txtMonthlyPayment")%></B>
is not sufficient to pay off a loan of
<B>$<% = Request.Form("txtTotalPrice")%></B>
at an interest rate of
<B><% = Request.Form("txtInterestRate")%>%</B><P>

<% End If
...
```

### The Message Queue Code

At this point in the script, we've got the results and written them into the returned page. All we need to do now is send them off to head office as well. We'll do the easy bit first and create the message body:

```
'create the message to send to head office
CRLF = Chr(13) & Chr(10)
strMsgBody = "Finance quote offered on " _
          & FormatDateTime(Now, vbGeneralDate) & CRLF _
          & "Total Price: " _
          & FormatCurrency(Request.Form("txtTotalPrice")) & CRLF _
          & "InterestRate: " _
```

```
        & Request.Form("txtInterestRate") & "%" & CRLF _
        & "Monthly Payment: " _
        & FormatCurrency(Request.Form("txtMonthlyPayment")) & CRLF _
        & "Number of Payments Required: " & CStr(intResult) & CRLF
...
```

Now we can create an instance of the **MSMQQueueInfo** object that we'll use to define (and if required create) our queue. The **PathName** includes the name of our head office machine:

```
...
'create a queue info object and set the path and name
Set objQueueInfo = Server.CreateObject("MSMQ.MSMQQueueInfo")
objQueueInfo.PathName = "daisy\FinanceQueue" 'remote head office queue
...
```

Next we attempt to create the queue. The **On Error Resume Next** statement will prevent the error that will occur if the queue already exists from breaking our code:

```
...
'try and create the queue in case it doesn't already exist
On Error Resume Next
objQueueInfo.Create
...
```

The next step is to open the queue. The **MSMQQueueInfo** object's **Open** method returns an **MSMQQueue** object, and we can set the values of the two constants we need (remember, ASP doesn't recognize the MSMQ named constants):

```
...
'use the MSMQQueueInfo object to open the FinanceQuote queue
Dim objQueue
MQ_SEND_ACCESS = 2    'declare the 'send' and 'deny' constants
MQ_DENY_NONE = 0
Set objQueue = objQueueInfo.Open(MQ_SEND_ACCESS, MQ_DENY_NONE)
...
```

Finally, providing the queue was opened successfully, we can create our new **MSMQMessage** object and set its properties before calling its **Send** method. We're only using a low priority for this logging operation. The last step is to close the queue, write a message into the returned page, and add the closing HTML stuff:

```
...
'see if queue opened OK, and if so create and send message
If objQueue.IsOpen Then
  Set objMessage = Server.CreateObject("MSMQ.MSMQMessage")
  objMessage.Priority = 2
  objMessage.Label = "Finance Quote on " _
                  & FormatDateTime(Now, vGeneralDate)
  objMessage.Body = strMsgBody
  objMessage.Send objQueue
  objQueue.Close
  Response.Write "Quote details also logged at head office."
```

```
  Else
     Response.Write "Could not send quote details to head office."
  End If
%>

<P><A HREF="finance_useasp.htm">Continue</A>
</BODY>
</HTML>
```

### The Resulting Page And Message

Here's the result of our ASP code, as seen in the browser. The confirmation message is a little misleading because it really only indicates that the queue was opened successfully. An error in the **Send** process wouldn't be detected because of the **On Error Resume Next** statement—one reason why we referred to this technique earlier as 'quick and dirty':

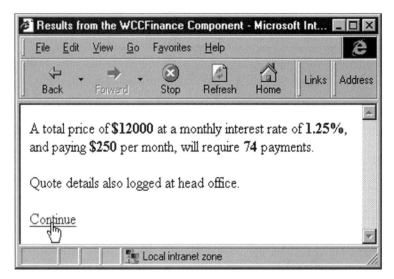

To confirm that the message was sent, we can view it in MQ Explorer:

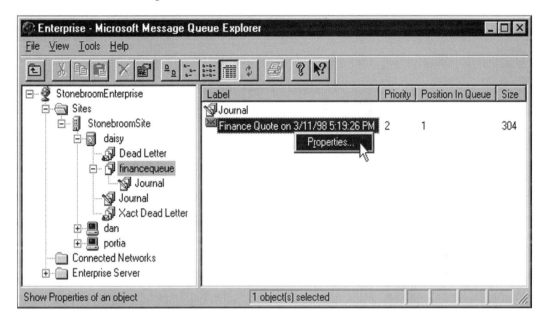

Right-clicking the message and selecting Properties shows details about the message. In the Body tab of this dialog, we can view the first 256 bytes of the message body:

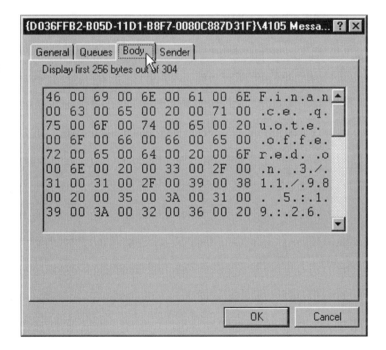

## *Receiving And Reading the Message*

We know that our message was delivered to the destination queue OK, because we've seen it in MQ Explorer. However, our application will usually want to do something with the messages, and so we need to be able to receive and read them using code. We've produced a simple program in Visual Basic that will read our message on the destination machine.

### *Creating The Simple Message Reader*

To work with MSMQ in Visual Basic (and other languages) it's easier if we provide the programming environment with a reference to the MSMQ type library. In the Project | References dialog, we can select the Microsoft Message Queue Object Library. This will allow us to use the MSMQ named constants in our code, view the MSMQ objects in Object Browser, and get pop-up tips as we type in our code:

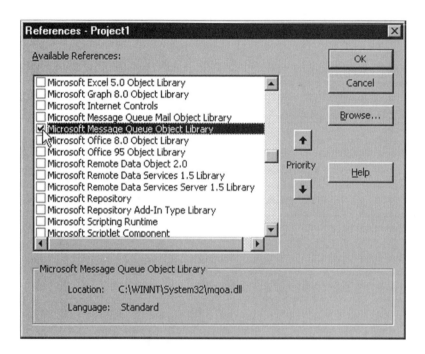

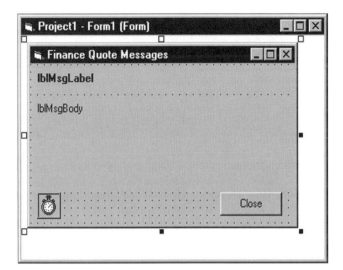

The application itself is a simple single form, compiled into a standard EXE project. The form itself contains a couple of labels that will display the values of the message's **Label** and **Body** properties, a button to close the program down, and a **Timer** control:

And because we have a reference to the MSMQ type library, VB knows about the objects that are available as we type the code into the form's Code window:

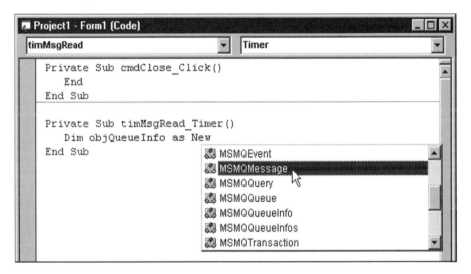

### The Message Reader Code

The Visual Basic code itself is simple. There's a subroutine to close the application down when we click the Close button:

```
Private Sub cmdClose_Click()
    End
End Sub
```

All the rest of the work is done in the **Timer** event of the timer control on the form. We've set the **Interval** property to **5000** in the timer's Properties dialog so that it occurs every five seconds. The code that runs each time the timer fires first creates a **MSMQQueueInfo** object and points it at the **FinanceQueue** queue on the local machine. Remember, this application is running at head office, and we created the queue there in our ASP page:

```
Private Sub timMsgRead_Timer()
   On Error GoTo timMsgRead_Error
   Dim objQueueInfo As New MSMQQueueInfo
   objQueueInfo.PathName = ".\FinanceQueue"
   ...
```

Then it creates a **MSMQQueue** object to refer to the queue with, and opens the queue. Next it creates a **MSMQMessage** object to hold the received message. Finally, it retrieves the topmost message by calling the queue object's **Receive** method, displays the values of the **Label** and **Body** properties in the label controls on the form, and closes the queue again:

```
   ...
   Dim objQueue As MSMQQueue
   Set objQueue = objQueueInfo.Open(MQ_RECEIVE_ACCESS, MQ_DENY_NONE)
   If objQueue.IsOpen Then
       Dim objMessage As New MSMQMessage
       Set objMessage = objQueue.Receive(ReceiveTimeout:=1000)
       lblMsgLabel = objMessage.Label
       lblMsgBody = objMessage.Body
       objQueue.Close
   End If
   Exit Sub
timMsgRead_Error:
   lblMsgLabel = "Error reading message"
   lblMsgBody = ""
   Exit Sub
End Sub
```

And here's the result. It would be easy enough now to write the value of the message's **Body** property to either a text file or a local database:

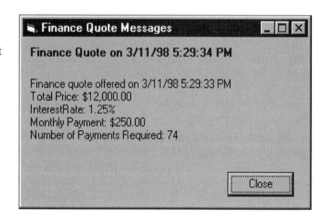

# Summary

In this chapter we've explored the concepts of message queuing, and seen how they are implemented in Microsoft Message Queue Server (MSMQ). Message Queuing provides two major advantages in distributed applications:

- ❑ **Communication between disparate systems and components.**
- ❑ **Connectionless communication with guaranteed delivery.**

We looked at each of these features in turn, and saw in overview how we can take advantage of them in a Windows DNA-based application. We then went on to examine MSMQ in more detail, to understand how it works and how we use it in our own applications.

Finally we put MSMQ to the test, both by using the tools that are supplied with it, and by adapting a simple component (which we first met back in Chapter 2) to use its basic features. This shows how easy it is to implement, requiring only a few lines of code for each process we carry out.

Message Queuing is a broad topic, and one that we can't cover the full ramifications of in one chapter. However, we have indicated why it is so useful, and how we can use it ourselves to provide better response and improved reliability when we create distributed applications–especially those that rely on transaction servers such as MTS.

In the next chapter, we'll implement the messaging features you've seen in this chapter in our sample Wrox Car Co application. This will include a practical example of how we can combine message queuing with transactions controlled by MTS.

# Queuing the Application

At the end of Chapter 4 we completed an application allowing us to use components to place orders in a local data store as well as a remote data store. It's quite obvious that this application suffers from a number of flaws—the major one being that the entire order process aborts if the head office data store is inaccessible.

The previous chapter explained message queuing, and how it can be used to add a more robust communications layer to your client/server applications. In simple terms this means we will be able to send messages from our Showroom to our Head Office, without worrying about what happens in between. Just like posting a letter, we don't care how it gets to its destination, just so long as it does.

Given this new communication method, we now have to consider how we can use it in the Wrox Car Co Ordering application to provide a better method of notifying Head Office of our orders.

In this chapter we will be:

❑ Examining the application design and how it needs to be changed to encompass message queuing
❑ How we can use Microsoft Message Queue Server in our new components
❑ How we can monitor Message Queue queues for incoming messages
❑ Rebuilding some of the components to take into account messaging

We won't be completely rebuilding the application, just enhancing the Head Office ordering side, as this is where we can utilise message queuing best. We will also be modifying the Showroom components to add a bit more functionality.

The queuing application is built around two machines, one of them being an Independent Client machine, however, you will be able to run all of the code if you only have one machine. The only thing you will not be able to do is simulate the total network failure that an Independent Client can cope with.

# The Design

Before we introduce some of the new message queue features, let's have a recap on the old design and look at its flaws. Let's start with the diagram of how the ordering works:

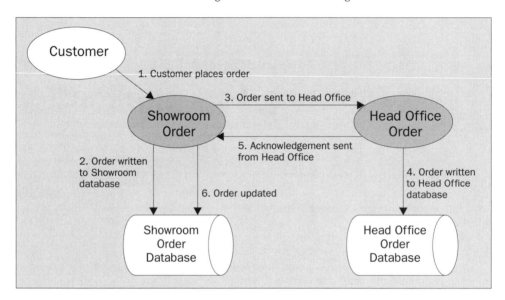

This shows the order in which the actions happen, but there's one important thing to note—the two components are actually running at the showroom. It's only the Head Office Order Database that is physically located at the head office. This is our single biggest worry, since if at any time we cannot communicate with head office, we cannot place any orders—clearly unacceptable. So what we need is some way to actually send the order to head office, and let them process it there—something like this:

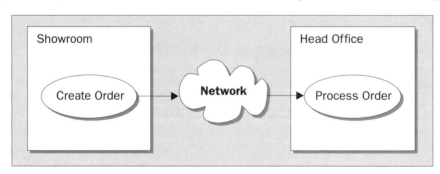

This gives us a really clear split between what happens at the showroom and what happens at head office. However, since we are no longer in control of placing the order at head office we need some way to confirm whether the order has been received, and if so what the head office order number and delivery date are. So what we are going to do is put Microsoft Message Queue Server in the middle and let it handle the delivery of the messages. We will have to code some new components to handle the messaging, as well as writing some specific code to process the order at head office.

As an overview we now have something like this:

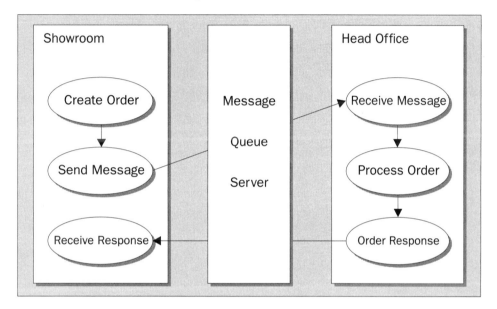

Now, when we place an order at the showroom we actually send a message, which is  received at head office. The order is processed and a response sent back to the client. MSMQ handles all of the messaging for us.

# Message Queue Set Up

In the previous chapter we discussed Message Queues, and now it's time to see how we are going to use these. We are going to have three queues—one at Head Office, and two locally at the showroom.

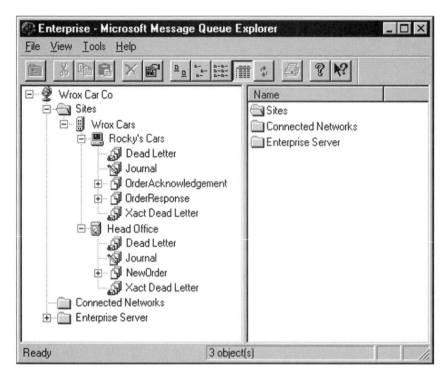

The above diagram shows the Message Queue Explorer for the Wrox Car Co. You can see there are two machines in the Wrox Cars site: Rocky's Cars, which is the showroom, and which has two queues: OrderAcknowlegement and OrderResponse. Head Office has just one queue, NewOrder. The table below shows what the icons mean:

| Icon | Description |
| --- | --- |
|  | MSMQ Enterprise. This comprises of all related sites. |
|  | Site. May contain multiple MSMQ controllers and/or clients. |
|  | Primary Enterprise Controller. The main controlling machine. |
|  | Client. A client machine that may or may not be disconnected from the network. |

| Icon | Description |
|------|-------------|
| | Normal Queue. A repository for messages |
| | Dead Letter Queue. Where messages are moved to if the exceed their expiry date. |
| | Journal Queue. Where message are place to inform of message delivery and receipt. |
| | Folder. Indicates a collection of items. |

Looking at the queues you can probably see how the ordering process is going to work. When we place an order we are going to send it to the Head Office  NewOrder queue. Head Office will send a message in the OrderAcknowledgement queue when they get the order and a response in the OrderResponse queue once the order has been processed. When you create the queues you need to make sure that NewOrder is a Transactional queue—you can do this by simply checking the box in the New Queue dialog:

The other two queues should not be transactional.

*Although we created the queues on two separate machines, you can create them on just one machine if you wish.*

# Transactions

So why is only one queue transactional? Wasn't one of the intentions of the previous application that transaction encompassed everything we did so that nothing was lost? Yes it was, but this approach needs modifying when dealing with message queuing. Let's think back to the original application. The transaction was started at the showroom, and we then put the order into the showroom database and then directly into the head office database. There, we immediately knew the response from the head office order component (the delivery date and order number). But this was a potential failure point if the link to head office was unavailable.

So we are using message queuing to provide fault-tolerance in case of network failure. Using message queuing, however, brings a problem. We are now sending a message to head office placing the order.

We have no way of knowing how long that message might take to get there, especially if the network is down. It might be immediate, but it might be two or three days. Who can tell? How do we then incorporate a transaction to cover the whole ordering process, including the head office? Obviously we can't. Having a transaction that has no guaranteed finish time is 'A Bad Thing'. Anyone who does this should Go Directly to Jail. Do not pass Go. Do not collect $200. Having a transaction that spans a large amount of time means that the data store is in a potentially unstable state, and that MTS is holding object references until the transaction commits. This may be acceptable for one person, but another person doing the same thing means no resource reuse. Performance drops and   scalability is reduced.

But don't despair. Using a transactional queue allows us to send messages that participate in MTS transactions. So what we can do is send the order to head office in a transactional queue. MSMQ will accept the message and tell MTS the transaction is OK (that is, it issues its own **SetComplete**), and MSMQ guarantees the delivery of the message. So as far as the showroom is concerned the order has been accepted. If MSMQ cannot guarantee the delivery of the message it will abort the transaction. So we will now have two transactions—one at the showroom where the order is placed locally and sent to head office, and one at head office accepting the order. The two transactions are unconnected, since there could be a considerable time gap between the two events.

# Component Design

Let's look at the showroom in more detail, concentrating on the **HeadOfficeOrder** component— remember that previously it just called a stored procedure held on the head office database to insert the order details. Now it has to create a message. We're also going to need a way of monitoring the acknowledgement and response queues, so we'll have a new **OrderMonitor** component for that. And now that we are sending a message to head office we'll need some sort of application there, as well as something to process the order once it's received. Let's see how these will fit together, looking first at the showroom:

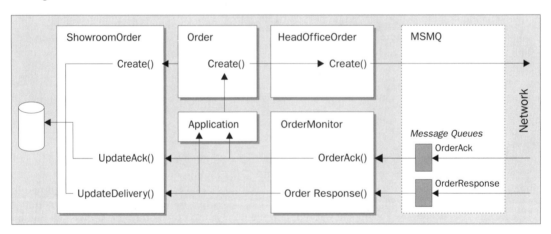

We now have a slightly more complex  setup but it's still very well structured. From the application we still call the **Order.Create()** as before, which in turn calls **ShowroomOrder.Create()** and **HeadOfficeOrder.Create(),** the latter of which now sends an MSMQ message. The new **OrderMonitor** component is responsible for monitoring the two local message queues, and when messages arrive, calling two new methods in **ShowroomOrder.OrderAck()** will update the

Acknowledged flag to identify that the order has been acknowledged by head office, and **UpdateDelivery()** will update the head office order number and the delivery date. We deliberately made the acknowledgement separate from the response, because the acknowledgement allows us to know that the order has been received at head office, and they may choose to respond at a later date. **OrderMonitor** also notifies the main application, allowing the screen to be updated.

OK, let's have a look at the new head office side of things.

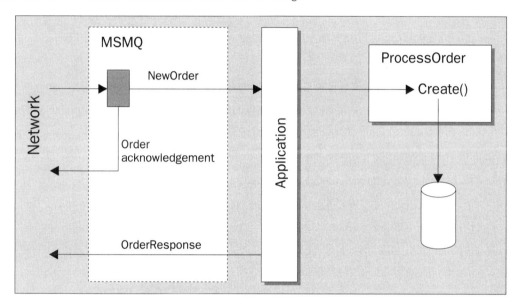

This is simpler, but works in a similar way. The head office application will monitor the **NewOrder** queue for incoming orders, and it will call **ProcessOrder.Create()** to create the order. MSMQ sends the order acknowledgement back to the showroom (in the **OrderAcknowledgement** queue) when the order is removed from the queue, and the application will send the response (in the **OrderResponse** queue) once the order has been processed. We've also changed the functionality of the head office ordering side, since we no longer reject orders when the requested car is out of stock. We knew from the start that it wasn't an ideal business scenario, but it was put in just to illustrate a programming trick. Now we actually accept the order but mark the delivery date as "Out of stock". Head office will be able to update the date when they have one available–you'll see how we do this later.

# Offline Usage

One of the advantages of the new design is that we have fault tolerance. This allows us to cope with a communications failure between the showroom and head office. This is a great boon, since it allows orders to be placed even whilst the network is down. Now, let's look at setting this up. Actually, you probably already have. If you have installed an Independent Client then you don't need to do anything else to allow you to work offline. MSMQ handles this silently for you. However, there is one major thing to watch out for, because whilst offline you cannot use any function that would need to access the Message Queue Information Store, as this is held on the server, which you cannot see whilst offline.

This isn't actually too much of a limitation because the only methods we've used so far that you might want to use are **Create** and **LookupQueue**. The former creates queues, which we won't be doing in the application—we assume that the queues are already created for us. The latter looks up queues in the information store, which again we won't need, as we know what the queue names are. However, there is a problem opening queues using the **PathName** property, because this causes a network query. In the previous chapter we briefly mentioned the use of **FormatName**, and because we want our showroom application to work whilst offline, this is what we must do.

We've chosen to do this by using the public format name and specifying the ID of the queue. You can find this out by looking at the properties for the queue in the MSMQ Explorer—just select a queue, right-mouse click and select  Properties.

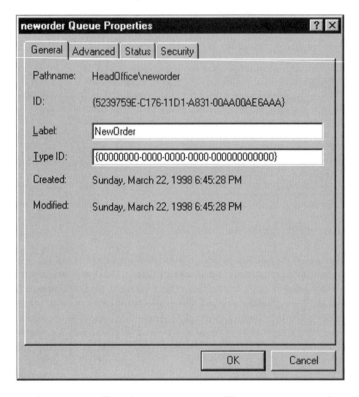

The funny long number next to ID is the one you want. There are two simple ways to use this information. The quick way is just to create a separate module with these numbers stored as constants, and then add the module into each project that needs to open these:

```
Public Const mcstrNewOrder          As String _
                                    = "5239759E-C176-11D1-A831-00AA00AE6AAA"
Public Const mcstrOrderResponse     As String _
                                    = "52397599-C176-11D1-A831-00AA00AE6AAA"
Public Const mcstrOrderAck          As String _
                                    = "52397595-C176-11D1-A831-00AA00AE6AAA"
```

This is an ugly solution and, in any case, the queue IDs can change. For example, if you move a queue from one machine to another, or delete the queue and then recreate it, the ID will change. This would mean recompiling your program. Not nice.

The second solution only requires a little more work initially, but adds a great deal of flexibility. Instead of hard coding these ID numbers we will use the **LookupQueue** method to get them, and we will store the result in the registry. OK, it means we have to be connected to the Information Store for the first time through, but that's not really too much of a problem, since you've got to connect to the IS to install the MSMQ client software. So we will use some common code to do this for us.

# Common Code

Like all good programmers we are creating some common routines that will be used in several components. So not only are we using components to improve future development, we are also using common routines to speed up the development of the components. This is one of those areas where we always say 'Oh, I'll get around to a code library some day' but we never do. So now is the time to start.

# The Queue IDs

We mentioned above how we are going to have some common code to look up queue names and IDs for us. What we are going to do is replace a whole chunk of code with a single routine called **MessageQueueOpen**. This will be given a queue name to open and it will first look in the registry for the queue name, and if found return the queue ID. The ID can then be used to open the queue. If the queue name isn't found in the registry we can then use **LookupQueue** to query the IS for the name. This will happen the first time the program is run on a particular machine, and it is at this point you need to be connected to the IS. Once the name has been looked up, its ID is stored in the registry for future lookups. Let's see how it's done. It's a normal **BAS** file that we just add to each component.

The first thing we do is declare the names of the queues. These can be hard coded as they are central to the application and will not be changing. We also declare a constant to be used as the default value should a queue name not be found in the registry.

```
Public Const mcstrNewOrder          As String = "NewOrder"
Public Const mcstrOrderResponse     As String = "OrderResponse"
Public Const mcstrOrderAck          As String = "OrderAcknowledgement"

' registry information
Private Const mcstrRegNotFound      As String = "<Not Found>"
```

Now comes the main function. This accepts two arguments. The first is the name of the queue to be opened, and the second is the access mode of the queue. This defines whether the queue is opened to send messages or to read message. **MQACCESS** is a predefined type that becomes available when you include a reference to the MSMQ code library. Notice that the return type of the function is **MSMQQueue**, because it will actually return the open queue object.

```
Public Function MessageQueueOpen(ByVal strQueueName As String, _
    ByVal intAccess As MQACCESS) As MSMQQueue
```

We turn on error handling because opening the queue might fail, and we need to be able to trap this. We then need some variables. The first variable is to hold the ID of the queue, the second an **MSMQQueueInfo** structure, and the third a flag to see if we've tried to open the queue before. You'll see this used in a moment.

```
On Error GoTo MessageQueueOpen_Err

Dim strGUID         As String              ' GUID of queue
Dim infQ            As New MSMQQueueInfo    ' queue information
Dim bFirstTry       As Boolean             ' true if first time
```

Since it's the first time we've tried to open the queue we set a flag.

```
bFirstTry = True
```

Now we lookup the queue name in the registry. We're using the same registry functions we created for the previous application, back in Chapter 4. We are passing in the queue name and the 'not found' string, which will be returned if the queue name is not found in the registry. The **RegistryRestore** function will return the value of the registry key (in this case the queue ID) as its return value.

```
' find the queue GUID in the registry
strGUID = RegistryRestore(strQueueName, mcstrRegNotFound)
```

Then we can check to see if the queue ID is the same as the 'not found' string. If it is, then this string was returned by **RegistryRestore**, and the queue name was not found in the registry, so we call **GetQueueID** to get the ID, and then we save the ID to the registry. We'll be looking at **GetQueueID** in a little while.

```
If strGUID = mcstrRegNotFound Then
    ' not found, so find it by name and return the guid
    strGUID = GetQueueGUID(strQueueName)

    ' save it in the registry
    RegistrySave strQueueName, strGUID
End If
```

At this stage we have the ID of the queue. It was either in the registry, or we used **GetQueueGUID** to get it from the IS. So we can now set the **FormatName** and open the queue using the MSMQ **Open** method. We return the queue object that we've just opened.

```
' now open the queue
infQ.FormatName = "PUBLIC=" & strGUID
Set MessageQueueOpen = infQ.Open(intAccess, MQ_DENY_NONE)
```

If everything worked then we can clear the object reference and exit.

```
MessageQueueOpen_Exit:
    If Not infQ Is Nothing Then
        Set infQ = Nothing
    End If
    Exit Function
```

Now onto the error routine. What we want to do is detect if the queue failed to be opened. This won't be because we have got the queue name wrong because we are using the ID to open the queue, so it must be if the ID is wrong. How could that happen? Remember we mentioned that deleting a queue and recreating it would change the ID. The queue exists, but the ID will have changed, in which case we want to look up the ID of the queue and try and open it again. If it fails now, we can then assume the queue is unavailable for some reason.

So, when we only check the error number once—when the 'first time' flag is true, indicating it is the first time we have tried to open the queue. The error number we need to check is **MQ_ERROR_QUEUE_NOT_FOUND**, telling us the queue could not be found.

```
MessageQueueOpen_Err:
    ' if it's not registered then we might have found an entry in the
    ' registry, but the queue does not exist.  This can occur if the
    ' queue is deleted and recreated.  So find it and try again.
    If bFirstTry And Err.Number = MQ_ERROR_QUEUE_NOT_FOUND Then
```

At this stage we couldn't open the queue (the first time) so we set the first time flag to False and then call **GetQueueGUID** to get the queue ID from the IS. We then save it to the registry, and try and open the queue again. If this fails the error gets trapped and we arrive back at **MessageQueueOpen_Err**.

```
        ' set first time flag so we don't keep trying to open the queue
        bFirstTry = False

        strGUID = GetQueueGUID(strQueueName)

        ' save it in the registry
        RegistrySave strQueueName, strGUID

        ' now open the queue
        infQ.FormatName = "PUBLIC=" & strGUID
        Set MessageQueueOpen = infQ.Open(intAccess, MQ_DENY_NONE)
        Resume MessageQueueOpen_Exit
    End If
```

We arrive here in one of two situations. The first is where the queue couldn't be opened and the first time flag is False, meaning we have tried to open it twice, and the second is if there was some other error trying to open the queue that didn't result in the **MQ_ERROR_QUEUE_NOT_FOUND** error code. In either case it's fatal, so we can raise an error.

```
        ' definitely can't open the queue
        If Not infQ Is Nothing Then
```

```
            Set infQ = Nothing
        End If
        Err.Raise Err.Number, "MessageQueueOpen", Err.Description
        Resume MessageQueueOpen_Exit

    End Function
```

So that's it. Although it looks complex it's really quite simple:

- ❑  1. Get the queue ID from the registry
- ❑  2. If not in the registry, look up the queue ID
- ❑  3. Open the queue
- ❑  4. If queue failed to open, look up queue ID
- ❑  5. Open queue
- ❑  6. If queue still failed to open, raise an error

What we haven't looked at yet is how we actually lookup the queue ID from the IS. This is pretty simple, and you've seen examples of this already, but let's look at it anyway. The **GetQueueGUID** function will accept the queue name and will return the ID. We then declare the variables used to query the IS.

```
    Private Function GetQueueGUID(strQueueName As String) As String

        Dim qryQ        As New MSMQQuery       ' queue query info
        Dim infQueues   As MSMQQueueInfos      ' queue infos from query
        Dim infQ        As MSMQQueueInfo       ' info of found queue
        Dim infQTmp     As MSMQQueueInfo       ' temp copy of queu info
        Dim intQueues   As Integer             ' count of queues found
```

The first thing to do is look up the queue name in the IS.

```
        ' find the queues with matching names
        Set infQueues = qryQ.LookupQueue(Label:=strQueueName)
```

Then we find the first queue that the lookup returned. In our case there will only be one.

```
        ' get the first queue returned
        infQueues.Reset
        Set infQTmp = infQueues.Next
```

Then we look through all of the queues returned. But didn't we say there would be only one? Yes, but we just want to guarantee that we find the correct queue.

```
        ' loop through the queue
        While Not (infQTmp Is Nothing)
            Set infQ = infQTmp
            intQueues = intQueues + 1
            ' get the next queue
            Set infQTmp = infQueues.Next
        Wend
```

Having looped through the queues we check to ensure that only 1 was found, and if we didn't find it we raise an error.

```
    ' check to see how many queues were returned, and fail
    ' if we didn't get only one
    If intQueues <> 1 Then
        Err.Raise vbObjectError + 10, "GetQueueGUID", _
                  "Did not find only one queue!"
    End If
```

If we did find only 1 queue we return the ID, as held in the **QueueGuid** property. Brackets surround this string, so we strip those off first, as they are not required to open the queue.

```
    ' return the GUID (strip off the surrounding {})
    GetQueueGUID = Mid$(infQ.QueueGuid, 2, Len(infQ.QueueGuid) - 2)

End Function
```

That's it. We could have done this in fewer lines of code, but remember this is a generic piece of code. We've built in some error checking to cope with a few errors, so it can easily be reused.

# The String Bag

Before we start looking at how the components are coded, we need to examine another aspect of MSMQ. The previous chapter explained how the **Body** property of a MSMQ Message can store a simple Variant type, that is – a string, array of bytes, numeric type, currency, date or persistent ActiveX object. We have a little problem because we want to send several pieces of information in our message—in fact, everything that is passed in as arguments to **HeadOfficeOrder.Create()**. This quite clearly doesn't fit into one of the simple types. So what do we do? The simplest way, when you only want to send one message with several items, is to package the items up somehow, and this is what we've done with the **StringBag**.

The interface has more to it than our previous components, but it's in fact very simple. Its role is to package up items into a string, and we can then use this string in the message **Body**. Let's look at the code in detail:

```
Private mcolProperties     As Collection      ' properties
Private mcolKeys           As Collection      ' values

Private mstrSeparator      As String          ' seperator
```

Firstly we have a collection to store the properties. These are the values of the items we wish to store. Next we have a collection for the keys, and these are how we identify the items. This is a bit like the fields in a recordset where **mcolKeys** stores the field names and **mcolProperties** holds the values. **mstrSeparator** is used to separate the keys and values from each other when they are all contained in a single string.

When the class is initialized we set the separator to character 0, and then create the collections to hold our keys and values.

```
Private Sub Class_Initialize()

    mstrSeparator = Chr$(0)
    Set mcolProperties = New Collection
    Set mcolKeys = New Collection

End Sub
```

Now it is initialized, we can add items to it.

```
Public Sub Add(ByVal strKey As String, ByVal strValue As String)

    mcolProperties.Add strValue, strKey
    mcolKeys.Add strKey, strKey

End Sub
```

The **Add** method takes two arguments–the key and the value. The value, **strValue**, is added to **mcolProperties**, using **strKey** as the key–this allows us to extract the value by using the key to identify it. We also add the keys to their own collection, **mcolKeys**, allowing us to loop through the keys later.

Once all of the items have been added to the **StringBag** we can use the **Serialize** method to convert them into a single string.

```
Public Function Serialize() As String

    Dim strOutput      As String
    Dim vntKey         As Variant
    Dim strKey         As String
    Dim strItem        As String

    ' Iterate through all of the keys
    For Each vntKey In mcolKeys
        strKey = CStr(vntKey)
        strItem = mcolProperties(strKey)

        ' add the key/value pair to the output string
```

```
            strOutput = strOutput & strKey & mstrSeparator & _
                               strItem & mstrSeparator
        Next

        Serialize = strOutput

    End Function
```

What we are doing here is looping through the collection creating a single string of the values. This is why we need a separate collection for the keys, because when you loop through a collection you get the values back, and not the keys. So we loop through the keys collection extracting each key in turn. We then use that key to lookup the value in the properties collection. So now we have a key and a value, which we can add to the string. Each item is separated by the separator string so that later we will be able to split them up again. So what we have is a string that looks like this:

```
<key><separator><value><separator><key><separator><value><separator>
```

The keys and values are stored together as a pair, but still separated.

Of course, if we have a method to turn these items into a string, we also need a method to turn them back again. What we'll be doing here is looping through the string, looking for the separator character, and every time we find it we'll extract the item to the left of the separator, and then take this item away from the string. So firstly we loop whilst the string has some characters left in it.

```
    Public Sub DeSerialize(ByVal strString As String)

        Dim strKey        As String        ' name of the key
        Dim strValue      As String        ' value of the key
        Dim lngSeperator  As Long          ' position of the seperator

        ' whilst we still have a string
        While (strString <> "")
```

Now we can find the separator character, aborting if we can't find one.

```
            ' find the seperator
            lngSeperator = InStr(strString, mstrSeparator)

            ' abort if no separator
            If (lngSeperator = 0) Then
                Err.Raise vbError + 1, "StringBag.DeSerialise", _
                                       "Missing separator in string"
                Exit Sub
            End If
```

Once we have the position of the separator, everything to the left of it is the key, so we extract the key, and then remove it from the string.

```
            ' extract the key and remove it from the string
            strKey = Left(strString, lngSeperator - 1)
            strString = Mid(strString, lngSeperator + 1)
```

We now have to find the next separator, as this will be after the value. Again we abort if no separator is found.

```
' now find the value
lngSeperator = InStr(strString, mstrSeparator)

' abort if no separator
If (lngSeperator = 0) Then
    Err.Raise vbError + 1, "StringBag.DeSerialise", _
                           "Missing separator in string"
    Exit Sub
End If
```

Now we know where the value ends so we extract the value, and remove it from the string.

```
' extract the value and remove it from the string
strValue = Left(strString, lngSeperator - 1)
strString = Mid(strString, lngSeperator + 1)
```

All that's left to do is add the key and value to the collections by calling the **Add** method.

```
' now add the key and value to the collection
Add strKey, strValue
Wend

End Sub
```

The very last method allows us to extract values from the collections.

```
Public Function Item(ByVal strKey As String) As String

    Item = mcolProperties(strKey)

End Function
```

This simply looks up the value in the properties collection for the key supplied.

At this stage we have everything we need to convert separate items into a single string and back again. Here's how it might be used to store the values in a message body:

```
Dim clsStringBag    As New StringBag

clsStringBad.Add "Key1", "Value1"
clsStringBad.Add "Key2", "Value2"

msg.Body = clsStringBag.Serialize
```

And to extract the message body we could do this:

```
Dim clsStringBag    As New StringBag
```

```
ClsStringBag.DeSerialize msg.Body

strValue1 = clsStringBag.Item ("Key1")
```

We'll be using this class at both the showroom and head office. This was created as an ActiveX DLL in the normal way. The only question to ask is whether this should be inserted as a component into an MTS package. The natural behavior of this component is in-process, so it doesn't really seem sensible to register it with MTS. It's also not transactional, as it isn't using any databases: there would be no benefit from MTS managing the resources. In this case we'll just create the component and register it in the good old-fashioned way.

```
regsvr32 StringBag.dll
```

Or alternatively, you could create a setup program that would register it for you. We've included a batch file to make this slightly easier for you—see Appendix A for more details.

# The Showroom

Now that we have looked at the design of the components and the common piece of code we are going to use, it's time to look at the components themselves. We'll start with the new code to send the message to head office, then move on to how we actually monitor message queues, and then the changes made to the showroom ordering component.

# Sending the order message

Creating the order uses a similar **Create** method, but the arguments are slightly different. We do not need to have any output parameters for the order number and delivery date, as all we are doing here is packaging the order details into a message and sending it to head office. They will respond with these details when they are ready, and we'll see that when we look at the order monitoring component.

One thing to note is that this component doesn't just consist of a single class any more. We've added the queuing module, with the generic queue opening routine.

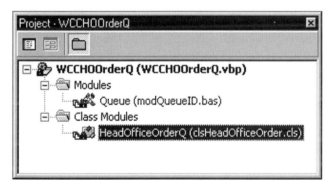

You've already seen the code for the Queue module, so we'll just look at the component.

```
Public Function Create(ByVal GarageName As String, _
                       ByVal GarageAddress As String, _
                       ByVal GarageTown As String, _
                       ByVal GarageState As String, _
                       ByVal GarageZipCode As String, _
                       ByVal GarageOrderNumber As Long, _
                       ByVal SalesPerson As String, _
                       ByVal CustomerName As String, _
                       ByVal CustomerAddress As String, _
                       ByVal CustomerTown As String, _
                       ByVal CustomerState As String, _
                       ByVal CustomerZipCode As String, _
                       ByVal CustomerPhone As String, _
                       ByVal CarID As Long, _
                       ByVal ColorID As Long) As Boolean
```

The first thing we do is set the error handling and declare our variables.

```
On Error GoTo Create_Err

Dim objContext     As ObjectContext          ' MTS Object context
Dim msgOrder       As New MSMQMessage         ' order message
Dim queSend        As New MSMQQueue           ' new order sending queue
Dim infResponse    As New MSMQQueueInfo       ' response queue
Dim infAck         As New MSMQQueueInfo       ' acknowledge queue
Dim queTemp        As New MSMQQueue           ' temporary queue

Dim objStringBag   As New WroxStringBag.StringBag  ' property storage
```

Then, as with our previous set of components, we get the context of MTS, allowing us to participate in the active transaction.

```
' get the MTS object context for transaction
Set objContext = GetObjectContext
```

Now we can open the destination queue–this is the **NewOrder** queue on the Head Office machine, so we call the central queue opening routine. We're passing in the name of the head office queue– as defined in the queue module.

```
' open the destination queue
Set queSend = MessageQueueOpen(mcstrNewOrder, MQ_SEND_ACCESS)
```

Next we set the Acknowledgement and Response queue **FormatName**s. MSMQ will automatically send a message to the acknowledgement queue when the new order is read from the queue at head office. Again we use the central routine to get the queue information. We don't actually need the queue open here, but we have a central routine to get this information so we use that.

```
' set the response and ack queues
Set queTemp = MessageQueueOpen(mcstrOrderAck, MQ_RECEIVE_ACCESS)
infAck.FormatName = queTemp.QueueInfo.FormatName
```

```
      queTemp.Close
      Set queTemp = MessageQueueOpen(mcstrOrderresponse, MQ_RECEIVE_ACCESS)
      infResponse.FormatName = "PUBLIC=" & mcstrOrderResponse
      queTemp.Close
```

Now we use the **StringBag** we looked at earlier to store all of the values that were passed into the function. We're using the parameter name as the key.

```
    ' add all of the items to the string bag
    With objStringBag
        .Add "GarageName", GarageName
        .Add "GarageAddress", GarageAddress
        .Add "GarageTown", GarageTown
        .Add "GarageState", GarageState
        .Add "GarageZipCode", GarageZipCode
        .Add "SalesPerson", SalesPerson
        .Add "CustomerName", CustomerName
        .Add "CustomerAddress", CustomerAddress
        .Add "CustomerTown", CustomerTown
        .Add "CustomerState", CustomerState
        .Add "CustomerZipCode", CustomerZipCode
        .Add "CustomerPhone", CustomerPhone
        .Add "CarID", CStr(CarID)
        .Add "ColorID", CStr(ColorID)
    End With
```

We can now construct the message that we are going to send. This is in fact the details of the new order.

```
    ' construct the message
    With msgOrder
        .Label = GarageName & ": Order number " & CStr(GarageOrderNumber)
        .Body = objStringBag.Serialize
        .AppSpecific = GarageOrderNumber
        .Delivery = MQMSG_DELIVERY_RECOVERABLE
        .Ack = MQMSG_ACKNOWLEDGMENT_FULL_RECEIVE
        Set .AdminQueueInfo = infAck
        Set .ResponseQueueInfo = infResponse
    End With
```

Let's look at these in more detail:

❑ The **Label** is the garage name plus the garage order number. This will appear in the queue and allows us to easily see where the order is from.

❑ The **Body** is the serialised details of the order, as stored in the **StringBag**. Remember, this is a string of key and value pairs.

❑ **AppSpecific** is the showroom/garage order number. This property can be used to store any long integer value. We could have passed this as a value in the **StringBag**, but this is quite useful for holding order numbers, etc.

❑ **Delivery** specifies how to deliver the message. We've chosen recoverable, in case of network failure. This is particularly important as this application is designed to work offline, and if you switch the showroom machine off then the messages will be saved.

❑ Setting **Ack** allows MSMQ to send an automatic acknowledgement message upon head office reading the new order message.

❑ **AdminQueueInfo** specifies the queue into which the acknowledgement message is sent.

❑ **ResponseQueueInfo** specifies the queue for the actual order response (delivery date and order number).

We are not specifying any timeouts for this message because we want it to be delivered, no matter how long it takes. This is perfectly safe to do if you know that the messages will be removed from the queue eventually.

Now we have all of the message details sorted out we can send the message. We specify **MQ_MTS_TRANSACTION** to allow the message send to participate in an existing MTS transaction.

```
' send message to remote queue
msgOrder.Send queSend, MQ_MTS_TRANSACTION
```

All that's left to do is close the message queue, tell MTS that the transaction has completed successfully, and exit.

```
' close queue
queSend.Close

Create = True

' tell MTS it's ok
objContext.SetComplete

Create_Exit:
' clean up and exit
If Not objContext Is Nothing Then
    Set objContext = Nothing
End If
If Not objStringBag Is Nothing Then
    Set objStringBag = Nothing
End If

Exit Function

Create_Err:
' tell MTS it's not ok
objContext.SetAbort

Create = False

Err.Raise Err.Number, "WWCCHOOrderQ.Create", Err.Description

Resume Create_Exit
```

That's all there is to sending our order to head office. All that's needed now is to compile the component and install it into an MTS package. Don't forget to set the properties first:

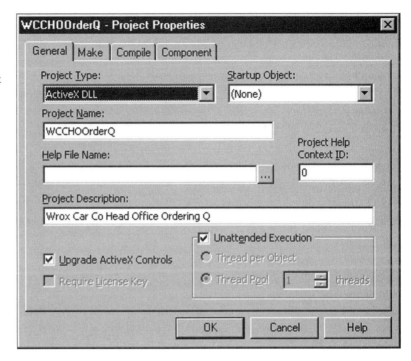

We've added a Q to the end of the Project Name and Description, since this will let you keep the existing components, as well as making this more readily identifiable as the Message Queue components. You might also like to create a new MTS package, just to keep these components separate, although this isn't necessary.

## Creating an Order

Having changed the head office ordering component to send a message, the main order component needs updating to take this into account. It's not that different from the previous version, but we no longer have to check for the out of stock error messages, nor do we update the showroom order with the delivery date and order number. Let's look at what has changed.

The **Create** method has changed, and now requires fewer parameters:

```
Public Function Create(ByVal GarageName As String, _
                 ByVal GarageAddress As String, _
                 ByVal GarageTown As String, _
                 ByVal GarageState As String, _
                 ByVal GarageZipCode As String, _
                 ByVal SalesPerson As String, _
                 ByVal PricePaid As Currency, _
                 ByVal CustomerName As String, _
                 ByVal CustomerAddress As String, _
                 ByVal CustomerTown As String, _
                 ByVal CustomerState As String, _
                 ByVal CustomerZipCode As String, _
                 ByVal CustomerPhone As String, _
```

```
                    ByVal CarID As Long, _
                    ByVal ColorID As Long, _
                    ByRef ShowroomOrderNumber As Long, _
                    Optional SRConnectionString As Variant) As Boolean
```

We no longer require a parameter for the head office order number or delivery date, as we don't know when these will be supplied, and it is no longer the responsibility of this component. We also don't need the optional connection string for the head office database, since we don't care where it is. Elsewhere, the calls to the two component **Create** methods have changed too:

```
' create the showroom order
Set objSROrder = objContext.CreateInstance("WCCSROrderQ.ShowroomOrderQ")
objSROrder.Create CarID, ColorID, SalesPerson, PricePaid, _
                CustomerName, CustomerAddress, CustomerTown, _
                CustomerState, CustomerZipCode, CustomerPhone, _
                strSROrderID, SRConnectionString

' create the head office order
Set objHOOrder = objContext.CreateInstance("WCCHOOrderQ.HeadOfficeOrderQ")
objHOOrder.Create GarageName, GarageAddress, GarageTown, _
                GarageState, GarageZipCode, strSROrderID, _
                SalesPerson, CustomerName, CustomerAddress, _
                CustomerTown, CustomerState, CustomerZipCode, _
                CustomerPhone, CarID, ColorID

' extract the local order number
ShowroomOrderNumber = CLng(strSROrderID)
```

That's all the component does now. It calls the showroom component to create the order locally, and the head office component to create the order remotely. It no longer has any responsibility for updating the local order details. This seems to fit a little better with the overall design.

# Waiting for a Response

Now that we have sent the order to head office, we really need some way of seeing when to read the message and what the head office response is. At the end of the previous chapter you saw the use of a Visual Basic Timer object to continuously poll the queues to examine their contents. Luckily for us, MSMQ has provided an **events** object–**MSMQEvent**–which allows MSMQ to notify us when messages appear in the queue. This is a far better solution because now we can simplify our code, and leave the monitoring up to MSMQ.

To use this event notification you declare a variable of type **MSMQEvent**, but you don't declare it in the way we have declared our previous MSMQ objects. This time you have to use the **WithEvents** keyword (there's more on this at the end of the chapter):

```
Private WithEvents evtResponse  As MSMQEvent
```

This tells Visual Basic that the object will raise events. Once you've declared an object like this it will appear in the objects drop down of the code window, and its events will appear in the   events drop down:

```
WCCOrderMonitorQ - OrderMonitorQ [Code]                        _ □ ×
evtResponse                         ▼   Arrived                        ▼
                                        Arrived
    Private Sub evtResponse_Arrived(ByVal Q  ArrivedError
```

You can then write code to be run when these events are fired. There are only two events: **Arrived**, which is fired when a message is in the queue, and **ArrivedError**, which is fired when an error is generated (such as a message timeout expiring, or an error when the queue is receiving the message). We're only dealing with the **Arrived** event here.

Let's see how this is used in the order monitoring component. Firstly, we declare the queue and event objects. We have two queues that we will be monitoring—one for the acknowledgement and one for the response.

```
' queues and events
Private queResponse              As MSMQQueue
Private queAck                   As MSMQQueue
Private WithEvents evtResponse   As MSMQEvent
Private WithEvents evtAck        As MSMQEvent
```

Now we declare some events of our own, to allow us to notify our calling routine that messages have arrived. This allows us to call the **OrderMonitor** from the main application, and be notified of messages so we can update the screen accordingly. The **OrderReponse** event passes back the order number, the delivery date and the head office order number. The **OrderAck** event passes back the order number and the class of the message. The class would allow us to determine what type of acknowledgement message was received—we're not actually using it in our application, but we've included it for completeness.

```
' to communicate back to caller
Event OrderResponse(OrderNumber As Long, DeliveryDate As String, _
                    HOOrderNumber As String)
Event OrderAck(OrderNumber As Long, Class As Long)
```

Next, we declare an object to hold the showroom ordering component. This allows us to update the acknowledged flag and the order details.

```
' the showroom ordering object
Private objShowroom                 As WCCSROrderQ.ShowroomOrderQ
```

The first procedure is the class initialization. This is where we actually set up the notification of messages arriving in the queue. We create a new queue and event object for the acknowledgement queue. Then we open the queue and use the **EnableNotification** method to tell the queue that we want to be notified when messages are in the queue, and we pass in the event object we have just created. This allows MSMQ to connect the queue to the events, so when a message arrives in the queue, the event object receives the notification.

```
' set up response queue events
' firstly for the acknowledgement
Set queAck = New MSMQQueue
```

```
        Set evtAck = New MSMQEvent
        Set queAck = MessageQueueOpen(mcstrOrderAck, MQ_RECEIVE_ACCESS)
        queAck.EnableNotification evtAck
```

Next we do the same for the response queue.

```
    ' now for the response
    Set queResponse = New MSMQQueue
    Set evtResponse = New MSMQEvent
    Set queAck = MessageQueueOpen(mcstrOrderResponse, MQ_RECEIVE_ACCESS)
    queResponse.EnableNotification evtResponse
```

Finally we clean up the queue info objects and exit.

```
    Set infResponse = Nothing
    Set infAck = Nothing

End Sub
```

That's all there is to start the notification process, but now we need to put some code into the event procedures. We'll start with the acknowledgement queue first.

```
    Private Sub evtAck_Arrived(ByVal Queue As Object, ByVal Cursor As Long)
```

The first parameter, **Queue**, is a **MSMQQueue** object that represents the queue which raised this event. The second parameter, **Cursor**, identifies the cursor position in the queue–this is not used in Visual Basic and, in fact, doesn't even appear in the documentation. For the inquisitive amongst you though, a cursor is just like a recordset giving you the current record. In the MSMQ environment this gives you the current message in the queue.

Since a message has arrived in the queue we need to declare a message object, and then we use Receive to receive the message as shown in the examples in the previous chapter. This is no different from receiving a message any other way. We are setting the **WantBody** argument of **Receive** to **False** since this is only an acknowledgement message–there is nothing in the **Body**. **WantBody** allows us to read the header information of a message without extracting the **Body**, that is, the contents. This is faster than extracting the message body, even if there is nothing in it.

```
    Dim msgAck        As MSMQMessage        ' acknowledgement message

    ' extract the message from the queue
    Set msgAck = Queue.Receive(WantBody:=False)
```

Now we know that the order has been acknowledged by head office, we can set the acknowledged flag in the local order so we create a new instance of the **ShowroomOrder**. We then call the **UpdateAck** method, passing in the **AppSpecific** property of the message–remember we used this to store the **OrderID**. As soon as it's done we clean our reference to the showroom order, so MTS can free its resources.

```
        ' update the acknowledgement in the showroom order
```

```
Set objShowroom = New WCCSROrderQ.ShowroomOrderQ
objShowroom.UpdateAck (msgAck.AppSpecific)
Set objShowroom = Nothing
```

Now that the acknowledgement has been written to the local order, we raise our own **OrderAck** event to allow our calling routine (the application) to do something. You'll see what it does a little later. We pass the **OrderID** and the **Class** of the message.

```
' now tell the caller what happened
RaiseEvent OrderAck(msgAck.AppSpecific, msgAck.Class)
```

We've now finished processing here, so we need to set the notification again. MSMQ doesn't keep this—as soon as one notification has been handled it is removed, so we need to set it again to make sure that we can respond to the next order.

```
' and reset notification on the queue
queAck.EnableNotification evtAck
```

And finally we clean our reference to the message object.

```
Set msgAck = Nothing

End Sub
```

You'll probably be able to guess that the event for the response is very similar in structure.

```
Private Sub evtResponse_Arrived(ByVal Queue As Object, ByVal Cursor As
Long)

    Dim msgResp      As MSMQMessage      ' response message
    Dim vardate      As Variant          ' the delivery date
```

The first difference is that we use a normal **Receive** here, allowing the **Body** to be put into the message object.

```
' extract the message from the queue
Set msgResp = Queue.Receive
```

Once again we instantiate the showroom order object. This time we will be updating the delivery date and the head office order number.

```
' update the showroom order details
Set objShowroom = New WCCSROrderQ.ShowroomOrderQ
```

Firstly, we check the message **Label** is a valid date. Head office has used the label to store the delivery date, and the message body to specify the head office order number. Although this might seem odd, there seems little point in using the **StringBag** for only two pieces of information when we have two properties that we can use. So we check it's a valid date—that's because if the car is out of stock head office will accept the order, but mark the delivery date as 'Out of stock'. That way the order is placed and confirmed, but with an unconfirmed delivery date.

```
' the label will contain the delivery date or 'Out of Stock'
If IsDate(msgResp.Label) Then
    vardate = msgResp.Label
Else
    vardate = Null
End If
```

Having checked the date, we now call the **UpdateDelivery** method of the showroom order object, passing in the **OrderID**, the head office order number, and the delivery date (or null). We then clear the reference to our object.

```
objShowroom.UpdateDelivery msgResp.AppSpecific, msgResp.Body, vardate
Set objShowroom = Nothing
```

Again, we now tell the calling routine that a response has been received. We pass the same information that we received.

```
' now tell the caller what happened
RaiseEvent OrderResponse(msgResp.AppSpecific, msgResp.Label,
msgResp.Body)
```

And once more we have to reset the notification before exiting.

```
' and reset notification on the queue
queResponse.EnableNotification evtResponse

Set msgResp = Nothing

End Sub
```

The only procedure not yet covered is the termination of the class, where we clean up any references to our objects.

```
Private Sub Class_Terminate()

    Set queResponse = Nothing
    Set queAck = Nothing
    Set evtResponse = Nothing
    Set evtAck = Nothing

End Sub
```

So that's how you have MSMQ notify you when messages arrive. These two event procedures extract the message from the queue, call a method in the showroom order object to update some details, and then exit, resetting the notification.

The location of this component can also come under question. Let's think about MTS components for a minute. To achieve the best from MTS they are stateless and are generally quick to complete. This component uses no data store connections, is stateless, but has a very long lifetime—in fact we want it to run all of the time, otherwise the local orders will not be updated. So once again the question we should ask is; does this fit within MTS? Well, not really. In fact the only advantage of putting it into MTS is if you want to use MTS as an object broker and you are accessing the component remotely. So this should be registered as a normal in-process server:

```
regsvr32 WCCOrderMonitorQ.DLL
```

# Updating the local order

Since you've seen how the new methods in the showroom order component are used, now is a good time to see how they are coded. Let's look at **UpdateAck** first, where the **OrderID** is passed in to identify which order has been acknowledged by head office.

```
Public Function UpdateAck(ByVal OrderID As Variant, _
                    Optional ConnectionString As Variant) As Boolean

    On Error GoTo UpdateAck_Err

    Dim objCommand          As New ADODB.Command    ' Command to execute
    Dim objContext          As ObjectContext        ' MTS Object context
```

As with our first set of components we get the MTS object context and set the ADO **Command** object. We are using a stored procedure to perform the update, so we use **Refresh** to get the parameters from the procedure.

```
    ' get the MTS object context for transaction
    Set objContext = GetObjectContext

    With objCommand
        ' set the command type
        If IsMissing(ConnectionString) Then
            .ActiveConnection = RegistryRestore("Showroom", "Not Set")
        Else
            .ActiveConnection = ConnectionString
        End If
        .CommandType = adCmdStoredProc
        .CommandText = "usp_OrderUpdateAck"

        ' go and get the parameters.
        .Parameters.Refresh
```

Once the parameters have been retrieved we set the `OrderID` and then execute the `Command`.

```
    ' now set the parameters
    .Parameters("@OrderID").Value = OrderID

    ' and now run the command
    .Execute
End With
```

And as usual we confirm the transaction and clean up.

```
    UpdateAck = True

    ' tell MTS it's ok
    objContext.SetComplete

UpdateAck_Exit:
    ' clean up and exit
    If Not objCommand Is Nothing Then
        Set objCommand = Nothing
    End If
    If Not objContext Is Nothing Then
        Set objContext = Nothing
    End If
    Exit Function

UpdateAck_Err:
    UpdateAck = False

    ' tell MTS it's not ok
    objContext.SetAbort

    Err.Raise Err.Number, "WCCSROrder.UpdateAck", Err.Description
    Resume UpdateAck_Exit

End Function
```

The `UpdateDelivery` method is very similar. This time we are passing in the head office order number and the delivery date as well as the `OrderID`. The only other differences are the stored procedure name and the parameters.

```
Public Function UpdateDelivery(ByVal OrderID As Variant, _
                        ByVal HOOrderNumber As Variant, _
                        ByVal DeliveryDate As Variant, _
                        Optional ConnectionString As Variant) _
            As Boolean

    On Error GoTo UpdateDelivery_Err

    Dim objCommand      As New ADODB.Command    ' Command to execute
    Dim objContext      As ObjectContext        ' MTS Object context

    ' get the MTS object context for transaction
    Set objContext = GetObjectContext
```

```
        With objCommand
            ' set the command type
            If IsMissing(ConnectionString) Then
                .ActiveConnection = RegistryRestore("Showroom", "Not Set")
            Else
                .ActiveConnection = ConnectionString
            End If
            .CommandType = adCmdStoredProc
            .CommandText = "usp_OrderUpdateDelivery"

            ' go and get the parameters.
            .Parameters.Refresh

            ' now set the parameters
            .Parameters("@OrderID").Value = OrderID
            .Parameters("@HOOrderNumber").Value = HOOrderNumber
            .Parameters("@DeliveryDate").Value = DeliveryDate

            ' and now run the command
            .Execute
        End With

        UpdateDelivery = True

        ' tell MTS it's ok
        objContext.SetComplete

UpdateDelivery_Exit:
        ' clean up and exit
        If Not objCommand Is Nothing Then
            Set objCommand = Nothing
        End If
        If Not objContext Is Nothing Then
            Set objContext = Nothing
        End If
        Exit Function

UpdateDelivery_Err:
        UpdateDelivery = False

        ' tell MTS it's not ok
        objContext.SetAbort

        Err.Raise Err.Number, "WCCSROrder.UpdateDelivery", Err.Description
        Resume UpdateDelivery_Exit

End Function
```

# Component Creation and Location

When compiling the components, we've again made sure that they have different names from the components we created in Chapter 4. We could have kept all the same names and replaced these original components, but we thought it more sensible to name them differently, so you can keep track of all the components. What we now have is this:

| Component | Description | Location |
|-----------|-------------|----------|
| `WCCCars` | Original car functions. | Original MTS package. |
| `WCCFinance` | Original finance functions. | Original MTS package. |
| `StringBag` | Property storage and serialization. | Manually registered on each machine that requires it. |
| `WCCHOOrderQ` | Queued head office ordering. | New MTS package |
| `WCCSROrderQ` | Queued showroom ordering | New MTS package |
| `WCCOrderMonitorQ` | Order queue monitoring | Manually registered on the showroom machine. |
| `WCCOrderQ` | Main queued ordering | New MTS Package |

So that's how we use message queuing in the showroom components. We have created a new showroom order component that sends messages to head office. We have created a new order monitoring component that can notify us when head office respond to our order, and we have created two new methods to update the order accordingly. Now let's have a look at how these components are used in the application.

# The Application

You might think that because of all of the changes made to the components the showroom application will change quite a lot too. In fact, most of the work has already been done—this is one of the great things about component-based systems. In the existing form the only changes have been to the actual ordering section:

```
Set oOrder = CreateObject("WCCOrderQ.OrderQ")
oOrder.Create mstrGarageName, mstrGarageAddress, _
            mstrGarageTown, mstrGarageState, _
            mstrGarageZipCode, _
            cboSales, txtPrice, _
            txtName, txtAddress, _
            txtTown, txtState, _
            txtZipCode, txtPhone, _
            GridCellContents(5), _
            lstColor.ItemData(lstColor.ListIndex), _
            lngOrderID, _
            mstrShowroom

frmMonitor.OrderSent lngOrderID
```

As you can see we now create the new queued version of the ordering component, and the parameters are slightly different. We don't need the head office order number or the delivery date. The new line at the bottom refers to a method on a new form, **frmMonitor**, and we'll look at this now.

We've created a new form for monitoring the orders because of the possible delay between placing the order and receiving an acknowledgement or response. We might have placed several orders before receiving anything back from head office, so updating the new order form would not be suitable. What we need is a way to keep track of the orders sent and the response from head office:

This keeps track of the showroom order number, the date the order was sent, whether the order has been acknowledged by head office, and what their order number and delivery dates are. It will also list all unconfirmed orders when it first starts. Again, this is to cope with the delay in getting a response—for example, if we place an order last thing at night, it might not be confirmed until the morning. Therefore when we start the application in the morning we want it to show any orders that haven't been confirmed. Let's look at the code.

First we have some grid column numbers. These just make the code more readable and maintainable, and simply indicate which column in the grid a certain field is in. We're using the standard MSFlexGrid for this.

```
Private Enum GridColumn
    mconColOrderNumber = 0
    mconColDateSent = 1
    mconColAck = 2
    mconColHOOrder = 3
    mconColDelivery = 4
End Enum
```

And now we have the order monitoring component. Notice that we use **WithEvents** as this component raises events. If you've not used **WithEvents** before then please take a quick skip forward to the end of the chapter, where there's a more detailed explanation.

```
Private WithEvents objMonitor        As WCCOrderMonitorQ.OrderMonitorQ
```

The first thing to look at is what happens when the form loads:

```
Private Sub Form_Load()

    ' set up the grid and show the existing outstanding orders
    GridInitialise
    GridResize
    ShowOrders

    ' start the monitor
    Set objMonitor = New WCCOrderMonitorQ.OrderMonitorQ

End Sub
```

The first two lines we'll skip over—they just set up the grid columns and sizes. The next ; **ShowOrders**, reads in the unconfirmed orders. The final thing here is to instantiate the order monitoring component—this will start the monitoring of the MSMQ queues.

Let's begin by looking at **ShowOrders**.

```
Private Sub ShowOrders()

    Dim recR       As New ADODB.Recordset      ' unconfimed records
    Dim lngOrderID As Long                      ' showroom order id
    Dim strAck     As String                    ' acknowledgement string
```

Firstly we open a recordset, based on a stored procedure. This simply lists the orders where the delivery date has not been filled in. Ideally this should be a method of a business object, but you've seen how to do that already, so we've just used a straight stored procedure.

```
    ' get a list of outstanding orders
    recR.Open "usp_OrdersNotConfirmed", _
              RegistryRestore("Showroom", "Not Set"), _
              adOpenForwardOnly, adLockReadOnly, adCmdStoredProc
```

Now we can start to loop through the orders.

```
    ' loop through the orders
    While Not recR.EOF
        lngOrderID = recR("OrderID")
```

We must check the acknowledged flag, because an order with an empty delivery date could have been acknowledged by head office but not confirmed (out of stock perhaps) or it might not have even been acknowledged (a network failure).

```
        ' check to see if has been acknowledged
        If IsNull(recR("Acknowledged")) Then
            strAck = ""
        Else
            strAck = "Acknowledged"
        End If
```

We then add the order details to the grid. **SetGridCell** just updates the cell items for a particular order.

```
        ' add the order to the grid
        grdOrders.AddItem lngOrderID
        SetGridCell lngOrderID, mconColDateSent, _
                    Format$(recR("OrderDate"), "Short Date")
        recR.MoveNext
    Wend
```

```
            recR.Close
            Set recR = Nothing

    End Sub
```

That's all there is to it—we're simply getting a list of records and filling a grid.

OK so we now have a grid, which might have some orders in it already, and we've started the queue monitoring component. What happens when a message arrives in the queue, and the monitoring component raises an event?

If you remember back to the order monitoring component, we defined an event called **OrderAck**, and then when a message arrived in the acknowledgement queue we raised this event. Well, this is where that event gets fired. Since the order monitor has already updated the databases, all we have to do is update the grid.

```
    Private Sub objMonitor_OrderAck(OrderNumber As Long, Class As Long)

        ' update the acknowledged column
        SetGridCell OrderNumber, mconColAck, "Acknowledged"

    End Sub
```

There's a very similar procedure for the **OrderResponse** event:

```
    Private Sub objMonitor_OrderResponse(OrderNumber As Long, _
                        DeliveryDate As String, HOOrderNumber As String)

        ' update the delivery date and head office order number columns
        SetGridCell OrderNumber, mconColDelivery, _
                            Format$(DeliveryDate, "Short Date")
        SetGridCell OrderNumber, mconColHOOrder, HOOrderNumber

    End Sub
```

This just updates two columns in the grid—the delivery date and the order number.

The last thing to look at is the **OrderSent** method of the form—remember we called this directly after creating the order:

```
    Public Sub OrderSent(OrderNumber As Long)

        ' add a new order to the grid
        grdOrders.AddItem OrderNumber
        SetGridCell OrderNumber, mconColDateSent, Format$(Date, "Short Date")

    End Sub
```

This simply adds a new order to the grid, and then fills in the column details. So why are we doing this rather than monitoring the **NewOrder** queue? One very simple reason—we cannot guarantee seeing the order in the **NewOrder** queue before head office removes it from the queue.

Consequently, if we were monitoring the **NewOrder** queue we might never actually see any new orders. It is for this reason that we add new orders to the Order Monitor grid directly. After all, we have just created the order ourselves, so there is really no need to monitor the queue.

That's all there is to it. If you have a look at a slightly different diagram showing the components it becomes much clearer:

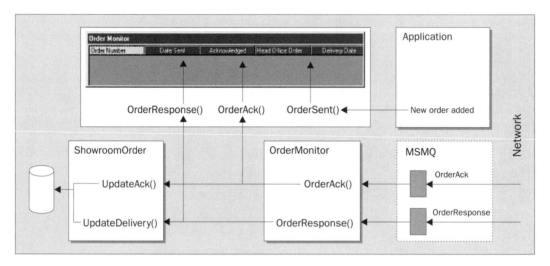

## The Message Flow

Now you've seen how it all fits together, let's have a look at this working. We'll start with placing an order:

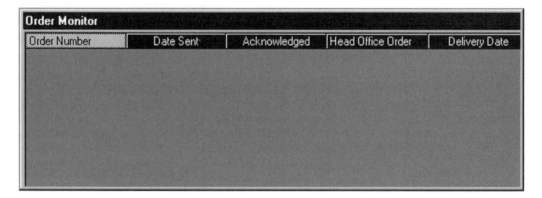

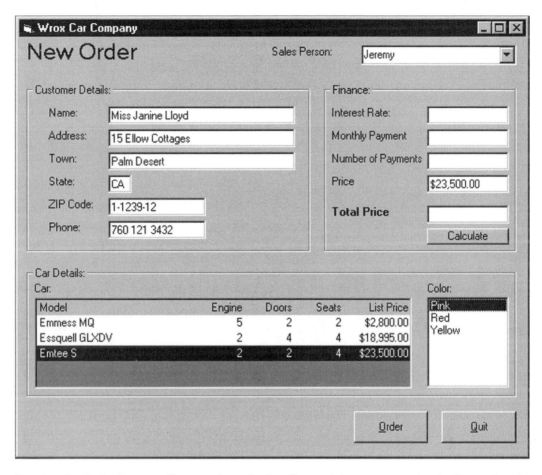

Pressing the Order button will create the order locally, send the message to head office and update the grid. At this stage the grid looks like this:

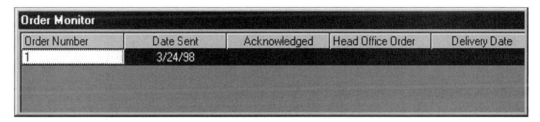

The order has been sent to head office, but has not yet been confirmed. Looking at the NewOrder queue in the MSMQ Explorer confirms our order is there. You might have to click on the NewOrder queue or press F5 to refresh the queue so it shows new messages.

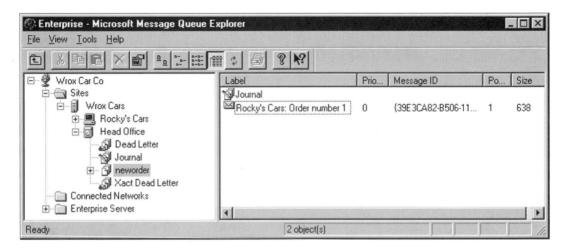

Once the order has been received by head office (that is, read from the queue) the acknowledgement message is sent back and the grid updated:

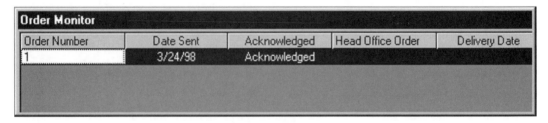

If you had the MSMQ Explorer open and were quick you might have seen the acknowledgement message in the queue:

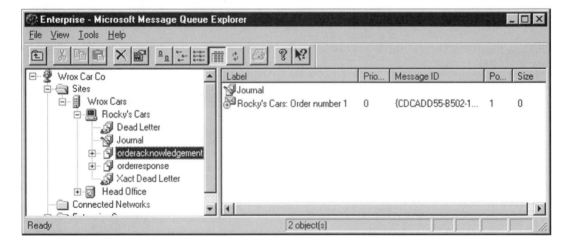

Once head office have processed the order the grid is updated with the head office details. If you picked a car that was out of stock (the Esquel GTXi in Red starts out this way) then you'll notice that head office give an order number, but do not confirm the delivery date:

If the car was in stock, the delivery date is confirmed:

Again if you were quick in MSMQ Explorer you might see the response message in the queue:

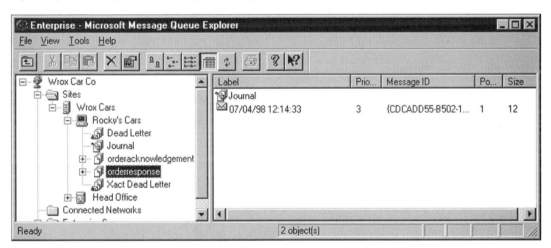

Remember that head office use the **Label** property for the delivery date, and the Body of the message for their order number. You can see this by right-mouse clicking on the message and selecting Properties, then viewing the Body tab:

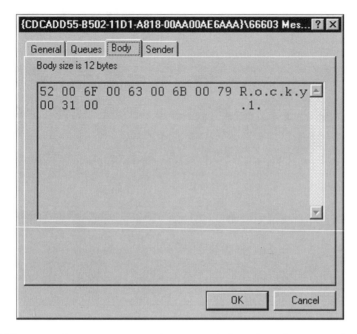

If you would like to see these messages in the queues before they disappear, the simple solution is to just comment out the line where we instantiate the order monitoring object. This is in the **Form_Load** procedure of the monitoring form:

```
' start the monitor
'Set objMonitor = New WCCOrderMonitorQ.OrderMonitorQ
```

If you comment this line out before running the application, then no monitoring takes place, and the acknowledgement and response messages are not removed from the queue. Don't forget to uncomment this later though.

# The Web Application

We've spent a lot of time examining the Visual Basic application for the showroom, but if you cast your mind back to Chapter 4 we also created a web based ordering screen. This was intended as a copy of the Visual Basic one, so it seems only right that we should update that too. However, one thing we have to bear in mind is that the architecture has changed quite a lot since the first ASP file we wrote.

Let's think about the main issue; receiving instant notification of the order being placed. We now send a message and the order monitoring component will process the responses from head office. Does it make any sense to have this coded in HTML? No, because it's a component and can be reused. But, does it make sense for this to be running in several places? Again, no. If you imagine the typical showroom, there might be several machines with the ordering software running on them. Having the monitor running on each machine seems excessive—all that you really want is a display of the orders, perhaps split between confirmed and unconfirmed. So what you should have is a single component (or program) that continuously runs and processes the responses from head office. In fact the existing component can be used for this, and could be included in a standard Visual Basic program that runs continuously on the MSMQ machine. This would process the acknowledgements and delivery date details, freeing the ordering screen from this task. The ordering screen can then take out any references to the monitor, and then each machine can have ordering and monitoring.

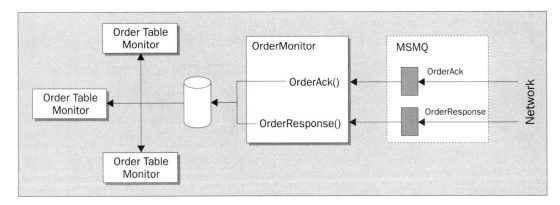

We won't actually do this split here, but all it involves is including the component (or even the whole of **frmMonitor**) in a new Visual Basic application, which could be placed in the  StartUp group of the machine. What we will do though, is look at the changes to the ASP ordering file, and then we'll create an HTML Scriptlet to use as the Order Table Monitor.

## Ordering the Car

Let's start with the ordering first. The changes here are actually very similar to the Visual Basic part. Nothing has changed in **WCCNewOrder.asp**, which is the visual portion of the web application, and we don't need to do much to **WCCOrder.asp**. Like the components we've create a new file for this, called **WCCOrderQ.asp** just to keep it distinct from the original version.

The first thing we do is  extract the order details from the **Form** object.

```
<SCRIPT LANGUAGE=VBScript RUNAT=Server>

' get the user details
sSalesPerson    = Request.Form("SalesPerson")
cPrice          = Request.Form("Price")
sName           = Request.Form("Name")
sAddress        = Request.Form("Address")
sTown           = Request.Form("Town")
sState          = Request.Form("State")
sZipCode        = Request.Form("ZipCode")
sPhone          = Request.Form("Phone")
lCarID          = Request.Form("CarID")
lColorID        = Request.Form("ColorID")
```

Now we place the order locally.

```
set oOrder = Server.CreateObject("WCCSROrderQ.ShowroomOrderQ")
oOrder.Create lCarID, lColorID, _
```

```
                    sSalesPerson, CCur(cPrice), _
                    sName, sAddress, _
                    sTown, sState, _
                    sZipCode, sPhone, _
                    sOrderID, _
                    sShowroom
```

And then we dispatch the order message to head office.

```
set oHOOrder = Server.CreateObject("WCCHOOrderQ.HeadOfficeOrderQ")
oHOOrder.Create sGarageName, sGarageAddress, _
                sGarageTown, sGarageState, _
                sGarageZipCode, sOrderID, _
                sSalesPerson, _
                sName, sAddress, _
                sTown, sState, _
                sZipCode, sPhone, _
                lCarID, lColorID

Set oOrder = Nothing
Set oHOOrder = nothing
```

And finally notify the user of what happened.

```
Sub OnTransactionCommit()

    Response.Write "<P>Order Dispatched"

End Sub

Sub OnTransactionAbort()

    Response.Write "<P>Unknown Error: Order not placed"

End Sub

</SCRIPT>
```

So that's it—even simpler than the previous version. Since we don't yet know the head office order details, let's look at creating a scriptlet to monitor the order table.

## Monitoring the Orders

Since we are building a reusable component let's make it really reusable. Let's have something that will monitor any data store table and build an HTML table, and refresh it periodically. If we are going to do that, we need to identify the data store, the actual data to return, and how often it should be refreshed. That will give us this interface:

| WCCTableMonitor |
| --- |
| ◇Connect : String |
| ◇SQL : String |
| ◇RefreshInterval : Integer |
| |
| ◆Start() |

We've also included a method, **Start**, to start the refresh process. So how about the code then—remember a scriptlet is a straight HTML file, so we'll call this **WCCTableMonitor.htm**.

> *A Scriptlet is simply a component written in HTML and a scripting language. It differs from normal HTML by having an interface just like normal components, and can be embedded onto HTML forms using the OBJECT tag.*

The first thing we do is include an RDS Data Control—this allows us to get a set of data from the server. The **CLASSID** is the unique identifier for the data control and will be the same on your machine.

```
<HTML>
<BODY BGCOLOR=SILVER>

<! RDS Advanced Data Control >
<OBJECT ID=adcO CLASSID="clsid:BD96C556-65A3-11D0-983A-00C04FC29E33"
    STYLE="position:absolute; height:1; width:1">
</OBJECT>
```

Next we define a placeholder for the table we are going to create. This is an empty table at the moment as it will be created dynamically.

```
<TABLE ID=tblTable BORDER=1 RULES=GROUPS WIDTH=100%>
</TABLE>
```

Then we include a hidden field. We do this because the RDS Data Control needs a bound field before it will return any data. If you don't have a bound field it seems to work fine, but you don't get any data back.

```
<INPUT TYPE=TEXT ID=txtHidden datasrc=#adcO datafld=OrderID
style="visibility:hidden">
```

And now we start the scripting. The data type constants from **adovbs.inc** have been included directly into the script here. We'll be using them later to detect what the field types are. To use **adovbs.inc** as an include file we would have had to have made this an ASP file, which wouldn't matter that much, but it seems silly to go through the extra parsing phase at the server when we don't need it. Also we don't need all of the constants, so this makes our scriptlet smaller.

```
<SCRIPT LANGUAGE=VBScript>
Option Explicit

' ------------------------------------------------------------
'---- DataTypeEnum Values from adovbs.inc ----

Const adEmpty = 0
. . .
Const adLongVarBinary = 205
' ------------------------------------------------------------
```

Now let's declare a couple of variables. The first will hold the refresh interval, and the second holds the id of the timer.

```
' Property variables
Dim mintRefreshInterval            ' rds refresh interval

' refresh timer id
Dim mlngIntervalID                 ' refresh interval id
```

And now we can declare our interface. When using VBScript you can create properties by including **public_put** or **public_get** in front of the property name. Using **public_put** gives you a write only property, **public_get** a read only property, and both together a read/write property.

Our first property is the **RefreshInterval**—this is how often the table is refreshed. Internally the timer works in milliseconds, so we multiply the property value by 1000. **Window.setInterval** runs the identified procedure every **n** milliseconds—here the procedure is the **Refresh** method of the RDS Data Control, to refresh the data.

```
Function public_put_RefreshInterval(intRefreshInterval)

    mintRefreshInterval = intRefreshInterval * 1000

    ' clear the old interval and set a new one
    ' but skip starting it off if first time in
    If Not IsEmpty(mlngIntervalID) Then
        Window.clearInterval (mlngIntervalID)
        mlngIntervalID = Window.setInterval ("adcO.Refresh", _
                                         mintRefreshInterval)
    End If

End Function
```

Next comes the connect string, to identify the data store.

```
Function public_put_Connect (strConnect)

    Document.All("adcO").Connect = strConnect

End Function
```

And then the SQL string to create the table from. This can be a stored procedure, a table name or even a SQL statement.

```
Function public_put_SQL (strSQL)

    Document.All("adcO").SQL = strSQL

End Function
```

And finally for the interface, the **Start** method, to start the refresh process.

```
Function public_Start()

    Document.All("adcO").Refresh

    ' set the interval timer
    mlngIntervalID = Window.setInterval ("adcO.Refresh", _
                                         mintRefreshInterval)

End Function
```

That's the interface finished, so now we look at the code that builds the table. We only want to do this once the data has been read into the RDS Data Control, and we can use the **onDatasetComplete** event for this, which is fired when the data has been loaded.

What we are going to do here is cycle through all of the records in the data store table and build a string of HTML tags that define an HTML table.

```
Sub adcO_onDatasetComplete()

    Dim adcOrders          ' orders data control
    Dim recO               ' orders recordset
    Dim strT               ' table html string
    Dim intFields          ' number of fields in recordset
    Dim intField           ' current field number
    Dim fldF               ' current field object
    Dim strValue           ' field value
```

The first thing we do is set **recO** to point to the recordset of the data. This will speed up our reference to the data.

```
    Set adcOrders = Document.All("adcO")
    Set recO = adcOrders.Recordset
```

Then we build the table header. To do this we loop through the **Fields** collection, making each column name contain the **Field Name**.

```
    strT = "<TABLE ID=tblTable BORDER=1 RULES=GROUPS WIDTH=100%>" & _
           "<THEAD BGCOLOR=GRAY><TR ALIGN=CENTER>"

    ' each each field as a table column name
    For Each fldF In recO.Fields
        strT = strT & "<TD>" & fldF.Name & "</TD>"
    Next
    strT = strT & "</TR></THEAD>"
```

Now we need to add the data to the table. Firstly we find out how many columns there are, and then we start the loop through the records.

```
    intFields = recO.Fields.Count - 1
    strT = strT & "<TBODY>"
    While Not recO.EOF
        strT = strT & "<TR ALIGN=CENTER>"
```

Now we loop through each field, and format it according to its type. This is where the data type constants come in. We are doing this because it is a generic routine, so we don't know what is in each field.

```
        For intField = 0 to intFields
            strValue = recO(intField)

            Select Case recO(intField).Type
            Case adDBDate, adDBTimeStamp, adDBTime, adDate
                If Not IsNull(strValue) Then
                    strValue = FormatDateTime (strValue, 2)
                End If

            Case adBoolean
                If strValue = "True" Then
                    strValue = "Yes"
                Else
                    strValue = "No"
                End If

            Case adCurrency
                If Not IsNull(strValue) Then
                    strValue = FormatCurrency(strValue)
                End If

            Case adBigInt, adDecimal, adDouble, adNumeric, adSingle, _
                adSmallInt, adTinyInt, adUnsignedBigInt, adUnsignedInt, _
                adUnsignedSmallInt, adUnsignedTinyInt
                If Not IsNull(strValue) Then
                    strValue = FormatNumber (strValue)
                End If

            End Select
```

We check the **Type** property of each field so that we can format it correctly. Date and Time types are formatted using **FormatDateTime**, which uses the date and time settings of the local machine. Boolean values are converted from **True** and **False** into **Yes** and **No**, as these are more readable. Currency values are formatted using **FormatCurrency**, which again uses the local machine settings, and finally any other numeric types are formatted with **FormatNumber**. All other types are assumed to be strings and no formatting takes place.

Once formatted, we can add it as a cell to the HTML table, and continue looping.

```
            strT = strT & "<TD>" & strValue & "</TD>"
        Next
        strT = strT & "</TR>"
        recO.MoveNext
    Wend
```

And once all rows and columns have been done, we can end the table, and set the **OuterHTML** property of the table to the new table string. This will replace the original blank table, with our fully populated and formatted table.

```
        strT = strT & "</TBODY></TABLE>"

        Document.All("tblTable").OuterHTML = strT

    End Sub

    </SCRIPT>
```

The very last thing the scriptlet does is detect whether we are running in a scriptlet or have been opened directly. If in a scriptlet we give ourselves a scrollbar, as the table we create could well exceed the size of the object it's placed in. We also remove the borders to give ourselves that little bit extra room.

```
    <SCRIPT LANGUAGE=VBScript FOR="Window" EVENT="onLoad">

        ' Add a scroll bar, as the table may be larger
        ' than the area containing it
        If InScriptlet Then
            Window.External.ScrollBar = True
        End If

        ' renmove scriptlet borders
        Document.Body.Style.marginTop = 0
        Document.Body.Style.marginLeft = 0
        Document.Body.Style.marginBottom = 0
        Document.Body.Style.marginRight = 0

    </SCRIPT>

    <SCRIPT language=JavaScript>
        var InScriptlet = (typeof(window.external.version)=="string");
    </SCRIPT>

    </BODY>
    </HTML>
```

That's all there is to it. You can now embed this into another HTML page using the standard OBJECT tag.

```
    <OBJECT ID= Monitor DATA="WCCTableMonitor.htm"
        WIDTH=100% HEIGHT=45%" TYPE="text/x-scriptlet">
    </OBJECT>
```

You can then set the properties and start the refresh.

```
Monitor.RefreshInterval = 5
Monitor.Connect = "driver={SQL Server};server=PIGLET;database=WroxCarCo"
Monitor.SQL = "usp_OrdersUnconfirmed"
Monitor.Start
```

In the file **WCCTableMonitor.htm**, we also need to add:

```
Function public_put_Server (strServer)
   Document.All("adcO").Server = strServer
End Function
```

In fact, because it is generic we can create a single HTML page with two copies of the script; one that shows confirmed orders and one that shows unconfirmed orders.

```
<B>Orders yet to be confirmed</B>
<OBJECT ID=tblUnconfirmed DATA="WCCTableMonitor.htm"
    WIDTH=100% HEIGHT=45%" TYPE="text/x-scriptlet">
</OBJECT>
<HR>
<B>Confirmed Orders</B>
<OBJECT ID=tblConfirmed DATA="WCCTableMonitor.htm"
    WIDTH=100% HEIGHT=45%" TYPE="text/x-scriptlet">
</OBJECT>

<SCRIPT LANGUAGE=VBScript>

Sub Window_onLoad()

    tblUnconfirmed.RefreshInterval = 5
    tblUnconfirmed.Connect = sShowroom
    tblUnconfirmed.Server = "http://<%=Request.ServerVariables _
            ("SERVER_NAME")%>"
    tblUnconfirmed.SQL = "usp_OrdersUnconfirmed"
    tblUnconfirmed.Start

    tblConfirmed.RefreshInterval = 5
    tblConfirmed.Connect = sShowroom
    tblConfirmed.Server = "http://<%=Request.ServerVariables _
            ("SERVER_NAME")%>"
    tblConfirmed.SQL = "usp_OrdersConfirmed"
    tblConfirmed.Start

End Sub

</SCRIPT>
```

This gives two continuously updating tables:

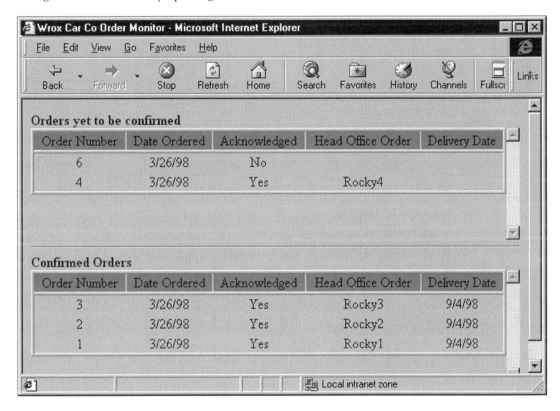

And that's all there is to it. A simple, generic table monitoring scriptlet that can be used in any HTML page. You can see that with a little pre-planning you can creating some simple generic components in HTML that can speed development and ease maintenance.

*If you'd like to learn more about scriptlets have a look at Instant Scriptlets (ISBN 1-861001-38-X) also from Wrox Press.*

# Head Office

The head office application is one area that we haven't looked at before. Now we have distinct processes to be run at head office, there are two things that need doing. The first is to monitor the **NewOrder** queue, and the second is to process the orders. In real life this would probably be a small part of a large application, but we only need to concentrate on the queuing aspects here.

# Processing the Order

We'll look at the order processing component first, because you've seen most of this before—it's the Head Office Ordering component from Chapter 4. Remember that when we first used this component, it connected to the remote head office data store to create the order. A few things have changed, but it's still very similar:

```
Public Function Create(ByVal GarageName As String, _
                       ByVal GarageAddress As String, _
                       ByVal GarageTown As String, _
                       ByVal GarageState As String, _
                       ByVal GarageZipCode As String, _
                       ByVal GarageOrderNumber As Long, _
                       ByVal SalesPerson As String, _
                       ByVal CustomerName As String, _
                       ByVal CustomerAddress As String, _
                       ByVal CustomerTown As String, _
                       ByVal CustomerState As String, _
                       ByVal CustomerZipCode As String, _
                       ByVal CustomerPhone As String, _
                       ByVal CarID As Long, _
                       ByVal ColorID As Long, _
                       ByVal ResponseQueue As String, _
                       ByRef OrderNumber As Variant, _
                       ByRef DeliveryDate As Variant, _
                       ByRef OrderID As Variant, _
                       ByRef NumberInStock As Variant, _
                       Optional ConnectionString As Variant) As Boolean
```

Most of the parameters are the same, being the order details, but there are a few new ones. The first new one is **ResponseQueue**, which is used to hold the **FormatName** of the MSMQ Response Queue. The response queue is passed to head office by the showroom so that the order number and delivery date can be sent back in a message to a specific queue. We need to store this as part of the order to enable the head office application to respond at a later date, for example, if a car is out of stock. This would require manual intervention to decide the delivery date. The other new parameters are output parameters, which will hold the head office order number, the delivery date, the order id and the number of cars in stock. You'll see where the last two are used later.

The next difference is the stored procedure name:

```
.CommandText = "usp_OrderInsertQ"
```

As with the components, we've added a **Q** to the end to make it obvious that this is for the queued version of the application. Then we have the parameters for the ADO Command object—only the new ones are shown here.

```
.Append comC.CreateParameter("@ResponseQueue", adVarChar, _
                              adParamInput, 255, ResponseQueue)
.Append comC.CreateParameter("@OrderNumber", adVarChar, _
                              adParamOutput, 10)
.Append comC.CreateParameter("@DeliveryDate", adDBTimeStamp, _
                              adParamOutput, 8)
```

```
.Append comC.CreateParameter("@OrderID", adInteger, _
                            adParamOutput, 8)
```

These are the same as the new parameters described earlier.

Once the command has been executed, the code is also slightly different.

```
NumberInStock = .Parameters("Return")
OrderNumber = .Parameters("@OrderNumber")
If IsNull(.Parameters("@DeliveryDate")) Then
    DeliveryDate = ""
Else
    DeliveryDate = .Parameters("@DeliveryDate")
End If
OrderID = .Parameters("@OrderID")
```

We are now returning three parameters back to our caller, and we also check for a null delivery date–this would happen if the car were out of stock.

Let's have a look at the stored procedure that this runs, as this has changed too. We'll skip the parameters since they match the ones above.

The first thing is to declare any variables. We need one for the number of cars in stock and for the current date.

```
DECLARE @InStock    integer
DECLARE @Today      datetime

SELECT @Today = GETDATE()
```

Now we can insert the order details into the order table, in exactly the same way as we did before.

```
INSERT INTO tblOrder (GarageName, GarageAddress, GarageTown,
                      GarageState, GarageZipCode, GarageOrderNumber,
                      SalesPerson, CustomerName, CustomerAddress,
                      CustomerTown, CustomerState, CustomerZipCode,
                      CustomerPhone, fkCarID, DateOrdered, fkColorID)
VALUES (@GarageName, @GarageAddress, @GarageTown, @GarageState,
        @GarageZipCode, @GarageOrderNumber, @SalesPerson,
        @CustomerName, @CustomerAddress, @CustomerTown, @CustomerState,
        @CustomerZipCode, @CustomerPhone,
        @CarID, @Today, @ColorID)
```

Then we set the **OrderID** parameter to the actual order id created. In the order table the order id field is an identity column and **@@IDENTITY** represents the last identity value inserted.

```
SELECT @OrderID = @@IDENTITY
```

Now we decrease the number of cars in stock. We'll look at this stored procedure after this one.

```
EXEC @InStock = usp_StockDecrementQ @CarID, @ColorID
```

Now we can create the head office order number– this is the first five characters of the garage name plus the order id.

```
SELECT @OrderNumber = SUBSTRING (@GarageName, 1, 5) + _
                      CONVERT(varchar(5), @OrderID)
```

And now we can decide whether the order can be fulfilled or not. If there are enough cars in stock, then we can set the delivery date (we assume it takes 14 days to get the car ready).

```
IF @InStock > 0
BEGIN
    -- Only update the delivery if we have a car in stock
    SELECT    @DeliveryDate = DATEADD(day, 14, @Today)
    UPDATE    tblOrder
    SET       DeliveryDate = @DeliveryDate
    WHERE     OrderID = @OrderID
END
```

If there aren't enough in stock we update the **ResponseQueue** field. Now, when we update the delivery date at a later date we'll know which queue to send the response to.

```
ELSE
BEGIN
    -- Update the response queue, so we can respond to
    -- the order at a later date
    UPDATE    tblOrder
    SET       ResponseQueue = @ResponseQueue
    WHERE     OrderID = @OrderID
END
```

The last thing to do is return the number of cars in stock.

```
RETURN    @InStock
```

That's it for that stored procedure–you can see it's a little more intelligent than the last version. We've also improved the stored procedure that reduces the number of cars in stock. Previously, this stored procedure raised an error if the order couldn't be fulfilled, but now we've added some more rules to allow it to cope with this.

One thing that hasn't changed is the procedure declaration–it still needs the car ID and color ID, and we still need a variable to hold the number of cars in stock.

```
CREATE PROCEDURE usp_StockDecrementQ
            @CarID              int,
            @ColorID            int
AS
    DECLARE     @NumberInStock     integer
```

Now we find out how many cars there are.

```
SELECT     @NumberInStock = InStock
FROM       tblCarColor
WHERE      fkCarID = @CarID
AND        fkColorID = @ColorID
```

This is where we add the new rule, because if there aren't enough in stock we add one to the number on order.

```
IF @NumberInStock < 1
BEGIN
     -- not in stock therefore add to on order count
     UPDATE     tblCarColor
     SET        OnOrder = OnOrder + 1
     WHERE      fkCarID = @CarID
     AND        fkColorID = @ColorID
END
```

If there are enough in stock we can reduce the count by 1.

```
ELSE
BEGIN
     -- in stock so decrement stock count
     UPDATE     tblCarColor
     SET        InStock = InStock - 1
     WHERE      fkCarID = @CarID
     AND        fkColorID = @ColorID
END
```

Now we can return the new number in stock.

```
RETURN @NumberInStock - 1
```

These changes are actually very sensible, since the component and its associated stored procedures now have a degree of intelligence and don't fail when they can't cope with something simple.

There's also a new method in the order processing component, **UpdateDeliveryDate**, which updates the delivery date for a given order:

```
Public Function UpdateDeliveryDate(ByVal OrderID As Long, _
                                   ByVal DeliveryDate As Date, _
                                   Optional ConnectionString As Variant) _
               As Boolean
```

We won't look at the code here since it is very much the same as some other components we've created—it simply creates an ADO Command object and executes a stored procedure, passing in the **OrderID** and **DeliveryDate**. We'll be using this method when we need to manually update the delivery date, for cars that are out of stock.

# Waiting for an Order

For the head office order monitoring we have some similar features to the showroom monitor. Let's look at the code and then we'll see it in action.

The first thing to notice is that we declare the queue and event objects, as we did before.

```
Private queNewOrder              As MSMQQueue     ' queue of orders
Private WithEvents evtNewOrder   As MSMQEvent     ' event of orders
```

And again we have a list of the column's numbers. This isn't strictly necessary, but it makes the code more friendly.

```
Private Enum GridColumn
    mconColOrderID = 0
    mconColGarage = 1
    mconColGarageOrderNo = 2
    mconColHOOrderNo = 3
    mconColDateOrdered = 4
    mconColDeliveryDate = 5
    mconColResponseQueue = 6
End Enum
```

Now when the form loads you'll see some more familiar lines of code. Firstly, we create a new queue info object and set the **PathName** to point to the **NewOrder** queue on the local machine. Notice that we don't need to use the GUID here, because the head office is the main MSMQ server and contains the information store, so we don't have to worry about it being offline. Of course in the real world, servers often become unavailable as the cleaner pulls the power out so she can plug in her vacuum cleaner, so we really should have built in some code to check this. This would allow us to display a nice message rather than an ugly, incoherent message from MSMQ itself.

The first thing to do is create the queue and event objects, and then start the queue notification.

```
Private Sub Form_Load()

    ' create the queue and event objects
    Set queNewOrder = New MSMQQueue
    Set evtNewOrder = New MSMQEvent

    ' open the queue and start notification
    Set queNewOrder = MessageQueueOpen(mcstrNewOrder, MQ_DENY_NONE)
    queNewOrder.EnableNotification evtNewOrder
```

And finally we can set up the grid columns and fill the grid with unconfirmed orders.

```
    ' set up the grids
    GridInitialise
    GridResize
    OrdersNotConfirmed

End Sub
```

The **OrdersNotConfirmed** does much the same as the showroom version, except it runs a stored procedure on the head office, which returns any orders that don't have a delivery date, and it places them in the grid. So that's it for the start—we can now sit and wait for orders to arrive in the queue, and when they do the **evtNewOrder_Arrived** event is fired. This extracts the message from the queue, passes it to the **ProcessOrder** procedure, and then resets the notification.

```
Private Sub evtNewOrder_Arrived(ByVal Queue As Object, _
                                ByVal Cursor As Long)

    Dim msgReceived      As New MSMQMessage      ' message received

    ' extract the message from the queue and process it
    Set msgReceived = Queue.Receive

    ProcessOrder msgReceived

    ' set up the monitoring again
    queNewOrder.EnableNotification evtNewOrder

End Sub
```

**ProcessOrder** accepts the MSMQ message that has just been delivered. The first variable is for the **StringBag**—remember this was used to serialize the order details into a string, and now we will use it to reverse that process. The second variable is the order processing component, and then we have some variables to use as the output parameters for the order processing component.

```
Private Sub ProcessOrder(ByVal msgRec As MSMQMessage)

    Dim clsStringBag      As New WroxStringBag.StringBag      ' string bag
    Dim objOrder          As WCCOrderProcessQ.Process         ' order proc

    Dim strOrderNumber    As String          ' order number
    Dim strDeliveryDate   As String          ' delivery date
    Dim lngOrderID        As Long            ' order id
    Dim lngInStock        As Long            ' number in stock
```

The first thing to do is unpack the order details from the **Body** of the message. We are using exactly the same string bag as before, which will take the string of key and value pairs, and split them into its collections.

```
    clsStringBag.DeSerialize msgRec.Body
```

Now we can create the order processing component and create the order. We use the string bag to access the values that were unpacked in the previous step. Remember that the **AppSpecific** property of the message holds the showroom order number, and notice that we are passing in the **FormatName** of the **ResponseQueueInfo**. This is the name (or GUID) of the queue that the showroom would like the order response in.

```
    Set objOrder = CreateObject("WCCOrderProcessQ.Process")
    objOrder.Create clsStringBag.Item("GarageName"), _
                    clsStringBag.Item("GarageAddress"), _
                    clsStringBag.Item("GarageTown"), _
```

```
                        clsStringBag.Item("GarageState"), _
                        clsStringBag.Item("GarageZipCode"), _
                        msgRec.AppSpecific, _
                        clsStringBag.Item("SalesPerson"), _
                        clsStringBag.Item("CustomerName"), _
                        clsStringBag.Item("CustomerAddress"), _
                        clsStringBag.Item("CustomerTown"), _
                        clsStringBag.Item("CustomerState"), _
                        clsStringBag.Item("CustomerZipCode"), _
                        clsStringBag.Item("CustomerPhone"), _
                        CLng(clsStringBag.Item("CarID")), _
                        CLng(clsStringBag.Item("ColorID")), _
                        msgRec.ResponseQueueInfo.FormatName, _
                        strOrderNumber, strDeliveryDate, _
                        lngOrderID, lngInStock
        Set objOrder = Nothing
```

As soon as the order has been created we can update the screen. If there weren't enough cars in stock then we make sure the delivery date field says so.

```
        If lngInStock < 0 Then
            strDeliveryDate = "Out of stock"
        End If
```

And then we add a row to the grid. **GridAddRow** is a function that adds a new row to the grid—we won't look at it in detail since it's very simple.

```
        GridAddRow lngOrderID, _
                    clsStringBag.Item("GarageName"), _
                    msgRec.AppSpecific, _
                    strOrderNumber, _
                    Format$(Now, "Short Date"), _
                    Format$(strDeliveryDate, "Short Date"), _
                    msgRec.ResponseQueueInfo.FormatName
```

Once the screen has been updated we can send a response to the showroom and exit.

```
        RespondToOrder msgRec.ResponseQueueInfo.FormatName, _
                    msgRec.AppSpecific, strDeliveryDate, strOrderNumber

    End Sub
```

Let's have a look at this **RespondToOrder** procedure, the parameters of which match up with the line of code above—the **FormatName** of the response queue, the showroom order number, the delivery date, and the head office order number. We'll be putting these into a message and sending it back to the showroom.

```
    Private Sub RespondToOrder(strFormatName As String, _
                    lngAppSpecific As Long, strLabel As String, _
                    strBody As String)
```

Firstly, we declare the message queue objects.

```
Dim infResponse       As New MSMQQueueInfo    ' response queue info
Dim queResponse       As New MSMQQueue        ' response queue
Dim msgResponse       As New MSMQMessage      ' response message
```

Then we open the queue.

```
infResponse.FormatName = strFormatName
Set queResponse = infResponse.Open(MQ_SEND_ACCESS, MQ_DENY_NONE)
```

And then we construct the message. Since we only need to send back three pieces of information we don't need to package them up with the string bag . The showroom order number goes back into the **AppSpecific** property, the delivery date into the **Label**, and the head office order number into the **Body**.

```
msgResponse.AppSpecific = lngAppSpecific
msgResponse.Label = strLabel
msgResponse.Body = strBody
```

All that's left to do is send the message off, close the queue, and  clean up our object references.

```
msgResponse.Send queResponse, MQ_NO_TRANSACTION

queResponse.Close
Set infResponse = Nothing
Set msgResponse = Nothing
Set queResponse = Nothing

End Sub
```

That's all there is to automatically responding to the order. You might have noticed that there appears to be no code to handle the acknowledgement, and you'd be right. There isn't any. MSMQ handles this for us, sending an acknowledgement message as soon as we r eceive the message from the queue. One less thing for us to worry about.

Let's see what this looks like:

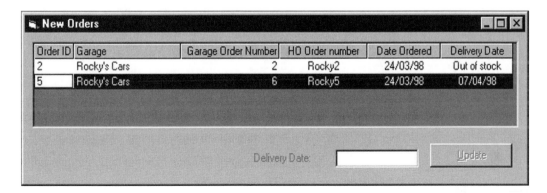

Pretty similar to the showroom monitor, except that there's a text field and a command button. This allows us to update the delivery date manually, and have this confirmation sent back to the showroom:

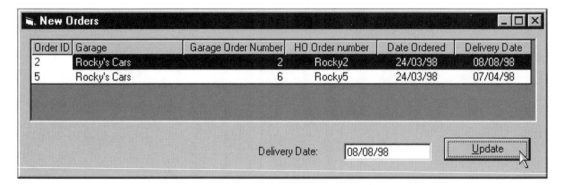

This sends a message to the same **OrderResponse** queue that was used when we automatically responded, so the showroom monitoring program will pick this up and update the local order as though the order had only just been placed. This is the only bit of code we haven't looked at yet, so let's look at it now.

Firstly the variables, including the order processing component.

```
Private Sub cmdUpdate_Click()

    Dim objOrder         As WCCOrderProcessQ.Process    ' order proc
    Dim intIdx           As Integer                     ' current row
    Dim lngOrderID       As Long                        ' Order ID
    Dim strResponse      As String                      ' Response queue
    Dim strHOOrderNumber As String                      ' HO Order number
    Dim strDate          As String                      ' delivery date
```

A little error checking, just to make sure the user typed in a valid date.

```
    If Not IsDate(txtDeliveryDate) Then
        MsgBox "Oops - invalid date.  Try again", , "Date Error"
        Exit Sub
    End If
```

Now we need to get the order ID. First we get the current row, and then call **GridCellContents** to extract the order ID from the correct column ( **mconColOrderID**).

```
    ' get the order id and number
    intIdx = grdOrders.Row
    lngOrderID = GridCellContents(intIdx, mconColOrderID)
```

Then we get the head office order number–remember we've allocated an order number even though the order couldn't be fulfilled.

```
    strHOOrderNumber = GridCellContents(intIdx, mconColHOOrderNo)
```

Then we format the date the user entered, and get the response queue details from the grid. You might have noticed that the response queue doesn't appear to be in the grid, but we've used an extra column and just made the column width 0. This allows us to store all of the information we need to update the order, even if we don't want it all shown on the screen.

```
strDate = Format$(txtDeliveryDate, "Short Date")
strResponse = GridCellContents(intIdx, mconColResponseQueue)
```

Now we create the order processing component, update the order, and fill in the date in the grid.

```
Set objOrder = CreateObject("WCCOrderProcessQ.Process")
objOrder.UpdateDeliveryDate lngOrderID, strDate
SetGridCell lngOrderID, mconColDeliveryDate, strDate

Set objOrder = Nothing
```

And finally, we respond to the order. This uses the same procedure shown earlier, except now we pass in the user entered date.

```
' now send a message back to the showroom
RespondToOrder strResponse, _
               GridCellContents(intIdx, mconColGarageOrderNo), _
               strDate, strHOOrderNumber

End Sub
```

So that's it. At the head office we now have a component to process the order, and an application that monitors incoming orders. We have a fully distributed, fault-tolerant application with very little effort.

# Events

This is just a little explanation if you haven't used user events within Visual Basic components. We're all used to events in Visual Basic, but most of the time these seem to be generated by the system. However, when creating components you often want the component to generate events of its own, so it can communicate back to the routine that instantiated it.

For example, imagine the Visual Basic class **Man**. We'll give **Man** two methods. **Walk** and **ChewGum**. We could use this class like so:

```
Private objMan As New Man

objMan.Walk

. . .

objMan.ChewGum
```

Now let's assume our **Man** is not very bright. Let's assume he can't **Walk** and **ChewGum** at the same time. Doing so results in a **FallOver**, and you need to communicate this back to your calling routine. This is where the event comes in. In our class we can define an event called **FallOver**. The whole class would now be:

```
Public Event FallOver (strDirection As String)

Private m_bWalking     As Boolean

Public Sub Walk()

    m_bWalking = True

    ' code to walk

End Sub

Public Sub ChewGum()

    If m_bWalking Then
        RaiseEvent FallOver ("Face")
    End If

    ' code to chew gum

End Sub
```

Now if the **ChewGum** method is invoked and we are already walking, then the **Man** will **FallOver** (this time on his face, but it could easily be his butt).

Now our code to use **Man** becomes:

```
Private WithEvents objMan As New Man

Private Sub objMan_FallOver (sDirection As String)

    MsgBox "Your man fell on his " & sDirection

End Sub

objMan.Walk

. . .

objMan.ChewGum
```

Notice we've added **WithEvents** to the declaration of **Man**. This allows this instance of **Man** to receive events. So we can create an event procedure to respond to the event, and tell us which direction our **Man** fell. When in Visual Basic **objMan** will appear in the objects list in the code window, and its events will appear in the event list.

Although a simple example, this is actually quite a powerful feature, and is really the best way for a component to communicate to its calling routine.

# Summary

Although the techniques and programming used in this chapter are quite simple, we've actually covered an awful lot of ground. We first examined why the original design wouldn't work when queuing was introduced. But we've seen how flexible this queuing is, and that designing your applications around it is worthwhile. Obviously it's best to start this design process from the beginning, but we all know that doesn't happen every time (or even that often), but the actual programming required to build queuing systems is extremely easy.

What we've seen is that message queuing allows us to communicate with other applications in a loose time frame. The only thing we worry about is the message getting there, and in cases where the application is built around a local area network, then that's probably not too much of a worry either. The recoverable delivery option though, allows this to happen, so even if your network does fail, your messages are safe.

You've also seen that you don't have to build complex monitoring programs, because the MSMQ events tell you when messages have arrived. You can use this like we have to update a form, or to silently update data, or even to pop up messages on the screen to alert users of the message. If you think about it you could even use MSMQ as the basis for a workflow application. All you need is a separate queue for each distinct stop along the workflow route. The originator could send the initial message to the first queue, which would alert the next person in the chain. When they have finished with the message they can send it to the next, and so on. A powerful, and easy to create, system. With a little imagination you could use message queuing for quite a lot of applications.

We've now come to the point where we really have a good DNA application, but there's one major topic that we haven't covered yet. Security. It's a big issue, and often a worry for network managers, so how do you deal with security issues in the DNA world? That's where the next chapter comes in.

# Securing Your DNA Applications

Ask a programmer whose job it is to implement the appropriate levels of security for a distributed application and they'll tell you it's the responsibility of the network administrator. Ask the network administrator and they'll tell you that they don't know how the program works, and that it's the programmer's job. If this sounds a familiar situation in your business then you're not alone. After fighting with the technology for as long as it takes to build any reasonably complex application, the average programmer is often pleased just to get it all working.

Of course you're not just an *average* programmer, but no doubt the previous paragraph has at least a ring of truth to it. Security in Windows NT is a system-wide issue, and your applications depend on a lot of operating system configurations as well as the code you write within the application.

In this and the next chapter we'll examine how Windows NT and the **Distributed interNet Applications** (DNA) architecture fit together to allow you to provide a secure environment for your applications. This isn't going to be an exhaustive exploration of every issue, because if you've got this far you'll already be familiar with the main concepts of Windows NT and the ways in which its security features can be used. Instead, we'll be concentrating on the topics concerned with technologies like **Active Server Pages**, **Microsoft Transaction Server**, and **Microsoft Message Queue Server** that we've been using in this book. Since implementing security in these areas is tightly integrated with Windows NT security, we'll show you in overview how all the parts fit together.

In this chapter you'll find:

- ❑ An overview of Windows NT Integrated Security features
- ❑ The three core concepts of security: Authentication, Encryption, and Auditing
- ❑ The particular issues that are involved in Web-based applications
- ❑ The ways that we can implement these core concepts in our applications

In the next chapter we'll move on to look at the security issues involved with MTS and MSMQ, and take a brief look at some of the ways that we need to protect our data sources. In both chapters, we provide you with a guide to the things you should be considering, and point you in the right direction if you want to find out more information about them.

To start with, we'll briefly see how Windows NT Integrated Security fits together.

# Windows NT Integrated Security

One of the strengths of Windows NT is the way that the built-in security features extend beyond the limits of the operating system to encompass other products and services running on it. All of the Microsoft BackOffice® products can plug into NT to get details of the files and resources that each user should have access to. This includes services such as Internet Information Server and SQL Server, as well as the MTS and MSMQ services that we'll focus on later in this chapter.

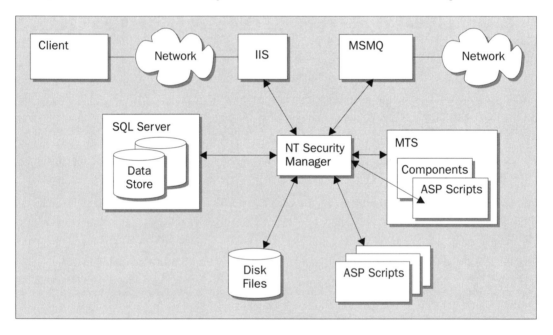

The major bonus here is that each user only has one  logon to perform. Each application or service can query Windows NT to see what resources the current user can access. Notice that we're talking here about *applications* rather than just Web sites. While the following applies just as well to sites that simply display information and distribute files, our DNA applications will generally enjoy a much closer relationship with the operating system and the services that it makes available.

# Security - The Three Core Concepts

All the aspects of security that we'll be examining in this chapter focus around three core concepts:

❑ **Authentication** is all about identifying the user precisely and reliably when they log onto the system, and when they access any resource within it. If NT cannot identify individual users, it can't tell what resources they should be allowed to access.

❑ **Encryption** consists of storing and passing information from one place to another in such a way that it cannot be read by anyone who intercepts it. Usernames and passwords are stored in encrypted form within Windows.

❑ **Auditing** is the technique of recording what goes on inside the operating system as users request and work with the resources it makes available to them. In particular it's used to identify where, when and how undesirable accesses were either attempted or even achieved.

In this first section of the chapter, we're mainly concerned with authentication and auditing. We'll come to encryption later, when we look at Internet Information Server.

# Security Basics

In Windows NT4 the security features are a development of the original Microsoft LAN Manager roots, while in NT5 it changes completely to use a technology called **Kerberos**—a standardized system that has been under development by MIT and other software manufacturers for some time. NT5 also gains a new system of storing security and other information called the **Active Directory Service**.

However, the underlying way that the security features are implemented does not concern us in this book. We're only interested in those things that should be considered when building DNA applications. This includes understanding the way that NT organizes details about each user, and the ways that it can control access to resources.

## Domains And WorkGroups

Traditional PC networks involved the concept of a **workgroup**. In this situation, each machine stored its own copy of the permissions available to each user, identified each user as they logged onto the machine, and controlled access to the resources in just that machine. The major problem here was that, for a new user to be able to access resources on several machines, you had to update each machine with that user's details.

This is unlike a more usual client/server mainframe or mini-based environment where details of all users are kept on the server, and each client logs directly onto the server itself. To achieve this within a networked PC environment, there has to be one computer that is defined as the controller, and which stores all the security information.

Of course, in Windows NT, this is the **Primary Domain Controller** (PDC). All the other PCs on the network can also keep their own **local** security information (generally just for the resources they themselves contain), but the PDC stores the global information for all users for all common resources. A **Backup Domain Controller** (BDC) can also be set up to keep a read-only copy of the information, to help spread the load during busy periods, or to be promoted to the Primary Domain Controller if the existing one should fail.

> *For information about planning domains, trust relationships, and the other issues that are involved, see the Help file for User Manager, and the Books Online on the Windows NT Server CD-ROM. Alternatively, look out for one of the many books on the market that cover this topic in depth.*

### Network Protocols, Firewalls and Proxy Servers

If your network is connected to the Internet, or to another external network, then you will also need to consider installing **firewall** or **proxy server** software, and multiple network cards, into the gateway machine. This hides the internal network from the outside world, while allowing internal users access to the external network.

There are whole books about network and Internet security, and if you are responsible for setting up the interface between your network and the outside world you should read up on these important topics. Look out for Professional Web Security (ISBN 1-861-00182-7) from Wrox Press, or visit Microsoft's Web site at http://www.microsoft.com/proxy/guide/firewall.asp.

# Users, Groups and User Manager

Windows stores a range of details about each user that has access to resources on the network in a **user account**. This includes the password and username that they log on with, their home directory (that is, the directory that appears as the root directory when they log on to the server), the periods in the day during which they can log on, and a range of other information.

The user account uniquely identifies each user –this helps the operating system to decide which users have permission to use which resource on the network server(s). However, to avoid having to enter all the information about each user individually, NT allows each user to be added to one or more groups of users, by defining **group accounts**. Members of a group inherit the permissions defined for that group. It's possible for user accounts to be given permissions on an individual basis as well, though it's not a good idea to do so.

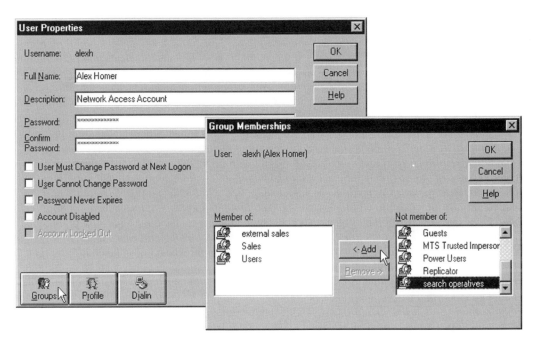

It's important to remember that nobody ever logs onto the system using a *group* account, but only as a *user*. The groups are there simply to allow permissions for a resource to be granted or revoked to all the user accounts assigned to that group as one operation: this is a big time-saver if you have a lot of users to administer. If you remove access to a particular resource from a group, then all the members of that group lose access to it. However, if a user is a member of more than one group, and the other group still has access to it, then they will retain this access permission.

## *Group And User Account Characteristics*

Each group and user account is created and modified with the Windows User Manager program. Once an account has been created, it is assigned characteristics through the Account Policy dialog (available from the Policies menu):

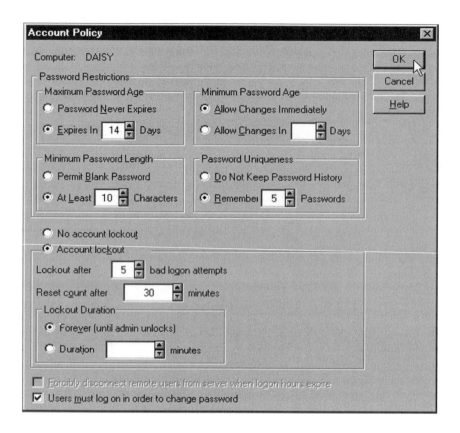

## Good Practice With Accounts

The options available in User Manager mean that you can limit user access to all the resources on the machine at the lowest level, and provide a core secure environment. Since the root of all security is the accurate and reliable identification of each user (i.e. **authentication**), you should take advantage of features like the minimum password length, password expiry periods, password renewal policies, and so on.

The usual advice for creating a basic secure environment includes:

❑ Always **format your drives using the NT File System (NTFS)** when you install NT and all other files. This provides the opportunity to allocate permissions to individual files separately.

❑ Make sure you have **installed all the current Service Packs** for both Windows NT and other integrated applications. The Microsoft Security Web page at **http://microsoft.com/security/** contains bulletins about newly discovered areas of security risk for which you can often download fixes, or protect your server by tweaking its configuration.

❑   **Secure the administrator's access** by creating a new account with a username that does not
   include the words Administrator or admin–there's no point in giving half the game away to an
   intruder–and by using a long and mixed case password. (You might even like to include some
   non-alphabetic characters but be sure that the keyboards on all your machines produce these
   characters from the same keys!) Then set up a complex 'mixed case plus numeric characters'
   password for the built-in Administrator account, after ensuring that any services installed on the
   system that use it to log onto NT have this password set up as well.

❑   **Ensure that the built-in** Guest **account is disabled**. If you want to provide 'public' access to parts
   of the system, create a new account for this purpose.

❑   **Create group accounts** for each type of access you want to offer to users. For a DNA
   application, where almost all access is via the Web server, you will only need one special
   account for this, plus a few user groups – as you'll see later in this chapter. Where possible, avoid
   giving permissions for resources to individual user accounts, because it's easy to lose track of
   permissions that are different from the group.

❑   **Lock down each account** as tightly as possible by limiting the log on periods, and the machines
   that they can log on from. Make sure NT demands that they use long and complex passwords
   that have to be changed regularly. And on a non-technical level, also **make sure that users keep
   their passwords safe and private**.

The limitations that you apply to each group will, of necessity, have to match the needs that the users
are required to make of the system. For more information and general guidelines on basic security,
check out **http://microsoft.com/ntserver/guide/secure_ntinstall.asp**, or the Help
files for NT's User Manager program.

> *One common suggestion is to* **disable** *the built-in Administrator account. However, this can be
> dangerous, because any account that* **you** *create can be deleted by someone with appropriate
> permissions, while the built-in Administrator account cannot. If you (by accident) or someone
> else (perhaps intentionally) were to delete the only existing account that has full administrator
> level permissions, then you'll be at sea without a paddle. You can't rename the  the built-in
> Administrator account without the  psuedo-administrator account so it's time for a full re-
> install...*

# Directory And File Security

Once NT can reliably identify ( **authenticate**) every user, it can control the resources that they have
access to. The details of which user can access a given resource are maintained internally by NT as
**Access Control Lists** (ACLs).

The first and most obvious of these resources are the files and directories stored on the network
drives. Under NTFS, each individual file and directory can be assigned **permissions** using the
Security page, in the appropriate Properties dialog in Windows NT Explorer. By assigning access
permissions only to selected groups of accounts, you deny access to that file or directory to all users
who do not belong to those groups (unless you assigned permission directly to that user's account):

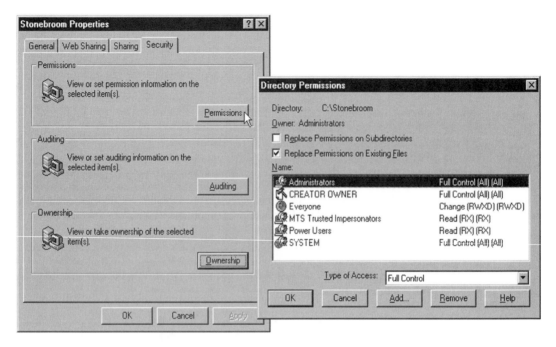

When you install NT, the default permission setting is to allow the special global account, Everyone, full access to all files and directories, meaning that there are no limitations. Remove this when you add user groups to a directory or file. You can also specify different types of access, such as Full Control, Read, Write or Change. You can also choose Special Access, in which you define the actions that can be performed down to a more granular level.

In other applications, the kinds of permissions you can assign to each group or user vary – for instance it doesn't make sense for a network printer to have a Read permission. In MSMQ, we have events like Create Queue and Receive Dead Letter.

# Windows NT Audit Logging

The worst way to find out if your system is secure enough is to discover that somebody has broken in and damaged it. However, if they break in and steal something without causing your server to fall over, you might never know – at least until it appears in the newspapers or in one of your competitors' new products.

## Audit Logging For Users And Resources

To find out if anything untoward is happening, like unwelcome visitors in the night, you can implement **auditing** on your system. This logs events to a disk file that you can examine at your leisure to see what's going on. A typical example is the WWW log that is produced by most Web servers. However, this is often better at providing information about legitimate visitors than unwelcome ones. In Windows NT, we can use the Audit Log to audit more obvious tasks.

Audit logging is available for a range of events. As part of each user account's profile you can record events, such as the success or failure of that user to log on or off the system, all attempts to shut down the server or change security policies, and of course their accesses to a range of resources. This dialog is available from the Policies | Audit menu:

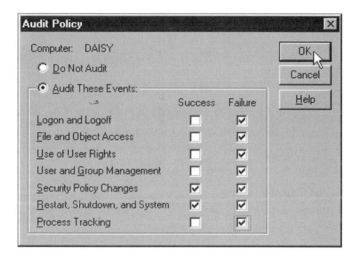

As well as logging the actions by user, you can log actions taken by groups of users on a specific resource, such as a file or directory. This is done from the Security page of the Windows NT Explorer Properties dialog for that file or directory (the dialog we saw when looking at file and directory security in the previous section):

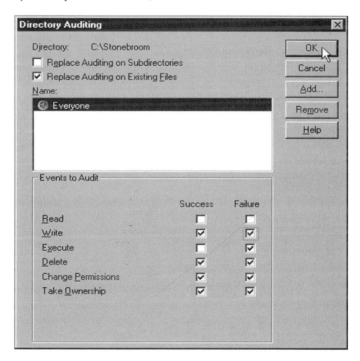

Other applications and services can write different events to the audit log. For example, MSMQ can log details of messages that failed to arrive, or attempts by users to access queues for which they have no permissions. The audit log can be viewed using Event Viewer (on the Administrative Tools section of the Start menu). Select Security from the Log menu.

One other technique is to use the Windows Performance Monitor tool to watch and record actions taking place– especially those involving the transmission of data over the network. There are also many separate applications that you can purchase for this task to offer more detailed information.

> *For a general view of all the security features implemented in Windows NT and the BackOffice applications and services, see*
> **www.microsoft.com/security/MSProductSecurity.htm**

# Securing Internet Information Server

**Internet Information Server** (IIS) is the built-in Web server for Windows NT, and version 4 (the current version of the product at the time of writing) adds many new features that allow fine-grained control over the way it works. It's now easy to set up separate **virtual sites**, specifying a different IP address and URL for each one; set script and executable permissions by directory; it's also easy to force executable programs to run in a separate area of memory from the Web server, and to tightly control user access to each part of each site that you host.

> *The IIS snap-in for the Microsoft Management Console (MMC) can be installed on a remote machine and it can be administered from there. See the Remote Administration topic (under Server Administration, Web and FTP Sites) in the Help files for more information.*

# The Internet Security Framework

As well as providing all the features required to distribute files and documents over the Internet or any other TCP/IP-enabled network, IIS sits in between your visitors and the Windows NT security manager. Together with several security technologies that we'll briefly visit in this section of the chapter, it offers a total package of system services that can be used to set up levels of security appropriate to your application. This is referred to as the **Internet Security Framework** (ISF).

# Handling Anonymous Users

While locking down your server and resources to prevent unauthorized access is fine for a local Intranet scenario, it's not much good if you intend to provide information and access to your applications for the great unwashed masses out on the Internet. This requires some way for visitors to log into your site anonymously. Even if they identify themselves–for example, by filling in a form– you still won't have a user account for them to log on to.

To achieve this, IIS has it's own account in NT which it uses to access resources on behalf of all anonymous visitors. By default this account is named IUSR_<*machinename*>–for example IUSR_KLINGON if you're a Star Trek fan –and has a randomly generated password. Anyone requesting a page or other resource from your server via IIS automatically gains the permissions that the IUSR account has.

This means, of course, that you need to set appropriate permissions for this account for each resource on your machine. Remember that the IUSR account will have access to any resources where the Everyone account is enabled:

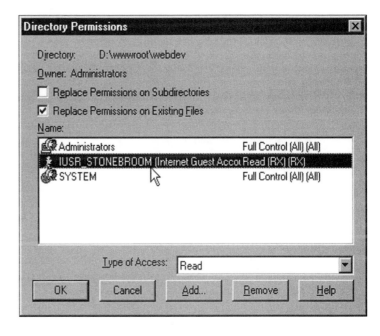

*To select a user account from the dialog that appears when you click* Add, *you have to click the* Show Users *button.*

# Identifying Users In IIS

For a Web-based *application*, rather than just a Web site, you'll need to be able to identify individual visitors, rather than having the IUSR account access resources on their behalf. This can be done in several ways, but ultimately comes back to linking each visitor with a valid Windows NT user account, other than the default IUSR anonymous account. This is where **authentication** over the Web comes into play.

## Web-based User Authentication

The simplest way to limit access to a file or resource on your Web server is to use the same authentication methods as users meet when they log onto their local network. Because all anonymous access is via the special IUSR account, you can prevent IIS from being able to access any resource, such as a file, by removing the IUSR and Everyone accounts from the list of those that have access to it. The NT security manager will prevent IIS from reading the file, and IIS will send back an Access Denied error message to the browser.

Under normal circumstances, you would expect the user to simply see an Access Denied message displayed in their browser. However, modern browsers are cleverer than that. When IIS sends the Access Denied message it can also include (in the HTTP headers) information about what types of authentication methods it supports. The browser can then send back a username and password, which can be used instead of the default IUSR account, to access the file or resource.

Most browsers will first send back the username and password that the user logged onto the client machine with—their standard network or logon username and password. If this results in another Access Denied message, the browser will prompt them with a dialog for another username/password combination to try.

This means that assigning permission for a resource only to a specific group of users, and removing the Everyone and IUSR accounts, will force the browser to present a username/password combination that authenticates the user in NT as a member of that group (as long as one of the authentication methods are enabled—we'll look at this next).

If they are logged on to their machine and home network with a suitable username and password (i.e. one that is also in the groups that have permission for this resource), they will automatically and transparently get access—their single 'NT Integrated Security' logon will be used. If they logged onto their own local network with a different password/ username combination (or used a lone machine, and didn't log on at all) they will only be able to access the resource on this machine as an authenticated NT user when they supply an appropriate username and password.

### Basic and Challenge/Response Authentication

Browsers other than Microsoft's Internet Explorer 3.0 or later transmit the username and password across the network to IIS in clear ASCII text form. This is obviously a critical disadvantage, because anyone out on the Internet monitoring the connection could read the details. This is called **Basic authentication**, and is usually avoided where possible.

Internet Explorer 3.0 and later also provide **Challenge/Response authentication**, where the client can convince the server that it knows the relevant username and password without actually transmitting it across the network—in much the same way as it does when you log on to your own LAN. Internet Explorer automatically chooses Challenge/Response over Basic authentication when talking to IIS, though it will use Basic authentication if Challenge/Response is not enabled (or with other Web servers, if it is not available).

> *Challenge/Response authentication involves the browser proving to the server that it knows the username and password of a suitable NT account, without sending the actual password over the network. Instead it encrypts the password locally using a complex 'one way' algorithm which creates a string that cannot be unencrypted with the same algorithm. The server applies the same algorithm to the password it holds for that user, and if the results are the same the client must know the password. However, anyone obtaining the encrypted version of the password cannot deduce the original, even if they know the algorithm that created it.*

You decide whether to support Basic and/or Challenge/Response authentication using the Microsoft Management Console (MMC)—in the Directory Security page of the Properties dialog for that directory. The preferred choice, if you can control which browsers will access your application, is to enable just Challenge/Response authentication. At the moment support for Challenge/Response authentication is limited to Internet Explorer 3 or higher:

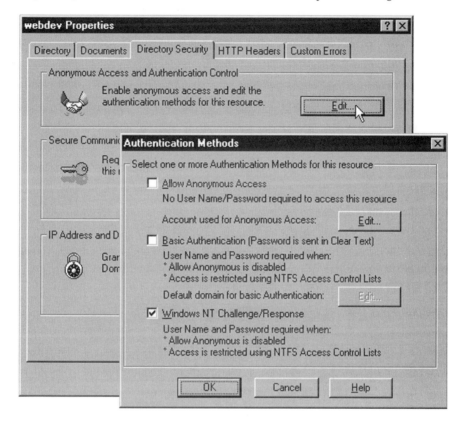

## Authentication In ASP And Custom Components

If you need to do more complex tasks that can be accomplished by just logging a user onto an NT account, you can take advantage of another technique. The HTTP header information that the browser sends along with each request it makes to your server can be used to get information about a logged-on user.

The standard HTTP header information includes a whole list of values—such things as the client's IP address and host name, their logon string (i.e. their username) and the authentication method used to identify them, the type of browser they are using, etc. Some of the HTTP values may be blank, but you can get a lot of useful information from the ones that aren't.

### The ASP ServerVariables Collection

The full set of HTTP values appears in the ASP **Request** object's **ServerVariables** collection. As an example of how we can use it, this ASP script produces a page containing the more useful ones:

```
<HTML>
<HEAD><TITLE>Reading the ServerVariables Collection</TITLE></HEAD>
<BODY>
<B>The contents of some of the ServerVariables collection are:</B><P>

<TABLE CELLPADDING=0 CELLSPACING=0>
<%
  Response.Write "<TR><TD>AUTH_PASSWORD = " _
      & Request.ServerVariables("AUTH_PASSWORD") & "</TD></TR>"
  Response.Write "<TR><TD>AUTH_TYPE = " _
      & Request.ServerVariables("AUTH_TYPE") & "</TD></TR>"
  Response.Write "<TR><TD>AUTH_USER = " _
      & Request.ServerVariables("AUTH_USER") & "</TD></TR>"
  '... etc
%>
</TABLE>
</BODY>
</HTML>
```

*A full list of all the **ServerVariables** collection members is included in the IIS Help pages. Look up ServerVariables in the Index.*

And here are the results when the client has logged on to Windows NT with an appropriate username and matching password (in other words where the Everyone and IUSR accounts had been removed from the directory's access list). Notice that because we logged in using Challenge/Response authentication, the **AUTH_PASSWORD** entry is empty:

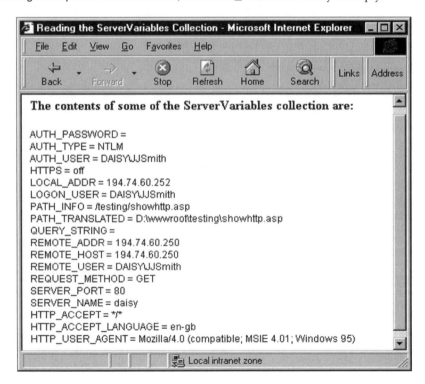

This means that we can redirect visitors, or control access to resources, using the information we obtain. In the following example, we're redirecting all connections that come in through the default port 80 to the default user areas of our site:

```
<%
   If Request.ServerVariables("SERVER_PORT") = "80" Then
     Response.Redirect "/defaultuser/welcome.htm"
   End If
%>
<HTML>
<HEAD>Welcome to the Wrox Car Company Dealer Pages</HEAD>
<BODY>
... rest of page for non-default port requests ...
</BODY>
</HTML>
```

Here, we're only including a link to the administration site if they successfully logged on to NT as user JJSmith:

```
<HTML>
<HEAD><TITLE>Navigation Control Using ServerVariables</TITLE></HEAD>
<BODY>
<H3>User Options:</H3>
<A HREF="">Change Display Configuration</A><BR>
<A HREF="">Change Display Colors</A><BR>
<A HREF="">Change Keyboard Configuration</A><BR>

<% If Request.ServerVariables("AUTH_USER") _
   = UCase(Request.ServerVariables("SERVER_NAME")) & "\JJSmith" Then %>

<A HREF="">Administer All Users</A><BR>
<A HREF="">Administer Logon Information</A>

<% End If %>

</BODY>
</HTML>
```

### Authentication Within Custom Components

We can get a reference to the ASP **ScriptingContext** object from wihin a custom component. The **ScriptingContext** object is a globally available object, which is generated for each ASP page request. Through it, we can then get a reference to the current **Request** object. ASP will execute a method of our component named **onStartPage** and pass it the **ScriptingContext** reference whenever a request for an ASP page is made. In Visual Basic this looks like:

```
Dim objRequest As ScriptingContext      'to hold the ASP scripting context

Public Sub onStartPage(objContext As ScriptingContext)
  Set objRequest = objContext.Request 'store reference to Request object
End Sub

Function GetUserName()   'returns the logon or username
   GetUserName = objRequest.ServerVariables("REMOTE_USER")
End Function
```

Bear in mind that many Web users dial into the Internet via an Internet Service Provider (ISP) that allocates IP addresses on demand from their own block of addresses—hence such a user's IP address will be different each time they visit your site. It means that you can't reliably identify users within your application from just their IP address unless you know that they have a permanent connection, or an ISP that implements non-dynamic address allocations.

> *For more information about using the ASP* **ServerVariables** *collection check out the IIS section of the Option Pack or Windows NT5 Help pages.*

# Secure and Encrypted Communication

The other major technique that you need to be able to apply to your site, if you want to pass sensitive information from client to server and vice versa, is how to provide a secure communication path between the two. This is where we come to look at **encryption**, and it is a huge topic in total. Here we'll take an overview of how it works—just enough so that you can see what is required to set it up.

## A Simple Guide to Encryption

There are two basic techniques for encrypting information, **symmetric encryption** (usually called *secret key* encryption) and **asymmetric encryption** (usually called *public key* encryption). We've chosen the names symmetric and asymmetric encryption because they are less confusing than secret key and public key encryption—ultimately both methods use a 'secret' key.

### Symmetric Encryption

**Symmetric encryption** is the oldest and best-known technique , based on the one you used at school to encode your love letters or 'secret gang' messages. A secret key, which can be a number, a word, or just a string of random letters, is applied to the text of a message so as to change the content in a particular way. It might be as simple as shifting each letter along by a set number of places in the alphabet. As long as both sender and recipient know the secret key, they can encrypt and decrypt all messages that use this key.

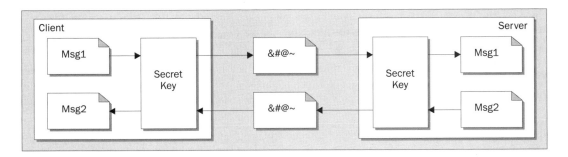

### Asymmetric Encryption

The problem with secret keys is how do you exchange them over the Internet or large network while preventing them from falling into the wrong hands? Anyone who knows the secret key can decrypt the messages. The answer is asymmetric encryption, where there are *two* related keys–a key pair. A **public key** is made freely available to anyone who might want to send you a message. A second **private key** is kept secret, so that only you know it.

The way it works is that any message (text, binary files, documents,  etc) encrypted using the **public** key can *only* be decrypted by applying the same algorithm to it, only using the matching **private** key. Vice versa, any message encrypted using the **private** key can only be decrypted using the matching **public** key.

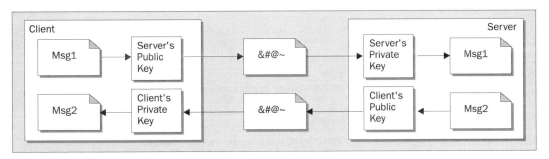

This means that you don't have to worry about passing public keys over the Internet– after all they're supposed to be public. The one problem with asymmetric encryption, however, is that it's quite slow compared to symmetric encryption, because it requires far more processing power to both encrypt and decrypt the content of the message.

## About Digital Certificates

In order to use asymmetric encryption, there has to be a way for users to discover each other's public keys. The usual technique is the use of **digital certificates**, or certificates for short. A certificate is simply a package of information that identifies a user or a server, containing things like the organization name, the  organization that issued the certificate, the user's email address, country, and of course their public key.

When a server and client require a secure encrypted communication, they send a query over the network to the other party, who sends back a copy of their certificate. The other party's public key can simply be extracted from the certificate. However, certificates can do more than this. Here we come back to authentication, because a certificate can also be used to uniquely identify the holder.

### Certificate Authorities

Recognized and trusted organizations, called **Certificate Authorities** (CAs), issue certificates to individuals and corporations. These certificates contain not only details about the holder and their public key, but also the public key of the CA. Because reputable CAs apply rigorous checks to see that applicants actually are who they claim to be (using tax and business registers, etc.) you are deemed to be able to trust the information in certificates they issue to be accurate. They also make available (through their Web site) their own **public** key certificate–this is called their **root certificate**. Many browsers come with the popular CA root certificates already installed:

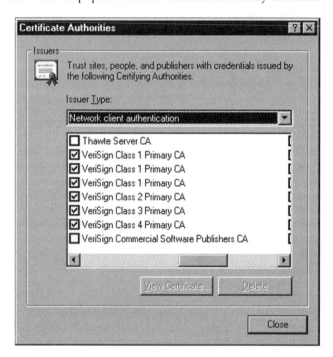

Before issuing a user who wishes to be certificated with their own personal certificate, the CA digitally 'signs' the certificate using their (the CA's) **private** key. This means that if you can decrypt this signature using the CA's **public** key, you know that it's a valid certificate from that CA.

### Verifying Certificates

So, one party can provide the other with their certificate, and at the same time send them an extract of it, which is encrypted with that party's **private** key. This extract is usually called the **message digest**. The recipient can then check that they are who they claim to be by decrypting the message digest using the **public** key in the certificate, and seeing if the results agree with the certificate contents. If they do, the sender must know the private key that matches this certificate, and so they must be the legitimate holder of the certificate. All this usually happens behind the scenes automatically, but if you want to work with certificates you need to know the principles.

> *Of course this all falls apart if the real holder of the certificate has allowed someone else to discover their private key, and it indicates how important it is to keep your own private keys safe. For a detailed explanation of the principles of digital certificates, check out the Tutorials available at* `http://www.verisign.com/repository/index.html`.

## Using Digital Certificates

One way of easily adding security to our DNA applications is to use certificates in our communication with clients. This can be done in two main ways.

- ❑ Firstly, we can use digital certificates to authenticate visitors and to allow them to authenticate our server—so that both sides are convinced that they actually are connected to who they think they are.

- ❑ Secondly, we can also use digital certificates to encrypt the communication, by using the other party's public keys that they contain. However, as we mentioned earlier, asymmetric (public key) encryption is slow. Instead, we use a combination of encryption methods to make it all work much more quickly.

We'll look at these two techniques next. The process of setting up a digital certificate on your server is quite complex, and is not covered in detail here. For more information check out the Help files for both IIS and Certificate Server that are supplied with the NT4 Option Pack and as part of NT5.

> *Server certificates and client certificates are fundamentally the same. IIS can use the certificates that are stored in the browser, which is installed on the server. This is one reason why you must install IE4 on your server when you install the Windows NT4 Option Pack.*

### Authentication And NT Account Mapping

In the Secure Communications dialog (available from the IIS Properties dialog) for a directory or virtual site, you can tell IIS whether to accept certificates for that directory, and whether to actually demand them:

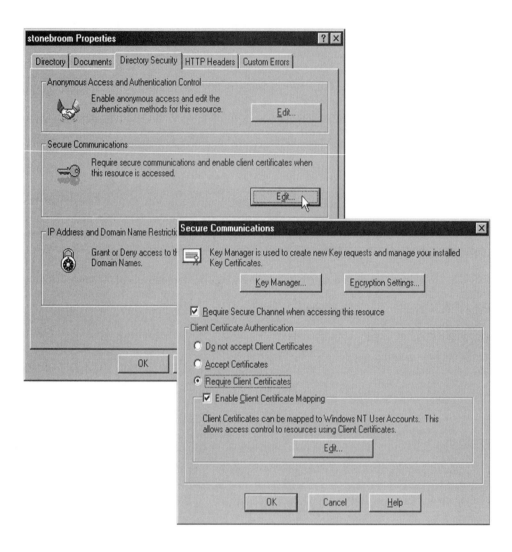

When IIS connects with a client that requires access to this directory(1), it will send the client its own (server) certificate together with a request for the client's certificate(2). The client checks the server's certificate against its copy of the appropriate CA root certificate(3), then sends confirmation of success back to the server together with a copy of its client certificate(4). The server can then verify the client's certificate against its copy of the appropriate CA root certificate(5), and, once it's happy with the result, start normal communication with the client(6):

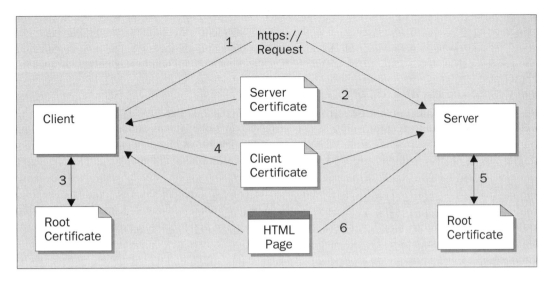

The clever part is that IIS can use the contents of the client's certificate to map that user to an existing NT user account on the server. This can be done as a basic one-to-one mapping, where a separate account is required for each client. In the Secure Communications dialog, turn on **Enable Client Certificate Mapping** and click **Edit**. Here, we've linked the certificate for our salesperson to the Windows NT **external sales** account:

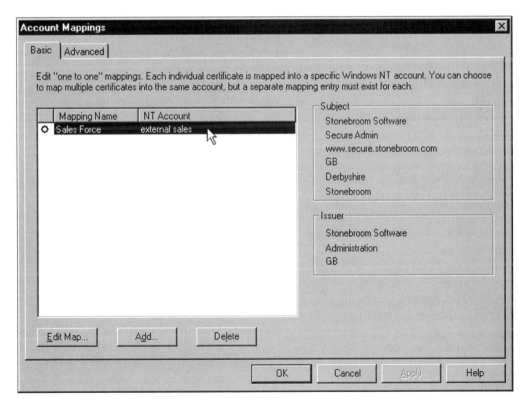

You can also set up a many-to-one mapping using the Advanced page of this dialog. In this case, certain parts of the certificate are matched (rather like wildcards) to a single user account. For example, you could map all users who have Joe's Car Co as the Organization in their certificate to a NT user single account that provides access to data appropriate to all employees of that company.

### Secure Communication With SSL Or PCT

The above discussion has only used certificates to identify the client and server to each other. As well as this, we can use the information in the certificate to implement secure encrypted communication. The common standard for this is **Secure Sockets Layer** (SSL), but IIS also supports the upcoming **Private Communication Technology** (PCT) standard as well.

By setting the Require Secure Channel option in the Secure Communications dialog that we saw in the previous section, we instruct IIS to set up encrypted communication with the browser. This requires that the browser connect to an address that uses the `https://` rather than `http://` protocol in the URL. The connection is made, and the server and client exchange certificates, in the same way as we saw earlier.

However, now there is one extra step. One party (usually the client) creates a new and unique session key, and encrypts it using the other party's public key—obtained, of course, from their certificate. The other party can decrypt it using their private key, and from that point on this 'secret' key is used to encrypt all communication between the client and server. This is symmetric encryption, which is much faster than asymmetric (public key) encryption. At the same time the browser will display a 'lock' symbol, and sometimes a message, to show that a secure connection is established.

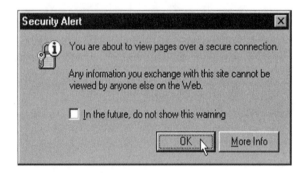

The secret session key is only used for the current secure connection, and is destroyed when the browser shuts down or when it leaves the secure site. A new one is created for each connection, so although symmetric encryption is easier for an intruder to crack, the keys will be constantly changing.

SSL and PCT are useful in many situations—for example, they are used by MSMQ to pass encrypted messages between servers. They also allow secure authentication for browsers that don't support the Challenge/Response method. Once the secure connection is established, you can use Basic authentication to collect username/password combinations from the user as they access different resources without risk.

### Using Digital Certificates With ASP

While certificates provide a way to automatically map visitors to a specific Windows NT user account, they can be used in a more flexible way with ASP. The ASP **Request** object provides a collection called **ClientCertificate**, which is normally empty when users access your site anonymously. However, when they present a client certificate along with their request for a resource, the values it contains are placed into the **ClientCertificate** collection.

The following example simply lists all the members of the **Request.ClientCertificate** collection in the browser, by looping through it with a **For Each ... Next** construct:

```
<HTML>
<HEAD><TITLE>Reading a Client Certificate</TITLE></HEAD>
<BODY>
<B>The contents of your Client Certificate are:</B><P>
<TABLE CELLPADDING=0 CELLSPACING=0>
<%
For Each keyItem In Request.ClientCertificate()
   strValue = Request.ClientCertificate(keyItem)
   If Len(strValue) > 90 Then strValue = Left(strValue, 60) & ".. etc."
   Response.Write "<TR><TD>" & keyItem & " = " & strValue & "</TD></TR>"
Next
%>
</TABLE>
</BODY>
</HTML>
```

The result when accessing a secure site of a local software provider looks like this:

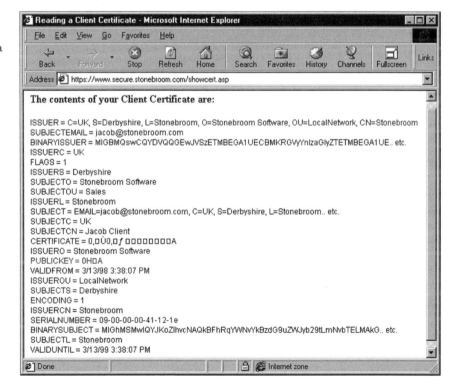

287

*You can see that the issuer of this certificate was not a publicly renowned CA like Verisign or Thawte Consulting, but in fact our own company—this is a **self-issued certificate**. The values shown are those of the client's certificate (the one they presented to our server with the request for this page) and you can see that the ISSUER and SUBJECT (client) values are basically the same. You'll see more of how this is done when we look at Windows **Certificate Server**.*

So if we can retrieve the details of the client's certificate, we can use them to change the way our application behaves. For example, we can redirect all visitors from an organization called Joes Car Company to a specific area of our Web site using:

```
<%
strOrg = Request.ClientCertificate(SUBJECTO)  'organization
If strOrg = "Joe's Car Company" Then
    Response.Redirect "/JoesCars/Default.htm"
End If
%>
```

A more mundane use is to welcome your visitors by name:

```
<%
strName = Request.ClientCertificate(SUBJECTCN)  'common name
strLocat = Request.ClientCertificate(SUBJECTL)  'location
%>
...
<H2>Hello <% = strName %><H2>
We hope the weather in <% = strLocat %> is better than it is here!
```

*And of course you might like to keep a record of your visitors' email addresses for future communication. All the information in their certificate is available, though remember that it will only be presented if you set up your server to Require A Client Certificate—as we have done in our earlier example. If you select Accept Certificates, the browser will not send one even if it has a suitable one available.*

## Windows NT Certificate Server

In an earlier example, you saw a site set up to provide authentication and encryption by using digital certificates. Normally, to obtain a certificate, you would visit a CA's Web site and fill in the details required. However, now you can issue your own digital certificates using the new **Certificate Server** service that is supplied with the Windows NT4 Server (not Workstation) Option Pack, and as an integral part of Windows NT5.

At the time of writing, Certificate Server suffered a couple of limitations—particularly the inability to create a certificate hierarchy based on a CA's root certificate. However you can use it to create your own root certificate, and use Certificate Server to automatically generate and distribute client certificates to your visitors. The problem is that because your certificates are rooted outside a widely known CA, visitors will get a warning in their browser that the certificate is not from a known issuer.

Whether this really is a problem depends on what you are using the certificates for. They will still provide secure communication across the network using encryption, so they are useful for Intranet and Extranet applications even if you decide against using them on the Web as a whole.

*If you are planning to set up your own CA using Certificate Server, remember that it's the CA itself that people have to trust and respect, not just the certificates. If the CA is unknown or cannot be trusted, the certificates it issues are worthless for the purpose of reliably identifying users.*

### Installing Root Certificates

When you install Certificate Server, it prompts for the details of your company and automatically generates your enterprise's root certificate. From that, you can create client and server certificates by applying for them via a special Web page that is supplied with Certificate Server. You can also use the Certificate Server Web pages to install your root certificate on other machines (which you'll need to do if they are to be able to verify your client and server certificates), and to monitor requests for certificates from users. The main menu page is in the folder where you installed Certificate Server:

As an example, here the browser is fetching the root certificate for the DAISY enterprise from our server using the special Web page supplied with Certificate Server:

Once installed, it appears in the list of certificate authorities in the  browser's Internet Options | Content | Authorities dialog:

### *Delivering Client Certificates*

The next step is for the user to apply for a client certificate. This is done from another of the standard Certificate Server pages, where clients fill in the details about themselves that will appear in the certificate:

The certificate request is then submitted to Certificate Server. By default, it will just issue a valid certificate by return, and this is automatically installed in the browser. Afterwards, the user can view the installed client (or Personal) certificates from the Internet Options | Content | Personal dialog:

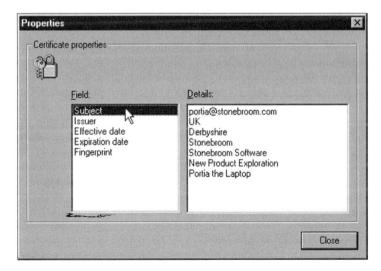

*Of course, we can personalize the Certificate Server Web pages to suit our own enterprise, and even create new ones using the same URLs as targets for the links in our new pages.*

## Installing Server Certificates

Server certificates are really just the same as client certificates, but are installed on the server so that IIS can use them instead of the browser. To get IIS to recognize the root certificates that are supplied with IE4, you run the **iisca.exe** program that comes with Certificate Server (and is placed in your **\winnt\system32** directory) in an NT Command window.

### Using Windows NT Key Manager

To request and install a server certificate in IIS, you use the Key Manager utility. From the Directory Security page, available from any directory's Properties dialog, open the Secure Communications dialog (the one we used to require a client certificate earlier) and click Key Manager. Here we can create a new key, which can be processed by Certificate Server to produce a server certificate. This starts a Wizard that collects all the information required:

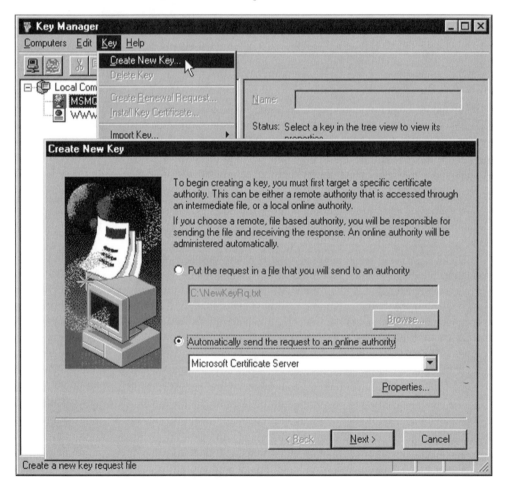

*The Wizard can also be used to create key requests for submission to an independent CA for verification.*

Once your new certificate is returned from a CA it is installed using the Install Key Certificate option in Key Manager. If you're using Certificate Server it will return and begin installing your new key certificate automatically. Part of the installation process is to bind the certificate to the appropriate Web site. If you host multiple Web sites on your server, a server certificate can be bound to one or more of these. Alternatively it can be used with all 'unassigned' requests.

However, when you implement a separate section of your server as a secure area, it's often useful to create it as a separate virtual site and assign a different IP address to it. The Server Bindings dialog appears as you install your certificate, and here we're assigning it to a virtual site:

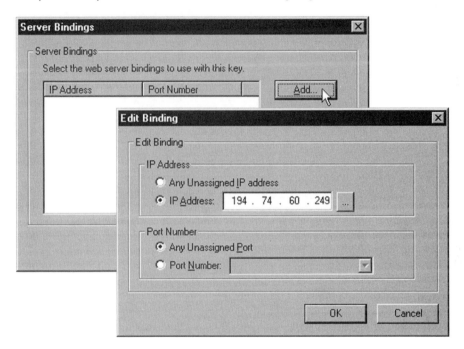

Once complete the certificate and binding appear in Key Manager. Notice the certificate for Microsoft Message Queue Server ( MSMQ) that is already there. This is created and installed as part of the MSMQ setup, and is used for encrypting messages as they are passed between and stored in message queues:

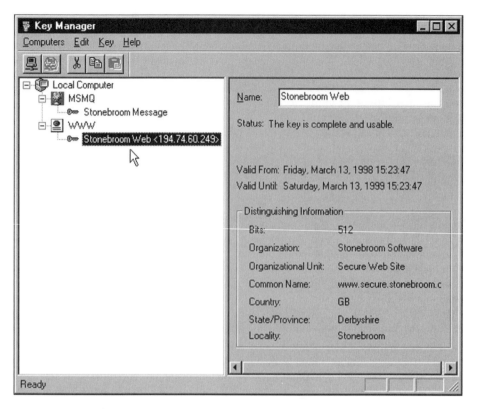

This is another reason why you need to know a little about certificates, and we'll come back to it when we look at MSMQ Security issues later on.

### Certificate Issuing Policies

For the certificates you issue to be of any value, you'll want to confirm the details about users who request certificates before you issue them. By default—as you've just seen—Certificate Server will accept the request and issue a certificate immediately. This is useful while you set up and test the system, then when you are ready you can configure Certificate Server to do more detailed checking of requests.

Detailed control of certificate issuing can be achieved by creating **custom policy modules** as COM components in VB or C++, and installing them into Certificate Server. For more information see the Writing Custom Policy Modules section of the Certificate Server Help pages.

## Other IIS Security Features

There are a couple of other ways you can control access to your Web server, though they are generally less useful—however, you may find that they fit in with your applications. In particular, the first of these can be used when you implement an Extranet, where you only want to permit access for a selected set of customers.

## Limiting Access By IP Address

If you only want to allow particular users or groups of users to access your site, you can use the IP Address and Domain Restrictions dialog to grant access only to specific IP addresses, and deny all others. An alternative, though generally less useful, strategy is to deny access to specific IP addresses and allow access to all others:

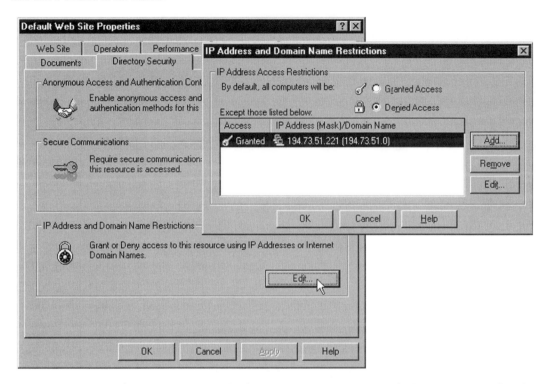

However, recall that (as we discussed earlier) many Web users dial into the Internet via an ISP who allocates IP addresses on demand, and so this type of user's IP address will be different each time they visit your site.

## Using Non-Default Port Numbers

The default port that the WWW service listens on is port 80 (and port 443 for SSL/PCT requests). You can set IIS to listen on other ports as well, and remove port 80 if required. This way visitors will have to know and specify as part of the URL the correct port number in order to gain access to your site, for example **http://yoursite.com:8671/default.htm**. You change the default port allocations in the Properties dialog for that directory, or use the Advanced dialog to set up multiple ports:

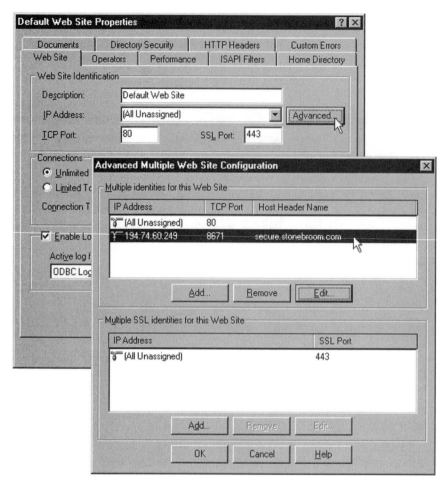

This isn't going to do much good if you then publish the full URL, but may be useful if you want to hide your site from casual browsers, or from search engines and agents that generate random IP numbers to see if any servers respond. Anyone can search the publicly available lists of domain name allocations to find you site's IP address anyway, but using a non-standard port makes it that bit harder to gain access.

## Good Practice With IIS

There are some general points that you should keep in mind when setting up IIS:

❑ **Disable any Internet services that you don't need**, for example Telnet, Gopher, and–where appropriate–FTP. FTP is not able to encrypt logon passwords, so it always presents a security risk. If you need to enable FTP, make sure you remove Execute permission (in the NT Explorer Properties | Security | Permissions dialog) for any FTP-accessible directories to prevent programs that are uploaded from being run on your server.

❑ **Review any virtual roots (aliases) that are set up** to ensure that they don't allow access to files in directories or subdirectories below the target directory, unless this is appropriate. Normally, visitors will be unable to access any directories outside the virtual Web and FTP roots (by default **\InetPub\WWWRoot** and **\InetPub\FTPRoot**), but a virtual directory can point anywhere.

❑ **Disable Execute permission on all WWW directories** unless they include DLLs or other CGI executable files that need to be executed as part of your application. You might even want to disable Script permission for directories that don't include scripts. Make sure that Write permission (which is off by default) has not been turned on, and that Directory Browsing is not enabled.

❑ **Keep scripts and executable files in separate directories** and remove the Read access permission from this directory. If scripts contain sensitive information, such as data source passwords and connection strings, you might even want to create server components (as shown in Chapter 2) to encapsulate the information and carry out the task instead.

❑ Decide whether you need to use the **IP filtering feature** to grant or deny access to specific visitors, and if you should use a **non-default port number** to make your Web server less visible to casual visitors.

❑ **Apply the appropriate Windows NT permissions** to each directory in your site, and even to specific files, for each account group and the IUSR account (using the NT User Manager program). If the IUSR account does not have access permission for a file it will force visitors to identify themselves with usernames and passwords that NT does recognize.

*In IIS 3, there was only one option for Execute permission in a virtual directory (or Alias). This had to be set (ticked) for ASP and other scripts to be executed, and this allowed executable programs to run as well. In IIS4 there are two options available in the Properties dialog for any directory (not just virtual directories). The Script option allows ASP and other scripts to run, while the Execute option allows executable programs such as **.exe** and **.dll** files to run.*

*For a detailed explanation of the security features implemented in Internet Information Server see the topic Security in the Server Administration section of the IIS documentation.*

# Summary

While this isn't a book about Windows security, you can't hope to build secure DNA applications unless you are aware of the issues involved once you step outside the safe confines of your corporate office network. Although existing security procedures may be in place on your LAN, they often aren't sufficient to properly protect the resources it contains once you start to use it as an Intranet for Windows DNA-style applications.

More to the point, once the great divide is crossed and you offer access to either a limited number of people (as an Extranet), or the whole world via the Internet, you need to be a lot more concerned with securing your system as a whole.

In this chapter we've overviewed the concepts of Windows NT Integrated Security, and seen the major issues that are involved in protecting other resources from intruders. In particular we've seen how Internet Information Server (IIS) fits into the picture, and how you can create specialist security features within your components and ASP scripts to offer even finer access control.

We covered:

❑ An overview of Windows NT Integrated Security features.
❑ The three core concepts of security: Authentication, Encryption, and Auditing.
❑ The particular issues that are involved in Web-based applications.
❑ The ways that we can implement these core concepts in our applications.

In the next chapter we'll complete our look at security topics with a particular focus on Component, MTS, and MSMQ issues. You'll see how the concepts we've covered in this chapter are firmly bound into the way that security is implemented within the working parts of your application—the parts that you as a programmer create.

# Configuring MTS, MSMQ and SQL Server

In the previous chapter we looked (albeit briefly) at the issues involved in authenticating users for our applications, through Windows NT and Internet Information Server (IIS). Now we can move on to see how this affects the design and construction of a DNA-based application. DNA applications follow a structured three-tier approach to design and implementation. Although this is considerably simpler than the multi-layer designs of some traditional applications, it still requires some careful planning as to how each tier will interface with those above and below it.

In this chapter, we'll finish off the 'teaching' section of this book with a look at a whole range of issues that affect how successfully and reliably your applications work when you move them from that development server out into the 'real world'.

The issues fall into three main areas, mirroring the three parts of a DNA application that we basically ignored in the previous chapter. The areas are **Microsoft Transaction Server** (MTS), **Message Queue Server** (MSMQ), and your chosen **Data Source**. Before we go into these in detail, however, we'll spend a little time looking at the way that communication between them and other components works—with the emphasis on the way that each one authenticates the 'user' that invokes them.

So, this chapter covers:

- ❑ How the layers and components of a DNA application authenticate each user
- ❑ Configuration and security issues concerned with Microsoft Transaction Server
- ❑ Configuration and security issues concerned with Message Queue Server
- ❑ Security issues connected with exposing data sources over the Web

We'll begin with an overview of the authentication process, to see where we need to configure each layer and how we should approach it.

# Communication Between Components

When we build and test DNA applications, it's easy to just log in as the local system administrator and run the application. In many cases, we might even do this on the machine that hosts the underlying services, such as IIS, MTS, MSMQ and SQL Server. It's fast and there are no network delays, and—more to the point—the application doesn't keep complaining about user permissions and denying access to components or files. In a complex application it is hard enough to get it all together, without any extra grief caused by NT being awkward about who gets to access what resources.

This is fine until you move the application to its real working environment where it all falls over because the security environment, server configuration, and NT Services settings are different. To avoid this, you need to be familiar with the way that DNA allows the application components to authenticate each other, without relying on specific user permissions.

# DNA Authentication Processes

In essence our DNA applications are three-tiered, providing a **client layer**, a **business rules layer**, and a **data store layer**. However, in reality, there are several individual components within the business rules layer that have to be able to communicate with each other. We're talking about components in the widest sense here—they could be custom compiled components (in VB, C++ or Java, for example), Service software such as ODBC drivers, ASP scripts, etc.

These components pass information back and forth, and can create instances of other components in order to use their services. Ultimately, they will talk to a data store of some kind, perhaps through a message queue. Alternatively, they may interface with legacy systems via SNA Server or a similar bridging software layer. At each point of contact along the line, there will be a check that the calling component has the appropriate Windows NT authorization to use the services of the next component.

However, DNA (through MTS, MSMQ, SQL Server, etc.) defines ways of configuring each component-to-component interface to provide two big advantages:

- ❑ A more flexible yet secure environment for your application
- ❑ Easier administration and maintenance while the application is in use

We'll see how this is achieved in the remainder of this chapter.

## *The Different User Contexts*

In the following diagram, you can see the most common interfaces where the authentication and checking of permissions is applied:

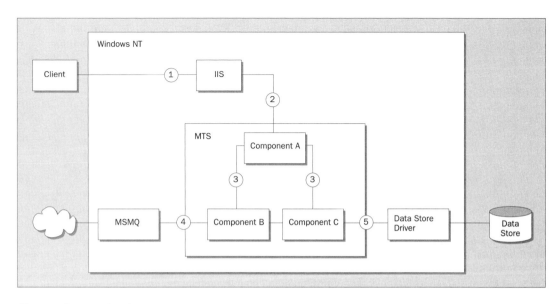

The numbers in the diagram represent:

❑ **1** - The client accessing our application can be authenticated in a variety of ways. They access the server via IIS, and this can also encrypt the communication if appropriate. This is where we left off in the previous chapter, when we looked at NT Authentication and IIS security. The end result is that we will either have identified the user via NT and IIS, or they will be accessing our application as an anonymous users under the IUSR_*machinename* account allocated to IIS.

❑ **2** - IIS now interfaces with one or more components on the server to create the returned page. These could be running stand-alone on the server, in which case the user context from IIS–a validated NT account or the IUSR account–must have access to the component's files (including any system components such as ADO and OLEDB drivers). In our example, however, the components are running inside MTS, and this changes the way the authentication process works. We use the MTS Explorer to define a set of **roles** for each **package** and map NT accounts to these roles. The components in each package can use this information to check the permissions for users that access them.

❑ **3** - If a component creates an instance of another component, or just uses its services, it must have permission to do so. We can assign a user context (an NT account) to each MTS package, and MTS will use that account to access other components outside the package rather than the original user's account. If the components are running within the *same* package, however, permissions are not checked.

❑ **4** - If a component needs to work with MSMQ it must have the appropriate permissions to access queues and to send messages. If security has been enabled in MTS, and an NT user account has been assigned to the package containing this component, the user context that will be presented to MSMQ will be that of the MTS *package* account, not the original NT *user* account.

❑ **5** - Finally, to access a data store, a component will again assume the user account context assigned to its package. These details will be passed on to the data store, which must have appropriate permission set up for that account–again, not the original NT user. It's also possible that the data store driver software will access the data store using a different account if this is set up within the driver software, as is sometimes the case with ODBC drivers.

*Integrated security with SQL Server and IIS on different machines has certain caveats applied to it. Resources that require Challenge/Response authentication to access resources on another physical NT machine will not be able to do so unless the machine running IIS is a domain controller. This implies that you will not be able to connect to SQL Server on another physical NT machine if the IIS Machine is not the controller for the domain. In this case, basic authentication can be used instead of Challenge/Response, and users won't be able to access Web pages and connect to the SQL Server with their NT user accounts. This limitation ties back to the inability to delegate. When IIS attempts to make the Name Pipes connection to SQL Server, it will not be able to encrypt a token because it does not have the user's password to use as the encryption key.*

### User Impersonation

The important point to realize is that the account used to access components or services downstream from the user does not have to be the actual user's account. This works in much the same way as when we map multiple users to a single Windows NT account within IIS–either with Certificates or through the anonymous IUSR account. In our DNA application, we can use the features of MTS to map multiple users to one or more Windows NT accounts that are created solely with the purpose of accessing downstream components and resources.

All this swapping of account contexts may seem like it's only making the whole process more complex. Of course, when you are logged on as the system administrator, or if you haven't enabled security on the components and the services they use, there's no problem–it all runs like clockwork. In the next section we'll see how we make sure it still runs like clockwork when we come to deploy it in the 'real world'.

# Configuring Transaction Server

In the previous section of this chapter we've seen how MTS can impersonate users of the application by presenting a different NT account to the components or services it accesses. However, this isn't mandatory–you can use MTS with this feature disabled and rely on the traditional method of each resource identifying the original user via NT's security manager. In fact this is the default setting for MTS.

MTS also offers a third way of managing users and controlling access to other resources. This takes advantage of the ability of MTS to identify the original user through methods of the **ObjectContext** object created for each component. To use this technique you write code within the component to retrieve information about the original user, and hence you can change the behavior of the component based on the user. So, we have three situations to consider:

- ❏ Traditional configuration and user access control through individual Windows NT accounts. These can be separate user accounts , accounts that are mapped to one or more NT accounts through certificates, or the anonymous IUSR account.
- ❏ Package-level and component-level access control through roles defined for each package and/or component. This is termed **declarative security**.
- ❏ Component-level access control using code within a component. This is referred to as **programmatic security**, and can be combined with declarative security to provide the most flexible solutions.

# Traditional Security Configuration

We won't spend time here looking at the traditional security configuration techniques in detail, because they are just the ones you use when creating applications that don't incorporate MTS. Instead, they depend on each component file and resource being allocated the appropriate permissions under Windows NT for the accounts that the application will run under. For a Web-based application, this will usually be the IUSR account, unless you need to limit access to individual users or groups of users. The techniques for mapping users to groups were described in the previous chapter.

A couple of points to watch out for are that you need to assign Read and/or Execute permissions for all the individual components and resources required for your application. This includes many of the files in the **Winnt** and **System32** directories, as well as the specialist components in the **Program Files\Common Files\System** directories, where the ADO and OLEDB components are stored. There may also be other components that are specific to your applications.

# Declarative Security Configuration

To take advantage of the security and configuration technologies that MTS brings to the party, you should seriously consider using **declarative security**. This is the technique we described in the previous section of the chapter, where each component within a package checks the validity of each user against a set of roles defined for that package. It also uses its own special account to access other components.

## MTS Roles and Identities

MTS defines the concept of **roles** for each package installed within it. These roles are simply lists of NT user groups and accounts that should have access to components in that package. If the user isn't authenticated as one of the users in the list, or as a member of one of the groups, they are denied permission to use the component.

> *In general—as with traditional Windows NT security methods—it's best to create groups and assign individual users to the appropriate groups, rather than assigning permissions directly to user accounts. This is the technique we'll be describing. Bear in mind that user accounts can be assigned to objects as well, if this is required in your application—such as the IUSR account or specific special user accounts. Be sure to use DOMAIN accounts and groups, and **not** local machine accounts which may not be available when the application is moved to its final location.*

When a component calls the services of another component or service, it does so using a 'user' account. As we've seen, this doesn't have to be the original user's account. In declarative security, we allow the component to act on the original user's behalf by defining a different account to be used in this context. This account is the **identity** of the package that contains the component.

### A Roles and Identity Example

As an example, which shows more clearly what the **identity** of a package does, take the Wrox Car Co application. Here we might have two types of user. One would be the sales staff in the showroom using an interface that allows them to query customer and car details, and place orders with the head office. The second would be anonymous users out on the Web who could place an order for a car, but could only query car details and not customer details.

The two types of user could access the application through different sets of components. However, as the act of placing an order is identical, the main components would be the same. The difference would only be in the 'top-level' components that they accessed directly. This means that we can set up roles and identities that allow each type of user access only to the appropriate components:

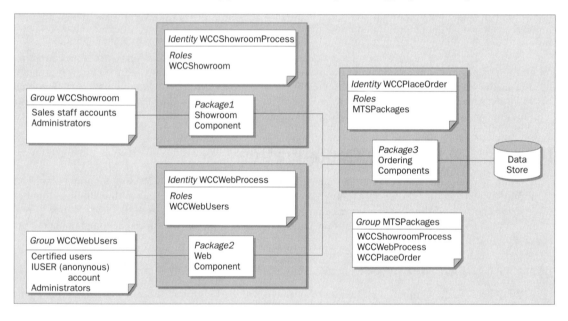

In the diagram, you can see that we have created three NT account groups. The group WCCShowroom contains the individual accounts for the sales staff in the showroom and the system administrator. The group WCCWebUsers contains three accounts. The first is the anonymous IUSR account, and the second is an account that is set up solely to be used with mappings from client certificates (you'll recall from the previous chapter that IIS can map selected parts of a users client certificate to a Windows NT account). Finally, the third account is that of the system administrator.

The last account group, MTSPackages, also contains three accounts. These accounts are the identities that are assigned to the different MTS packages in the application. As you'll see next, this group makes it easier to set up the access permissions for 'second-level' packages, and specify the login information for SQL Server or any other data source.

The MTS package containing the component accessed by showroom staff has only the WCCShowroom group assigned to its **roles**. Therefore only users in this group will be able to access the component. The **identity** of this package is WCCShowroomProcess, which is a member of the MTSPackages group. This account will be used to access the components in the third package.

Likewise, the MTS package containing the Web user component will only be accessible to members of the WCCWebUsers group. The **identity** of this package is WCCWebProcess, which is also a member of the MTSPackages group–and this account will be used to access the components in the third package.

The third package has the group MTSPackages assigned to its **roles,** and has the account WCCPlaceOrder as its **identity**. It will use this account to access SQL Server. In SQL Server we give this group access to the tables and stored procedures required to actually place the order.

The end result of all this is that showroom staff and Web visitors can only access and run the components in their own 'top-level' package, i.e. Package1 or Package2. They don't have an account in the MTSPackages group, so they cannot directly access either the second-level components (in Package3) or the database.

> *We could also have used an intermediate group, say WCCOrderProcess, and assigned the WCCShowroomProcess and WCCWebProcess accounts to it. Then we would specify this group in the **roles** for the third component, instead of MTSPackages. This may be appropriate in a more complex application. It's also appropriate to have more than one group assigned to the roles of a package if you want to allow different permissions to members of each group.*

### Role Membership Of Components

After assigning groups (or individual users) to the **roles** of a package, we define the mapping between individual components in the package and these roles. When declarative security is enabled, only the components that are mapped to the roles of the package will be able to perform authorization checking.

Using MTS Explorer we define this mapping for each component. This means that if a package has more than one role defined for it, each component can be mapped to a different role–allowing a finer level of control than when there is a single role defined for a package. You'll see we create roles, add users to them, and map them to components a little later.

> *Components don't have their own **identity**. They always assume the identity of the package that they are contained in when declarative security is in use.*

### Package Identity and Connection Pooling

There is one other benefit of using a single NT account (or a limited number of accounts) to access the data source. Most ODBC and OLEDB data store drivers implement connection pooling, which greatly increases efficiency when regular access to the data is required–something very likely in a Web-based application.

Normally, the user name and password are part of the connection string used to access the data store, and this means that each connection can only be reused by the same account. On an Intranet where you have a large number of user accounts, the different username and password combinations will require a new connection to be created each time. One way round this is to create account groups based on the permissions required, and allocate all users to an appropriate group—reducing the number of different connection strings. However under MTS, where the data access components can all run under the same **identity** for all users, connection re-use is much more likely and so the connection pooling feature provides a real performance boost.

## Administrative Security - The System Package

MTS provides a special package named System, which controls administrative access to MTS Explorer itself. By default, any user who has access to the machine where MTS is installed (or another machine if remote administration is enabled) can change the configuration of packages and components. We can prevent this by enabling security on the System package, so that only the users who appear in the roles of the System package will be able to administer MTS.

There are two pre-defined roles for the System package, Administrator (full access) and Reader (read-only access). You should add your administrator account to the System package's Administrator role, and any other relevant accounts to the Administrator and Reader roles, then enable security on the System package in the same way as you would for any other package.

Once declarative security is enabled, only members of the System package Administrator role will be able to administer MTS and the other packages installed in it. It's vitally important to ensure that you have assigned at least the Administrators group to the System roles, otherwise you will be locked out. After changing the settings, restart the package or reboot your server to initialize them.

> **Read this twice and remember it—always add the Administrators group or your own group or account to the System package Administrator role before enabling declarative security for a package. Otherwise you will be locked out and will have to re-install MTS to regain control.**

## Assigning Roles and Identities

To perform package and component configuration, we use the MTS Explorer snap-in for the Microsoft Management Console (MMC). Here we've opened out the tree to show the WCCFinanceTest package we installed back in Chapter 3. You can see that MTS Explorer provides our package with two main folders, Components and Roles:

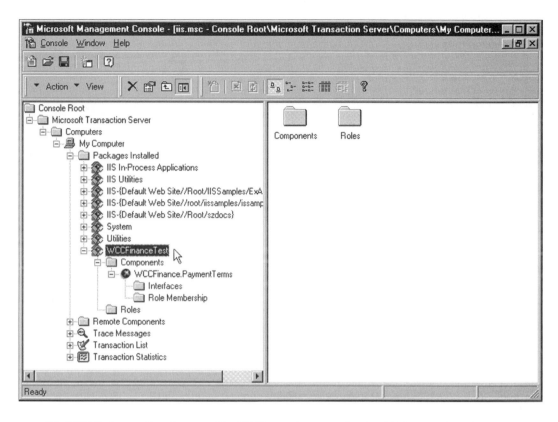

*The **MTS Software Development Kit** (SDK) contains a set of scriptable **Automation objects** that you can install into MTS. These allow you to write scripts to automate the operations that you normally carry out in MTS Explorer. For more details see the Automating MTS Administration section of the MTS Administrator's Guide.*

## Creating Roles for a Package

This first step is to add the roles we need to the package. In our case there is just one,
WCCWebUsers. Role names must be unique within a package, though the same role name can be
used in different packages. To open the New Role dialog right-click the Roles folder and select New
| Role, or use the drop-down Action menu in the toolbar:

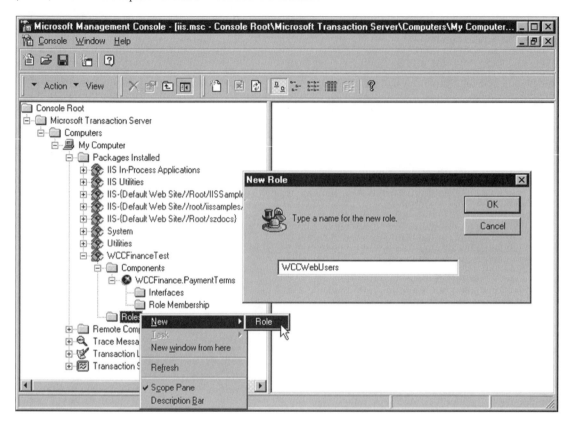

### Adding Users to Package Roles

Once the role is created we can add the appropriate users to it. Here, we're adding the IUSR account directly, plus the two groups Administrators and Certificated users. To open the Add Users and Groups dialog right-click the new Users folder for the appropriate role and select New | User, or use the drop-down Action menu in the toolbar:

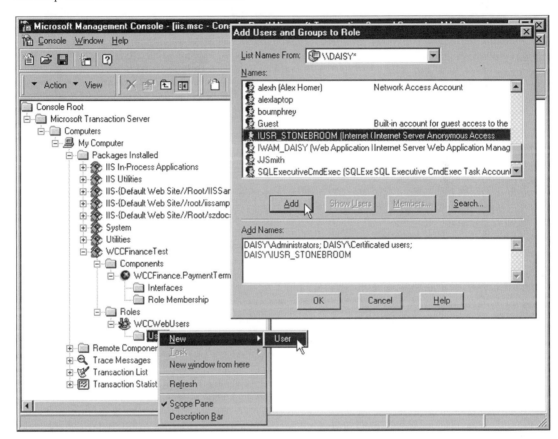

Here's the result with our three users added to the WCCWebUsers role. Of course the real reason for including this screenshot was just to see the hats:

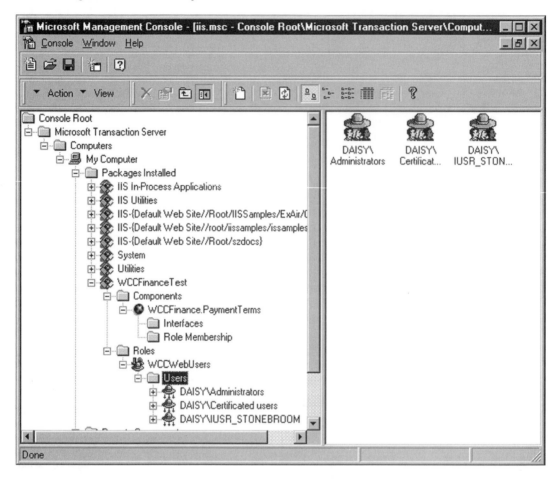

### Assigning Role Membership for Components

Now that we've created the roles and added the users to them, we can specify which components in the package will use each role for authorization checking. To open the Select Roles dialog right-click the Role Membership folder for the component and select New | Role, or use the drop-down Action menu in the toolbar. Only components selected in this dialog will use the roles to check that users have valid access permission:

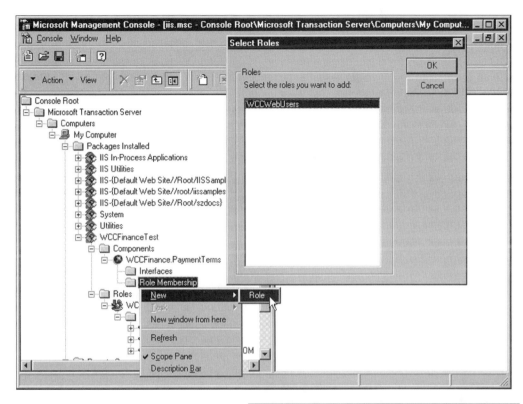

### Enabling Declarative Security

The final step is to activate declarative
security for the package by enabling
authorization checking. This is done in
the Properties dialog for the package
itself. To open the Properties dialog
right-click the name of the package and
select Properties, or use the drop-down
Action menu in the toolbar. The Security
tab contains the checkbox that enables
authorization checking. We also have a
choice of five levels of authentication,
with the default being Packet:

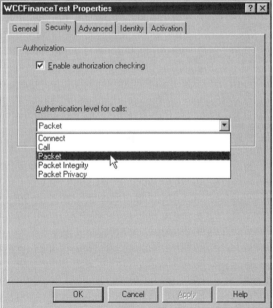

*The other settings are only really useful with remote components, and in general you can use the default setting for all your applications. For more details look at the* Setting MTS Package Properties *topic in the* Creating MTS Packages *section of the MTS* Administrator's Guide.

### Enabling Security at Component Level

By default all components in a package will use declarative security once it is enabled for the package. However, we can change this setting for individual components. This is done with the Properties dialog for the component itself. To open a component's Properties dialog right-click the name of the component and select Properties, or use the drop-down Action menu in the toolbar:

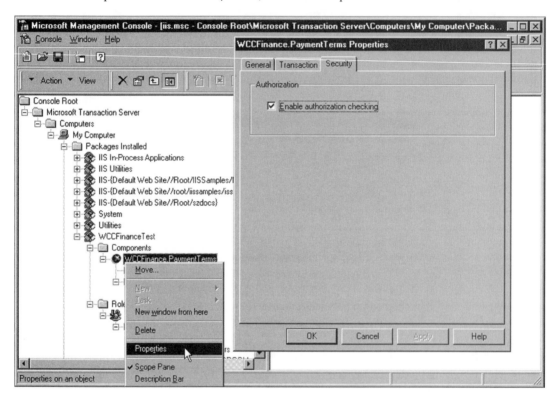

### Creating the Identity for a Package

We use the Properties dialog of a package to assign an **identity** to that package. In the Identity tab, the Account setting defaults to Interactive User–in other words the package will use the account that accessed it in the first place to access other components and resources. To set the package identity we specify the account we want the package to use by selecting This User and filling in the details:

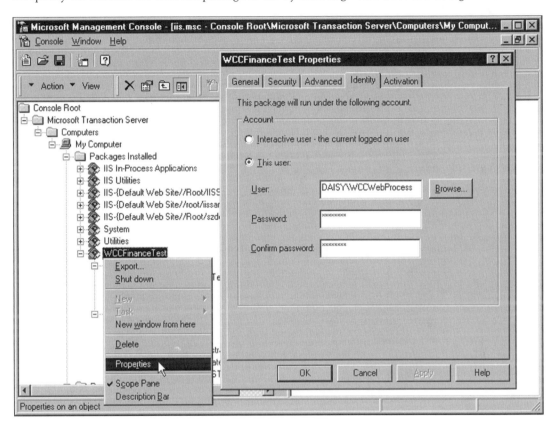

### Package Activation Settings

Components can be run either in the client's memory space (as a **library package**) or within the dedicated server memory space (as a **server package**). This is defined in the Activation tab of the Properties dialog for the package. The default setting is Server Package. Running components in the client's process improves performance, especially when many calls are made to the component. However, you can't use declarative or programmatic security when a component is being run within a Library Package.

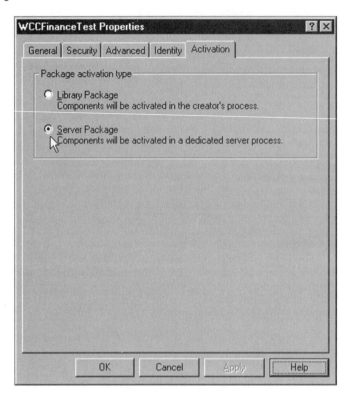

And here's the final result showing all the roles, role members and users for the WCCFinanceTest package. Our component only has the default **interface**, but if it had more than one interface we could assign users and groups to each interface separately. This gives the finest level of control of all, but it is not usually required except in the most complex of components:

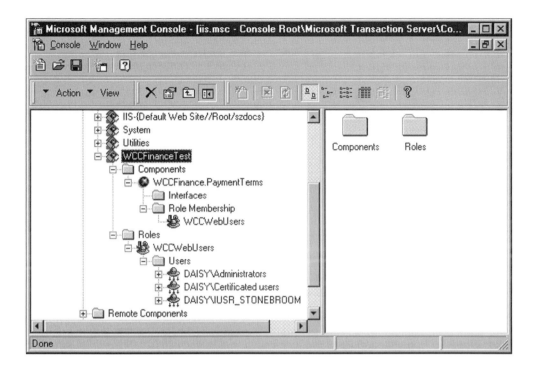

### Setting the Identity Account Properties

As we saw earlier, each package **identity** is a valid Windows NT account. To enable MTS to use the account to access other components or services, you must ensure that it has the appropriate settings. This is done using the Windows NT User Manager application (which we saw in the previous chapter). In the New User dialog, when you create the account, make sure you enter a suitable password to prevent users from being able to log on and impersonate the account if they know the username. In the same dialog set the User Cannot Change Password and Password Never Expires options:

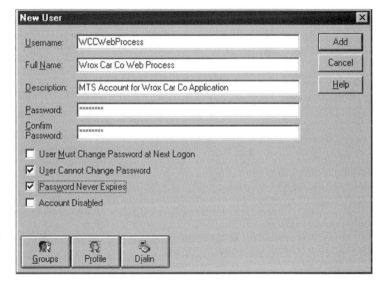

Then click the Groups button and add this account to the Users group, as well as to the group you created for all MTS packages–in our earlier example this was MTSPackages.

Back in the User Manager main window, open the Policies | User Rights dialog, turn on the Show Advanced User Rights option and select 'Log on as a batch job'. Assign this user right to the accounts that will be used as identities, so that MTS can instantiate and execute the components and log onto other resources as part of a transaction:

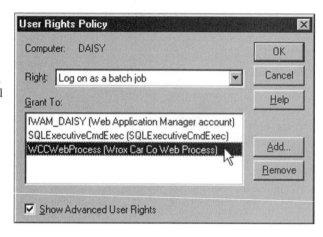

### Setting DCOM Permissions for Distributed Packages

If you have installed **remote packages** on other machines (something we haven't tackled in this book), you also need to set the appropriate permissions using the DCOM configuration utility. Run **dcomcnfg.exe** from your **Winnt\System32** directory, and make sure that you assign the correct default authorization and impersonation levels.

Unless you have a thorough understanding of DCOM authentication levels, it is recommended that you leave the Default Authentication Level setting of your package at the MTS default of Packet. The Default Impersonation Level must be set to Impersonate:

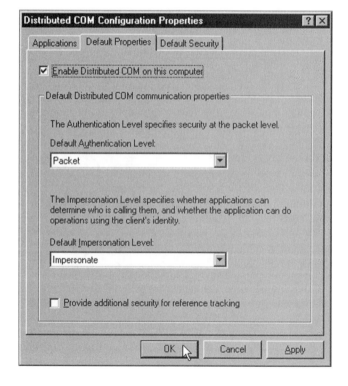

*For more details about the DCOM options available in MTS, check out the* Setting MTS Authentication Levels *section of the* Creating MTS Packages *topic in the* Microsoft Transaction Server Administrator's Guide.

# Programmatic Security Techniques

As well as using declarative security in MTS by adding roles to packages, we can add code to a component that exerts finer control over the way it behaves. An excellent example of this in our Wrox Car Co application would be where we wanted to control access in different ways for different 'ranks' of people in the showroom. For example, we might want to limit the total size of an order if it was being placed by a salesperson, and permit only managers to place fleet orders (say more than one car to the same customer).

## Why Use Programmatic Security?

To do this with only declarative security would mean creating a separate component, placing it in a separate package, and having salespersons and managers log on and use the appropriate component. Instead we can add both user account groups ( Sales staff and Showroom managers) to the roles of the component and then differentiate between them inside the component using **programmatic security**.

We can even use the MTS objects to get the username of the caller, although this technique is generally frowned upon. If we hard-code account names into the component we have to rebuild it when the account details change—when a new manager joins the company for example. By using the MTS roles, we just add users to, and remove them from, the NT groups assigned to the roles for this component's package.

## How Programmatic Security Works

To use programmatic security we take advantage of methods and other objects that MTS makes available within our components, via the **ObjectContext** object. The two methods are:

❑ **IsSecurityEnabled** - returns **True** if security is enabled for the component, or **False** if not. This method always returns **False** for components installed in Library packages—i.e. those that are running in the client's address space.

❑ **IsCallerInRole** - accepts a string that is the name of a role and returns **True** if the current user account is a member of that role. Note that this is the account used to activate the component, and so may not be the original user's account. It could be the **identity** of another component.

Using these methods is easy enough. However, bear in mind that an error should prevent access, and not allow it by default. In other words, your code needs to be fail-safe. The sequence of events is to check first that the component is running under MTS, then that security is enabled, and finally see if the caller is listed in the specified role of the package. The following example returns **True** if the user is part of the role specified in the **strRoleName** argument, and **False** if not:

```
Function ValidateCaller(strRoleName As String) As Boolean
    On Error GoTo Validate_Error
    Dim objContext As ObjectContext
    Set objContext = GetObjectContext()
```

```
    'if objContext is Nothing we're not running in MTS
    If objContext Is Nothing Then
        ValidateCaller = False
        Exit Function
    End If
    'see if security is enabled
    If objContext.IsSecurityEnabled() = False Then
        IsInRole = False
        Exit Function
    End If
    'OK, so call the IsCallerInRole method
    ValidateCaller = objContext.IsCallerInRole(strRoleName)
    Exit Function
Validate_Error:
    ValidateCaller = False
    Exit Function
End Function
```

We could then use this function to limit fleet sales in our Wrox Car Co application to members of the
Showroom managers NT account group with:

```
...
If intNumberCars > 1 Then
    If ValidateCaller("Showroom managers") Then
        'OK to process order
    Else
        'Error, user is not a manager
    End If
End If
...
```

### Finding The Original and Direct Users

The **Security** property of the **ObjectContext** object returns a reference to the component's
**SecurityProperty** object. This provides four methods, all of which we can use to get details of
the original user account that started off the process within which our component is executing.

There are two situations to consider. The **original process** is the process that started off the whole
chain of events. This will be the user who accessed the application via IIS in our Web based
examples. In effect, the name of the original process is that of the 'real' user's account.

The **base process** is that which initiated the current process. If we are in a component inside a
transaction, for example, the base process will be the component that initiated the transaction. It will
always be a component or user outside the current package, but may not be the same as the original
process.

For each of these two processes, we can retrieve the account username for either the **caller** or the
**creator**. In general these will be the same. They will differ when one process creates an instance of a
component and then passes a reference to it on to another component, which then calls a method in
the new component. In this case the **creator** and the **caller** are different processes, and so could have
different usernames.

| | |
|---|---|
| `GetOriginalCallerName` | The username of the original process that called the currently executing method. |
| `GetOriginalCreatorName` | The username of the original process that directly created the current object. |
| `GetDirectCallerName` | The username of the base process that called the currently executing method. |
| `GetDirectCreatorName` | The username of the base process that directly created the current object. |

As an example, look at the following (somewhat contrived) example. The diagram shows a process **A**, which creates an instance of an object **C**. It then passes a reference to this object on to process **B**, which calls a method in that object. Object **C** then calls a method in object **D**, creating an instance of it in the process:

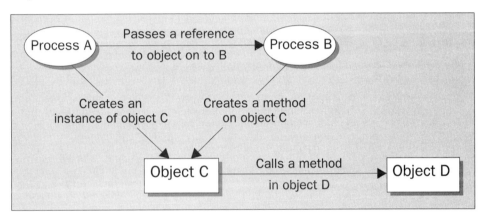

In this case, within the security context of object **D**, the **original caller** is process **B** while the **direct caller** is object **C**. The **original creator**, however, is process **A**; and the **direct creator** is object **C**.

To get the username of the original caller, we could use the code:

```
Dim strUserName As String
Dim objContext As ObjectContext
objContext = GetObjectContext()
strUserName = objContext.Security.GetOriginalCallerName()
```

As we noted earlier, using these methods to retrieve details of user accounts for 'real' users (i.e. people, rather than package identities) is generally not a good idea. It means that you will have to change the code if you need to add or remove users in the future. It's far better to design the security structure of the application around declarative security and the two **ObjectContext** methods **IsSecurityEnabled** and **IsCallerInRole**. Then you can use the Windows NT User Manager to add and remove users, and the changes will automatically be picked up by MTS.

As you've seen in this section of the chapter, MTS security techniques are at the heart of any DNA application. Using declarative security, combined where appropriate with programmatic security, means that we can exert fine control over which users can access our application, and which parts of the application they can use. The next step is to consider how we configure other parts of our application to work securely with MTS.

# Configuring Message Queue Server

We first met **Microsoft Message Queue Server** (MSMQ) back in Chapter 5. There we described how we use the range of ActiveX objects that it exposes to create and locate queues, and to send and receive messages. MSMQ poses another problem from the standpoint of security. We'll generally be using it in situations where the network between the various parts of our distributed application is slow or unreliable. In the majority of cases, this means the Internet or other wide-area network (WAN).

# MSMQ Message Security

Our earlier examples used public MSMQ queues and unencrypted messages, simply sending text or objects between one site and another. We chose to send them using **RECOVERABLE** delivery methods because this provides the most robust environment. However, it means that the messages are held on disk in all the machines that handle it while travelling between the source and destination queues.

Worse than that, we used unsecured public queues, so any inquisitive user could access the queue with an appropriate application and read, change or remove the messages it contains before our application gets to see them. Obviously, we have to consider configuring MSMQ to keep the messages private and safe from interference.

## An Overview of MSMQ Security

What follows is a brief look at the different aspects of security and configuration that you'll need to take into account when you create your own MSMQ enterprise. The levels of security you adopt, and the way that you configure each part of the enterprise, will depend on what kind of messages you will be sending, the nature of the network over which they'll travel, and of course the size and complexity of your organization.

> *The MSMQ Help files contain a lot of detailed information about setting up each security feature. The topic* Securing Your MSMQ Enterprise *(under* Administrators Guide *in the* Message Queue Server *section of the contents) provides a good starting point. There's also a section named* MSMQ Security Services *under the* MSMQ Guide *heading in the* Programmers Reference *section.*

### The Enterprise and Domains

Windows NT is a domain-based system, where all the machines within a domain can use the security services of the domain controllers to check global access rights of users for any part of the domain. This provides a tidy way to control access to the entire domain from one machine—the **primary domain controller** (PDC).

Unfortunately MSMQ doesn't sit well with the domain security model, as its main purpose is to allow messages to be passed between computers that are at opposite ends of a slow or unreliable network. Thus, the places where MSMQ is least useful are likely to be within your own local domain. You're only like to use the MSMQ within the same domain when the domain itself is widely distributed, perhaps using the Internet or leased lines to connect users.

> **MSMQ can only provide a fully secure environment for computers that log onto an NT domain. Workgroup users cannot use MSMQ secured queues or message authentication features, although message encryption and all the other MSMQ features are still available.**

In many cases, messages will have to cross domain boundaries. This is where the notion of an MSMQ **enterprise** differs from that of the Windows NT **domain**. In the following diagram there are two domains, labeled **A** and **B**. Each domain contains one or more MSMQ **sites**, with their own selection of other **servers** and **clients**. Together they make up our theoretical enterprise:

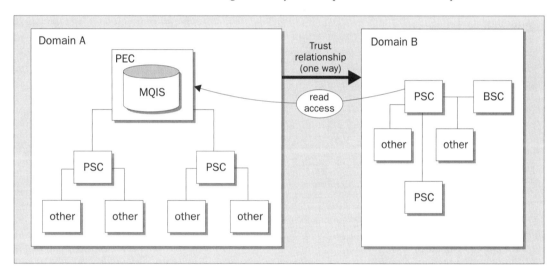

PEC - *Primary Enterprise Controller*
PSC - *Primary Site Controller*
BSC - *Backup Site Controller*

An MSMQ enterprise is centered on the **Message Queue Information Store** (MQIS). In Windows NT4 this is based on a SQL Server database, though it will migrate to Active Directory in NT5. However, the problem still remains. Each site controller keeps a read-only copy of the enterprise information, replicated from the MQIS. To do this, it needs to have access permissions to the Primary Enterprise Controller (PEC) in domain **A**. The result is that you must ensure that a **trust relationship** has been set up so that the domain containing the PEC (domain **A** in our example) trusts all the other domains within the enterprise.

### Admin and User Access Permissions

MSMQ allows the Enterprise Administrator (the person who installed MSMQ) to control the permissions for all other users, who by default have read-only permission to the MQIS and the other objects within the enterprise. To be able to do anything other than send a message to an existing queue (for which permission is enabled for all users by default), you must assign appropriate permissions to your users.

> *Remember that if you are using MTS with declarative security enabled, the users will be the accounts you assigned to the **identity** of the components that access the MSMQ service, not the 'real' original users.*

In particular, the Get Properties permission is required to be able to search for a queue and retrieve its properties. Other permissions include Peek Message, Receive Message and Receive Journal, to view and retrieve messages and journals from queues; and Create Queue, Set Properties and Delete Queue for manipulating queues.

The Enterprise Administrator can assign permissions to each Site Administrator that allow them to deal with the setting of permissions within a single site. In fact this is the recommended way to set up an enterprise. Create two Windows NT account groups in User Manager, one for Enterprise Administrators and one for Site Administrators, then add the appropriate users to each group. In MSMQ Explorer on the enterprise controller, give the Enterprise Administrators group Full Control permission for all the sites, connected networks and computers in the enterprise.

Then give the Site Administrators (who should also have Windows NT Administrator permissions for that site) Full Control permission for the site and each computer in that site. This allows them to install and configure computers in their own site, but prevents them from adding sites or changing the enterprise configuration.

> *There may be occasions where MSMQ will be used without any requirements for security, such as in a small office environment. In this situation you can run it in an unsecured fashion by giving the Windows NT Everyone group Full Control for the entire enterprise. This is set in MSMQ Explorer, in the Security tab of the Properties dialog for the primary enterprise controller machine.*

### Message Authentication

When MSMQ is installed it adds all the CA root certificates registered in Internet Explorer 4 to the MSMQ service. These are used to digitally sign messages that are in transit, and allow the receiving queue manager to positively identify the message sender and be assured that the message has not been tampered with en route. The process is transparent, and if the message cannot be verified it is automatically deleted from the receiving queue and returned to the sender. This is referred to as **internal certificate** authentication. We'll look at how it's done in code later in the chapter.

A message that is successfully sent and received with authentication has its **IsAuthenticated** property set to **1**, and **HashAlgorithm** property set to a value indicating the authentication type used. The default, unless specified when sending the message, is the message digest authentication technique MD5. MSMQ also sets the values of the **SenderID** and **SenderIDType** properties, which identify the user by their internal security identifier. In general, however, you would only need to use the **IsAuthenticated** property—and only then if the queue is configured to accept both authenticated and non-authenticated messages. If it is configured to accept only authenticated messages, an attempt to send a non-authenticated message will result in an error at the sending application.

*At the time of writing, the authentication and encryption methods available in MSMQ were limited, and liable to change. For the latest details check out the* Authentication and Encryption *topics in the* Securing Your MSMQ Enterprise *section of the* Microsoft Message Queue Server Administrator's Guide.

*MSMQ can also use **external certificates** from other CA's. However, in this case the verification is not automatic, and it is left up to the receiving application to validate the message.*

### Message Encryption

As well as authenticating the message to ensure that it hasn't been changed, we can instruct MSMQ to encrypt messages while they are in transit. Again, this is reasonably transparent from the programmers' and users' points of view. We just set the `PrivLevel` property (and optionally the `EncryptAlgorithm` property) of the message to specify that it should be encrypted by MSMQ before it is sent. When received by the destination queue it is automatically unencrypted. Queues can be configured to accept both encrypted messages and unencrypted messages, or to accept just one or the other. Again, we'll see how it's done in code later in the chapter.

Notice that the messages are *not* held in encrypted form within the receiving queue. This allows the receiving applications to peek and retrieve messages without the delays that would appear if they all had to be unencrypted each time. Therefore it's important to set appropriate access permissions to receiving queues to protect the messages they contain.

*Like authentication, the encryption process uses certificates and the Microsoft* Base Cryptographic Provider *service that is installed with MSMQ (and with Internet Explorer). Both the authentication and encryption of messages affect performance of MSMQ, and should only be used where necessary.*

### Auditing Events

Like many Windows services and NT itself, MSMQ can create **audit log** entries that allow administrators to monitor the actions taken by users and their applications. Audit control settings are changed in MSMQ Explorer. Each type of object (Message, Queue, Computer, Site, etc.) can create audit entries, for example a queue can be set up to log the receiving of messages, the reading and changing of properties, and the deletion of queues. The audit log entries take the form of messages placed into the Windows NT Event Log, and can be viewed using Event Viewer in the usual way. Computers can be set up to log things like the creation of queues, the receiving of dead letters and journals, and attempts to change properties or set permissions.

One point to watch is that the audit log messages are written to the audit log of the computer that performs the operation, and this will not generally be the Primary Enterprise Controller. For example, audit entries for the creation of a queue and the setting of its properties are logged on the machine that actually *creates* the queue. And if this is a *remote* queue (on a different machine) the actions of opening the queue to send or receive messages will be logged on the computer that *contains* the queue instead.

# Managing Security in MSMQ Explorer

As you will have gathered from the previous sections of this chapter, there is a lot to security in MSMQ. We won't be covering it all in depth here, but instead we'll provide you with a guide to where and how you set up access permissions and audit logging for your enterprise. All these tasks are done in the MSMQ Explorer that we worked with back in Chapter 5.

## Setting the Enterprise Properties

Almost all the configuration and security settings for the enterprise are in the Enterprise Properties dialog. To open this right-click on the top-level Enterprise entry and select Properties. In the Security tab there are the three standard buttons used to set the Permissions, Auditing and Ownership of the object—in this case the enterprise as a whole. In the Permissions dialog we can add our Enterprise Administrators group, and make sure that the Everyone group has only Read permissions.

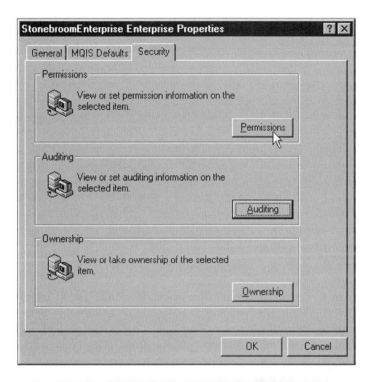

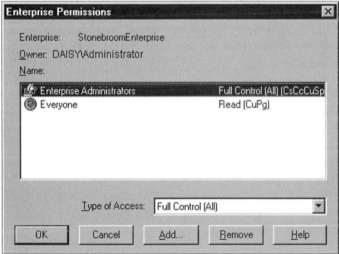

*It's here that you would assign the Everyone group Full Control to provide a non-secured small office-type environment if this was appropriate to your business.*

### Enterprise Auditing

In the same Properties
dialog we can set up the
auditing defaults for the
enterprise by adding
users and groups to the
list and setting the
checkboxes for the
events we want to audit:

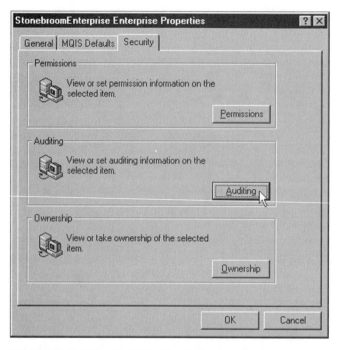

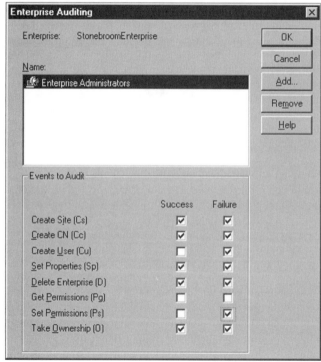

### General Enterprise Defaults

Still in the Properties dialog, we can use the General and MQIS Defaults tabs to set other global options for the enterprise. This includes the replication intervals between internal ( intra-site) and external (inter-site) machines in the enterprise, and the lifetime (or timeout) for all messages. The default intra-site interval is 2 seconds, and the default inter-site interval is 10 seconds, but the ideal settings depend on the traffic levels and latency of your networks. The lifetime of messages is 90 days, but you can limit it down to a number of hours if this is appropriate for your applications. One nice touch is that when you change the setting in the drop-down list, it converts the number of days into hours and vice-versa. You can throw you calculator away now:

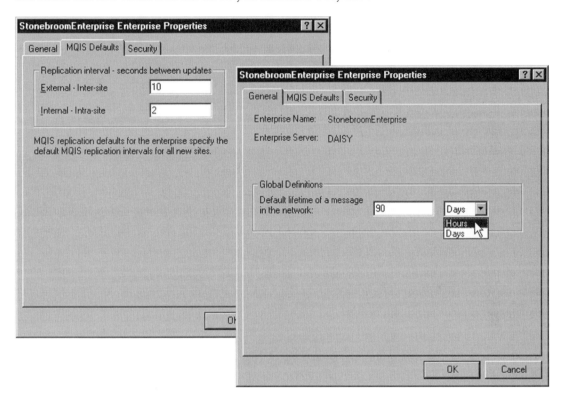

## Setting Properties for a Site

In the Properties dialog for each site within the enterprise you set the permissions and control audit events for that site—in exactly the same way as for the enterprise. In this case, however, you'll add the Site Administrators group to the Permissions dialog (and the Enterprise Administrators group if they are not also members of the Site Administrators group). We've also provided special access permissions to another group that maintains the site. They have restricted permissions compared to the Site Administrators:

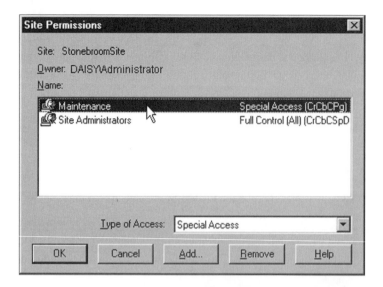

Setting the Type of Access for an account or group to Special Access opens the Special dialog (you can also double-click the account name). Here we're allowing Maintenance users to carry out a subset of the tasks available for a site:

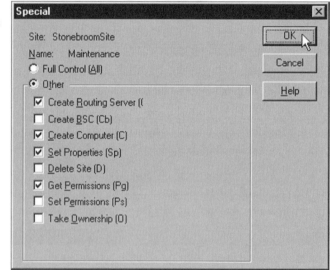

### Setting Route Connection Costs

You'll recall that in Chapter 5 we discussed the way that MSMQ can 'cost' routes so as to distribute messages in the most efficient way. This is set up for each site in the Connections dialog. Here we're adding routes and costs for a fictitious enterprise that spans the USA:

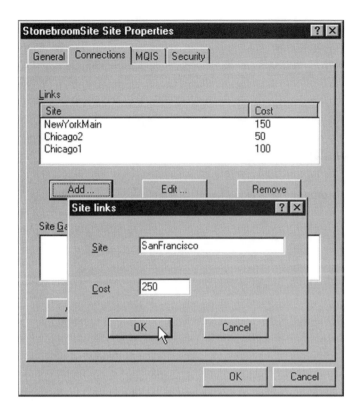

*This dialog is also used to define* Site Gates *between one enterprise and another. For more information on route costs and* Site Gates, *check out the MSMQ Help files. A series of topics under* Routing, *in the* Understanding MSMQ *section of the* Administrators Guide, *contains information on all the message routing options.*

## Setting Properties for a Queue

In MSMQ Explorer we can also set and change the properties for a queue. As well as the usual Security settings, there is a page where we can specify the total maximum size for messages and journals, as well as controlling if the queue will accept only Authenticated messages (when un-checked the queue will accept both authenticated and un-authenticated messages). We can also set the Privacy Level of the queue and the Base Priority here:

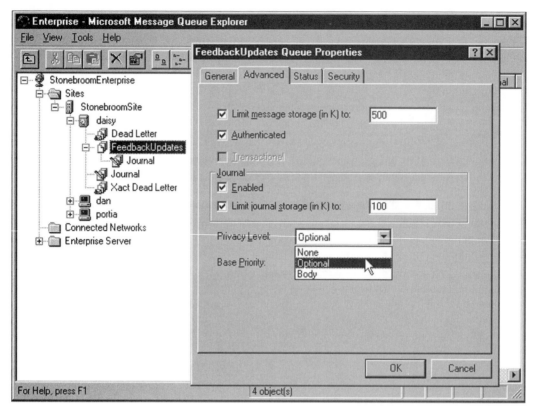

As we saw back in Chapter 5, the priority of a message controls the order in which it will be delivered, compared with the other messages that have different priority settings. Messages with the highest priority are delivered first. If no priority is specified when the message is created, the value of **Base Priority** is assigned to it.

The setting for **Privacy Level** determines whether messages sent to the queue can be encrypted. **Optional** means that the queue will accept both encrypted and unencrypted messages. **Body** means that all messages sent to this queue must be encrypted, and any attempts to send one that isn't will result in an error.

> *The* **Transactional** *option is only enabled if we create the queue as a transactional queue in the first place.*

A queue's properties can be set in code when you create a queue dynamically within your application (i.e. when you are the owner of the queue). We'll see how this is done in the next section.

# Sending and Receiving Secure Messages

We saw how to send and receive messages using both ASP and Visual Basic in the previous chapter. Here we'll concentrate just on the extra steps required to create messages that are authenticated, and messages that are encrypted.

## Using MSMQ Message Authentication

To create a queue that will only accept authenticated messages in **Visual Basic**, we could use the following code. The line that encrypts the queue is highlighted:

```
Dim objQueueInfo As New MSMQQueueInfo
Dim objQueue As New MSMQQueue
'set the name and label of the queue to create
objQueueInfo.PathName = ".\TestQueue"
objQueueInfo.Label = "My Authenticated Message Queue"
```

```
'set the queue to only accept authenticated messages
objQueueInfo.Authenticate = MQ_AUTHENTICATE
```

```
'now create the queue object
objQueueInfo.Create
Set objQueue = objQueueInfo.Open(MQ_SEND_ACCESS, MQ_DENY_NONE)
If objQueue.IsOpen Then
  'OK to send a message
End If
```

The **Authenticate** property can take one of two values: **MQ_AUTHENTICATE** (**1**) which creates a queue that will only accept authenticated messages, and **MQ_AUTHENTICATE_NONE** (**0** - the default) which will accept both authenticated and un-authenticated messages.

In **Active Server Pages**, we have to use the **Server.CreateObject** method to create the MSMQ objects, and the actual values of the MSMQ named constants. To create a queue that will only accept authenticated messages with ASP we can use the following:

```
Set objQueueInfo = Server.CreateObject("MSMQ.MSMQQueueInfo")
Set objQueue = Server.CreateObject("MSMQ.MSMQQueue")
'set the name and label of the queue to create
objQueueInfo.PathName = ".\TestQueue"
objQueueInfo.Label = "My Authenticated Message Queue"
```

```
'set the queue to only accept authenticated messages
objQueueInfo.Authenticate = 1
```

```
'now create the queue object
objQueueInfo.Create
Set objQueue = objQueueInfo.Open(2, 0) 'send and deny_none
If objQueue.IsOpen Then
  'OK to send a message
End If
```

### Changing a Queue's Authentication Property

The authentication level can be changed while the queue is open by changing the value of the **Authenticate** property and calling that particular **MSMQQueueInfo** object's **Update** method. Other applications can check the current setting of the queue's properties by calling the **MSMQQueueInfo** object's **Refresh** method and then reading the property values.

### Sending Authenticated Messages

To create and send an authenticated message with **Visual Basic** we could use:

```
...
If objQueue.IsOpen Then
  'OK to send a message
  Dim objMessage As New MSMQMessage
  objMessage.Label = "Authentication Test Message"
  objMessage.Body = "This is a test of authentication"

  'instruct MSMQ to authenticate the message on receipt
  objMessage.AuthLevel = MQMSG_AUTH_LEVEL_ALWAYS
  'tell it which authentication hash algorith to use (optional)
  objMessage.HashAlgorithm = MQMSG_CALG_MD5

  objMessage.Send objQueue
  objQueue.Close
End If
```

The **AuthLevel** property can be set to **MQMSG_AUTH_LEVEL_ALWAYS** (**1**) to instruct MSMQ to authenticate the message on receipt, and **MQMSG_AUTH_LEVEL_NONE** (**0** - the default) if it doesn't need to be authenticated. The **HashAlgorithm** property defines which authentication method will be used. A dozen different encryption algorithms are defined, but not all are implemented at the time of writing and no doubt the list will change. The default for authenticated messages is MD5 (**&H8003**).

To create and send an authenticated message with **Active Server Pages** we could use:

```
...
If objQueue.IsOpen Then
  'OK to send a message
  Set objMessage = Server.CreateObject("MSMQ.MSMQMessage")
  objMessage.Label = "Authentication Test Message"
  objMessage.Body = "This is a test of authentication"

  'instruct MSMQ to authenticate the message on receipt
  objMessage.AuthLevel = 1
  'tell it which authentication hash algorith to use (optional)
  objMessage.HashAlgorithm = &H8003    'MD5 authentication

  objMessage.Send objQueue
  objQueue.Close
End If
```

### Receiving Authenticated Messages

To receive a message and check its authentication status and security information in **Visual Basic**, we could use:

```
Dim objQueueInfo As New MSMQQueueInfo
Dim objQueue As MSMQQueue
objQueueInfo.PathName = ".\TestQueue"
'set the name of the queue and open it
Set objQueue = objQueueInfo.Open(MQ_RECEIVE_ACCESS, MQ_DENY_NONE)
If objQueue.IsOpen Then
```

```
  Set objMessage = objQueue.Receive
  strInfo = "The message '" & objMessage.Label
  If objMessage.IsAuthenticated Then
    strInfo = strInfo & "' has been successfully authenticated by MSMQ." _
          & Chr(13) & "The Sender ID is " & objMessage.SenderID _
          & Chr(13) & "The ID Type is " & objMessage.SenderIDType
  Else
    strInfo = strInfo & "' has not been authenticated."
  End If
  MsgBox strInfo

End If
```

To receive a message and check its authentication status and security information using **Active Server Pages** we could use:

```
Set objQueueInfo = Server.CreateObject("MSMQ.MSMQQueueInfo")
Set objQueue = Server.CreateObject("MSMQ.MSMQQueue")
'set the name of the queue and open it
objQueueInfo.PathName = ".\TestQueue"
Set objQueue = objQueueInfo.Open(1, 0)
If objQueue.IsOpen Then
```

```
strInfo = "The message '" & objMessage.Label
  If objMessage.IsAuthenticated Then
    strInfo = strInfo & "' has been successfully authenticated by MSMQ." _
          & "<BR>The Sender ID is " & objMessage.SenderID _
          & "<BR>The ID Type is " & objMessage.SenderIDType
  Else
    strInfo = strInfo & "' has not been authenticated."
  End If
  Response.Write strInfo
```

```
End If
```

## Sending and Receiving Encrypted Messages

Creating a queue that will only accept **encrypted** messages is similar to creating one that uses authentication—and in fact you may want to combine the two security features. In the following sections of code we've omitted the lines that are repeated from the earlier example, to avoid excessive duplication.

To create a queue for encrypted messages in **Visual Basic** we could use:

```
...
objQueueInfo.PathName = ".\TestQueue"
objQueueInfo.Label = "My Encrypted Message Queue"
```

```
'set the queue to only accept encrypted messages
objQueueInfo.PrivLevel = MQ_PRIV_LEVEL_BODY
```

```
'now create the queue object
objQueueInfo.Create
...
```

The **PrivLevel** property defines the privacy of the queue's messages. The values are **MQ_PRIV_LEVEL_NONE** (**0** - the default) which allows only un-encrypted messages to be sent, **MQ_PRIV_LEVEL_OPTIONAL** (**1**) which allow both encrypted and un-encrypted messages to be sent, and **MQ_PRIV_LEVEL_BODY** (**2**) which allows only encrypted messages to be sent.

To create a queue that will only accept encrypted messages with **Active Server Pages** we could use:

```
...
objQueueInfo.PathName = ".\TestQueue"
objQueueInfo.Label = "My Encrypted Message Queue"
'set the queue to only accept encrypted messages
objQueueInfo.PrivLevel = 2
'now create the queue object
objQueueInfo.Create
...
```

### Sending Authenticated Messages

To create and send an encrypted message with **Visual Basic** we could use:

```
...
objMessage.Label = "Encryption Test Message"
objMessage.Body = "This is a test of encryption"
'instruct MSMQ to encrypt the message
objMessage.PrivLevel = MQMSG_PRIV_LEVEL_BODY
'tell it which encryption algorith to use (optional)
objMessage.EncryptAlgorithm = MQMSG_CALG_RC4
objMessage.Send objQueue
objQueue.Close
...
```

The **PrivLevel** property here is similar to the **PrivLevel** property of the queue, but uses different named constants. The options are **MQMSG_PRIV_LEVEL_NONE** (**0** - the default) for messages that are not encrypted, and **MQMSG_PRIV_LEVEL_BODY** (**1**) for messages that are encrypted. Again there are a dozen different encryption algorithms defined, but not all are implemented at the time of writing. The default for encrypting messages is RC2 ( **&H6602**).

> *For the latest details on implemented authentication and encryption algorithms, check out the* Authentication *and* Encryption *topics in the* Securing Your MSMQ Enterprise *section of the* Microsoft Message Queue Server Administrator's Guide.

To create and send an encrypted message with **Active Server Pages** we would use:

```
...
objMessage.Label = "Encryption Test Message"
objMessage.Body = "This is a test of encryption"
'instruct MSMQ to encrypt the message
objMessage.PrivLevel = 1   'encrypted
'tell MSMQ which encryption algorith to use (optional)
```

```
objMessage.EncryptAlgorithm = &H6801    'RC4 encryption

objMessage.Send objQueue
objQueue.Close
...
```

### Receiving Authenticated Messages

To receive a message and check its encryption level and type in **Visual Basic**, we could use:

```
...
objQueueInfo.PathName = ".\TestQueue"
Set objQueue = objQueueInfo.Open(MQ_RECEIVE_ACCESS, MQ_DENY_NONE)
If objQueue.IsOpen Then

    Set objMessage = objQueue.Receive
    strInfo = "Message '" & objMessage.Label
    If objMessage.PrivLevel = MQMSG_PRIV_LEVEL_BODY Then
      strInfo = strInfo & "' is encrypted using the algorithm " _
            & CStr(objMessage.EncryptAlgorithm) & "."
    Else
      strInfo = strInfo & "' is not encrypted."
    End If
    MsgBox strInfo

End If
```

Here's the result with a small test program that combines all of the code samples shown above. It creates, sends and receives an encrypted message:

To receive a message and to check its encryption level and encryption type in **Active Server Pages** we might use:

```
...
objQueueInfo.PathName = ".\TestQueue"
Set objQueue = objQueueInfo.Open(1, 0)
If objQueue.IsOpen Then

    Set objMessage = objQueue.Receive
    strInfo = "Message '" & objMessage.Label
    If objMessage.PrivLevel = 1 Then
      strInfo = strInfo & "' is encrypted using the algorithm " _
```

```
                 & CStr(objMessage.EncryptAlgorithm) & "."
   Else
     strInfo = strInfo & "' is not encrypted."
   End If
   Response.Write strInfo

 End If
```

This is the result given by combining the ASP code samples above. It produces a page that creates an encrypted queue, sends an encrypted message to it, and then retrieves the message:

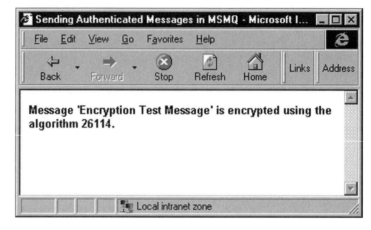

# Data Source Security Issues

The final stage in our application is usually accessing the data store. In our examples we've used SQL Server because this is often the database of choice for DNA applications. However, the DNA architecture is designed to offer seamless access to all kinds of data stores, from relational databases like Access, Oracle, and Informix, to Exchange Server and Active Directory Services. Microsoft are promoting this as the **Universal Data Access** (UDA) concept.

In the remainder of this chapter, we'll take a brief look at some issues involved in protecting your data from unwelcome attentions when you use it in Web-based applications. This is only an overview, and you should use it in conjunction with information specific to the data source you are using.

## Accounts And Logins

The techniques for setting up security and handling logins on each kind of data store will differ, but the overall principles are the same. In particular, providing that declarative security is in use in MTS , the account used to access the data store driver (such as ODBC or OLEDB) will be the same—irrespective of the data store in use.

In SQL Server 6.5 we can choose between **Integrated** security (SQL Server uses the security information stored in Windows NT, and you manipulate it with User Manager just like any other Windows NT Service), **Standard** security (SQL Server maintains it's own set of security information), and **Mixed** (a combination of both). In other database systems you may only have the manufacturers own security implementation, or it may interface with Windows NT.

## SQL Server Standard Security

While **Integrated** security is usually the best choice, as it allows user permissions to be controlled from User Manager along with all other security information, **Standard** security can be used successfully in a DNA-based application. In fact, because MTS provides **impersonation** of users by mapping them to a limited number of user accounts, it is usually simple enough to keep the total number of logins and their security permissions under control.

In SQL Server, the Enterprise Manager tool allows you to create new Logins (accounts) and assign permissions to them for each object in your database:

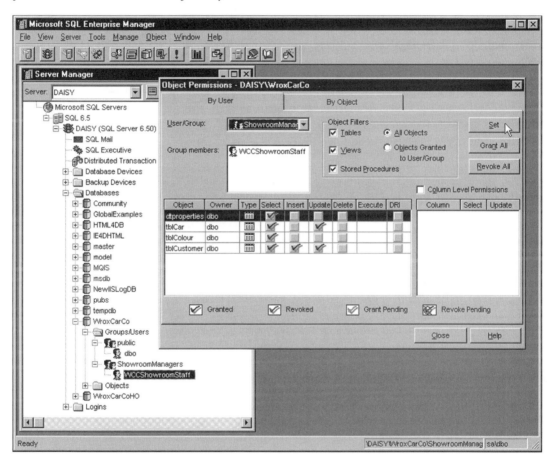

Setting appropriate permissions to the separate objects in your database is vital. However, in SQL Server and most other data sources, you can generally set individual permissions right down to field level if required:

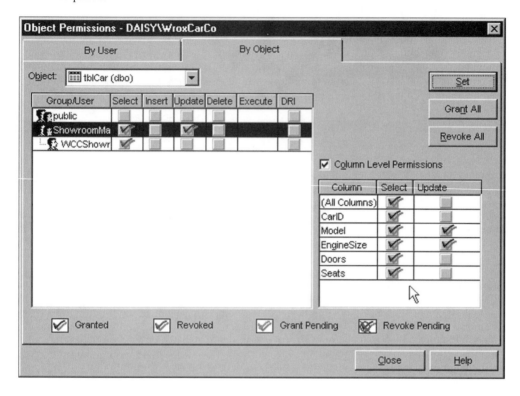

*The network protocol that SQL Server is configured to use also has a big impact on how it integrates with IIS. The two most likely protocols to be used are Named Pipes and TCP/IP Sockets. Named Pipes is an authenticated protocol, while TCP/IP is not.*

# Some Tips and Hints for Data Sources

Some things to consider when using SQL Server, or any other data sources, are:

❑ **Protect the system administrator account** with a strong password, just as you would the administrator account in Windows NT. SQL Server allows users to connect to it over the network (including the Internet) using the client-side tools supplied with it. If they crack your administrator account they can do almost anything you can with the database contents.

❑ **Create Views, Queries, or Stored Procedures** that contain only the information you wish to make available to a particular account group. For example, if an ASP page only needs to   access a couple of fields in a large table you should consider creating a view that contains only those fields, or a query or stored procedure that returns a   recordset containing only those fields. In general, except for the simplest of tables, you should avoid accessing the table directly.

❑ **Assign appropriate permissions to every object in the database**. Even if some tables are not accessed by Web users, set up strong passwords on them. Use the ability of the database's own security system to allocate permissions on an object-by-object basis (even down to field level), including views, queries and stored procedures.

❑ **Create a custom data access component** rather than using ASP code if you need to collect information from several places and work with it before returning it to the caller (such as formatting values or summarizing the contents). A component can hide details of the origin of the data from intruders (i.e. the passwords, table names, System DSNs, connection strings, etc.) much better than an ASP script, and will generally be faster.

❑ **Avoid providing users with File DSNs** on their own machines wherever possible. These contain information about the source of the data, and may tempt users to experiment with trying to obtain access to sensitive information.

# Remote Data Services

One particular area of concern is the new **Remote Data Service** technology that provides client-side data-binding for Web pages over HTTP. This is a very powerful new technique, and allows you to create Web pages that provide fast and responsive access to data on your server. These pages can be used to edit the data, and the updates are automatically made back on the server. We've used it to our advantage in the Wrox Car Co sample application.

## RDS Security Risks

RDS is completely unlike any previous technique for displaying and updating data over the Web. With CGI applications, Perl scripts and ASP, we are used to sending just an HTML page containing the results of a query to a data source, and not a 'real' recordset that could be manipulated on the client. RDS is more like the traditional client/server model, where actual recordsets are moved across the network to the client.

### Preventing Remote Data Updates

In traditional Web applications, there was no way users could update the source data directly. This required an equivalent server-side component (application or script) that collected the information they submitted from a form in the page, and the component updated the data source. In RDS, however, the browser will quite happily update the data itself—so you need to make sure that you set appropriate permissions.

If the data is available for read-only purposes, use the database security methods to lock it against all updates by specifying Read permission. You can do this in the ODBC driver for some data sources (like Microsoft Access for example). If it's supposed to be read-only for some people but updateable to others, make sure you have separate accounts for the two groups with the correct permissions on all objects in the database.

### Distributing Connection Information

As well as the danger of the client automatically being able to update data on your server, RDS also introduces a new area of risk. In order for the client-side page to connect to the data source and build a recordset on the client, it has to have the connection information. When you put the database name, username and password in the page, you are inviting them into your database as surely as if you gave them the keys to the building.

There's no easy way round this. When the user loads a page of data created by an ASP script, they have no indication at all of where the data came from—it's just HTML code and text. If you use RDS, however, you have to tell the browser where to get the data from. No matter how you try to hide this (for example using a client-side ActiveX control that the user downloads to make the connection) you can't stop them from modifying the HTML or copying the information to create their own query page.

> *RDS pages are usually simple HTML files with the* `.htm` *file extension. RDS works just as well when pages like this are loaded from a local hard disk as when loaded from your server over the Web.*

This means that you must be even more vigilant about the permissions available to users for that database. You might like to consider creating a special account with no password, and using that in cases where RDS data access is required. Within each database allow this account only the minimum level of permissions, and always use read-only unless the users have to be able to update the tables.

### Distributing Table Structure Information

As well as the connection information, RDS pages often contain SQL strings that are sent to the data source to create the recordset for the page. This is a prime example of where you should be using **views**, **queries** or **stored procedures** to create the relevant recordsets.

For example, if you want to provide a staff telephone list using fields from the main employees and departments tables, create a view that contains only the fields required for the list. Don't be tempted to give the user an SQL string in the page containing the real table names. They might just guess that the employees table contained a **Salary** column, and create their own RDS page to see what's in it. Even if the table is read-only, so that they can't change the contents, you would probably want to prevent them seeing it at all.

> *Remember that the SQL string and the HTML attributes within an RDS page provide the field names of the recordset. You can change the names of the fields within a query or stored procedure from those in the source tables, so that the user cannot apply them to the original table should they be able to get access to it.*

### RDS and MTS Impersonation

One real security hole with RDS, at present, occurs when it is used with Microsoft Transaction Server. This is an underlying issue with COM, which caches identities of components between process calls. What this means in practice is that, if you access a component through the RDS **DataSpace** object, MTS will cache the security context. If someone else then accesses the component in the same way, they will run in the security context of the first user. This problem is due to be fixed with Windows NT5, and at the time of writing there was no ' hotfix' or patch available.

# Summary

In this chapter we've built on the security outlines for Windows NT and IIS that we looked at in Chapter 7 to encompass the 'working parts' of a DNA application. In particular, we've seen how the **declarative security** feature in Microsoft Transaction Server (MTS) can be used to simplify the control of user permissions between the various middle-tier business rules components that the application uses.

We've also shown how to use programmatic security to make each component more flexible—that is add code to the component that will differentiate between different users and groups, and then change the component's behaviour accordingly. By combining these two methods with the ways we used **server variables** and **certificates** back in Chapter 7, we have a wide choice of techniques available for managing user access.

In this chapter we also revisited the structure of a Microsoft Message Queue Server (MSMQ) **enterprise**, from the point of view of configuring it to provide a secure environment for distributed messaging. We saw how we can protect each part of the enterprise, right down to queue level, with the built-in Windows NT security features. We also looked at the ways we can authenticate and encrypt messages that we pass over the network.

Finally, we took a very brief look at some of the issues involved at the data-source end of our DNA applications. In particular this was oriented towards SQL Server, but the general recommendations are just as valid—no matter which relational database system you use. And, of course, other types of data store, such as Exchange, Active Directory, or other specialist applications, will each have their own special requirements and security features.

Overall, in this chapter, we've covered:

- ❑ How the layers and components of a DNA application authenticate each user
- ❑ Configuration and security issues concerned with Microsoft Transaction Server
- ❑ Configuration and security issues concerned with Message Queue Server
- ❑ Security issues connected with exposing data sources over the Web

We've now come to the end of the 'teaching' part of this book, and we'll finish with a final implementation of our Wrox Car Company application by showing you how we move it from the showroom out onto the Internet, and let people order their new car from the comfort of their own home.

# 9

# Going Public On The Web

In this book we've gone from nowhere to creating a DNA-based application that uses transactions and message queuing. The application provides a compact, robust, easily extensible and re- usable core of business functions and rules, implemented as components in a range of formats and languages.

We've built components using Active Server Pages, Visual Basic, and HTML Scriptlets; and client-side interfaces with HTML and Dynamic HTML, VBScript, JavaScript, and Visual Basic. We've handled data using SQL Server stored procedures, using custom VB components through ADO, and using client-side data-binding with RDS. We even explored the technique of sending recordsets to the client through the data factory interface, and packaged them up using a custom VB routine we called a **StringBag**.

So what's left to do now? Well, in this chapter we're going to take that final step and put our application's core components to work as part of a publicly-accessible Web application. We'll look at the issues involved in this, take a view on how we plan the final product, and see how we've implemented it in our example.

In this final chapter you'll see:

- ❑  The issues we need to consider when we decide to go public on the Web
- ❑  Some of the ways that we handle large numbers of concurrent users
- ❑  How we interface a new application with existing core components
- ❑  How the Wrox Car Company public application is implemented

We'll start with a look at what applications like this are really designed to achieve.

# What Do We Want From the Web?

If you've seen any of the commercials from the world's largest computer company, you'll probably be amused by the concept that many people don't know what a presence on the Web is meant to achieve. However, this is probably the first question that you need to ask yourself when you think about designing Web applications.

- ❑ **Is It Corporate Presence?** Are we just there 'because we have to be', or because everyone else is?
- ❑ **Is It An Advertisement?** Are we just looking for a relatively cheap way to showcase our products or services?
- ❑ **Is It To Provide Information?** Do we want to use the web to provide technical support, product guides, fixes, or free downloadable files?
- ❑ **Is It Supposed To Make Money?** Is our Web site supposed to be a productive part of the business, or just a cost it has to sustain?

## Making Money Using The Web

We're not going to argue benefits of the various categories here, because the only one that really interests us is in this book the last one. We're involved in applications, and in particular applications that handle customer orders. So if we're going out publicly onto the Web, we really want to do so in a way that gives the best return on the not-inconsiderable investment it involves.

During the last year or so it has become obvious that the Web provides a way to sell products, and that the public at large (or at least a proportion of them) will buy using the Internet—look at the huge number of sales being notched up by Dell Computers, for example. Well, why not implement the same capabilities for our fictional car company?

Besides, once we've tempted a prospective customer into our site, we are wasting opportunities if we don't try our hardest to part them from their money on the spot. After all, this is just what our carefully-trained salespersons try to do in the showroom! So, in this chapter, we'll look at how we can persuade our visitors to order their new car from our Web site directly.

# Designing A Public Web Application

The Wrox Car Company applications we've built in previous chapters have been focused on the requirements of our business and the staff we employ. In the showroom, our sales people use the computer simply to place orders that they've persuaded the customer to place, and to check on the delivery status of orders placed previously. The whole concept was one of a functional, robust and reliable application that would carry out all the tasks of placing the order both on the showroom and head office systems. For the Web, however, we need to do more than this.

# A Showcase That Sells

A consumer-oriented application, often referred to as an **e-commerce** application, needs to do a lot more than just be functional. In particular it needs to provide an attractive and persuasive showcase for the products—after all there's no salesperson standing behind the user to explain why they should purchase one of our cars.

So, as well as the functionality we've already seen in the previous chapters, we need to add a section that displays the cars and lets the customer choose which suits them, and how much it will cost. We also have to think about the way the application will work for our clients, for example, whether it will be responsive over their Internet connection, and whether it will work on their browser. And of course, can our server support the (hopefully) thousands of users that will be running it?

## *The Sections Of A Public Web Application*

The first step is to think about how we can divide up our application. These divisions are not supposed to be visible to the user, who expects the entire site to be integrated and provide a consistent environment. Instead, they are designed to allow us to build and maintain the sections more easily, and interchange them in the same way as we would interchange components in the 'back end' processing parts of the application. Some general sections might be:

- ❑ The product showcase section, which sells the product to the customer
- ❑ The order entry section, where they enter their order, payment, and other details
- ❑ The processing section, where their order is physically stored on our systems

We might also have sections for customer feedback, support, inquiries, etc.—though for simplicity we haven't implemented these in our Wrox Car Co sample application.

### The Product Showcase Section

If we're going to actually sell anything, we need to provide an interface that is attractive, responsive, and will persuade potential customers to part with their hard-earned cash. In the Wrox Car Co application, we open with a list of the cars and some small graphics, together with a simple animation to catch the eye:

Customers can select a car model and get more information about it by clicking the Details button. To make it more exciting we allow them to choose a color and see what the car looks like in that color. (OK, so our graphics are a little less sophisticated that you'd see in a professionally designed page, but you get the idea):

*If you want to see just what is possible, take a look at the CarPoint site at http://carpoint.msn.com. It uses an ActiveX control called Surround Video, which lets you view and pan around the inside and outside of the cars.*

We can also offer specially tailored finance packages on our cars. A simple page allows users to choose how they would like to pay for the car, and see what it will cost each month. This uses a combination of techniques, including the **WCCFinance** component that we built earlier in the book:

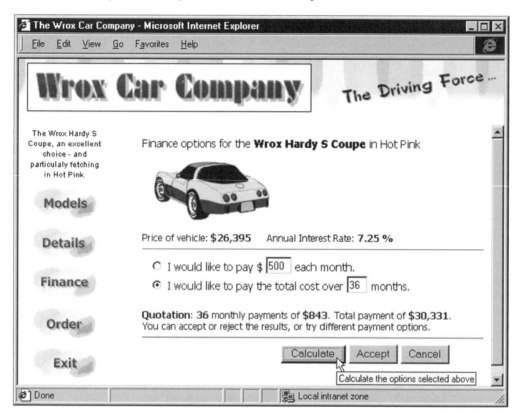

*If you're wondering why clicking on a car doesn't immediately open the Details page, it's done to allow user to select the Finance page instead if they wish.*

### The Order Entry Section

We make it easy for users to place an order for a car with a button on the main page. This presents them with a choice: they can order via our secure site (which uses SSL and certificates to provide encrypted communication) or through the normal anonymous HTTP protocol. Many users are nervous about submitting information over the Web, and this helps to allay their fears. If they opt for the secure site, we use the contents of their client certificate to pre-fill some of the order details as well:

### The Order Processing Section

The order is submitted to our order processing components, and a response is returned to indicate if this was successful. Normally this part of the process is the most difficult to implement. However, because we've already created a complete DNA-compliant core order processing function as a set of components (which we used with the showroom application earlier in the book), we've already got everything we need.

This is, of course, one of the main reasons for sticking rigidly to a design philosophy like DNA—we reuse existing components and business logic functions without having to worry about how they work. As was in fact the case with the Wrox Car Co Web application, the developer who builds the client interface section doesn't need to know anything about how the back-end business functions work.

# Scalability Issues And Responsiveness

While making the pages look attractive is a prime function, what's equally important is how we handle the data that we need for our application and at the same time make using the interface as responsive as possible. One of the best ways to put people off browsing your Web site is to build it in such a way that each page takes an age to load in their browser. Our public application needs to load quickly, and—more important—respond quickly to user actions. While they will probably be prepared to give the first page a chance to load, they won't accept long delays each time they open another page.

## The Intranet vs The Web

On top of this, we need to think about the effects on our server. When implementing applications at the showroom, we have a server for each showroom and only the sales staff and managers in the showroom will access it. This will also probably be over a high-bandwidth local network or Intranet, so it's easy to achieve good connection performance and provide a powerful enough server to handle the known number of users.

As for the head office, we've implemented the communication between our application and the database located there using message queuing. Even if the head office server is under intense loading all day from its local users, it will catch up during slack periods or overnight. Again, here, scalability is not likely to be a major problem.

When we go public on the Web, however, the situation is very different. We can't predict the number of users or the traffic patterns. At the same time, we probably can't afford to install gigabit-bandwidth lines and multiple servers just in case it gets busy at some times of the day. Instead we need to consider how we can build the application interface so as to apply the minimal load to our server and our Internet connection.

## Browsing vs Ordering

In the examples you've seen earlier in this book we used a variety of techniques to get data from the server to the client and back again. Unlike the showroom applications, where the prime purpose is to submit data, our public Web application will spend most of its time reading information from our server as users browse the car models, view details of each one, and examine the finance packages that are available. Only on limited occasions will an order be submitted to our server—although of course we'd like this to happen as often as possible!

So our design needs to take this factor into account. We need to think about how we can most effectively use the components we've got to provide information about our products to the user, and then process any orders that they place:

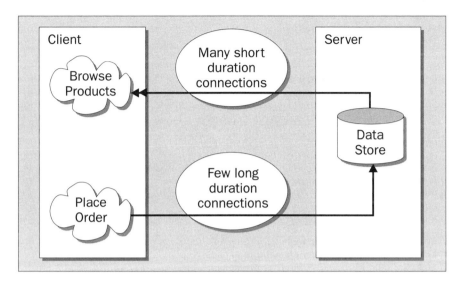

The diagram shows where the largest loading on our server comes from, and it is this that we need to plan for.

### Server Load While Placing An Order

When it comes to placing the order, we can't do much to reduce the number of connections. We need to store the details of every order or we'll create a lot of unhappy customers. However placing an order involves multiple table and multiple database updates, and here we are dependent on the latency of the data sources and the connections to them.

We can aim to reduce the duration of each connection by using the techniques you've seen already in this book—in particular message queuing, which allows the operation to complete successfully without having to wait for the remote data source to signal a successful update.

### Server Load While Browsing The Products

The duration of each individual connection when browsing will tend to be short because the server just has to retrieve the data (a recordset, HTML page or graphic file), send it to the client, and then disconnect. As long as any tasks our server has to run, such as stored procedures or custom components, operate as efficiently as possible we can't do much else to reduce the duration of each connection. What we can do is try to reduce the *number* of connections.

## Minimizing Client Connections

To be able to reduce the number of connections that the client makes to our server when browsing, we can cache the data on the client rather than sending it each time they request a different page. To see how, consider the ways that we've used to retrieve data in the previous chapters of this book.

### Client-side ActiveX Controls

The early chapters about components showed a simple component **WCCFinance** that calculated the number of payments required for a loan. We used this as an Active Server Component running in ASP on the server, which required a connection and a return HTML page each time the user wanted to do a calculation. We also used it (unchanged) as a client-side ActiveX control, which ran on the client's system. This way they had just one connection to our server to load the page (albeit extended the first time by the duration required to download the control), and they could do as many calculations as they liked without reconnecting to the server.

The downside here is that the browser must support ActiveX controls, and the user must be prepared to accept them. This is a particular problem with unsigned controls like our sample **WCCFinance** control. However the reduction in connections and resulting increase in responsiveness is a real bonus.

### Server-side Business Objects

Of course, some business objects, such as the **WCCCars** component that returns a recordset of details for all the car models, is designed to run only on the server. In this case we were forced to use ASP to create an HTML page, or send the recordset directly to a VB client-side application.

How the business object retrieves that data from the data store isn't that important when it runs server-side, as long as it does it in the most efficient way. We used ADO and an OLEDB driver to connect to a stored procedure in SQL Server, but the techniques you choose are dependent on your data store and available drivers.

### Remote Data Services

One of the topics we discussed way back in Chapter 1 was the split between client-side and server-side processing in DNA-based applications. We've used the 'half-way' technique of Remote Data Services in several earlier examples, including our Wrox Car Co showroom application.

It provides a perfect opportunity to spread some of the processing onto the client, by caching data recordsets there rather than fetching selected parts of the recordset through separate and repeated connections to the server. However RDS does carry some concerns over security, it's not as flexible as ADO, and it's not always as fast as you might like over a less-than-ideal network connection. In our Wrox Car Co application we use a form of RDS, together with a totally different way of caching data, to reduce the number of connections required. You'll see more when we come to look at the application in detail later in this chapter.

# Designing For Responsiveness

As well as moving data from the server to the client during browsing, we also have to send other files. In particular graphics can make an application appear to respond slowly, and this can give a poor impression of our site and our products. While you can't speed up the users connection, you can use the time that they spend reading a page to advantage.

One way is to make sure that graphics are cached early on, and this is what we do in our Wrox Car Co Web application. As the user is reading the introductory page, with its animated titles and list of models, we are downloading and caching the larger graphics required for the car details pages. Unfortunately, how successfully we can do this, therefore reducing the number of connections required in other ways, depends on the client browser's capabilities.

## Browser Compatibility Issues

To reduce client connections as far as possible means making maximum use of the client browser's features. This means that you need to decide early on which browsers you are going to support. Until there is a more universal level of compatibility between different versions this is not an easy task.

### Changing The Color Of An Image

For example, consider how we might go about changing the color of an image, like we do with the car images in our application. The universal approach would be to have a graphic in each color for each car. However, this means that we have to load around ten times as many graphics if the user chooses to see all the colors. Besides, with the exceptions of the latest browsers, we can't change a graphic without reloading the page—so even more server connections are required.

In Internet Explorer 4 and higher, we can use color light filters to change the image color, but these are not ideal as, without a lot of image-specific coding, they tend to affect the whole image. The way we've chosen to do it is perhaps the simplest of all. We make the ' colored area' of the car transparent in the image (a standard 256 color GIF file), place it in a table cell, and change the background color of the cell on demand. This is fast, looks acceptable, and requires no server interaction. With more professionally designed graphics it would, of course, look even better.

### Writing Pages Dynamically On The Client

If we are going to cache the data about the cars and colors locally on the client, we need to have a way of creating the pages dynamically in line with this data—and without connecting to the server each time. This can be done easily using client-side scripting, probably with JavaScript or VBScript. This means that we need a browser that supports scripting and provides a relatively standard object model to script to.

### Updating Page Content Dynamically

Finally, we wanted to provide features that make the user experience more intuitive—by indicating which model was selected with a different color title, and by changing the text content of parts of a page as they worked with that page. Again we could easily do this with ASP and a round trip to the server, but we're looking to decrease the number of client connections, not increase them. The answer is Dynamic HTML, which is supported from version 4 in both mainline browsers from Netscape and Microsoft.

> *This book isn't designed to be a discussion of browser compatibility, and we'll take this subject no further here. If you want to know more about this topic look out for other Wrox Press books such as* Instant HTML 4.0 Programmers Reference *(ISBN 1-861001-56-8); and* Instant Dynamic HTML Programmers Reference *which is available in two editions—for Netscape Navigator (ISBN 1-861001-19-3) and Microsoft Internet Explorer (ISBN 1-861000-68-5).*

### Choosing Your Target Browser

At the end of the day, we chose to build our application to run on Internet Explorer 4/5. That's not to say that we couldn't have done the same with Navigator 4 or 5, which also support client-side scripting and a version of Dynamic HTML. What would be considerably more difficult, though by no means impossible, would be to build it in such a way that it ran on any modern browser. This is where you need to consider your target market, and the way your application will be implemented.

> *We're not proud of our choice to support only one browser, but this book (and this chapter) is about implementing and interfacing with back-end services rather than which browser we actually end up supporting. You'll have to make the difficult choices yourself, balancing features and benefits in line with the intended market for your own applications. The techniques we used can be modified to suit your choice of browser, or extended to offer more cross-browser support as required.*

# The Wrox Car Company Web Application

You've seen some screen shots of the completed Wrox Car Company application earlier in this chapter, so you'll have a good idea of what it includes. You can run the application directly from our own Web site at **http://rapid.wrox.co.uk/books/1460/** (together with other samples from this book), or download it and install it on your own system. Appendix A contains instructions on setting up the server-side database and configuring the components on your own server.

> *Note that the Finance ActiveX control is not signed, so you must set your browser's security level to Low if you want to use the control within the application. There are more details about this control on our Web site where you'll find the application.*

What we're interested in looking at here is how our application is designed to implement the features we considered earlier in this chapter. You won't find detailed descriptions of the HTML tags we used; but you will see how we used client-side scripting, Dynamic HTML, and Internet Explorer-specific features to achieve a minimum number of server connections and maximum responsiveness.

## Loading The Start Page

Like most applications we have a **default.htm** file in the application directory, which starts the application running by loading the main page. Because we're only supporting one browser (IE4/5) we need to check that the user has this browser to prevent the pages appearing to be broken when run on other incompatible browsers.

### Checking the Browser Version

Here's the complete **default.htm** page. We use client-side code to detect the browser version and load the main **wroxcars.asp** page into the full browser window if it's IE4 or better. If not, we display a message telling the user what happened:

```
<HTML>
<HEAD>
<TITLE>Loading, please wait..</TITLE>
```

```
<SCRIPT LANGUAGE="VBScript">
blnIE4 = False
strUA = navigator.userAgent
'use Microsoft's recommended browser type detection code:
intMSIE = Instr(strUA, "MSIE ") + 5
If intMSIE > 5 Then
  If CInt(Mid(strUA, intMSIE, Instr(intMSIE, strUA, ".") _
     - intMSIE)) >= 4 Then blnIE4 = True
End If
If blnIE4 Then top.window.location.href="wroxcars.asp"
</SCRIPT>

</HEAD>
<BODY>
<CENTER>
 <H3>Sorry, this application requires Internet Explorer 4 or higher.</H3>
 You can download the latest version of Internet Explorer from:<BR>
 <A HREF="http://www.microsoft.com/ie/">http://www.microsoft.com/ie/</A>
</CENTER>
</BODY>
</HTML>
```

# The Frameset Page

Our application uses a frameset page **wroxcars.asp**, which contains three frames to hold the pages that the user sees. These are the 'banner' frame and page at the top containing our logo and animation, the 'menu' frame and page containing the navigation buttons, and the 'main' frame where the list of models, details, finance information and order form are displayed. The frameset HTML code is shown below. Notice that we don't actually load the main page in the HTML–you'll see why in a while:

```
...
<FRAMESET ROWS="80,*">
 <FRAME SRC="banner.htm" SCROLLING=NO FRAMEBORDER=NO
        FRAMESPACING=0 BORDERCOLOR=white>
 <FRAMESET COLS="150,*">
  <FRAME NAME="menu" SRC="menu.htm" SCROLLING=NO
         FRAMEBORDER=NO FRAMESPACING=0 BORDERCOLOR=white>
  <FRAME NAME="main" SRC="" SCROLLING=AUTO FRAMEBORDER=NO
         FRAMESPACING=0 BORDERCOLOR=white>
 </FRAMESET>
</FRAMESET>
...
```

Even though it's a frameset, we wanted to achieve the border-less appearance that is so popular at the moment. To do this we set **FRAMEBORDER=NO** in the frameset and in each frame, and **FRAMESPACING=0** and **BORDERCOLOR=white** for each frame as well.

## Global Variables And Procedures

We're going to be caching information locally, on the client, so we need some global variables to store it and make it available to all the other pages in the frameset. The best place for this is in the frameset page itself, **wroxcars.asp**. We can then access it from anywhere else using either **parent.**_variablename_ or **top.**_variablename_. Because (as you saw earlier) we've arranged for our page to always be loaded into the full browser window, we can use **top.**_variablename_ in our code.

### The Database Connection String

We're going to need a database connection to get the data about the cars and colors, and we declare this to ASP at the top of the page. This has to be changed to suit your server, so putting it here makes it easy to find:

```
<%
'the database connection string, change to suit your database
strConnection = "driver={SQL Server};server=yourservername;" _
               & "database=WroxCarCo;UID=username;PWD=password"
%>
```

### Other Global Variables

While the connection string is only required by ASP, the other variables are required by the client-side application so they need to be stored in script on the client. We do this next, within the **<HEAD>** section of the page:

```
<HTML>
<HEAD>
<TITLE>The Wrox Car Company</TITLE>

<SCRIPT LANGUAGE="VBScript">
'global variables for navigation

Dim selectedModel       'the currently selected CarID
Dim selectedColor       'the currently selected ColorID
Dim financePayment      'the current calculated monthly payment
Dim financeMonths       'the current calculated number of months
Dim financeTotal        'the current calculated total payment
Dim interestRate        'the interest rate
ReDim arrCars(7,100)    'array to hold details of all cars
ReDim arrColors(2,500)  'array to hold all car-to-color mappings

selectedModel = 0       'initialize the global variables
selectedColor = 0
totalPrice = 0
financePayment = 0
financeMonths = 0
financeTotal = 0

'change this to suit, also requires new finance.txt file for payments
interestRate = 7.25
...
```

_We're storing the interest rate as a hard-coded number here (in the main_ **wroxcars.asp** _file), but this could also be created dynamically by the server each time if required. However there are other issues involved, which we'll discuss when we come to look at the Finance page later on._

### The Global Procedures

As well as storing variables globally in the frameset page, we can put procedures that are accessible from other pages there as well. We're storing the details of the cars and colors in two dynamic arrays, **arrCars(7,100)** and **arrColors(2,500)**, which we declared in the previous section of code. These will hold all the details about all the cars and colors, including the **CarID** and **ColorID** values for each one.

We're also storing the car and color that the user has selected in the two global variables, **selectedModel** and **selectedColor**, and so we need to be able to translate these key values into array indexes at several points in the application (i.e. when we want to get information about the currently selected car or color from the arrays):

```
...
Function CarArrayIndex()
'returns the array index of the currently selected car model
intArrayIndex = -1
intNumCars = UBound(arrCars, 2)
For intLoop = 0 To intNumCars
  If selectedModel = arrCars(0, intLoop) Then
    intArrayIndex = intLoop
    Exit For
  End If
Next
CarArrayIndex = intArrayIndex
End Function

Function ColorArrayIndex()
'returns the array index of the currently selected color
intArrayIndex = -1
intNumColors = UBound(arrColors, 2)
For intLoop = 0 To intNumColors
  If selectedColor = arrColors(1, intLoop) Then
    intArrayIndex = intLoop
    Exit For
  End If
Next
ColorArrayIndex = intArrayIndex
End Function
...
```

## Caching Data Client-side

The next step is to store the car and color data client-side. Remember that this is an **ASP page** that also contains **client-side script**. We can create this client-side script code dynamically using ASP code on the server when we build the page (just as we would create tables of values, for example). In our case, we use ASP to create the client-side script that fills the arrays with values.

### Caching The Car Details

To retrieve the car information from our database we use the same technique as we did in the showroom applications. This involved the custom business component **WCCCars**, which returns a recordset containing all the details of all the cars. However, instead of using it to create a table as we did for the showroom application, we use the recordset to fill the **arrCars** array:

```
...
Sub window_onload()
'fill the arrays of cars and colors
<%
CRLF = Chr(13) & Chr(10) 'carriage return
QUOT = Chr(34)             'double quote character
Set recCars = Server.CreateObject("ADODB.Recordset")
Set objCars = Server.CreateObject("WCCCars.Cars") 'our business object
Set recCars = objCars.GetAll(strConnection)       'get all car records
recCars.Open
'loop through all the car records filling the array
intArrayRow = 0
recCars.MoveFirst
While Not recCars.EOF
  Response.Write "arrCars(0, " & intArrayRow & ") = " _
                 & recCars("CarID") & CRLF
  Response.Write "arrCars(1, " & intArrayRow & ") = " & QUOT _
                 & recCars("Model") & QUOT & CRLF
  Response.Write "arrCars(2, " & intArrayRow & ") = " _
                 & recCars("EngineSize") & CRLF
  Response.Write "arrCars(3, " & intArrayRow & ") = " _
                 & recCars("Doors") & CRLF
  Response.Write "arrCars(4, " & intArrayRow & ") = " _
                 & recCars("Seats") & CRLF
  Response.Write "arrCars(5, " & intArrayRow & ") = " _
                 & recCars("Price") & CRLF
  Response.Write "arrCars(6, " & intArrayRow & ") = " _
                 & QUOT & recCars("Picture") & QUOT & CRLF
  Response.Write "arrCars(7, " & intArrayRow & ") = " & QUOT _
                 & recCars("Description") & QUOT & CRLF
  recCars.MoveNext
  intArrayRow = intArrayRow + 1
Wend
Set recCars = Nothing
Set objCars = Nothing
'put code in page to redimension cars array to correct size
Response.Write "ReDim Preserve arrCars(7, " & intArrayRow - 1 & ")" & CRLF
...
```

Once this page gets to the client it looks like the following code. As far as the browser is concerned it is client-side VBScript. And once we've iterated through all the records, keeping count of the number with our **intArrayRow** variable, we can resize the array to the correct size—recall it started out as **arrCars(7,100)**:

```
Sub window_onload()
' fill the arrays of cars and colors
arrCars(0, 0) = 1
arrCars(1, 0) = "Esquel GTXi"
arrCars(2, 0) = 94
arrCars(3, 0) = 2
arrCars(4, 0) = 4
arrCars(5, 0) = 18995
arrCars(6, 0) = "car1.gif"
arrCars(7, 0) = "A sporting yet all-purpose car that gives ... etc."
... rest of car details here ...
```

```
arrCars(0, 4) = 5
arrCars(1, 4) = "Deanay Pickup"
arrCars(2, 4) = 80
arrCars(3, 4) = 2
arrCars(4, 4) = 6
arrCars(5, 4) = 24995
arrCars(6, 4) = "van1.gif"
arrCars(7, 4) = "When it comes to those DIY jobs, moving ... etc."
ReDim Preserve arrCars(7, 4)
...
```

### Caching The Color Details

Now we do the same to fill the array of colors. As in the showroom application, we use the SQL Server stored procedure **usp_AllColorsForAllCars** to return a recordset. Now, however, we're putting the values into our **arrColors** array:

```
...
strSQL = "usp_AllColorsForAllCars"    'stored procedure
Set oConn = Server.CreateObject("ADODB.Connection")
oConn.Open strConnection
Set recColors = oConn.Execute(strSQL)
'loop through all the color records filling the array
intArrayRow = 0
recColors.MoveFirst
While Not recColors.EOF
  Response.Write "arrColors(0, " & intArrayRow & ") = " _
                 & recColors("fkCarID") & CRLF
  Response.Write "arrColors(1, " & intArrayRow & ") = " _
                 & recColors("ColorID") & CRLF
  Response.Write "arrColors(2, " & intArrayRow & ") = " & QUOT _
                 & recColors("Color") & QUOT & CRLF
  recColors.MoveNext
  intArrayRow = intArrayRow + 1
Wend
Set recColors = Nothing
Set oConn = Nothing
'put code in page to redimension colors array to correct size
Response.Write "ReDim Preserve arrColors(2, " & intArrayRow - 1 & ")" _
               & CRLF
%>
...
```

Once this part of the page gets to the browser it looks like this:

```
...
arrColors(0, 0) = 1
arrColors(1, 0) = 1
arrColors(2, 0) = "White"
arrColors(0, 1) = 2
arrColors(1, 1) = 1
arrColors(2, 1) = "White"
...
arrColors(2, 17) = "Dark Orange"
...
```

```
arrColors(2, 29) = "Powder Blue"
...
arrColors(2, 46) = "Black"
ReDim Preserve arrColors(2, 46)
End Sub
```

### Loading The Main Car Models Page

Now that we've got all the data safely stored in our two arrays, we can load the 'list of models' page **carmodels.htm** into the main window. We didn't do it before because we need the values in the arrays to build this page dynamically, and the browser can run script code and the HTML parsing engine as separate processes. This could have meant that the browser loaded the model list page before the values had been placed in the arrays by the client-side script:

```
...
'now load the car models page
frames("main").location.href = "carmodels.htm"

End Sub
</SCRIPT>
```

# The Car Model List Page

With all our data available, we can now create a list of cars models. This is the page **carmodels.htm** that we loaded at the end of the frameset page's **window_onload()** event. As all the data is cached on the client in our arrays, we need to use client-side script code to build the page dynamically.

## Building Pages Dynamically

The main part of the model list page is a table containing the name and description of each car, and a small image. To make it look attractive we alternated the image alignment between left and right. This means that we can't just loop through the array using the same code for each model, we have to do two in each pass. Here's the complete script section that creates the table—the second row is just a mirror of the first:

```
<TABLE ID="tblModels" STYLE="border-style:none" CELLPADDING=10>

<SCRIPT LANGUAGE="VBScript">
'build the table of car models
BS = Chr(47)     'slash character '/'
QUOT= Chr(34)    'double quote
intNumCars = UBound(top.arrCars, 2)
intThisCar = 0
Do While intThisCar <= intNumCars
    'table row with picture on left
    Document.Write "<TR><TD ALIGN=RIGHT STYLE=" & QUOT & "cursor:hand" _
        & QUOT & "><IMG ID=" & QUOT & "Img" & top.arrCars(0, intThisCar) _
        & QUOT & " SRC=" & QUOT & "images/150" & top.arrCars(6, intThisCar) _
        & QUOT & " BORDER=0 HSPACE=15><P><" & BS & "TD>"
    Document.Write "<TD ALIGN=LEFT><SPAN ID=" & QUOT & "Car" _
        & top.arrCars(0, intThisCar) & QUOT & " CLASS=" & QUOT
    If top.arrCars(0, intThisCar) = top.selectedModel Then
```

```
            Document.Write "SELNAME"    'selected model
        Else
            Document.Write "MODNAME"    'not selected model
        End If
        Document.Write QUOT & ">The Wrox " & top.arrCars(1, intThisCar) _
            & "<" & BS & "SPAN><BR>" & top.arrCars(7, intThisCar) _
            & "<P><" & BS & "TD><" & BS & "TR>"
        'move to the next car (if there is one)
        intThisCar = intThisCar + 1
        If intThisCar <= intNumCars Then
            'table row with picture on right
            '{repeat of code above but with image and text swapped over}
        End If
        intThisCar = intThisCar + 1
    Loop
    </SCRIPT>

    </TABLE>
```

The result for one row of the table is shown here. A couple of things to notice are that there are no **<A>** tags in the code, because we're going to detect mouse clicks with script code, and we use a different style for the car name if it's the currently selected one (i.e. its **CarID** is the same as the value stored in the global variable **top.selectedModel**).

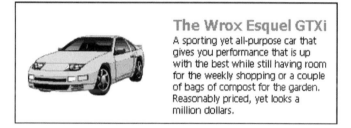

*You'll also see we use a string variable **BS** to write the slash character '**/**' into the page. HTML 4.0 says that when using client-side script to write HTML code into a page, any combination of '**</**' followed by a letter should be treated as the end of a script section. This would mean that the browser would stop writing the HTML at that point, and you'd get a syntax error caused by the 'real' **</SCRIPT>** tag. IE4 doesn't actually do this, but we're sticking to the rules here.*

### The Problem With Document.Write

Using client-side script to create the page's HTML code dynamically can be a real pain. It's easy to omit a closing '**>**' or double-quote and get a page that looks nothing like you expected. Unlike a page created with ASP, you can't 'view the source' and see what your code actually produced—all you see is the client-side script code.

To make life easier, we developed a very simple tool that allows you to see the actual HTML that is created in IE4 or better. It uses the fact that we can read the **innerHTML** property of an element to get a string containing the 'virtual' HTML that the browser uses to create the page. If we write this string back to the **innerText** (rather than **innerHTML**) property of another element, it isn't parsed by the browser but just displayed as text.

What we do is place a temporary **<DIV>** (document division) section around the entire contents of the **<BODY>** of the page, positioning it so that it doesn't change the layout of the existing elements:

```
</HEAD>
<DIV ID="ToBeRead" STYLE="position:absolute; left:0; top:0">
<BODY STYLE="background-color:white; text-align:center">
...
... page content here including <SCRIPT> sections with Document.Write
...
</BODY>
</DIV>
</HTML>
```

Then, in the script code in the page, we add a **window_onload** event (or add the code to an existing event) to open our special **read_doc.htm** page in a new browser window, and place the content of the page into it:

```
Sub window_onload()
   Set objNewWin = window.open("read_doc.htm")
   objNewWin.document.all("Output").innerText _
            = document.all("ToBeRead").innerHTML
End Sub
```

The **read_doc.htm** page contains a heading and some instruction on use. However, the main part is the **<DIV>** named **Output** into which we are placing the page content:

```
<DIV ID="Output">
... default text and insrtructions here
</DIV>
```

*You can run this page from our Web site at http://rapid.wrox.co.uk/books/1460/*

Here's the result from the first two rows of the car models page table. The last few lines of the script code we saw earlier, which creates the table, are highlighted. The remainder is the HTML that is created dynamically by that script code:

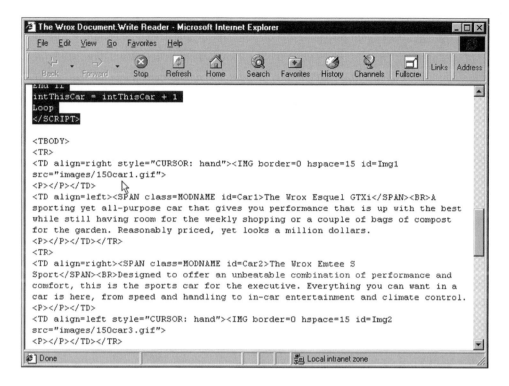

*It's interesting to note how the browser has changed the code we wrote to the page. (IE4 does this with all pages, including plain HTML ones, as it converts them from the text HTML source into the 'virtual' page it displays). For example, it sorts the attributes for each element into alphabetical order, and changes their case—all the style property names come out in capital letters, for example.*

## Caching Images

The car models list displays small images, named **150car1.gif**, **150car2.gif**, etc. However the details page uses a larger image, named **300car1.gif**, **300car2.gif**, etc., instead. When the user selects a model we want to display the details as quickly as possible, and we can do this by downloading and caching the larger images while they are viewing the model list. At the end of the model list page we create a set of hidden image tags:

```
...
<SCRIPT LANGUAGE="VBScript">
'preload the main car pictures for use later
For intLoop = 0 To intNumCars
  Document.Write "<IMG WIDTH=1 HEIGHT=1 SRC=" & QUOT & "images/300" _
    & top.arrCars(6, intLoop) & QUOT _
    & " STYLE=" & QUOT & "visibility:hidden" & QUOT & ">"
Next
</SCRIPT>
</BODY>
</HTML>
```

The resulting virtual HTML code looks like this—again IE4 has changed the case and ordering of some of the attributes:

```
<IMG height=1 src="images/300car1.gif" style="VISIBILITY: hidden" width=1>
<IMG height=1 src="images/300car3.gif" style="VISIBILITY: hidden" width=1>
<IMG height=1 src="images/300car4.gif" style="VISIBILITY: hidden" width=1>
<IMG height=1 src="images/300car2.gif" style="VISIBILITY: hidden" width=1>
<IMG height=1 src="images/300van1.gif" style="VISIBILITY: hidden" width=1>
```

## Indicating The Selected Model

The final task in the main page is to allow the user to select a car model, and indicate to them which model is currently selected. The small car images and the car model names are not actually hyperlinks, although we used the **STYLE="cursor:hand"** attribute to make them appear as if they are. So we need to detect a mouse-click on them another way. The standard IE4 Dynamic HTML technique is shown in the code below:

**The Wrox Hardy S Coupe**

This is the car for the enthusiast. As the name suggests, you need to revel in the basics of what a sports car is about. Noisy, uncomfortable, and it handles like a dog. But when it comes to performance, this car is the tops.

```
Sub document_onclick()
   Set objSource = window.event.srcElement
   If Left(objSource.id, 3) = "Car" Or Left(objSource.id, 3) = "Img" Then
      'a car image or name was clicked, get the CarID key
      intCarID = CInt(Mid(objSource.id, 4))
      'change the style of the car names as appropriate
      document.all("Car" & intCarID).className = "SELNAME"
      If top.selectedModel > 0 And top.selectedModel <> intCarID Then
         document.all("Car" & top.selectedModel).className = "MODNAME"
      End If
      'store the selection in the frameset page variables
      top.selectedModel = intCarID
      top.selectedColor = 0
      'update the 'salespersons comment' window
      strMessage = document.all("Car" & intCarID).innerText_
               & ", an excellent choice."
      top.frames("menu").document.all("divMessage").innerText = strmessage
   End If
   window.event.cancelBubble = true
   window.event.returnValue = false
End Sub
```

We can get the **CarID** from the **ID** attribute of the image or car name, because we put it there ourselves when we created the page. Then we only have to swap the text style of the previously selected item (if there was one and it's not the same as the current one) and the currently selected one. This makes the currently selected model name appear in red rather than gray–the style definitions are in the **<HEAD>** of the page and aren't shown in the code here.

The final task is to update the salesperson's comments that appear in the top left section of the page, above the navigation buttons. We do this by writing to the **innerText** property of a **<DIV>** on that page. We'll look at this page in detail later on.

# The Banner Heading Page

The banner heading page, **banner.htm**, is loaded at the start of the application, and contains a simple animation designed to catch the user's eye. All the techniques are standard IE4 Dynamic HTML, so we won't be spending time describing them in detail. For more information, check out our sister publication, Professional IE4 Programming (ISBN 1-861000-70-7). Here's the main section of the HTML code that creates the page:

```
<DIV ID="BannerDiv" STYLE="position:absolute; left:0; top:0; width:100%">
<IMG ID="CarImg" SRC="images/wcctowcar.gif" WIDTH="134" HEIGHT="61"
    STYLE="visibility:hidden; position:absolute; left:-150; top:5">
<IMG ID="CarImg2" SRC="images/wcctowcar2.gif"STYLE="visibility:hidden">
<IMG ID="HeadImg" SRC="images/wccheader.gif" WIDTH="370" HEIGHT="61"
    STYLE="visibility:hidden; position:absolute; left:-520; top:5">
</DIV>
```

Notice the **<DIV>** named **BannerDiv**, which encloses the entire content. We're going to move a graphic from left to right when this page loads, and then fade in a slogan when it disappears off the right-hand end of the page. This means that we need to know how wide the page is in pixels. While Netscape Navigator is good enough to expose this directly as a property, IE 4 isn't.

What we do is simply read the **pixelWidth** style property value of the enclosing **<DIV>** element. As the **<DIV>** is positioned at the extreme left and set to **100%** of the page width, this returns the width of the page in pixels:

```
'the DIV holding the page contents is sized to 100% of page width, so
intWindowWidth = document.all("BannerDiv").style.pixelWidth
```

## The Banner Page Animation

The animation consists of a series of actions:

- ❑ The first car image (with towrope) moves from left-to-right dragging the logo banner
- ❑ The banner stops 10 pixels in from the left, and the car image is swapped to one without a towrope
- ❑ This new car image moves to the right until it disappears off the page
- ❑ The slogan is faded into view next to the banner logo

As is usual in this kind of scenario, the timing of movement are controlled by the **setInterval** method of the browser. Here's the global variables that we use to hold references and flags between each timer event, and the code that initializes them:

```
<SCRIPT LANGUAGE="VBScript">

'declare the global variables
Dim objMyTimer      'reference to window.setInterval timer
Dim objCar          'reference to 'old car' image
Dim objHead         'reference to Wrox Car Co banner image
Dim blnLoaded       'flag to show if images are finished loading
Dim blnSwapped      'flag to show we've swapped to the 2nd car image
Dim intWindowWidth  'width of client window

Sub window_onload()
  window.status = "Welcome to the Wrox Car Company"
  Set objCar = document.all("CarImg")
  Set objHead = document.all("HeadImg")
  blnLoaded = False    'not yet loaded
  blnSwapped = False   'using first car image
  'the DIV holding the page contents is sized to 100% of page width, so
  intWindowWidth = document.all("BannerDiv").style.pixelWidth
  'start the interval timer
  objMyTimer = window.setInterval("moveImages()", 100, "VBScript")
End Sub
```

### Moving the Images

Each time the **setInterval** method fires an event, we run the **moveImages** subroutine. This is the full code:

```
Sub moveImages()
  If Not blnLoaded Then    'pictures not yet loaded so check again
    blnLoaded = (objCar.readyState = "complete" _
                 And objHead.readyState = "complete")
    objCar.style.visibility = "visible"   'make offscreen images visible
    objHead.style.visibility = "visible"
  Else
    If objCar.style.pixelLeft > intWindowWidth Then 'car is at right end
      window.clearInterval (objMyTimer)                  'so stop timer
      objCar.style.visibility = "hidden"                 'and hide it
      window.status = "Select a car and click 'Details' for information"
      startTransition   'start to fade in the slogan image
    Else
      objCar.style.left = objCar.style.pixelLeft + 3  'move the images
      If objHead.style.pixelLeft < 10 Then
        objHead.style.left = objHead.style.pixelLeft + 3
      Else
        If Not blnSwapped Then   'swap to second car image (no towrope)
          objCar.src = document.all("CarImg2").src
          blnSwapped = True
        End If
      End If
    End If
  End If
End Sub
```

And here's the result part-way into the animation:

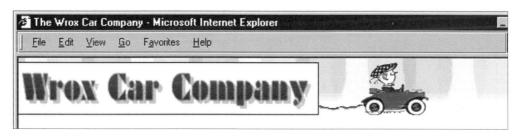

### Fading In The Slogan

The slogan is faded in using a **transition filter**. We add the filter to our image in the HTML that creates the page. The image isn't visible when loaded, because we include the **visibility:hidden** style property:

```
<IMG ID="Force" SRC="images/force.gif" WIDTH="200" HEIGHT="40"
    STYLE="visibility:hidden; position:absolute; left:420;
           top:15; filter: revealTrans(Transition=12, Duration=5)">
```

Once our car image has moved off-screen, our **moveImages** code calls our **startTransition** routine. This is the code:

```
Sub startTransition()
   'apply transition to 'lock' the image
   document.all("Force").filters(0).apply()
   'make it visible, but it's still locked
   document.all("Force").style.visibility = visible
   'play the transition to make it appear
   document.all("Force").filters(0).play()
End Sub
```

This first 'applies' the filter that we added to the image element in the HTML (elements can have more than one filter attached to them at a time and this selects the filter we want to use). Next it makes the image visible, but because the filter has been applied this 'locks' the image, which doesn't actually appear in the page. The final step is to 'play' the filter, which makes it gradually appear.

*You can learn all about IE4's animations and filters (along with all kinds of other techniques) from our sister book* Professional IE4 Programming, *ISBN 1-861000-70-7.*

# The Navigation Menu

The page in the left-hand window of our application, **menu.htm**, is a simple 'navigation bar' menu containing five 'buttons'. These are images within hyperlink **<A>** tags. There's also a small **<DIV>** that is used to display the kind of inane comments you would expect if you had the salesperson standing behind you in the showroom.

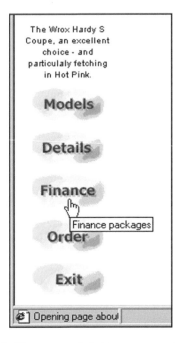

The HTML code that creates this page is simple enough. The car models list page can be loaded normally at any time, and will automatically use the current value of the global **selectedModel** variable to highlight the correct model. However notice that the next three options, Details, Finance and Order, are hyperlinks to JavaScript functions:

```
<DIV ID="divMessage" STYLE="position:absolute; left:10; top:5;
    width=100; height=65; text-align:center"></DIV>
<A HREF="carmodels.htm" TARGET="main"><IMG SRC="images/btn_models.gif"
    WIDTH="83" HEIGHT="40" ALT="List of models" STYLE="border:none;
    position:absolute; left:20; top:80"></A>
<A HREF="javascript:carDetail();"><IMG SRC="images/btn_details.gif"
    WIDTH="83" HEIGHT="40" ALT="View car details" STYLE="border:none;
    position:absolute; left:20; top:130"></A>
<A HREF="javascript:carFinance();"><IMG SRC="images/btn_finance.gif"
    WIDTH="83" HEIGHT="40" ALT="Finance packages" STYLE="border:none;
    position:absolute; left:20; top:180"></A>
<A HREF="javascript:carOrder();"><IMG SRC="images/btn_order.gif"
    WIDTH="83" HEIGHT="40" ALT="Place an order" STYLE="border:none;
    position:absolute; left:20; top:230"></A>
<A HREF="yourpages.htm" TARGET="_top"><IMG SRC="images/btn_exit.gif"
    WIDTH="83" HEIGHT="40" ALT="Exit the application"
    STYLE="border:none; position:absolute; left:20; top:280"></A>
```

*We used JScript rather than VBScript here because the hyperlinks are **JavaScript URLs** (JavaScript code or a JavaScript function name preceded by '**`javascript:`**'). However, you can also use a JavaScript URL to execute a function written in VBScript—but we fancied a change of language anyway...*

## Controlling Navigation

We don't want to allow the user to open the Detail or Finance page until they select a car model, or the Order page until they select a car model and color. This is easy enough to do in JavaScript. If the appropriate global variable(s) are still zero we display an error message. If it's OK to continue we just load the page they asked for:

```
<SCRIPT LANGUAGE="JavaScript">
<!--
function carDetail()
{
  if (top.selectedModel.valueOf() > 0)
    top.frames['main'].location.href = 'cardetail.htm'
  else
    alert('You must select a model of car first.');
}

function carFinance()
{
  if (top.selectedModel.valueOf() > 0)
    top.frames['main'].location.href = 'webfinance.htm'
  else
    alert('You must select a model of car first.');
}

function carOrder()
{
  if ((top.selectedModel.valueOf() > 0)
    && (top.selectedColor.valueOf() > 0))
    top.frames['main'].location.href = 'weborder.htm'
  else
    alert('You must select a car and a color first.');
}

//-->
</SCRIPT>
```

# The Car Details Page

Once the user selects a model of car, we can show them more information about it. This is done by loading the **cardetail.htm** page into the main frame of our application. The main section of this page is a table containing the large graphic of the vehicle and some details about it—including the colors it's available in:

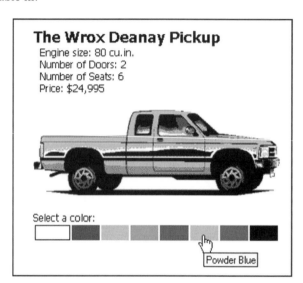

The code that creates this page is fundamentally similar to that in the car models list page, except now we just need to retrieve details about one car, not all of them. This is where the global **CarArrayIndex** routine comes in—we use it to find out which row of our **arrCars** array contains the details of the currently selected model:

```
<SCRIPT LANGUAGE="VBScript">
BS = Chr(47)    'slash character '/'
QUOT= Chr(34)   'double quote
intArrayIndex = top.CarArrayIndex()    'the array index of this car
Document.Write "<SPAN ID=" & QUOT & "CarName" & QUOT _
  & " CLASS=" & QUOT & "MAIN" & QUOT & ">The Wrox " _
  & top.arrCars(1, intArrayIndex) & "<" & BS & "SPAN><BR>"
Document.Write "  Engine size: " _
  & top.arrCars(2, intArrayIndex) & " cu.in.<BR>"
Document.Write "  Number of Doors: " _
  & top.arrCars(3, intArrayIndex) & "<BR>"
Document.Write "  Number of Seats: " _
  & top.arrCars(4, intArrayIndex) & "<BR>"
Document.Write "  Price: " _
  & FormatCurrency(top.arrCars(5, intArrayIndex), 0) & "<P>"
</SCRIPT>
. . .
```

The remainder of the code here creates the table containing the car name, image, and other details. Looking at it in our Document.Write Reader tool, you can see the client-side script code selected, and below it the resulting HTML:

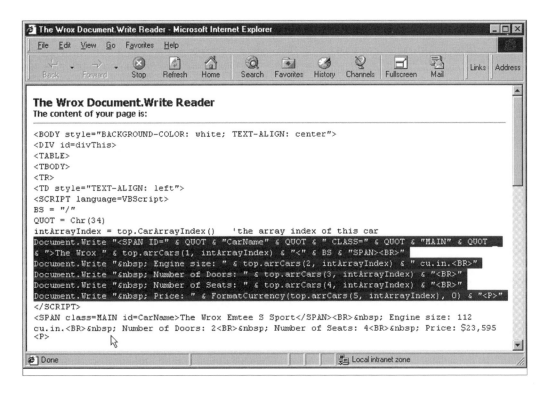

*You can download this 'tool' from the Resources section of our Web site at*
`http://rapid.wrox.co.uk/resources/`

## Inserting the Car Image

Following the car details is a short section that creates the single-cell table containing the car image. We give the table cell the **ID** of **tdCarImg**, and remove any padding or spacing so that the image completely fills the cell:

```
...
<TABLE CELLSPACING=0 CELLPADDING=0>
  <TR><TD ID="tdCarImg">

<SCRIPT LANGUAGE="VBScript">
Document.Write "<IMG SRC=" & QUOT & "images/300" _
   & top.arrCars(6, intArrayIndex) & QUOT & "><" & BS & "TD>"
</SCRIPT>

</TR>
</TABLE>
...
```

Now, when we change the color of the cell background, this new color will only be visible through the transparent parts of the car image.

## Inserting the Colors Table

Our database stores the color names as well as the color ID values, and we've cached these in our **arrColors** array. Fortunately (through good design at the outset) the color names are the same as the standard HTML color names, except for case and the inclusion of a space for some colors–i.e. the HTML color name **hotpink** is in our database as Hot Pink. We can convert from our version into HTML color names easily enough with a custom function named **unspaceColor**:

```
Function unspaceColor(strColorName)
  'convert real color name into IE4 'colorname' format
  strColor = LCase(strColorName)
  intSpace = InStr(strColor, " ")
  Do While intSpace
    strColor = Left(strColor, intSpace - 1) & Mid(strColor, intSpace + 1)
    intSpace = InStr(strColor, " ")
  Loop
  unspaceColor = strColor
End Function
```

So now it's a simple matter of building the table of colors from the contents of the **arrColors** array. This array holds three values in each row–the ID of a car that is available in this color, the ID of this color, and the color name. We only have to loop through the entire array looking for rows that have the same **CarID** as our currently selected model. Note that the table has the **cursor:hand** style property to indicate that colors can be clicked:

```
...
Select a color:
<TABLE ID="tbColors" STYLE="border-style:none; width:300px;
                            font-size:20; cursor:hand">
  <TR>

<SCRIPT LANGUAGE="VBScript">
'loop through the colors table selecting ones that apply to this car
intNumRecs = UBound(top.arrColors, 2)
For intColorRec = 0 To intNumRecs
  If top.arrColors(0, intColorRec) = top.selectedModel Then
    strColorName = unspaceColor(top.arrColors(2, intColorRec))
    Document.Write "<TD ID=" & QUOT & "Color" _
       & top.arrColors(1, intColorRec) & QUOT _
       & "STYLE=" & QUOT & "background-color:" & strColorName
    If strColorName = "white" Then
      Document.Write "; border-width:1px; border-style:solid; "_
         & "border-color:black"
    End If
    Document.Write QUOT & " TITLE=" & QUOT _
       & top.arrColors(2, intColorRec) & QUOT & "> <" & BS & "TD>"
  End If
Next
</SCRIPT>

  </TR>
</TABLE>
```

The script iterates through the array building each table cell. If the color is white, it also adds a black border so that the cell is visible on the white page. For each cell, it sets the title to the original color name from our array to act as a pop-up tool tip. Here's the result in our Document.Write Reader:

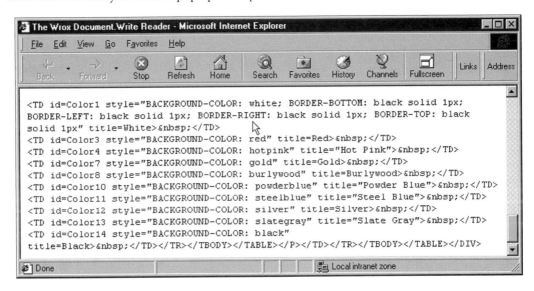

## Selecting A Color

When the user clicks on the table of colors, we have to store the ID of the color they selected and change the background color of the table cell that contains the car image. We also update the salesperson's comments to include the color they chose:

```
Sub tbColors_onclick()
    'change the color of the car by changing the table background color
    Set objSource = window.event.srcElement    'the cell that was clicked
    Set objCarCell = document.all("tdCarImg") 'cell holding car picture
    strNewColor = objSource.style.backgroundColor
    objCarCell.style.backgroundColor = strNewColor
    'update the global selected color in the frameset page
    top.selectedColor = CInt(Mid(objSource.id, 6))
    'update the salesperson's comments
    strMessage = document.all("CarName").innerText _
        & ", an excellent choice - and particulaly fetching in " _
        & objSource.title & "."
    top.frames("menu").document.all("divMessage").innerText = strMessage
    window.event.cancelBubble = true
    window.event.returnValue = false
End Sub
```

# The Finance Details Page

This page, **webfinance.htm**, is the most complex of the application, yet demonstrates another useful way of minimizing load on your server under high usage conditions. However, let's work through from the top and see how the page is built.

The page heading containing the car model (and color if selected) is created in the same way as in the Details page. Following it is a set of HTML 'form' controls. They aren't actually on a **<FORM>** because we won't be submitting anything. (If you build a page like this in Navigator you still have to include the **<FORM>** tags or the controls won't be displayed). Here's the result:

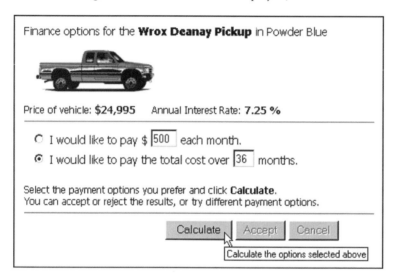

And here's the HTML code for the controls section (the part below the first horizontal rule):

```
...
<HR>
  <INPUT TYPE=RADIO ID="chkNumberMonths" NAME="CheckGroup" CHECKED>
I would like to pay $
<INPUT TYPE=TEXT ID="txtNumberMonths" VALUE="500" SIZE=3 MAXLENGTH=3>
each month.
<BR>
  <INPUT TYPE=RADIO ID="chkMonthlyAmount" NAME="CheckGroup">
I would like to pay the total cost over
<INPUT TYPE=TEXT ID="txtMonthlyAmount" VALUE="36" SIZE=2 MAXLENGTH=3>
months.
<DIV ID="divResults">
   Select the payment options you prefer and click <B>Calculate</B>.
</DIV>
<DIV ID="divInstructions">
   You can accept or reject the results or try different payment options.
</DIV>
<HR>
<DIV STYLE="text-align:right; width:90%">
<INPUT TYPE="BUTTON" ID="cmdCalculate" VALUE="Calculate"
       ONCLICK="calculateResults()"
```

```
                TITLE="Calculate the options selected above">
  <INPUT TYPE="BUTTON" ID="cmdAccept" VALUE="Accept"
         DISABLED ONCLICK="acceptResults()"
         TITLE="Accept the results displayed above">
  <INPUT TYPE="BUTTON" ID="cmdCancel" VALUE="Cancel"
         DISABLED ONCLICK="clearResults()"
         TITLE="Reject the results displayed above">
  </DIV>
  ...
```

Notice that we give the two **RADIO** buttons the same **NAME** (so that only one can be selected at a time), but different **ID**s. We can easily use the **ID** to tell which one was selected.

## Calculating Finance Packages

The first part of the script in the page declares some variables that will be global just for this page, followed by the **calculateResults** procedure that runs when the Calculate button is clicked:

```
<SCRIPT LANGUAGE="VBScript">
'variable to hold last quotation.
'accepted quotes are stored in frameset page variables
intNumberMonths = 0
curMonthlyPayment = 0
curTotalPrice = 0

Sub calculateResults()
  'runs when Calculate button is clicked
  document.all("cmdAccept").Disabled = True    'disable the Accept button
  document.all("cmdCancel").Disabled = True    'disable the Cancel button
  If document.all("chkNumberMonths").checked Then
    'calculate number of months to pay given payment amount
    strResult = calculateMonths()
  Else
    'calculate monthly payment given number of months
    strResult = calculatePayment()
  End If
  If InStr(strResult, "Sorry") > 0 Then    'couldn't calculate a result
    strResult = "<B>Error</B>: " & strResult
  Else
    strResult = "<B>Quotation</B>: " & strResult 'quote succeeded
    document.all("cmdAccept").Disabled = False    'enable Accept button
    document.all("cmdCancel").Disabled = False    'enable Cancel button
  End If
  document.all("divResults").innerHTML = strResult 'display the results
End Sub
```

All that **calculateResults** does is check which option was selected, and call the appropriate procedure to return the result as a string. If the string contains the word ' Sorry' we know that the calculation could not be completed. At the same time, the code enables and disables the Accept and Cancel buttons depending on the outcome of the calculation.

The two types of calculation involve two very different client-side techniques. The first of these is the one we originally saw back in Chapter 2. We provide a custom ActiveX control named **WCCFinance** on our server which is downloaded and installed on the client when the page is opened.

### The Client-side WCCFinance ActiveX Control

The **WCCFinance** control is inserted into the client page using an **<OBJECT>** tag. The first time that the user opens this page the control is downloaded from our Web site. Any supporting files that it requires (such as the VB5 runtime library) are downloaded directly from the special Microsoft site designed for just this purpose–the VB5 Application Setup program looks after all these details automatically. After the user has visited the page once, the control will be available directly on their machine for subsequent visits so there will be no delays:

```
<!-- our custom ActiveX control -->
<OBJECT ID="FinanceObject"
  CLASSID="CLSID:CBFC0DA5-A499-11D1-882B-00201834E2A6"
  CODEBASE="WCCFinance.cab#version=1,0,0,0">
</OBJECT>
```

The **calculateMonths** routine that uses the control is similar to the code we saw in Chapter 2, but now performs some extra error checking:

```
Function calculateMonths()
  'calculate number months given payment amount with custom control
  On Error Resume Next
  Set objFinance = document.all("FinanceObject")   'instantiate control
  If Not IsObject(objFinance) Then                  'couldn't instantiate
    strMesg = "This calculation requires an ActiveX control that "
            & "has not been properly installed" ..etc.
    Msgbox strMesg, vbInformation, "Finance Control Error"
    calculateMonths = "Sorry, cannot perform calculation."
    Exit Function
  End If
  curPaymentValue = document.all("txtNumberMonths").Value
  'check value is a number
  If Not IsNumeric(curPaymentValue) Then
    strMesg = "You must enter a number for the monthly amount."
    Msgbox strMesg, vbInformation, "Data Entry Error"
    document.all("txtNumberMonths").focus
    document.all("txtNumberMonths").select
    calculateMonths = "Sorry, cannot perform calculation."
    Exit Function
  End If
  objFinance.TotalPrice = top.arrCars(5, intCarIndex) 'price of car
  objFinance.InterestRate = top.interestRate / 12     'interest rate
  objFinance.MonthlyPayment = curPaymentValue         'payment amount
  intCalcMonths = objFinance.GetNumberPayments        'calculate result
  If intCalcMonths > 0 Then    'control returns number > 0 if succeeded
    'update page-level 'last quote' variables
    intNumberMonths = intCalcMonths
    curMonthlyPayment = curPaymentValue
    curTotalPrice = curMonthlyPayment * intNumberMonths
    strResult = "<B>" & intNumberMonths & "</B> payments of <B>" _
```

```
                    & FormatCurrency(curMonthlyPayment, 0) & "</B>. " _
                    & "Total payment of <B>" _
                    & FormatCurrency(curTotalPrice, 0) & "</B>."
       Else
         strResult = "Sorry, this is insufficient to meet the interest costs."
       End If
       calculateMonths = strResult
    End Function
```

Once the values have been calculated, we update the local variables in this page (not the global variables in the main frameset) and return the results as a formatted string. If we can't calculate a result we return a message including the word ' Sorry'. As you saw in the previous section, the return string is displayed in the page and the state of the buttons updated by the **calculateResults** procedure.

### The RDS Tabular Data Control

The second finance option is to specify the number of months to pay off the debt, and have the page calculate the payment. This isn't a trivial task, and requires use of the standard **PMT** financial function–something that is not supported in VBScript or JavaScript.

Instead, we've used Excel to create a simple comma-delimited text file containing the payments required for a $1000 loan over periods ranging from 6 months to 10 years at the interest rate (7.25%) hard-coded into the frameset page **wroxcars.asp**. This text file, **finance.txt**, is on our server within the application directory:

```
Months,Payment
6,171.19
7,147.30
8,129.37
9,115.44
10,104.29
11,95.17
12,87.57
...
117,13.00
118,12.94
119,12.87
120,12.80
```

*In our application, we used a hard-coded interest rate for simplicity. There is no reason why you can't store the rate on the server and retrieve it when you create the frameset page. However you will also have to provide a table (as shown above) for that rate, or modify the code to read from a multi-column table that contains all possible rates. As they say in all the best books, this is left for you to experiment with.*

**379**

To get the data into our application, we use Remote Data Services (RDS) as we did in the Chapter 2 example. However we have a simple text file rather than a database table, and so we can use the light-weight **Simple Tabular Data Control** (TDC) on the client, instead of the Advanced Data Control (ADC) we used earlier. This loads the entire text file from the server, caches it on the client, and accesses it there. The whole process only requires one connection to upload the relatively small file, and never needs to go back to the server again–just what we want to happen.

The TDC is inserted with an **<OBJECT>** tag, and we also include a hidden bound control to make sure it retrieves the data file (sometimes it may not retrieve the data file if there are no bound controls on the page, although this is more likely to happen with the ADC rather than the TDC):

```
<!-- the RDS Tabular Data Control -->
<OBJECT ID="FinanceData" WIDTH=1 HEIGHT=1
  CLASSID="CLSID:333C7BC4-460F-11D0-BC04-0080C7055A83">
  <PARAM NAME="FieldDelim" VALUE=",">
  <PARAM NAME="DataURL" VALUE="finance.txt">
  <PARAM NAME="UseHeader" VALUE=True>
</OBJECT>

<!-- may need a bound control to get TDC to retrieve records -->
<INPUT TYPE="TEXT" DATASRC="#FinanceData" DATAFLD="Months"
       STYLE="visibility:hidden">
```

The routine that uses the TDC is fundamentally similar to the **WCCFinance** routine, except that it also checks that the value for the number of months is within the range of the values in the text file. The following code is the **calculatePayments** function in our Finance page that is called if the user specifies the number of months they want to spread the payments over:

```
Function calculatePayment ()
   'calculate monthly payment given number of months using RDS text file
   On Error Resume Next
   intCalcMonths = document.all("txtMonthlyAmount").Value
   'check value is a number
   If Not IsNumeric(intCalcMonths) Then
   ... { create error message here }
   Exit Function
   End If
   'check value is in range for values in text file
   If (intCalcMonths < 6) Or (intCalcMonths > 120) Then
      ... { create error message here }
     Exit Function
   End If
   'create local recordset from TDC control to get the payments list
   Set oRs = document.all("FinanceData").Recordset
   If Not IsObject(oRs) Then    'couldn't create the control
     strMesg = "This calculation uses the ActiveX Tabular Data Control, "_
            & "which has not been properly installed on your system."
     Msgbox strMesg, vbInformation, "Finance Data Error"
     calculatePayment = "Sorry, cannot perform calculation."
     Exit Function
   End If
   ...
```

Once we're sure we can do the calculation, we open the TDC's recordset and loop through the records looking for the number of months entered by the user, then collect the payment for a $1000 loan over that period. Afterwards it's just a matter of multiplying this up to match the price of the car, building the return string, and updating the page-level 'last quote' variables:

```
   . . .
   'loop through the records looking for required number of months
   oRs.MoveFirst
   curPaymentValue = 0
   Do While Not oRs.EOF
      If oRs("Months") = intCalcMonths Then
         curPaymentValue = oRs("Payment")
      End If
      oRs.MoveNext
   Loop
   If curPaymentValue > 0 Then    'will be zero if not found
      intNumberMonths = intCalcMonths
      curMonthlyPayment = curPaymentValue _
                    * top.arrCars(5, intCarIndex) / 1000
      curTotalPrice = curMonthlyPayment * intNumberMonths
      strResult = "<B>" & intNumberMonths & "</B> monthly payments of <B>" _
            & FormatCurrency(curMonthlyPayment, 0) & "</B>. " _
            & "Total payment of <B>" _
            & FormatCurrency(curTotalPrice, 0) & "</B>."
   Else
      strResult = "Sorry, cannot calculate for this number of months."
   End If
   calculatePayment = strResult
End Function
```

### Accepting A Quote

Once we've done a successful quote, we allow the user to accept it by clicking the Accept button. This runs the **acceptResults** code, which updates the global variables in the frameset page, inserts a message into this page, and sets the state of the buttons to allow the user to cancel the quote if required:

```
Sub acceptResults()
   'update the global variables in the frameset page
   top.financePayment = curMonthlyPayment
   top.financeMonths = intNumberMonths
   top.financeTotal = curTotalPrice
   'enable/disable buttons as appropriate
   document.all("cmdAccept").Disabled = True
   document.all("cmdCancel").Disabled = False
   'and display accepted quote
   strResult = "<B>Accepted</B>: " _
            & Mid(document.all("divResults").innerHTML, 19)
   document.all("divInstructions").innerHTML = strResult
End Sub
```

Here's the result when they accept a quote:

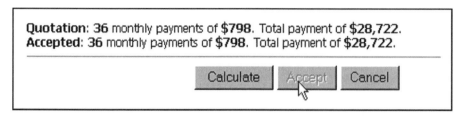

### Rejecting A Quote

To reject a quote we set the global frameset variables back to zero, disable both the Accept and Cancel buttons, and display the instructions again:

```
Sub clearResults()
    'zero the global variables in the frameset page
    top.financePayment = 0
    top.financeMonths = 0
    top.financeTotal = 0
    'disable the buttons
    document.all("cmdAccept").Disabled = True
    document.all("cmdCancel").Disabled = True
    'remove last quote and last accepted quote
    strResult = "Select the payment options you prefer ..." etc.
    document.all("divResults").innerHTML = strResult
    strResult = "You can accept or reject the results or ..." etc.
    document.all("divInstructions").innerHTML = strResult
End Sub
```

# Placing An Order

It's taken some time to get to this point, but now we come to the whole object of the exercise. Our Web application has persuaded the user that they want to order one of our cars, and we need to place this order in the showroom and head office databases.

The order process consists of two steps. The first is for the user to select their preferred method of placing the order, via our secure site accessed with a certificate (as introduced in Chapter 7) or through the standard site. The page **weborder.htm** gives them these options, plus the option to jump to the certificate enrollment page where they can obtain a certificate:

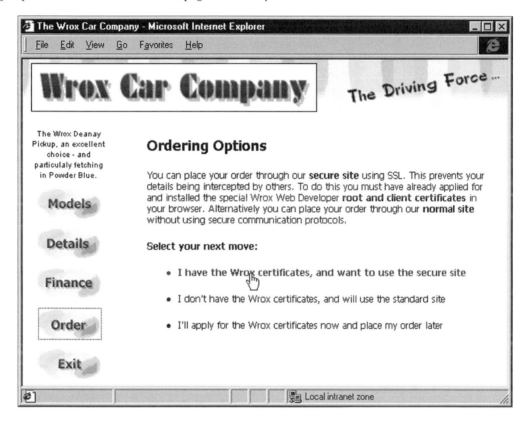

The list is created using HTML **<UL>** and **<LI>** elements in the usual way. However there are no hyperlinks, so we add the **STYLE="cursor:hand"** attribute, as well as an **ID** so that we can identify the entire list later in our code. We also give each option its own unique **ID**:

```
...
<UL ID="theList" STYLE="cursor:hand">
  <LI ID="option1">I have the Wrox certificates, and want
                   to use the secure site</LI><P>
  <LI ID="option2">I don't have the Wrox certificates,
                   and will use the standard site</LI><P>
  <LI ID="option3">I'll apply for the Wrox certificates now
                   and place my order later</LI><P>
</UL>
...
```

### Dynamic Style Changes

As the mouse pointer moves over the list options we use the standard Dynamic HTML technique to change the style of the text to bold red lettering, highlighting the option the mouse pointer is over:

```
Sub theList_onmouseover()
   'make option under cursor bold and red
   Set objItem = window.event.srcElement
   objItem.style.color = "red"
   objItem.style.fontWeight = "bold"
   window.event.cancelBubble = True
   window.event.returnValue = False
End Sub

Sub theList_onmouseout()
   'make option normal when cursor moves off
   Set objItem = window.event.srcElement
   objItem.style.color = "black"
   objItem.style.fontWeight = "normal"
   window.event.cancelBubble = True
   window.event.returnValue = False
End Sub
```

### Opening The Order Detail Page

When the user clicks on a link we can open the appropriate page in the main frame of our application window. If they select the secure site, this will be the page **placeorder.asp** stored in a directory within that area of our site. If they opt to use the standard site to place an order, this is an identical file within the same unsecured directory as the rest of the application.

> *To use the secure site, you must apply for the Wrox root and client certificates. You'll need to specify the URL of your own Web site to obtain the client certificate. If you don't have your own site, you can cheat by specifying a friend's site, or even our own site, but don't tell anybody else about this.*

The **placeorder.asp** file will display text boxes where they enter the information required to place the order. However they've already chosen the car model and color, so we can pre-fill these for them. This means that we need to be able to get at these values from code in the **placeorder.asp** page.

This is not a problem if the page is loaded from the same directory as the other pages (more specifically the frameset page **wroxcars.asp**), because we can get at the global variables **top.selectedModel**, **top.SelectedColor**, etc. However, if the page is loaded from a different domain (and, more importantly, a secure **https://** domain) we can't access variables or code in other pages—the browser security model will prevent this.

This is why we chose to use an ASP page for collecting user details because, in the case of a secure order, we won't be able to retrieve the global variables from code within it. Instead we'll pass the values to it through the URL **QueryString**. This is the code in the page **weborder.htm** which opens the **placeorder.asp** page in either the secure or normal directory, or redirects the user to the certificate enrollment site:

```
Sub theList_onclick()
  'get array indexes for selected car and color
  intCarIndex = top.CarArrayIndex
  intColorIndex = top.ColorArrayIndex
  'get total price, maybe including finance payments
  If top.financeTotal > 0 Then
    curTotalPrice = top.financeTotal
  Else
    curTotalPrice = top.arrCars(5, intCarIndex)
  End If
  'build query string to pass values on to placeorder.asp page
  strQuery = "?CarID=" & top.selectedModel _
           & "&CarName=" & top.arrCars(1, intCarIndex) _
           & "&ColorID=" & top.selectedColor _
           & "&ColorName=" & top.arrColors(2, intColorIndex) _
           & "&TotalPrice=" & curTotalPrice
  'jump to appropriate page depending on item selected
  strItem = window.event.srcElement.id
  Select Case strItem
    Case "option1": window.location.href = _
        "https://rapid.wrox.co.uk/securesite/placeorder.asp" & strQuery
    Case "option2": window.location.href = "placeorder.asp" & strQuery
    Case "option3": top.window.location.href = "/certsrv/"
  End Select
  window.event.cancelBubble = True
End Sub
```

This code creates a query string **strQuery**, and adds it onto the end of the URL used for placing an order. The string itself will contain the key values for the car model and color, the text names of the car model and color, and the total price including any finance payments. Depending on the user selections, it will look something like this:

```
placeorder.asp?CarID=4&CarName=Hardy S Coupe&ColorID=4
                  &ColorName=Hot Pink&TotalPrice=30331
```

*We could have tested for the presence of certificates and redirected the user automatically to the appropriate site, but this would be more complex. Normally the browser doesn't send any certificates, and the server doesn't request them. It would mean that we would have to use a different server directory that **requested** certificates, and then redirected the client back to the secure site that **requires** them.*

### Pre-filling The Order Details

The **placeorder.asp** files in the secure and normal directories are identical. Their task is to collect the rest of the details required to place the order from the user, and pass these on to our custom business functions back on the server which will place the order in the showroom database and post a message off to head office as well—in exactly the same way as the showroom application we saw in Chapter 6 did. Because of the way we designed the applications for this book, we can interchange the client without making any changes to the 'back end' services.

The HTML part of the page is simple enough. Note how we use the **READONLY** attribute to prevent the user changing the car, color or price information, and we include hidden fields for the car and color **IDs** (the key values). We also have a hidden field that is pre-filled with the word  Anonymous for the salesperson's name, just so that we get a value sent to the order processing components:

```
<%@ LANGUAGE="VBSCRIPT" %>
...
<FORM ID="frmOrder" ACTION="WCCOrderQ.asp" METHOD="POST">
<TABLE>
<TR>
 <TD STYLE="text-align:right">Vehicle Name:</TD>
 <TD STYLE="text-align:left">
  <INPUT TYPE=TEXT SIZE=20 READONLY NAME="CarName">
  <INPUT TYPE=TEXT NAME="CarID" STYLE="visibility:hidden; width:0">
 </TD>
</TR>
... { code for the rest of the HTML controls here }
<TR>
  <TD STYLE="text-align:right">Phone:</TD>
  <TD STYLE="text-align:left"><INPUT TYPE=TEXT NAME=Phone SIZE=20></TD>
</TR>
<TR>
  <TD COLSPAN=2 STYLE="text-align:right">
    <INPUT TYPE="BUTTON" ID="cmdOrder" VALUE="Place Order"
    ONCLICK="submitOrder()" TITLE="Place your order now">
  </TD>
</TR>
</TABLE>
</FORM>
```

### Pre-filling the Order Details

This is an ASP page, and we are sending it a query string containing the values we want filled in for some of the controls. We could write these values into the HTML as part of the  **<INPUT>** elements, but we chose to do it with some client-side script that runs when the page is loaded:

```
Sub window_onload()
    'fill in the car and color details from the query string
    document.all("CarName").Value = "<% = Request.QueryString("CarName") %>"
    document.all("CarID").Value = "<% = Request.QueryString("CarID") %>"
    document.all("ColorName").Value = _
                "<% = Request.QueryString("ColorName") %>"
    document.all("ColorID").Value = "<% = Request.QueryString("ColorID") %>"
    document.all("TotalPrice").Value = _
                "<% = CLng(Request.QueryString("TotalPrice")) %>"
<%
    'If cePresent (1) of Flags is set we have a client certificate
    If (Request.ClientCertificate("Flags") And 1) Then
%>

    document.all("Name").Value = _
```

```
                    "<% = Request.ClientCertificate("SubjectCN") %>"
    document.all("Town").Value = _
                    "<% = Request.ClientCertificate("SubjectL") %>"
    document.all("State").Value = _
                    "<% = Request.ClientCertificate("SubjectS") %>"
  <%
    End If
  %>
  End Sub
```

This produces a **window_onload()** subroutine in the page, which looks like the code below. Because the user chose the 'secure ordering' option, we can get some details from their client certificate as well:

```
Sub window_onload()
    'fill in the car and color details from the query string
    document.all("CarName").Value = "Hardy S Coupe"
    document.all("CarID").Value = "4"
    document.all("ColorName").Value = "Hot Pink"
    document.all("ColorID").Value = "4"
    document.all("TotalPrice").Value = "30331"
    document.all("Name").Value = "Alex Homer"
    document.all("Town").Value = "Stonebroom"
    document.all("State").Value = "Derbyshire"
End Sub
```

Here's the result when we actually did find someone who wanted to buy a pink car:

### Submitting The Order

The final section of the **placeorder.asp** page is a client-side routine that submits the order to our custom business objects when the Place Order button is clicked. If you look back at the HTML code of this page, you'll see that even though all the controls are on a **<FORM>**, the button isn't a **SUBMIT** button—it just runs our custom **submitOrder** procedure:

```
<INPUT TYPE="BUTTON" ID="cmdOrder" VALUE="Place Order"
```

```
      ONCLICK="submitOrder()" TITLE="Place your order now">
```

The **submitOrder** procedure checks that we got at least some input in each text box (except for the Phone box) and if not, displays a message. If everything else is OK, it submits the **<FORM>** to the same ASP page as we used in our showroom Web application, **WCCOrderQ.asp**, by calling the **submit** method of the form:

```
Sub submitOrder()
  blnOK = True  'check we got enough details
  If document.all("Name").Value = "" Then blnOK = False
  If document.all("Address").Value = "" Then blnOK = False
  If document.all("Town").Value = "" Then blnOK = False
  If document.all("State").Value = "" Then blnOK = False
  If document.all("ZipCode").Value = "" Then blnOK = False
  If Not blnOK Then
     strMesg = "Only the 'Phone' field is optional."
     MsgBox strMesg, vbInformation, "More Details Required"
  End If
  'submit the form to the ASP order script
  If blnOK Then document.all("frmOrder").submit
End Sub
```

At this point, the **WCCOrderQ.asp** page that we wrote in Chapter 6 takes over, and the order is registered with head office. Within a few days, our customer should be the proud possessor of a hot pink Hardy S. Coupe...

# Summary

In this final chapter, we've seen how we can interchange layers in an application without affecting the way it is built, and without having to know how it works underneath. Our new public Web application interface uses the same **WCCCars** component to get-up-to-date information about the cars we stock, and the same SQL Server stored procedure to get the color details, as the Web-based and Visual Basic interfaces we designed for use in our car showrooms did.

It also places the order using the same ASP page as the showroom application, and so the order is processed in exactly the same way. We can even run the showroom order monitor application from anywhere on the Web to get information about head office acceptance of the orders.

This freedom to interchange interfaces with business functions is one of the core concepts of the **Distributed interNet Applications** (DNA) architecture, and one of its major advantages when it comes to building distributed applications. Because of the **Component Object Model** (COM), all our components, ASP scripts, services and other objects can communicate very easily in standardized formats and across widely distributed networks.

We've come to the end of the book, and with it our exploration of **DNA, Components, Microsoft Transaction Server** and **Microsoft Message Queue Server**. To learn more about any of these topics, including the way they can be implemented in other languages like C++, Java, JavaScript, VBScript and Visual Basic, visit our Web Developer Resources and Reference site at **http://rapid.wrox.co.uk/**, and our main Wrox Press Books sites at **http://www.wrox.com/** and **http://www.wrox.co.uk**/.

# Installation Instructions & Database Design

This appendix provides a set of instructions for installing the databases and code samples. Please note that, although we've tried to cover this as clearly as possible, you are expected to have a certain amount of knowledge regarding databases and component design.

So what is actually included in the samples. It all revolves around several  top level directories.

- ❑ **Scripts**. The database scripts. These will build the databases for you.
- ❑ **Chapter 02**. Simple component usage.
- ❑ **Chapter 03**. Transacted finance component,
- ❑ **Chapter 04**. The code for chapter 4. This is the MTS application.
- ❑ **Chapter 05**. This is the Finance component.
- ❑ **Chapter 06**. The code for chapter 6. This is the MTS and MSMQ application.
- ❑ **Chapter 07**. This covers setting up security.
- ❑ **Chapter 08**. This is the encryption and authorization code.
- ❑ **Chapter 09**. The code for the final web application
- ❑ **Common**. For code that is common to more than one of the above directories.
- ❑ **Setup**. Not a full set up routine, but a small program to allow you to update the data source names for your databases.
- ❑ **Packages**. The completed MTS packages, which you can import directly into MTS.

We'll first give you a quick setup guide, as we're quite sure that you're just like every other developer in the world, who tends to ignore long installation instructions! Then we'll look at the directories in turn, so that you have a clear idea of what's included and how it is laid out. And finally, at the end we've also included a description of the database tables.

# Installation

Why haven't we provided a nice neat installation routine? The cynical amongst you might say laziness, but in fact there is a simple reason - flexibility. An installation routine simply wouldn't give you the flexibility to install the various components, queues, and database in the way you might like. We've said that one of the central ideas behind DNA programming is this loose approach to component location. By providing a few distinct routines and instructions you have the choice of where these are run.

# Quick Setup

For those of you who are really keen, this is what you need to do to get going:

## To create the databases

Open a Command Prompt on the server that hosts the database. Run the following commands:

```
HeadOfficeBuild.bat
ShowroomBuild.bat
```

NOTE: This assumes that the SQL Server user **sa** has no password. If it has a password or you wish to use a different user and password (that has privilege to create databases) then edit the **.bat** files. The -U flag specifies the SQL Server user name -P the password. For example:

```
isql -Uuser_name -Ppassword -i HODatabase.sql
```

# Create the Data Store Connection Strings

Run **Setup.exe** from the setup directory. This will allow you to specify the server names, user id's and passwords to use when connecting to the databases.

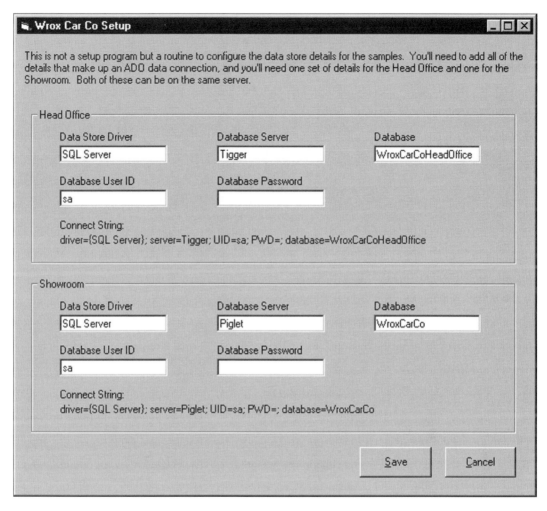

You shouldn't need to change Data Store Driver and Database, but you should enter the Database Server names for your SQL Server machines, as well as the user id's and passwords.

Pressing the Save button will store these details in the registry, where they will be read by the components. It will also create the include file for the asp components, in the following directories:

- ❑ **Chapter04\Application\Web**
- ❑ **Chapter06\Showroom\Application\Web**
- ❑ **Chapter09**

This file is **DataStore.inc**, and contains the connect strings for ADO.

# Transaction Server

There are ready built MTS packages under the Packages directory. They were exported from the MTS installation on the Wrox server. To install the packages you should follow these directions:

1. Start the Transaction Server Explorer.
2. Select the computer you wish to install the packages on, and select Packages.
3. From the Action menu select New, then Package (or right mouse click then New/Package).
4. Select Install pre-built packages.
5. Click the Add button, and select the PAK file from one of the following directories under the Packages directory:

   ❑ **Wrox Car Co**, for the standard components, as used in chapter 4.
   ❑ **Wrox Car Co Common**, for components that are common between the queued and non-queued applications.
   ❑ **Wrox Car Co Queued**, for the queued versions of the components.

You can install all of the packages, whichever application you wish to use. The queued components have different names and there is no conflict. The following, details which components are in which package:

| Package | Component | Description |
| --- | --- | --- |
| Wrox Car Co | WCCHOOrder.dll | Head Office ordering |
| | WCCOrder.dll | Combined ordering |
| | WCCSROrder.dll | Showroom ordering |
| Wrox Car Co Common | WCCCars.dll | General car routines |
| | WCCFinanceMTS.dll | Finance routines |
| Wrox Car Co Queued | WCCHOOrderQ.dll | Queued Head Office ordering |
| | WCCOrderProcessQ.dll | Head Office order processing |
| | WCCOrderQ.dll | Queued combined ordering |
| | WCCSROrderQ.dll | Queued showroom ordering |

## Un-Queued Visual Basic Application

To run the Visual Basic version of the application change directory to **Chapter04\Application\Visual Basic** and run **Showroom.exe**.

## Un-Queued Web Application

For the Web version of the application set up a virtual root to point to **Chapter04\Application\Web**, and then in Internet Explore open **WCCNewOrder.asp** from the new virtual root.

# Non MTS Components

The queued application requires two components that are not handled by MTS. These are **StringBag.dll** and **WCCOrderMonitorQ.dll**, and require registering manually. There are four BAT files in **Chapter06\Library** which you can double click to do this for you:

- ❏ **OrderMonitorRegister.bat**, to register the order monitor component.
- ❏ **OrderMonitorUnRegister.bat**, to un-register the order monitor component.
- ❏ **StringBagRegister.bat**, to register the String Bag component.
- ❏ **StringBagUnRegister.bat**, to un-register the String Bag component.

These simply call regsvr32.exe, and save you creating Command Prompts and getting your hands dirty.

If you implement the queued application on two machines, then the string bag should be registered on both machines. The order monitor only needs registering on the Showroom machine.

# Message Queues

You need to go into MSMQ Explorer and create the queues. If you're using two machines then put **NewOrders** on the Head Office machine and **OrderAcknowledgement** and **OrderResponse** on the Showroom machine. If you're only using one machine you can put all three queues on that machine. You'll also need a **FinanceQueue** for chapter 5. This can be on any machine, but the samples are based around running an ASP file, which creates the finance component, so it really ought to be on the same machine. Also, the **NewOrders** queue should be a Transacted Queue.

## Queued Visual Basic Application

To run the Visual Basic version of the application change directory to **Chapter06\Showroom\Application\Visual Basic** and run **Showroom.exe**.

## Queued Web Application

For the Web version of the application set up a virtual root to point to **Chapter06\Showroom\Application\Web**, and then in Internet Explorer open **WCCNewOrderQ.asp** from the new virtual root.

To run the order monitor open **WCCOrderMonitor.htm** from the same directory.

For the head office order processing application, change directory to **Chapter06\HeadOffice\Application** and run **HeadOffice.exe**.

# Scripts

The Wrox Car Co is designed around two databases, **WroxCarCo** and **WroxCarCoHeadOffice**. We built these on two separate machines, but they could reside on the same machine. Even when the application is queued using MSMQ you could still put both databases on one SQL Server, although you will need two machines to work with MSMQ if you want to see the Queue failure in operation.

There is a set of scripts that will automatically build both databases. They are split into a set for each database so that you can create them separately if you wish.

| Script | Description |
|---|---|
| `HeadOfficeBuild.bat` | Master script to build the head office database |
| `HODatabase.sql` | Head Office database devices and database creation SQL script |
| `HOTablesProcedures.sql` | Head Office tables and stored procedures SQL Script |
| `HODataInsert.sql` | Head Office data insertion SQL script |
| `ShowroomBuild.bat` | Master script to build the showroom database |
| `SRDatabase.sql` | Showroom database devices and database creation SQL script |
| `SRTablesProcedures.sql` | Showroom tables and stored procedures SQL Script |
| `SRDataInsert.sql` | Showroom data insertion SQL script |

There are two ways to create the databases. The first is the easiest, using the batch file supplied, which just runs the three SQL scripts in order:

```
isql -Usa -P -i HODatabase.sql
isql -Usa -P -i HOTablesProcedures.sql
isql -Usa -P -i HODataInsert.sql
```

Notice that this uses the User **sa** with a blank password. If you have put a password on your **sa** account you can supply the password after the - **P** argument, like so:

```
isql -Usa -Ppwd -i HODatabase.sql
isql -Usa -Ppwd -i HOTablesProcedures.sql
isql -Usa -Ppwd -i HODataInsert.sql
```

This assumes that **pwd** is the **sa** password.

If you don't know the **sa** password, then you can substitute another user account and password. One thing to note though, is that if you use another user account it must have permissions to create databases. If you are unsure about this you should consult your system administrator.

An alternative way of creating the databases is to run the scripts one at a time from within a query window (using Enterprise Manager or ISQL/w). You should run the **.sql** files in the order they are show in the table above. The first script will create the database for you (it creates a 10Mb Data Device and a 3 Mb Log Device). The second script will create the tables and stored procedures, and the final script inserts the data.

All scripts are standard SQL, and in fact SQL Server created the first two using the Generate Scripts option. There are very few restrictions and permissions on any of the objects. The global **public** group has been given permission, although you can change this if you wish.

# Chapter02

For the Chapter 2 sample you need to register the **WCCFinance.dll**. There is a file, **FinanceRegister.bat**, to do this for you. It simply calls **regsvr32.exe**, and running this file will register the component for use in ASP.

# Chapter03

Contains the Transacted Finance component.

# Chapter04

The Chapter04 directory contains the code described in, Chapter 4, where we looked at the straight MTS version of the application, without any queuing. The directory structure is as follows:

| Directory | Description |
|-----------|-------------|
| Finance | The Finance component |
| Cars | The Cars component |
| ShowroomOrder | The ShowroomOrder component |
| HeadOfficeOrder | The HeadOfficeOrder component |
| Order | The combined Order component |
| Library | The DLLs |
| Application\Visual Basic | The Visual Basic application |
| Application\Web | The Web application |
| Application\Images | Pictures of the cars |

We've supplied the DLLs and the fully built Visual Basic application, in case you want to rush ahead without building the components. If you want to build the components yourself, simply load each into Visual Basic and compile it into the **Library** directory. You can compile it elsewhere, but make sure you set the Compatible Project settings accordingly. All of the components should be run on the Showroom machine, so you can install them into a MTS Package on the appropriate machine. You should set the transactional capabilities for the components as shown:

| Component | Transactions |
|-----------|--------------|
| WCCCars | Not supported |
| WCCFinance | Not supported |
| WCCOrder | Requires new |
| WCCHOOrder | Supported |
| WCCSROrder | Supported |

# Chapter05

This just contains the component code and web pages for using the Finance component.

# Chapter06

The components for Chapter 6 are slightly more complex, as this contains the queued application, and there is now a separate set of code for the Head Office. There is also some common code and an associated directory.

| Directory | Description |
|---|---|
| CombinedMonitor | The Head Office and Showroom order monitoring combined |
| Common | Common routines |
| Common\Cars | The Cars component |
| Common\General | The message queue common code |
| Common\StringBag | Collection and String routines |
| HeadOffice | Head Office routines |
| HeadOffice\Application | Head Office application |
| HeadOffice\OrderProcess | Head Office order processing component |
| Showroom | Showroom routines |
| Showroom\Application\Visual Basic | The showroom Visual Basic application |
| Showroom\Application\Web | The showroom Web application |
| Showroom\Application\Images | Pictures of the cars |
| Showroom\Finance | The finance component |
| Showroom\HeadOfficeOrder | The HeadOfficeOrder component |
| Showroom\Order | The combined Order component |
| Showroom\OrderMonitor | The Order Monitor component |
| Showroom\ShowroomOrder | The ShowroomOrder component |
| Library | The DLLs |

Since there are two sets of components you need to make sure that they are installed on the correct machine:

| Showroom machine | Head Office machine |
|---|---|
| StringBag | StringBag |
| WCCSROrderQ | WCCOrderProcessQ |
| WCCOrderMonitorQ | |
| WCCOrderQ | |
| WCCHOOrderQ | |

There are two components that have to be registered manually, so create a Command Prompt, change directory to **Chapter 6\Library** and type the following:

```
regsvr32 StringBag.dll
regsvr32 WCCOrderMonitorQ.dll
```

If using two machines **StringBag** is needed on both machines.

The MTS components need the following transactional capabilities.

| Machine | Component | Transactions |
|---|---|---|
| Showroom | WCCOrderQ | Requires New |
| | WCCSROrderQ | Supported |
| | WCCHOOrderQ | Supported |
| Head Office | WCCOrderProcessQ | Requires New |

# Chapter07

This directory contains the **.asp** files for dealing with security, especially certificates.

# Chapter08

This chapter contains the Visual Basic code and pages for authenticating and encrypting messages.

# Chapter09

This is the final application. You'll see that it's intended to be used as an Internet application, and therefore works in a completely different way. It is fully described in Chapter 9.

# Common

This contains any Visual Basic code that is common to all chapters. As it stands, there is only one file, **Registry.bas**, which is used to read and write values from the registry. This is used in both the Chapter 4 (un-queued) and Chapter 6 (queued) components, and was therefore moved to a common directory.

# Setup

Setup is the Visual Basic program that writes the data store names to the registry and creates the **DataStore.inc** files.

# Database Description

This section outlines the database tables and stored procedures. You won't need to use these to create the databases, as the scripts do this for you, but it enables you to see at a glance the database structure.

## Head Office

The head office database is **WroxCarCoHeadOffice**. It stores the master list of cars, colors, and car/color combinations, along with the orders for all showrooms.

### tblCar

This stores the range and details of all of the cars.

| Column Name | Data Type | Length | Description |
|---|---|---|---|
| CarID | int IDENTITY | 4 | Unique Key |
| Model | varchar | 50 | Car model |
| EngineSize | smallint | 2 | Engine size |
| Doors | smallint | 2 | Number of doors |
| Seats | smallint | 2 | Number of seats |
| Price | numeric | 9 | List price |
| Picture | varchar | 255 | Path to a picture |
| Description | text | 16 | Description of car |

## tblColor

This stores all colors.

| Column Name | Data Type | Length | Description |
|---|---|---|---|
| ColorID | int IDENTITY | 4 | Unique Key |
| Color | varchar | 50 | Color description |

## tblCarColor

This stores which colors are available for which cars, and the stock availability for the Car/Color combination.

| Column Name | Data Type | Length | Description |
|---|---|---|---|
| CarColorID | int IDENTITY | 4 | Unique Key |
| fkCarID | int | 4 | ID of Car |
| fkColorID | int | 4 | ID of Color |
| InStock | smallint | 2 | Number in stock |
| OnOrder | smallint | 2 | Number on order |

## tblOrder

This stores the details for an order. The Garage and Customer details were included directly in here, rather than having separate tables to simplify the design. We agree that it's not normalized and this was done deliberately. We'd like to say it was designed like this to aid fast querying without having multiple table joins, but you wouldn't believe us.

| Column Name | Data Type | Length | Description |
|---|---|---|---|
| OrderID | int IDENTITY | 4 | Unique Key |
| GarageName | varchar | 50 | Name of showroom who placed the order |
| GarageAddress | varchar | 50 | Address of showroom who placed the order |
| GarageTown | varchar | 20 | Town of showroom who placed the order |
| GarageState | varchar | 2 | State of showroom who placed the order |
| GarageZipCode | varchar | 15 | Zip Code of showroom who placed the order |

| Column Name | Data Type | Length | Description |
|---|---|---|---|
| SalesPerson | varchar | 20 | Sales person at showroom who placed the order |
| CustomerName | varchar | 20 | Name of customer who placed order |
| CustomerAddress | varchar | 50 | Address of customer who placed order |
| CustomerTown | varchar | 20 | Town of customer who placed order |
| CustomerState | varchar | 2 | State of customer who placed order |
| CustomerZipCode | varchar | 15 | Zip Code of customer who placed order |
| CustomerPhone | varchar | 15 | Phone Number of customer who placed order |
| fkCarID | int | 4 | ID of car ordered |
| fkColorID | int | 4 | ID of color of car ordered |
| DateOrdered | datetime | 8 | Date order was placed |
| Ackowledged | datetime | 8 | Date the order been acknowledged |
| DeliveryDate | datetime | 8 | Date car will be delivered |
| GarageOrderNumber | int | 4 | Showroom order number |
| ResponseQueue | varchar | 255 | MSMQ Message Response Queue ID |

# Showroom

The showroom database is WroxCarCo. It stores a copy of the car and color tables from head office, as well as customer and order details.

**tblCar**, **tblColor** are identical to those of head office.

## tblCarColor

This stores which colors are available for which cars, and the stock availability for the Car/Color combination. It differs slight from the head office copy, as there is no **OnOrder** column.

| Column Name | Data Type | Length | Description |
|---|---|---|---|
| CarColorID | int IDENTITY | 4 | Unique Key |
| fkCarID | int | 4 | ID of Car |
| fkColorID | int | 4 | ID of Color |
| InStock | smallint | 2 | Number in stock |

## tblOrder

This stores the details of the orders at the showroom.

| Column Name | Data Type | Length | Description |
|---|---|---|---|
| OrderID | int IDENTITY | 4 | Unique Key |
| fkCustomerID | int | 4 | ID of Customer who placed the order |
| OrderDate | datetime | 8 | Date order was placed |
| fkCarID | int | 4 | ID of car ordered |
| fkColorID | int | 4 | ID of color of car ordered |
| SalesPerson | varchar | 20 | Sales person at showroom who placed the order |
| Ackowledged | bit | 1 | Has the order been acknowledged |
| DeliveryDate | datetime | 8 | Date car will be delivered |
| HOOrderNumber | int | 4 | Head Office order number |
| PricePaid | numeric | 9 | Actual price paid |

## tblCustomer

This stores the details of an individual customer.

| Column Name | Data Type | Length | Description |
|---|---|---|---|
| CustomerName | varchar | 20 | Name of customer who placed order |
| CustomerAddress | varchar | 50 | Address of customer who placed order |
| CustomerTown | varchar | 20 | Town of customer who placed order |
| CustomerState | varchar | 2 | State of customer who placed order |
| CustomerZipCode | varchar | 15 | Zip Code of customer who placed order |
| CustomerPhone | varchar | 15 | Phone No of customer who placed order |

# Microsoft ActiveX Data Objects 1.5 Library Reference

## Objects

| Name | Description |
| --- | --- |
| Command | A Command object is a definition of a specific command that you intend to execute against a data source |
| Connection | A Connection object represents an open connection to a data store |
| Error | An Error object contains the details about data access errors pertaining to a single operation involving the provider |
| Errors | The Errors collection contains all of the Error objects created in response to a single failure involving the provider |
| Field | A Field object represents a column of data within a common data type |
| Fields | A Fields collection contains all of the Field objects of a **Recordset** object |
| Parameter | A Parameter object represents a parameter or argument associated with a Command object based on a parameterized query or stored procedure |
| Parameters | A Parameters collection contains all the Property objects for a specific instance of an object |

*Table Continued on Following Page*

| Name | Description |
|------|-------------|
| `Properties` | A Properties collection contains all the Parameter objects of a Command object |
| `Property` | A Property object represents a dynamic characteristic of an ADO object that is defined by the provider |
| `Recordset` | A Recordset object represents the entire set of records from a base table or the results of an executed command. At any time, the Recordset object only refers to a single record within the set as the current record |

# Command

## *Methods*

| Name | Returns | Description |
|------|---------|-------------|
| `CreateParameter` | Parameter | Creates a command parameter |
| `Execute` | Recordset | Runs the query, SQL statement, or stored procedure specified in the **CommandText** property |

## *Properties*

| Name | Returns | Description | Type |
|------|---------|-------------|------|
| `ActiveConnection` | Connection | Indicates to which Connection object the specified **Command** currently belongs | Read/Write |
| `CommandText` | String | Contains the text of a command that you want to issue against a provider. | Read/Write |
| `CommandTimeout` | Integer | Indicates wait while executing a command before terminating the attempt and generating an error | Read/Write |
| `CommandType` | CommandTypeEnum | Indicates the type of a **Command** object. | Read/Write |
| `Name` | String | Indicates the name for a **Command** object | Read/Write |

| Name | Returns | Description | Type |
|---|---|---|---|
| **Parameters** | Parameters | Collection of **Parameters** | Read only |
| **Prepared** | Boolean | Indicates whether or not to save a compiled version of a command before execution. | Read/ Write |
| **Properties** | Properties | Collection of **Property** objects | Read only |

# Connection

## Methods

| Name | Returns | Description |
|---|---|---|
| **BeginTrans** | Integer | Starts a new transaction |
| **Close** | | Closes an open **Connection** and any dependent objects |
| **CommitTrans** | | Saves changes and ends the current transaction |
| **Execute** | Recordset | Runs the specified query, SQL statement, or stored procedure |
| **Open** | | Opens a **Connection** to a data source. |
| **OpenSchema** | Recordset | Obtains database schema information from the provider. |
| **RollbackTrans** | | Cancels changes made during the current transaction and ends the transaction |

## Properties

| Name | Returns | Description | Type |
|---|---|---|---|
| **Attributes** | Integer | Indicates one or more characteristics of the **Connection** object | Read/ Write |

*Table Continued on Following Page*

| Name | Returns | Description | Type |
|------|---------|-------------|------|
| CommandTimeout | Integer | Indicates wait while executing a command before terminating the attempt and generating an error | Read/ Write |
| ConnectionString | String | Contains the information used to establish a connection to a data source. | Read/ Write |
| ConnectionTimeout | Integer | Indicates how long to wait while establishing a connection before terminating the attempt and generating an error. | Read/ Write |
| CursorLocation | CursorLocationEnum | Sets or returns the location of the cursor engine. | Read/ Write |
| DefaultDatabase | String | Indicates the default database for a **Connection** object. | Read/ Write |
| Errors | Errors | Collection of errors that have occurred during the connection | Read only |
| IsolationLevel | IsolationLevelEnum | Indicates the level of isolation for a **Connection** object | Read/ Write |
| Mode | ConnectModeEnum | Indicates the available permissions for modifying data in a **Connection** | Read/ Write |
| Properties | Properties | Collection of **Property** objects | Read only |
| Provider | String | Indicates the name of the provider for a **Connection** object. | Read/ Write |
| State | Integer | Describes the current state of the **Connection** object. | Read only |
| Version | String | Indicates the ADO version number. | Read only |

# Error

## Properties

| Name | Returns | Description | Type |
|------|---------|-------------|------|
| Description | String | A descriptive string associated with an **Error** object | Read only |
| HelpContext | Integer | Indicates the help file and topic associated with an **Error** object | Read only |
| HelpFile | String | Indicates the help file and topic associated with an **Error** object | Read only |
| NativeError | Integer | Indicates the help file and topic associated with an **Error** object | Read only |
| Number | Integer | Indicates the number that uniquely identifies an **Error** object | Read only |
| Source | String | Indicates the name of the object or application that originally generated the error | Read only |
| SQLState | String | Indicates the help file and topic associated with an **Error** object | Read only |

# Errors

## Methods

| Name | Returns | Description |
|------|---------|-------------|
| Clear | | Removes all of the errors from the **Errors** Collection |
| Refresh | | Updates collection contents to reflect recent changes |

## Properties

| Name | Returns | Description | Type |
|------|---------|-------------|------|
| Count | Integer | Returns number of objects in the collection | Read only |
| Item | Error | Returns a specific member of the **Errors** collection by name or ordinal number. | Read only |

# Field

## *Methods*

| Name | Returns | Description |
|------|---------|-------------|
| AppendChunk | | Appends data to a large text or binary data **Field** object |
| GetChunk | Variant | Returns all or a portion of the contents of a large text or binary data **Field** object |

## *Properties*

| Name | Returns | Description | Type |
|------|---------|-------------|------|
| ActualSize | Integer | Indicates the actual length of a field's value | Read only |
| Attributes | Integer | Indicates one or more characteristics of the **Field** object | Read only |
| DefinedSize | Integer | Indicates the defined size of a **Field** object. | Read only |
| Name | String | Indicates the name for a **Field** object | Read only |
| NumericScale | Byte | Indicates the scale of Numeric values in a **Parameter** or **Field** object | Read only |
| OriginalValue | Variant | Indicates the value of a **Field** that existed in the record before any changes were made. | Read only |
| Precision | Byte | Degree of precision for Numeric values in a **Parameter** object or for numeric **Field** objects | Read only |
| Properties | Properties | Collection of **Property** objects | Read only |
| Type | DataTypeEnum | Indicates the operational type or data type of a **Field** object | Read only |
| UnderlyingValue | Variant | Indicates a **Field** object's current value in the database. | Read only |
| Value | Variant | Indicates the value assigned to a **Field** object | Read/Write |

# Fields

## *Methods*

| Name | Returns | Description |
|---|---|---|
| `Refresh` | | Updates collection contents to reflect recent changes |

## *Properties*

| Name | Returns | Description | Type |
|---|---|---|---|
| `Count` | Integer | Returns number of objects in the collection | Read only |
| `Item` | Field | Returns a specific member of the **Fields** collection by name or ordinal number. | Read only |

# Parameter

## *Methods*

| Name | Returns | Description |
|---|---|---|
| `AppendChunk` | | Appends data to a large text or binary data **Parameter** object |

## *Properties*

| Name | Returns | Description | Type |
|---|---|---|---|
| `Attributes` | Integer | Indicates one or more characteristics of the **Parameter** object | Read/Write |
| `Direction` | ParameterDirectionEnum | Indicates whether the **Parameter** represents an input, output, both, or a return value from an SP | Read/Write |
| `Name` | String | Indicates the name for a **Parameter** object | Read/Write |
| `NumericScale` | Byte | Indicates the scale of Numeric values in a **Parameter** or **Field** object | Read/Write |

*Table Continued on Following Page*

| Name | Returns | Description | Type |
|------|---------|-------------|------|
| **Precision** | Byte | Degree of precision for Numeric values in a **Parameter** object or for numeric **Field** objects | Read/Write |
| **Properties** | Properties | Collection of **Property** objects | Read only |
| **Size** | Integer | Indicates the maximum size, in bytes, of a **Parameter** object | Read/Write |
| **Type** | DataTypeEnum | Indicates the operational type or data type of a **Parameter** object | Read/Write |
| **Value** | Variant | Indicates the value assigned to a **Field**, **Parameter**, or **Property** object | Read/Write |

# Parameters

## Methods

| Name | Returns | Description |
|------|---------|-------------|
| **Append** | | Adds an object to the collection |
| **Delete** | | Removes an object from the collection |
| **Refresh** | | Updates collection contents to reflect recent changes |

## Properties

| Name | Returns | Description | Type |
|------|---------|-------------|------|
| **Count** | Integer | Returns number of objects in the collection | Read only |
| **Item** | Parameter | Returns a specific member of the Parameters collection by name or ordinal number. | Read only |

# Properties

## Methods

| Name | Returns | Description |
|------|---------|-------------|
| **Refresh** | | Updates collection contents to reflect recent changes |

## Properties

| Name | Returns | Description | Type |
|------|---------|-------------|------|
| Count | Integer | Returns number of objects in the collection | Read only |
| Item | Property | Returns a specific member of the **Properties** collection by name or ordinal number. | Read only |

# Property

## Properties

| Name | Returns | Description | Type |
|------|---------|-------------|------|
| Attributes | Integer | Indicates one or more characteristics of the Property object | Read/Write |
| Name | String | Indicates the name for a **Property** object | Read only |
| Type | DataTypeEnum | Indicates the operational type or data type of a **Property** object | Read only |
| Value | Variant | Indicates the value assigned to a **Property** object | Read/Write |

# Recordset

## Methods

| Name | Returns | Description |
|------|---------|-------------|
| AddNew | | Creates a new record for an updateable **Recordset** |
| CancelBatch | | Cancels a pending batch update |
| CancelUpdate | | Cancels any changes made to the current record or to a new record prior to calling the **Update** method |
| Clone | Recordset | Creates a duplicate **Recordset** object from an existing **Recordset** object |
| Close | | Closes an open **Recordset** and any dependent objects |
| Delete | | Deletes the current record or group of records |
| Find | | Find a record in a **Recordset** |

*Table Continued on Following Page*

| Name | Returns | Description |
|------|---------|-------------|
| GetRows | Variant | Retrieves multiple records of **Recordset** into an array |
| Move | | Moves the position of the current record in a **Recordset** object |
| MoveFirst | | Moves to the first record in a specified **Recordset** object and makes that record the current record. |
| MoveLast | | Moves to the last record in a specified **Recordset** object and makes that record the current record. |
| MoveNext | | Moves to the next record in a specified **Recordset** object and makes that record the current record. |
| Move Previous | | Moves to the previous record in a specified **Recordset** object and makes that record the current record. |
| Next Recordset | Recordset | Clears the current **Recordset** object and returns the next **Recordset** by advancing through a series of commands. |
| Open | | Opens a **Recordset** |
| Requery | | Updates the data in a **Recordset** object by re-executing the query on which the object is based. |
| Resync | | Refreshes the data in the current **Recordset** object from the underlying database. |
| Supports | Boolean | Determines whether a specified **Recordset** object supports a particular type of functionality. |
| Update | | Saves any changes you make to the current record of a **Recordset** object. |
| UpdateBatch | | Writes all pending batch updates to disk. |

## Properties

| Name | Returns | Description | Type |
|------|---------|-------------|------|
| AbsolutePage | PositionEnum | Specifies in which page the current record resides | Read/Write |
| AbsolutePosition | PositionEnum | Indicates position of a **Recordset**'s current record | Read/Write |
| ActiveConnection | Variant | Indicates to which **Connection** object the specified **Recordset** currently belongs | Read/Write |

| Name | Returns | Description | Type |
|------|---------|-------------|------|
| **BOF** | Boolean | Indicates that the current record position is before the first record in a **Recordset** object | Read only |
| **Bookmark** | Variant | Returns a bookmark that uniquely identifies the current record in a **Recordset** object or sets the current record in a **Recordset** object to the record identified by a valid bookmark. | Read/ Write |
| **CacheSize** | Integer | Indicates the number of records from a **Recordset** object that are cached locally in memory | Read/ Write |
| **Collect** | Variant | Default collection of field items. | Read/ Write |
| **CursorLocation** | CursorLocationEnum | Sets or returns the location of the cursor engine. | Read/ Write |
| **CursorType** | CursorTypeEnum | Indicates the type of cursor used in a **Recordset** object. | Read/ Write |
| **EditMode** | EditModeEnum | Indicates the editing status of the current record. | Read only |
| **EOF** | Boolean | Indicates that the current record position is after the last record in a **Recordset** object | Read only |
| **Fields** | Fields | Collection of **Fields** | Read only |
| **Filter** | Variant | Indicates a filter for data in a **Recordset.** | Read/ Write |
| **LockType** | LockTypeEnum | Indicates the type of locks placed on records during editing. | Read/ Write |
| **MarshalOptions** | MarshalOptionsEnum | Indicates which records are to be marshaled back to the server. | Read/ Write |

*Table Continued on Following Page*

| Name | Returns | Description | Type |
|------|---------|-------------|------|
| MaxRecords | Integer | Indicates the maximum number of records to return to a **Recordset** from a query. | Read/Write |
| PageCount | Integer | Indicates how many pages of data the **Recordset** object contains. | Read only |
| PageSize | Integer | Indicates how many records constitute one page in the **Recordset.** | Read/Write |
| Properties | Properties | Collection of **Property** objects | Read only |
| RecordCount | Integer | Indicates the current number of records in a **Recordset** object | Read only |
| Sort | String | Indicate the fields and direction for accessing the **Recordset** | Read/Write |
| Source | Variant | Indicates the source for the data in a **Recordset** object (Command object, SQL statement, table name, or stored procedure). | Read/Write |
| State | Integer | Describes the current state of the **Recordset** object. | Read only |
| Status | Integer | Indicates the status of the current record with respect to batch updates or other bulk operations. | Read only |

# Constants

## AffectEnum

| Name | Value | Description |
|------|-------|-------------|
| AdAffectAll | 3 | Operation affects all records in the recordset |
| AdAffectCurrent | 1 | Operation affects only the current record |
| AdAffectGroup | 2 | Operation affects records that satisfy the current **Filter** property |

## BookmarkEnum

| Name | Value | Description |
| --- | --- | --- |
| AdBookmarkCurrent | 0 | Default. Start at the current record |
| AdBookmarkFirst | 1 | Start at the first record |
| AdBookmarkLast | 2 | Start at the last record |

## CommandTypeEnum

| Name | Value | Description |
| --- | --- | --- |
| AdCmdStoredProc | 4 | Evaluates **CommandText** as a stored procedure |
| AdCmdTable | 2 | Evaluates **CommandText** as a table name |
| AdCmdText | 1 | Evaluates **CommandText** as text (ie a SQL command) |
| AdCmdUnknown | 8 | Evaluates **CommandText** as an unknown command type |
| AdCmdUnspecified | -1 | Indicates **CommandText** is unspecified |

## ConnectModeEnum

| Name | Value | Description |
| --- | --- | --- |
| AdModeRead | 1 | Indicates read-only permissions |
| AdModeReadWrite | 3 | Indicates read/write permissions |
| AdModeShareDenyNone | 16 | Prevents others from opening connection with any permissions |
| AdModeShareDenyRead | 4 | Prevents others from opening connection with read permissions |
| AdModeShareDenyWrite | 8 | Prevents others from opening connection with write permissions |
| AdModeShareExclusive | 12 | Prevents others from opening connection |
| AdModeUnknown | 0 | Default. Indicates that the permissions have not yet been set or cannot be determined |
| AdModeWrite | 2 | Indicates write-only permissions |

## ConnectPromptEnum

| Name | Value | Description |
|------|-------|-------------|
| AdPromptAlways | 1 | Always prompt for connection information |
| AdPromptComplete | 2 | Only prompt if not enough information was supplied |
| AdPromptCompleteRequired | 3 | Only prompt if not enough information was supplied, but disable any options not directly applicable to the connection |
| AdPromptNever | 4 | Default. Never prompt for connection information |

## CursorLocationEnum

| Name | Value | Description |
|------|-------|-------------|
| AdUseClient | 3 | Use client-side cursors supplied by the local cursor library. |
| AdUseClientBatch | 3 | Use client-side cursors supplied by the local cursor library. |
| AdUseNone | 1 | No cursor services are used. |
| AdUseServer | 2 | Default. Uses data provider driver supplied cursors. |

## CursorOptionEnum

| Name | Value | Description |
|------|-------|-------------|
| AdAddNew | 16778240 | You can use the **AddNew** method to add new records |
| AdApproxPosition | 16384 | You can read and set the **AbsolutePosition** and **AbsolutePage** properties |
| AdBookmark | 8192 | You can use the **Bookmark** property to access specific records |
| AdDelete | 16779264 | You can use the **Delete** method to delete records |
| AdHoldRecords | 256 | You can retrieve more records or change the next retrieve position without committing all pending changes |
| AdMovePrevious | 512 | You can use the **ModeFirst**, **MovePrevious**, **Move** and **GetRows** methods. |

| Name | Value | Description |
|---|---|---|
| AdResync | 131072 | You can update the cursor with the data visible in the underlying database with the **Resync** method |
| AdUpdate | 16809984 | You can use the **Update** method to modify existing records |
| AdUpdateBatch | 65536 | You can use the **UpdateBatch** or **CancelBatch** methods to transfer changes to the provider in groups |

## CursorTypeEnum

| Name | Value | Description |
|---|---|---|
| AdOpenDynamic | 2 | Opens a dynamic type cursor |
| AdOpenForwardOnly | 0 | Default. Opens a forward-only type cursor |
| AdOpenKeyset | 1 | Opens a keyset type cursor |
| AdOpenStatic | 3 | Opens a static type cursor |
| AdOpenUnspecified | -1 | Indicates an unspecified value for cursor type |

## DataTypeEnum

| Name | Value | Description |
|---|---|---|
| AdBigInt | 20 | An 8-byte signed integer |
| AdBinary | 128 | A binary value |
| AdBoolean | 11 | A Boolean value |
| AdBSTR | 8 | A null-terminated character string |
| AdChar | 129 | A String value |
| AdCurrency | 6 | A currency value. An 8-byte signed integer scaled by 10,000, with 4 digits to the right of the decimal point |
| AdDate | 7 | A Date value. A Double where the whole part is the number of days since December 31 1899, and the fractional part is a fraction of the day |
| AdDBDate | 133 | A data value (yyyymmdd) |
| AdDBTime | 134 | A time value (hhmmss) |

*Table Continued on Following Page*

| Name | Value | Description |
| --- | --- | --- |
| AdDBTimeStamp | 135 | A date-time stamp (yyyymmddhhmmss plus a fraction in billionths) |
| AdDecimal | 14 | An exact numeric value with fixed precision and scale |
| AdDouble | 5 | A double-precision floating point value |
| AdEmpty | 0 | No value was specified |
| AdError | 10 | A 32-bit error code |
| AdGUID | 72 | A globally unique identifier |
| AdIDispatch | 9 | A pointer to an Idispatch interface on an OLE object |
| AdInteger | 3 | A 4-byte signed integer |
| AdIUnknown | 13 | A pointer to an Iunknown interface on an OLE object |
| AdLongVarBinary | 205 | A long binary value |
| AdLongVarChar | 201 | A long String value |
| AdLongVarWChar | 203 | A long null-terminated string value |
| AdNumeric | 131 | An exact numeric value with a fixed precision and scale |
| AdSingle | 4 | A single-precision floating point value |
| AdSmallInt | 2 | A 2-byte signed integer |
| AdTinyInt | 16 | A 1-byte signed integer |
| AdUnsignedBigInt | 21 | An 8-byte unsigned integer |
| AdUnsignedInt | 19 | An 4-byte unsigned integer |
| AdUnsignedSmallInt | 18 | An 2-byte unsigned integer |
| AdUnsignedTinyInt | 17 | An 1-byte unsigned integer |
| AdUserDefined | 132 | A user-defined variable |
| AdVarBinary | 204 | A binary value |
| AdVarChar | 200 | A String value |
| AdVariant | 12 | An Automation Variant |
| AdVarWChar | 202 | A null-terminated Unicode character string |
| AdWChar | 130 | A null-terminated Unicode character string |

## EditcModeEnum

| Name | Value | Description |
|------|-------|-------------|
| AdEditAdd | 2 | Indicates that the **AddNew** method has been invoked and the current record in the buffer is a new record that hasn't been saved to the database |
| AdEditDelete | 4 | Indicates that the **Delete** method has been invoked |
| AdEditInProgress | 1 | Indicates that data in the current record has been modified but not saved |
| AdEditNone | 0 | Indicates that no editing is in progress |

## ErrorValueEnum

| Name | Value | Description |
|------|-------|-------------|
| AdErrBoundToCommand | 3707 | The application cannot change the **ActiveConnection** property of a **Recordset** object with a Commend object as its source |
| AdErrDataConversion | 3421 | The application is using a value of the wrong type for the current application |
| AdErrFeatureNotAvailable | 3251 | The operation requested by the application is not supported by the provider |
| AdErrIllegalOperation | 3219 | The operation requested by the application is not allowed in this context |
| AdErrInTransaction | 3246 | The application cannot explicitly close a **Connection** object while in the middle of a transaction |
| AdErrInvalidArgument | 3001 | The application is using arguments that are the wrong type, are out of the acceptable range, or are in conflict with one another |
| AdErrInvalidConnection | 3709 | The application requested an operation on an object with a reference to a closed or invalid **Connection** object |
| AdErrInvalidParamInfo | 3708 | The application has improperly defined a **Parameter** object |
| AdErrItemNotFound | 3265 | ADO could not find the object in the collection. |

| Name | Value | Description |
|------|-------|-------------|
| AdErrNoCurrentRecord | 3021 | Eith **BOF** or **EOF** is True, or the current record has been deleted. The operation requested by the application requires a current record |
| AdErrObjectClosed | 3704 | The operation requested by the application is not allowed if the object is closed |
| AdErrObjectInCollection | 3367 | Can't append. Object already in collection |
| AdErrObjectNotSet | 3420 | The object referenced by the application no longer points to a valid object |
| AdErrObjectOpen | 3705 | The operation requested by the application is not allowed if the object is open |
| AdErrProviderNotFound | 3706 | ADO could not find the specified provider |

## ExecuteOptionEnum

| Name | Value | Description |
|------|-------|-------------|
| AdOptionUnspecified | -1 | |

## FieldAttributeEnum

| Name | Value | Description |
|------|-------|-------------|
| AdFldCacheDeferred | 4096 | Indicates that the provider caches field calues and that subsequent reads are done from the cache |
| AdFldFixed | 16 | Indicates that the field contains fixed-length data |
| AdFldIsNullable | 32 | Indicates that the field accepts Null values |
| AdFldLong | 128 | Indicates that the field is a long binary field, and that the **AppendChunk** and **GetChunk** methods can be used |
| AdFldMayBeNull | 64 | Indicates that you can read Null values from the field |
| AdFldMayDefer | 2 | Indicates that the field is deferred, that is, the field values are not retrieved from the data source with the whole record, but only when you access them |

| Name | Value | Description |
|------|-------|-------------|
| `AdFldRowID` | 256 | Indicates that the field some kind of record ID |
| `AdFldRowVersion` | 512 | Indicates that the field time or **datestamp** used to track updates |
| `AdFldUnknownUpdatable` | 8 | Indicates that the provider cannot determine if you can write to the field |
| `AdFldUpdatable` | 4 | Indicates that you can write to the field |

## *FilterGroupEnum*

| Name | Value | Description |
|------|-------|-------------|
| `AdFilterAffectedRecords` | 2 | Allows you to view only records affected by the last **Delete**, **Resync**, **UpdateBatch**, or **CancelBatch** method |
| `AdFilterFetchedRecords` | 3 | Allows you to view records in the current cache. |
| `AdFilterNone` | 0 | Removes the current filter and restores all records to view |
| `AdFilterPendingRecords` | 1 | Allows you to view only the records that have changed but have not been sent to the server. Only applicable for batch update mode |
| `AdFilterPredicate` | 4 | |

## *GetRowsOptionEnum*

| Name | Value | Description |
|------|-------|-------------|
| `AdGetRowsRest` | -1 | Retrieve the remainder of the rows in the recordset |

## *IsolationLevelEnum*

| Name | Value | Description |
|------|-------|-------------|
| `AdXactBrowse` | 256 | Indicates that from one transaction you can view uncommitted changes in other transactions |
| `AdXactChaos` | 16 | Indicates that you cannot overwrite pending changes from more highly isolated transactions |

*Table Continued on Following Page*

| Name | Value | Description |
|---|---|---|
| AdXactCursorStability | 4096 | Performs retaining aborts, thus calling **RollbackTrans** automatically starts a new transaction. Provider dependant |
| AdXactIsolated | 1048576 | Default. Indicates that from one transaction you can view changes in other transactions only after they have been submitted |
| AdXactReadCommitted | 4096 | Default. Indicates that from one transaction you can view changes in other transactions only after they have been submitted |
| AdXactReadUncommitted | 256 | Indicates that from one transaction you can view uncommitted changes in other transactions |
| AdXactRepeatableRead | 65536 | Indicates that from one transaction you cannot see changes made in other transactions, but that requerying can bring new recordsets |
| AdXactSerializable | 1048576 | Indicates that from one transaction you cannot see changes made in other transactions, but that requerying can bring new recordsets |
| AdXactUnspecified | -1 | Indicates that the provider is using a different **IsolationLevel** than specified, but that the level cannot be identified |

## LockTypeEnum

| Name | Value | Description |
|---|---|---|
| AdLockBatchOptimistic | 4 | Optimistic batch updates. |
| AdLockOptimistic | 3 | Optimistic locking, record by record. The provider locks records when **Update** is called |
| AdLockPessimistic | 2 | Pessimistic locking, record by record. The provider locks the record immediately upon editing |
| AdLockReadOnly | 1 | Default. Read only, data cannot be modified |
| AdLockUnspecified | -1 | The clone is created with the same lock type as the original |

## MarshalOptionsEnum

| Name | Value | Description |
|------|-------|-------------|
| `AdMarshalAll` | 0 | Default. Indicates that all rows are returned to the server |
| `AdMarshalModifiedOnly` | 1 | Indicates that only modified rows are returned to the server |

## ObjectStateEnum

| Name | Value | Description |
|------|-------|-------------|
| `AdStateClosed` | 0 | Default. Indicates that the object is closed |
| `AdStateOpen` | 1 | Indicates that the object is open |

## ParameterAttributesEnum

| Name | Value | Description |
|------|-------|-------------|
| `AdParamLong` | 128 | Indicates that the parameter accepts long binary data |
| `AdParamNullable` | 64 | Indicates that the parameter accepts Null values |
| `AdParamSigned` | 16 | Default. Indicates that the parameter accepts signed values |

## ParameterDirectionEnum

| Name | Value | Description |
|------|-------|-------------|
| `AdParamInput` | 1 | Default. Indicates an input parameter |
| `AdParamInputOutput` | 3 | Indicates both an input and output parameter |
| `AdParamOutput` | 2 | Indicates an output parameter |
| `AdParamReturnValue` | 4 | Indicates a return value |
| `AdParamUnknown` | 0 | Indicates parameter direction is unknown |

## PositionEnum

| Name | Value | Description |
|------|-------|-------------|
| `AdPosBOF` | -2 | The current record pointer is at **BOF** |
| `AdPosEOF` | -3 | The current record pointer is at **EOF** |

*Table Continued on Following Page*

| Name | Value | Description |
|------|-------|-------------|
| AdPosUnknown | -1 | The **Recordset** is empty, the current position is unknown, or the provider does not support the **AbsolutePage** property |

## PropertyAttributesEnum

| Name | Value | Description |
|------|-------|-------------|
| AdPropNot Supported | 0 | Indicates that the property is not supported by the provider |
| AdPropOptional | 2 | Indicates that the user does not need to specify a value for this property before the data source is initialised |
| AdPropRead | 512 | Indicates that the user can read the property |
| AdPropRequired | 1 | Indicates that the user must specify a value for this property before the data source is initialised |
| AdPropWrite | 1024 | Indicates that the user can set the property |

## RecordStatusEnum

| Name | Value | Description |
|------|-------|-------------|
| AdRecCanceled | 256 | The record was not saved because the operation was cancelled |
| AdRecCantRelease | 1024 | The new record was not saved because of existing record locks |
| AdRecConcurrencyViolation | 2048 | The record was not saved because optimistic concurrency was in use |
| AdRecDBDeleted | 262144 | The record has already been deleted from the data source |
| AdRecDeleted | 4 | The record was deleted |
| AdRecIntegrityViolation | 4096 | The record was not saved because the user violated integrity constraints |
| AdRecInvalid | 16 | The record was not saved because its bookmark is invalid |
| AdRecMaxChangesExceeded | 8192 | The record was not saved because there were too many pending changes |
| AdRecModified | 2 | The record was modified |

| Name | Value | Description |
|---|---|---|
| `AdRecMultipleChanges` | 64 | The record was not saved because it would have affected multiple records |
| `AdRecNew` | 1 | The record is new |
| `AdRecObjectOpen` | 16384 | The record was not saved because of a conflict with an open storage object |
| `AdRecOK` | 0 | The record was successfully updated |
| `AdRecOutOfMemory` | 32768 | The record was not saved because the computer has run out of memory |
| `AdRecPendingChanges` | 128 | The record was not saved because it refers to a pending insert |
| `AdRecPermissionDenied` | 65536 | The record was not saved because the user has insufficient permissions |
| `AdRecSchemaViolation` | 131072 | The record was not saved because it violates the structure of the underlying database |
| `AdRecUnmodified` | 8 | The record was not modified |

## SchemaEnum

| Name | Value | Description |
|---|---|---|
| `AdSchemaAsserts` | 0 | Request assert information |
| `AdSchemaCatalogs` | 1 | Request catalog information |
| `AdSchemaCharacterSets` | 2 | Request character set information |
| `AdSchemaCheckConstraints` | 5 | Request check constraint information |
| `AdSchemaCollations` | 3 | Request collation information |
| `AdSchemaColumnPrivileges` | 13 | Request column privilege information |
| `AdSchemaColumns` | 4 | Request column information |
| `AdSchemaColumnsDomainUsage` | 11 | Request column domain usage information |
| `AdSchemaConstraintColumnUsage` | 6 | Request column constraint usage information |
| `AdSchemaConstraintTableUsage` | 7 | Request table constraint usage information |

*Table Continued on Following Page*

| Name | Value | Description |
|---|---|---|
| `AdSchemaForeignKeys` | 27 | Request foreign key information |
| `AdSchemaIndexes` | 12 | Request index information |
| `AdSchemaKeyColumnUsage` | 8 | Request key column usage information |
| `AdSchemaPrimaryKeys` | 28 | Request primary key information |
| `AdSchemaProcedureColumns` | 29 | Request stored procedure column information |
| `AdSchemaProcedureParameters` | 26 | Request stored procedure parameter information |
| `AdSchemaProcedures` | 16 | Request stored procedure information |
| `AdSchemaProviderSpecific` | -1 | Request provider specific information |
| `AdSchemaProviderTypes` | 22 | Request provider type information |
| `AdSchemaReferentialContraints` | 9 | Request referential constraint information |
| `AdSchemaSchemata` | 17 | Request schema information |
| `AdSchemaSQLLanguages` | 18 | Request SQL language support information |
| `AdSchemaStatistics` | 19 | Request statistics information |
| `AdSchemaTableConstraints` | 10 | Request table constraint information |
| `AdSchemaTablePrivileges` | 14 | Request table privilege information |
| `AdSchemaTables` | 20 | Request information about the tables |
| `AdSchemaTranslations` | 21 | Request character set translation information |
| `adSchemaUsagePrivileges` | 15 | Request user privilege information |
| `adSchemaViewColumnUsage` | 24 | Request column usage in views information |
| `adSchemaViews` | 23 | Request view information |
| `adSchemaViewTableUsage` | 25 | Request table usage in views information |

## SearchDirection

| Name | Value | Description |
|---|---|---|
| adSearchBackward | -1 | Search backward from the current record |
| adSearchForward | 1 | Search forward from the current record |

## SearchDirectionEnum

| Name | Value | Description |
|---|---|---|
| adSearchBackward | -1 | Search backward from the current record |
| adSearchForward | 1 | Search forward from the current record |

# Microsoft Transaction Server Type Library Reference

## Objects

| Name | Description |
|------|-------------|
| ObjectContext | Provides access to the current objects context |
| SecurityProperty | Used to determine the current object's caller or creator |

## ObjectContext

### Methods

| Name | Returns | Description |
|------|---------|-------------|
| CreateInstance | Variant | Creates an object using current object's context. |
| DisableCommit | | Indicates that the object is not yet finished its work and any attempt to commit the transaction will force an abort. |

| Name | Returns | Description |
|------|---------|-------------|
| EnableCommit | | Indicates that the object is not yet finished its work but would allow the transaction to commit. |
| IsCallerInRole | Boolean | Returns TRUE if the caller's Userid is included in the identified role. |
| IsInTransaction | Boolean | Returns TRUE if this object context has an active transaction. |
| IsSecurityEnabled | Boolean | Returns TRUE if security is enabled. |
| SetAbort | | Indicates that the object has completed its work and the transaction must be aborted. |
| SetComplete | | Indicates that the object has completed its work and a transaction can be committed. |

## Properties

| Name | Returns | Description | Type |
|------|---------|-------------|------|
| Count | Integer | Get number of named properties. | Read only |
| Item | Variant | Get a named property | Read only |
| Security | SecurityProperty | Returns the security object | Read only |

# SecurityProperty

## Methods

| Name | Returns | Description |
|------|---------|-------------|
| GetDirectCallerName | String | Returns the Name of the direct caller |
| GetDirectCreatorName | String | Returns the Name of the direct creator |

| Name | Returns | Description |
|------|---------|-------------|
| GetDirectCreatorName | String | Returns the Name of the direct creator |
| GetOriginalCallerName | String | Returns the Name of the original caller |
| GetOriginalCreatorName | String | Returns the Name of the original creator |

# Constants

## Error_Constants

| Name | Value | Description |
|------|-------|-------------|
| mtsErrCtxAborted | -2147164158 | The transaction was aborted |
| mtsErrCtxAborting | -2147164157 | The transaction is aborting |
| MtsErrCtxActivityTimeout | -2147164154 | The activity timed out |
| mtsErrCtxNoContext | -2147164156 | There is no object context |
| mtsErrCtxNoSecurity | -2147164147 | There is no security context |
| MtsErrCtxNotRegistered | -2147164155 | The context is not registered |
| MtsErrCtxOldReference | -2147164153 | The context has an old reference |
| MtsErrCtxRoleNotFound | -2147164148 | The role was not found |
| mtsErrCtxTMNotAvailable | -2147164145 | The Transaction Monitor is not available |
| mtsErrCtxWrongThread | -2147164146 | Execution on wrong thread |

## XactAttributeEnum

| Name | Value | Description |
|------|-------|-------------|
| adXactAbortRetaining | 262144 | Performs retaining aborts, so calling **Rollback** automatically starts a new transaction |
| adXactCommitRetaining | 131072 | Performs retaining commits, thus calling **CommitTrans** automatically starts a new transaction. Provider dependant. |

# Microsoft Message Queue Object Library Reference

This appendix aims to provide a complete reference for all the objects, with their methods and properties, and all the constants that you could conceivably need to use the Microsoft Message Queue.

## Objects

| Name | Description |
|---|---|
| MSMQApplication | Obtains the machine identifier |
| MSMQCoordinatedTransactionDispenser | Use to obtain an MSMQ DTC Transaction Object (MSMQTransaction) |
| MSMQEvent | Allows implementation of a single event handler to support multiple queues |
| MSMQMessage | A message to be queued |
| MSMQQuery | Allow the querying of existing public queues |
| MSMQQueue | An MSMQ Queue |
| MSMQQueueInfo | Provides Queue Management |

*Table Continued on Following Page*

| Name | Description |
|------|-------------|
| `MSMQQueueInfos` | Allows selection of public queues |
| `MSMQTransaction` | An MSMQ Transaction Object |
| `MSMQTransactionDispenser` | Used to create new MSMQ Internal Transaction Objects |

# MSMQApplication

## Methods

| Name | Returns | Description |
|------|---------|-------------|
| `MachineIdOfMachineName` | String | Global function used to map a machine pathname to a unique identifier. For example, this identifier can be used to construct a format name for a computer so that its journal queue can be opened. |

# MSMQCoordinatedTransactionDispenser

## Methods

| Name | Returns | Description |
|------|---------|-------------|
| `BeginTransaction` | IMSMQTransaction | Method used to obtain a new transaction from a transaction dispenser. |

# MSMQEvent

## Methods

| Name | Returns | Description |
|------|---------|-------------|
| `Arrived` | | User-defined method invoked when a message arrives at a queue. |
| `ArrivedError` | | User-defined method invoked when an error is returned while reading messages asynchronously. |

# MSMQMessage

## Methods

| Name | Returns | Description |
|------|---------|-------------|
| `AttachCurrentSecurityContext` | | Method used to associate the current security context with a message. |
| `Send` | | Method used to send a message to the destination queue. Can optionally be part of a transaction. |

## Properties

| Name | Returns | Description | Type |
|------|---------|-------------|------|
| `Ack` | Integer | Property indicating what kind of acknowledgement message is returned. Possible values defined by MQMSGACKNOWLEDGEMENT enumeration. | Read/ Write |
| `AdminQueue Info` | IMSMQQueue Info | Property indicating the administration queue for the message. | Read/ Write |
| `AppSpecific` | Integer | Property containing application-specific information. | Read/ Write |
| `ArrivedTime` | Variant | Property indicating when the message arrived at its destination queue. Type is Variant Date. | Read only |
| `AuthLevel` | Integer | Property indicating the authorization level of a message. Possible values defined by MQMSGAUTHLEVEL enumeration. | Read/ Write |
| `Body` | Variant | Property containing the message body. It is a Variant type and can contain any intrinsic type and persistent object. | Read/ Write |
| `BodyLength` | Integer | Property indicating the length (in bytes) of the message body. | Read only |

*Table Continued on Following Page*

| Name | Returns | Description | Type |
|---|---|---|---|
| Class | Integer | Property indicating the class of message. Possible values defined by MQMSGCLASS enumeration. | Read only |
| CorrelationId | Variant | Property indicating the correlation identifier (array of bytes) of the message. | Read/ Write |
| Delivery | Integer | Property indicating the delivery mode of a message. Possible values defined by MQMSGDELIVERY enumeration. | Read/ Write |
| Destination QueueInfo | IMSMQQueue Info | Property indicating the destination queue of the message. Typically used when reading response messages, or messages in machine journals or dead-letter queues. | Read only |
| EncryptAlgorithm | Integer | Property indicating which encryption algorithm to use when encrypting the message body of a private message. | Read/ Write |
| HashAlgorithm | Integer | Property indicating which hash algorithm to use when authenticating the message. | Read/ Write |
| Id | Variant | Property containing the MSMQ-generated identifier (array of bytes) of the message. | Read only |
| IsAuthenticated | Boolean | Property indicating whether a message was or was not authenticated. | Read only |
| Journal | Integer | Property indicating journaling option for message. Possible values defined by MQMSGJOURNAL enumeration. | Read/ Write |
| Label | String | Property indicating the label of the message. | Read/ Write |

| Name | Returns | Description | Type |
|------|---------|-------------|------|
| MaxTimeToReach Queue | Integer | Property indicating the amount of time MSMQ has to deliver the message to its destination queue. | Read/ Write |
| MaxTimeToReceive | Integer | Property indicating the amount of time the receiving application has to retrieve the message from its destination queue. | Read/ Write |
| Priority | Integer | Property indicating the priority level of a message. Range must be between MQ_MIN_PRIORITY and MQ_MAX_PRIORITY. | Read/ Write |
| PrivLevel | Integer | Property indicating the privacy level of a message. Possible values defined by MQMSGPRIVLEVEL enumeration. | Read/ Write |
| ResponseQueue Info | IMSMQQueue Info | Property indicating the response queue for the message. | Read/ Write |
| Sender Certificate | Variant | Property containing the security certificate of a message. Type is an array of bytes. | Read/ Write |
| SenderId | Variant | Property containing the sender identifier of the message. Type is an array of bytes. | Read only |
| SenderIdType | Integer | Property indicating what type of identifier is attached to the message. Possible values are defined by MSMQSENDERIDTYPE enumeration. | Read/ Write |
| SentTime | Variant | Property indicating when the message was sent. Type is Variant Date. | Read only |
| SourceMachine Guid | String | Property identifying the computer where the message originated. | Read only |

*Table Continued on Following Page*

| Name | Returns | Description | Type |
|------|---------|-------------|------|
| Trace | Integer | Property indicating tracing option for message. Possible values defined by MQMSGTRACE enumeration. | Read/Write |

# MSMQQuery

## Methods

| Name | Returns | Description |
|------|---------|-------------|
| LookupQueue | IMSMQQueueInfos | Produces a collection of public queues that match a specified selection criteria. Queries the MSMQ information store. |

# MSMQQueue

## Methods

| Name | Returns | Description |
|------|---------|-------------|
| Close | | Method to close an open instance of a queue. |
| Enable Notification | | Method to enable asynchronous notification of arriving messages. It can use the queue's implicit cursor. The user-defined MSMQEvent_Arrived event handler is invoked when a message arrives at the location specified by the optional Cursor parameter (default is first message in the queue), or a timeout occurs. The user-defined MSMQEvent_ArrivedError is invoked if the asynchronous message retrieval results in an error. |
| Peek | IMSMQMessage | Method to synchronously peek at the first message in the queue, regardless of the implicit cursor position. Optional parameters include ReceiveTimeout (default set to INFINITE), WantDestinationQueue (default set to False), and WantBody (default set to True). |

| Name | Returns | Description |
|------|---------|-------------|
| **Peek Current** | IMSMQMessage | Method to synchronously peek at the current message in queue (message pointed at by the implicit cursor). The implicit cursor is not advanced. Optional parameters include ReceiveTimeout (default set to INFINITE) and Transaction (default set to MTS Transaction). |
| **PeekNext** | IMSMQMessage | Method to synchronously peek at the next message in the queue. When called, the implicit cursor is first advanced and then the message is returned. Optional parameters include ReceiveTimeout (default set to INFINITE) and Transaction (default set to MTS Transaction). |
| **Receive** | IMSMQMessage | Method to synchronously retrieve a message from a queue. It always removes the first message in queue regardless of the position of the implicit cursor. Optional parameters include ReceiveTimeout (default set to INFINITE), Transaction (default set to MTS Transaction), WantDestinationQueue (default set to False), and WantBody (default set to True). |
| **Receive Current** | IMSMQMessage | Method to synchronously remove the current message from the queue. Retrieves the message at the position pointed to by the implicit cursor. Optional parameters include ReceiveTimeout (default set to INFINITE) and Transaction (default set to MTS Transaction). |
| **Reset** | | Method that resets the queue's implicit cursor to the beginning of the queue. |

## Properties

| Name | Returns | Description | Type |
|------|---------|-------------|------|
| **Access** | Integer | Property indicating the access mode of a queue. Possible values defined by MQACCESS enumeration. | Read only |
| **Handle** | Integer | Property indicating the internal MSMQ handle of an open queue instance. Useful for directly calling MSMQ APIs. | Read only |
| **IsOpen** | Boolean | Property indicating whether or not the queue object refers to an open instance of a queue. | Read only |

*Table Continued on Following Page*

| Name | Returns | Description | Type |
|------|---------|-------------|------|
| QueueInfo | IMSM QQueueInfo | Property referring to an **MSMQQueueInfo** instance describing the queue. | Read only |
| ShareMode | Integer | Property indicating the share mode of a queue. Possible values defined by **MQSHARE** enumeration. | Read only |

# MSMQQueueInfo

## Methods

| Name | Returns | Description |
|------|---------|-------------|
| Create | | Method that creates a new queue. The PathName property is required to create a queue. The FormatName property is updated when the queue is created. Optional parameters include IsWorldReadable (default set to False) and IsTransactional (default set to False). |
| Delete | | Method used to delete queue. The PathName property must be specified to delete a queue. |
| Open | IMSMQQueue | Method used to open a queue. The PathName property must be specified to open a queue. Parameters include Access (send, peek, or receive) and ShareMode (exclusive or all). |
| Refresh | | Method used to refresh the properties of a public queue from the MSMQ information store. |
| Update | | Method used to update the MSMQ information store with the public queue's current properties. |

## Properties

| Name | Returns | Description | Type |
|------|---------|-------------|------|
| Authenticate | Integer | Property that specifies whether or not the queue only accepts authenticated messages. If the authentication level of the message does not match the authentication level of the queue, the message is rejected by the queue. Possible values are defined by the **MQAUTHENTICATE** enumeration. | Read/ Write |

| Name | Returns | Description | Type |
|------|---------|-------------|------|
| **BasePriority** | Integer | Property that specifies the base priority for all messages sent to a public queue. The queue's base priority has no effect on the order of the messages in the queue, or how messages are read from the queue. | Read/ Write |
| **CreateTime** | Variant | Property that indicates the time and date when the queue was created. Type is Variant Date. | Read only |
| **FormatName** | String | Property that identifies the queue. The format name of a queue is generated by MSMQ when the queue is created, or generated later by the application. | Read/ Write |
| **IsTransactional** | Boolean | Property indicating whether the queue is transactional or non-transactional. If the queue is transactional, all messages sent to the queue must be part of a transaction. | Read only |
| **IsWorldReadable** | Boolean | Property that indicates who can read messages in the queue. If False, then the queue has the default MSMQ security: all users can send messages to the queue but only the owner of the queue can read messages from it. Otherwise all users can read its messages. | Read only |
| **Journal** | Integer | Property that specifies if the messages retrieved from the queue are copied to the queue's journal queue. Possible values are defined by the **MQJOURNAL** enumeration. | Read/ Write |
| **JournalQuota** | Integer | Property that specifies the maximum size (in kilobytes) of the journal queue. | Read/ Write |
| **Label** | String | Property indicating the label of the queue. | Read/ Write |

*Table Continued on Following Page*

| Name | Returns | Description | Type |
|------|---------|-------------|------|
| ModifyTime | Variant | Property that indicates the time and date when the queue's properties were last modified. Type is Variant Date. | Read only |
| PathName | String | Property indicating pathname (physical location) of the queue. | Read/ Write |
| PrivLevel | Integer | Property that specifies the privacy level that is required by the queue. The privacy level determines how the queue handles private (encrypted) messages. Possible values are defined by the **MQPRIVLEVEL** enumeration. | Read/ Write |
| QueueGuid | String | Property indicating the identifier of the public queue. | Read only |
| Quota | Integer | Property that specifies the maximum size (in kilobytes) of the queue. | Read/ Write |
| ServiceTypeGuid | String | Property identifying the type of service provided by the queue. | Read/ Write |

# MSMQQueueInfos

## Methods

| Name | Returns | Description |
|------|---------|-------------|
| Next | IMSMQQueueInfo | Method used to reset the implicit cursor to the start of a collection of queues produced by **MSMQQuery.LookupQueue**. |
| Reset | | Method used to reset the implicit cursor to the start of a collection of queues produced by **MSMQQuery.LookupQueue**. |

# MSMQTransaction

## Methods

| Name | Returns | Description |
|------|---------|-------------|
| Abort | | Method used to abort an MSMQ transaction. |
| Commit | | Method used to commit an MSMQ transaction. |

## Properties

| Name | Returns | Description | Type |
|------|---------|-------------|------|
| Transaction | Integer | Property that indicates the underlying "magic cookie" used by a transaction dispenser. | Read only |

# MSMQTransactionDispenser

## Methods

| Name | Returns | Description |
|------|---------|-------------|
| BeginTransaction | IMSMQTransaction | Method used to obtain a new transaction from a transaction dispenser. |

# Constants

## MQACCESS

| Name | Value | Description |
|------|-------|-------------|
| MQ_PEEK_ACCESS | 32 | Messages can only be looked at, and cannot be removed from the queue |
| MQ_RECEIVE_ACCESS | 1 | Messages can be retrieved from the queue or peeked at. |
| MQ_SEND_ACCESS | 2 | Messages can only be sent to the queue |

## MQAUTHENTICATE

| Name | Value | Description |
| --- | --- | --- |
| MQ_AUTHENTICATE | 1 | The queue only accepts authenticated messages |
| MQ_AUTHENTICATE_NONE | 0 | The default. The queue accepts authenticated and non-authenticated messages |

## MQCALG

| Name | Value | Description |
| --- | --- | --- |
| MQMSG_CALG_DES | 26113 | Hashing algorithm used when authenticating messages |
| MQMSG_CALG_DSS_SIGN | 8704 | Hashing algorithm used when authenticating messages |
| MQMSG_CALG_MAC | 32773 | Hashing algorithm used when authenticating messages |
| MQMSG_CALG_MD2 | 32769 | Hashing algorithm used when authenticating messages |
| MQMSG_CALG_MD4 | 32770 | Hashing algorithm used when authenticating messages |
| MQMSG_CALG_MD5 | 32771 | The Default. Hashing algorithm used when authenticating messages |
| MQMSG_CALG_RC2 | 26114 | Hashing algorithm used when authenticating messages |
| MQMSG_CALG_RC4 | 26625 | Hashing algorithm used when authenticating messages |
| MQMSG_CALG_RSA_KEYX | 41984 | Hashing algorithm used when authenticating messages |
| MQMSG_CALG_RSA_SIGN | 9216 | Hashing algorithm used when authenticating messages |
| MQMSG_CALG_SEAL | 26626 | Hashing algorithm used when authenticating messages |
| MQMSG_CALG_SHA | 32772 | Hashing algorithm used when authenticating messages |

## MQDEFAULT

| Name | Value | Description |
| --- | --- | --- |
| DEFAULT_M_ACKNOWLEDGE | 0 | Default value for the **Acknowledgement** property of a Message |
| DEFAULT_M_APPSPECIFIC | 0 | Default value for the **AppSpecific** property of a Message |
| DEFAULT_M_AUTH_LEVEL | 0 | Default value for the **AuthLevel** property of a Message |
| DEFAULT_M_DELIVERY | 0 | Default value for the **Delivery** property of a Message |
| DEFAULT_M_JOURNAL | 0 | Default value for the **Journal** property of a Message |
| DEFAULT_M_PRIORITY | 3 | Default value for the **Priority** property of a Message |
| DEFAULT_M_PRIV_LEVEL | 0 | Default value for the **PrivLevel** property of a Message |
| DEFAULT_M_SENDERID_TYPE | 1 | Default value for the **SenderId** property of a Message |
| DEFAULT_Q_AUTHENTICATE | 0 | Default value for the **Authenticate** property of a Queue |
| DEFAULT_Q_BASEPRIORITY | 0 | Default value for the **BasePriority** property of a Queue |
| DEFAULT_Q_JOURNAL | 0 | Default value for the **Journal** property of a Queue |
| DEFAULT_Q_JOURNAL_QUOTA | -1 | Default value for the **JournalQuota** property of a Queue |
| DEFAULT_Q_PRIV_LEVEL | 1 | Default value for the **PrivLevel** property of a Queue |
| DEFAULT_Q_QUOTA | -1 | Default value for the **Quota** property of a Queue |
| DEFAULT_Q_TRANSACTION | 0 | Default value for the **Transaction** property of a Queue |

## *MQERROR*

| Name | Value | Description |
|------|-------|-------------|
| MQ_ERROR | -1072824319 | Generic error code. |
| MQ_ERROR_ACCESS_ DENIED | -1072824283 | Access to the specified queue or computer is denied. |
| MQ_ERROR_BAD_ SECURITY_CONTEXT | -1072824267 | Security context specified by **PROPID_M_SECURITY_CONTEXT** is corrupted. |
| MQ_ERROR_BUFFER_ OVERFLOW | -1072824294 | Supplied message body buffer is too small. A partial copy of the message body is copied to the buffer, but the message is not removed from the queue. |
| MQ_ERROR_CANNOT_ IMPERSONATE_CLIENT | -1072824284 | MSMQ information store server cannot impersonate the client application. Security credentials could not be verified. |
| MQ_ERROR_COMPUTER_ DOES_NOT_SUPPORT_ ENCRYPTION | -1072824269 | Encryption failed. Computer (source or destination) does not support encryption operations. |
| MQ_ERROR_CORRUPTED_ INTERNAL_CERTIFICATE | -1072824275 | MSMQ-supplied internal certificate is corrupted. |
| MQ_ERROR_CORRUPTED_ PERSONAL_CERT_STORE | -1072824271 | Microsoft® Internet Explorer personal certificate store is corrupted. |
| MQ_ERROR_CORRUPTED_ SECURITY_DATA | -1072824272 | Cryptographic function (CryptoAPI) has failed. |
| MQ_ERROR_COULD_NOT_ GET_ACCOUNT_INFO | -1072824265 | MSMQ could not get account information for the user. |
| MQ_ERROR_COULD_NOT_ GET_USER_SID | -1072824266 | MSMQ could not get the specified sender identifier. |
| MQ_ERROR_DELETE_CN_ IN_USE | -1072824248 | Specified connected network (CN) cannot be deleted because it is defined in at least one computer. Remove the CN from all CN lists and try again. |
| MQ_ERROR_DS_ERROR | -1072824253 | Internal error with MQIS. |
| MQ_ERROR_DS_IS_FULL | -1072824254 | MSMQ information store is full. |

| Name | Value | Description |
|------|-------|-------------|
| `MQ_ERROR_DTC_CONNECT` | -1072824244 | MSMQ cannot connect to the Microsoft® Distributed Transaction Coordinator (MS DTC). |
| `MQ_ERROR_FORMATNAME_BUFFER_TOO_SMALL` | -1072824289 | Specified format name buffer is too small to contain the queue's format name. |
| `MQ_ERROR_ILLEGAL_CONTEXT` | -1072824229 | The `lpwcsContext` parameter of `MQLocateBegin` is not NULL. |
| `MQ_ERROR_ILLEGAL_CURSOR_ACTION` | -1072824292 | An attempt was made to peek at the next message in the queue when cursor was at the end of the queue. |
| `MQ_ERROR_ILLEGAL_FORMATNAME` | -1072824290 | Format name specified is not valid. |
| `MQ_ERROR_ILLEGAL_MQCOLUMNS` | -1072824264 | Indicates that `pColumns` is NULL. |
| `MQ_ERROR_ILLEGAL_MQQMPROPS` | -1072824255 | No properties are specified by the `MQQMPROPS` structure, or it is set to NULL. |
| `MQ_ERROR_ILLEGAL_MQQUEUEPROPS` | -1072824259 | No properties are specified by the `MQQUEUEPROPS` structure, or it is set to NULL. |
| `MQ_ERROR_ILLEGAL_OPERATION` | -1072824220 | The operation is not supported on this specific platform. |
| `MQ_ERROR_ILLEGAL_PROPERTY_SIZE` | -1072824261 | The specified buffer for the message identifier or correlation identifier is not the correct size. |
| `MQ_ERROR_ILLEGAL_PROPERTY_VALUE` | -1072824296 | Property value specified in the `PROPVARIANT` array is illegal. |
| `MQ_ERROR_ILLEGAL_PROPERTY_VT` | -1072824295 | VARTYPE specified in the VT field of the `PROPVARIANT` array is not valid. |
| `MQ_ERROR_ILLEGAL_PROPID` | -1072824263 | Property identifier in the property identifier array is not valid. |
| `MQ_ERROR_ILLEGAL_QUEUE_PATHNAME` | -1072824300 | MSMQ pathname specified for the queue is not valid. |
| `MQ_ERROR_ILLEGAL_RELATION` | -1072824262 | Relationship parameter is not valid. |

*Table Continued on Following Page*

| Name | Value | Description |
|------|-------|-------------|
| MQ_ERROR_ILLEGAL_RESTRICTION_PROPID | -1072824260 | Property identifier specified in **MQRESTRICTION** is invalid. |
| MQ_ERROR_ILLEGAL_SECURITY_DESCRIPTOR | -1072824287 | Specified security descriptor is not valid. |
| MQ_ERROR_ILLEGAL_SORT | -1072824304 | Illegal sort specified. |
| MQ_ERROR_ILLEGAL_SORT_PROPID | -1072824228 | Property identifier specified in **MQSORTSET** is not valid. |
| MQ_ERROR_ILLEGAL_USER | -1072824303 | User is not legal. |
| MQ_ERROR_INSUFFICIENT_PROPERTIES | -1072824257 | Not all properties required for the operation were specified. |
| MQ_ERROR_INSUFFICIENT_RESOURCES | -1072824281 | Insufficient resources to complete operation (for example, not enough memory). Operation failed. |
| MQ_ERROR_INTERNAL_USER_CERT_EXIST | -1072824274 | Internal user certificate exists |
| MQ_ERROR_INVALID_CERTIFICATE | -1072824276 | Security certificate specified by **PROPID_M_SENDER_CERT** is invalid, or the certificate is not correctly placed in the Microsoft® Internet Explorer personal certificate store. |
| MQ_ERROR_INVALID_HANDLE | -1072824313 | Specified queue handle is not valid. |
| MQ_ERROR_INVALID_OWNER | -1072824252 | Object owner is not valid. Owner was not found when trying to create object. |
| MQ_ERROR_INVALID_PARAMETER | -1072824314 | One of the IN parameters supplied by the operation is not valid. |
| MQ_ERROR_IO_TIMEOUT | -1072824293 | **MQReceiveMessage** I/O timeout has expired. |
| MQ_ERROR_LABEL_BUFFER_TOO_SMALL | -1072824226 | Message label buffer is too small for received label. |
| MQ_ERROR_LABEL_TOO_LONG | -1072824227 | Message label is too long. It should be equal to or less than |
| MQ_ERROR_MACHINE_EXISTS | -1072824256 | Machine with the specified name already exists. |

| Name | Value | Description |
|------|-------|-------------|
| `MQ_ERROR_MACHINE_NOT_FOUND` | -1072824307 | Specified machine could not be found in MQIS. |
| `MQ_ERROR_MESSAGE_ALREADY_RECEIVED` | -1072824291 | Message pointed at by the cursor has already been removed from the queue. |
| `MQ_ERROR_MESSAGE_STORAGE_FAILED` | -1072824278 | Recoverable message could not be stored on the local computer. |
| `MQ_ERROR_MISSING_CONNECTOR_TYPE` | -1072824235 | Specified a property typically generated by MSMQ but did not specify `PROPID_M_CONNECTOR_TYPE` |
| `MQ_ERROR_MQIS_READONLY_MODE` | -1072824224 | MQIS database is in read-only mode. |
| `MQ_ERROR_MQIS_SERVER_EMPTY` | -1072824225 | The list of MSMQ information store servers (in registry) is empty. |
| `MQ_ERROR_NO_DS` | -1072824301 | No connection with the Site Controller server. Cannot access the MQIS. |
| `MQ_ERROR_NO_INTERNAL_USER_CERT` | -1072824273 | No internal certificate available for this user. |
| `MQ_ERROR_NO_RESPONSE_FROM_OBJECT_SERVER` | -1072824247 | No response from MQIS server. Operation status is unknown. |
| `MQ_ERROR_OBJECT_SERVER_NOT_AVAILABLE` | -1072824246 | Object's MSMQ information store server is not available. Operation failed. |
| `MQ_ERROR_OPERATION_CANCELLED` | -1072824312 | Operation was cancelled before it could be started. |
| `MQ_ERROR_PRIVILEGE_NOT_HELD` | -1072824282 | Application does not have the required privileges to perform the operation. |
| `MQ_ERROR_PROPERTY` | -1072824318 | One or more of the specified properties caused an error. |
| `MQ_ERROR_PROPERTY_NOTALLOWED` | -1072824258 | Specified property is not valid for the operation (for example, specifying `PROPID_Q_INSTANCE` when setting queue properties). |

*Table Continued on Following Page*

**451**

| Name | Value | Description |
|---|---|---|
| `MQ_ERROR_PROV_NAME_`<br>`BUFFER_TOO_SMALL` | -1072824221 | The provider name buffer for cryptographic service provider is too small. |
| `MQ_ERROR_QUEUE_DELETED` | -1072824230 | Queue was deleted before the message could be read. The specified queue handle is no longer valid and the queue must be closed. |
| `MQ_ERROR_QUEUE_EXISTS` | -1072824315 | Queue (public or private) with the identical MSMQ pathname is registered. Public queues are registered in MQIS. Private queues are registered in the local computer. |
| `MQ_ERROR_QUEUE_NOT_`<br>`AVAILABLE` | -1072824245 | Error while reading from queue residing on a remote computer. |
| `MQ_ERROR_QUEUE_NOT_`<br>`FOUND` | -1072824317 | Public queue is not registered in MQIS. This error does not apply to private queues. |
| `MQ_ERROR_RESULT_`<br>`BUFFER_TOO_SMALL` | -1072824250 | Supplied result buffer is too small. **MQLocateNext** could not return at least one complete query result. |
| `MQ_ERROR_SECURITY_`<br>`DESCRIPTOR_TOO_SMALL` | -1072824285 | Supplied security buffer is too small. |
| `MQ_ERROR_SENDER_CERT_`<br>`BUFFER_TOO_SMALL` | -1072824277 | Supplied sender certificate buffer is too small. |
| `MQ_ERROR_SENDERID_`<br>`BUFFER_TOO_SMALL` | -1072824286 | Supplied sender identification buffer is too small to hold sender identification. |
| `MQ_ERROR_SERVICE_NOT_`<br>`AVAILABLE` | -1072824309 | Application was unable to connect to the Queue Manager. |
| `MQ_ERROR_SHARING_`<br>`VIOLATION` | -1072824311 | Sharing violation when opening queue. The application is trying to open an already opened queue that has exclusive read rights. |
| `MQ_ERROR_SIGNATURE_`<br>`BUFFER_TOO_SMALL` | -1072824222 | The signature buffer is too small. |

| Name | Value | Description |
|------|-------|-------------|
| MQ_ERROR_STALE_HANDLE | -1072824234 | Specified handle was obtained in a previous session of the Queue Manager service. |
| MQ_ERROR_SYMM_KEY_ BUFFER_TOO_SMALL | -1072824223 | The symmetric key buffer is too small. |
| MQ_ERROR_TRANSACTION_ ENLIST | -1072824232 | Cannot enlist transaction. |
| MQ_ERROR_TRANSACTION_ IMPORT | -1072824242 | MSMQ could not import the specified transaction. |
| MQ_ERROR_TRANSACTION_ SEQUENCE | -1072824239 | Transaction operation sequence is incorrect. |
| MQ_ERROR_TRANSACTION_ USAGE | -1072824240 | Either the queue or the message is not transactional. Transaction messages can only be sent to a transaction queue, and transaction queues can only receive transaction messages. |
| MQ_ERROR_UNSUPPORTED_ ACCESS_MODE | -1072824251 | Specified access mode is not supported. Supported access modes include **MQ_PEEK_MESSAGE, MQ_SEND_MESSAGE,** and **MQ_RECEIVE_MESSAGE.** |
| MQ_ERROR_UNSUPPORTED_ DBMS | -1072824302 | Current version of Database Management System is not supported |
| MQ_ERROR_UNSUPPORTED_ FORMATNAME_OPERATION | -1072824288 | Requested operation is not supported for the specified format name (for example, trying to open a queue to receive messages using a direct format name). |
| MQ_ERROR_USER_BUFFER_ TOO_SMALL | -1072824280 | Supplied buffer for user is too small to hold the returned information. |
| MQ_ERROR_WRITE_NOT_ ALLOWED | -1072824219 | Write operations to MQIS are not allowed while an MSMQ information store server is being installed. |

## MQJOURNAL

| Name | Value | Description |
|------|-------|-------------|
| MQ_JOURNAL | 1 | when a message is removed from the queue it is stored in the queue journal |

*Table Continued on Following Page*

| Name | Value | Description |
|---|---|---|
| MQ_JOURNAL_NONE | 0 | The default. Messages are not stored in a journal queue when they are removed from the queue |

## MQMAX

| Name | Value | Description |
|---|---|---|
| MQ_MAX_Q_LABEL_LEN | 124 | The maximum length of the queue label |
| MQ_MAX_Q_NAME_LEN | 124 | The maximum length of the queue name |

## MQMSGACKNOWLEDGEMENT

| Name | Value | Description |
|---|---|---|
| MQMSG_ACKNOWLEDGMENT_ FULL_REACH_QUEUE | 5 | Posts positive and negative acknowledgements depending upon whether or not the message reached the queue. This can happen when the time-to-reach-queue timer expires, or when a message cannot be authenticated |
| MQMSG_ACKNOWLEDGMENT_ FULL_RECEIVE | 14 | Post a positive or negative acknowledgement depending on whether or not the message is retrieved from the queue before its time-to-be-received timer expires. |
| MQMSG_ACKNOWLEDGMENT_ NACK_REACH_QUEUE | 4 | Posts a negative acknowledgement when the message cannot reach the queue. This can happen when the time-to-reach-queue timer expires, or a message can not be authenticated |
| MQMSG_ACKNOWLEDGMENT_ NACK_RECEIVE | 12 | Posts a negative acknowledgement when an error occurs and the message cannot be retrieved from the queue before its time-to-be-received timer expires. |
| MQMSG_ACKNOWLEDGMENT_ NEG_ARRIVAL | 4 | Indicates a negative message arrival |
| MQMSG_ACKNOWLEDGMENT_ NEG_RECEIVE | 8 | Indicates a negative message receive |
| MQMSG_ACKNOWLEDGMENT_ NONE | 0 | The default. No acknowledgement messages are posted. |
| MQMSG_ACKNOWLEDGMENT_ POS_ARRIVAL | 1 | Indicates a positive message arrival |
| MQMSG_ACKNOWLEDGMENT_ POS_RECEIVE | 2 | Indicates a positive message receive |

## MQMSGAUTHLEVEL

| Name | Value | Description |
|---|---|---|
| MQMSG_AUTH_LEVEL_ALWAYS | 1 | The message must be authenticated when it arrives at the destination queue |
| MQMSG_AUTH_LEVEL_NONE | 0 | The default. The message does not have to be authenticated when it arrives at the destination queue |

## MQMSGCLASS

| Name | Value | Description |
|---|---|---|
| MQMSG_CLASS_ACK_REACH_QUEUE | 2 | The original message reached its destination queue |
| MQMSG_CLASS_ACK_RECEIVE | 16384 | The original message was retrieved by the receiving application |
| MQMSG_CLASS_NACK_ACCESS_DENIED | 32772 | The sending application does not have access rights to the destination queue |
| MQMSG_CLASS_NACK_BAD_DST_Q | 32768 | The destination queue is not available to the sending application |
| MQMSG_CLASS_NACK_BAD_ENCRYPTION | 32775 | The destination Queue Manager could not decrypt a private (encrypted) message |
| MQMSG_CLASS_NACK_BAD_SIGNATURE | 32774 | MSMQ could not authenticate the original message. The original message's digital signature is not valid. |
| MQMSG_CLASS_NACK_COULD_NOT_ENCRYPT | 32776 | The source Queue Manager could not encrypt a private message |
| MQMSG_CLASS_NACK_HOP_COUNT_EXCEEDED | 32773 | The original message's hop count is exceeded |
| MQMSG_CLASS_NACK_NOT_TRANSACTIONAL_MSG | 32778 | A non-transaction message was sent to a transactional queue |
| MQMSG_CLASS_NACK_NOT_TRANSACTIONAL_Q | 32777 | A transaction message was sent to a non-transactional queue |
| MQMSG_CLASS_NACK_PURGED | 32769 | The message was purged before reaching the destination queue |
| MQMSG_CLASS_NACK_Q_DELETED | 49152 | The queue was deleted before the message could be read from the queue |

*Table Continued on Following Page*

| Name | Value | Description |
|------|-------|-------------|
| `MQMSG_CLASS_NACK_Q_ EXCEED_QUOTA` | 32771 | The original message's destination queue is full |
| `MQMSG_CLASS_NACK_Q_ PURGED` | 49153 | The queue was purged and the message no longer exists |
| `MQMSG_CLASS_NACK_ REACH_QUEUE_TIMEOUT` | 32770 | Either the time-to-reach-queue or time-to-be-received timer expired before the original message could reach the destination queue |
| `MQMSG_CLASS_NACK_ RECEIVE_TIMEOUT` | 49154 | The original message was not removed from the queue before its time-to-be-received timer expired |
| `MQMSG_CLASS_NORMAL` | 0 | Indicates a normal MSMQ message |
| `MQMSG_CLASS_REPORT` | 1 | Indicates a report message |

## MQMSGCURSOR

| Name | Value | Description |
|------|-------|-------------|
| `MQMSG_CURRENT` | 1 | Notification starts when a message is at the current cursor location |
| `MQMSG_FIRST` | 0 | The default. Notification starts when a message is in the queue |
| `MQMSG_NEXT` | 2 | The cursor is moved, then notification starts when a message is at the new cursor location |

## MQMSGDELIVERY

| Name | Value | Description |
|------|-------|-------------|
| `MQMSG_DELIVERY_ EXPRESS` | 0 | The default. The message stays in memory until it can be delivered |
| `MQMSG_DELIVERY_ RECOVERABLE` | 1 | In every hop along its route, the message is forwarded to the next hop or stored locally in a backup file until delivered, thus guaranteeing delivery even in the case of a machine crash |

## MQMSGIDSIZE

| Name | Value | Description |
| --- | --- | --- |
| MQMSG_CORRELATIONID_SIZE | 20 | Size of **CorrelationID** byte array |
| MQMSG_MSGID_SIZE | 20 | Size of **MessageID** byte array |

## MQMSGJOURNAL

| Name | Value | Description |
| --- | --- | --- |
| MQMSG_DEADLETTER | 1 | If the message time-to-be-received or time-to-reach-queue setting expires, keep the message in the dead letter queue on the machine where time expired |
| MQMSG_JOURNAL | 2 | If the message is transmitted (from the originating machine to the next hop), keep it in the machine journal on the originating machine |
| MQMSG_JOURNAL_NONE | 0 | The default. The message is not kept in the originating machine's journal |

## MQMSGMAX

| Name | Value | Description |
| --- | --- | --- |
| MQ_MAX_MSG_LABEL_LEN | 249 | Maximum length of the message **Label** property |

## MQMSGPRIVLEVEL

| Name | Value | Description |
| --- | --- | --- |
| MQMSG_PRIV_LEVEL_BODY | 1 | The message is a private (encrypted) message |
| MQMSG_PRIV_LEVEL_NONE | 0 | The default. The message is a non-private (clear) message |

## MQMSGSENDERIDTYPE

| Name | Value | Description |
| --- | --- | --- |
| MQMSG_SENDERID_TYPE_NONE | 0 | **SenderID** is not attached to the message |
| MQMSG_SENDERID_TYPE_SID | 1 | The default. The **SenderID** property contains a SID for the user sending the message |

## MQMSGTRACE

| Name | Value | Description |
|------|-------|-------------|
| MQMSG_SEND_ROUTE_TO_REPORT_QUEUE | 1 | Each hop made by the original message generates a report that is recorded in a report message, which is send to the report queue specified by the source Queue Manager |
| MQMSG_TRACE_NONE | 0 | The default. No tracing for this message |

## MQPRIORITY

| Name | Value | Description |
|------|-------|-------------|
| MQ_MAX_PRIORITY | 7 | Maximum queue priority |
| MQ_MIN_PRIORITY | 0 | Minimum queue priority |

## MQPRIVLEVEL

| Name | Value | Description |
|------|-------|-------------|
| MQ_PRIV_LEVEL_BODY | 2 | The queue accepts only private (encrypted) messages |
| MQ_PRIV_LEVEL_NONE | 0 | The queue accepts only non-private (clear) messages |
| MQ_PRIV_LEVEL_OPTIONAL | 1 | The default. The queue does not force privacy, and accepts both clear and encrypted messages |

## MQSHARE

| Name | Value | Description |
|------|-------|-------------|
| MQ_DENY_NONE | 0 | The queue is available to everyone for sending, peeking, or retrieving messages. |
| MQ_DENY_RECEIVE_SHARE | 1 | Messages can only be retrieved by this process. |

## MQTRANSACTION

| Name | Value | Description |
|------|-------|-------------|
| MQ_MTS_TRANSACTION | 1 | Specifies that the call is part of the current MTS transaction |
| MQ_NO_TRANSACTION | 0 | Specifies the call is not part of a transaction |

| Name | Value | Description |
|------|-------|-------------|
| MQ_SINGLE_MESSAGE | 3 | Sends a single message as a transaction |
| MQ_XA_TRANSACTION | 2 | Specifies that the call is part of an externally coordinated, XA compliant, transaction |

## MQTRANSACTIONAL

| Name | Value | Description |
|------|-------|-------------|
| MQ_TRANSACTIONAL | 1 | All messages sent to the queue must be done through an MSMQ transaction |
| MQ_TRANSACTIONAL_NONE | 0 | Default. No transaction operations can be performed on the queue |

## MQWARNING

| Name | Value | Description |
|------|-------|-------------|
| MQ_INFORMATION_DUPLICATE_PROPERTY | 1074659333 | Property already specified with same value. When duplicate settings are found, the first entry is used and subsequent settings are ignored. |
| MQ_INFORMATION_FORMATNAME_BUFFER_TOO_SMALL | 1074659337 | Supplied format name buffer is too small. Queue was still created. |
| MQ_INFORMATION_ILLEGAL_PROPERTY | 1074659330 | Specified identifier in property identifier array **aPropID** is not valid. |
| MQ_INFORMATION_OPERATION_PENDING | 1074659334 | Asynchronous operation is pending. |
| MQ_INFORMATION_PROPERTY | 1074659329 | One or more of the specified properties resulted in a warning. Operation completed anyway. |
| MQ_INFORMATION_PROPERTY_IGNORED | 1074659331 | Specified property is not valid for this operation (for example, **PROPID_M_SENDERID** is not valid; it is set by MSMQ when sending messages). |
| MQ_INFORMATION_UNSUPPORTED_PROPERTY | 1074659332 | Specified property is not supported by this operation. This property is ignored. |

## RELOPS

| Name | Value | Description |
|---|---|---|
| REL_EQ | 1 | The default. Queue searching operator. Find only items that are Equal to the search string |
| REL_GE | 6 | Queue searching operator. Find only items that are Greater than or Equal to the search string |
| REL_GT | 4 | Queue searching operator. Find only items that are Greater than the search string |
| REL_LE | 5 | Queue searching operator. Find only items that are Less than or Equal to the search string |
| REL_LT | 3 | Queue searching operator. Find only items that are Less than the search string |
| REL_NEQ | 2 | Queue searching operator. Find only items that are Not Equal to the search string |
| REL_NOP | 0 | Queue searching operator. |

# Glossary of Terms and Acronyms

As you're no doubt aware, the number of acronyms in current use increases at an astonishing rate. This is by no means a complete glossary , simply an attempt to provide translations for the most widely used acronyms. A full and up-to-date glossary is available from the Resource Tools page of our website, accessible from the Resources link on our home page, **www.rapid.wrox.com**.

## A

| | |
|---|---|
| ACID | **Data transaction properties**. For a transaction to be considered valid, it must be Atomic, Consistent, Isolated and Durable - hence the acronym. |
| ACL | **Access Control List**. Internal object used by Windows NT to store user permissions for an individual resource, such as a disk file or directory. |
| ADC | **Advanced Data Connector**. An Active Server Component, usually referred to as the Data Access Component, which can provide the interface between a script and a data source. |
| ADO | **ActiveX Data Objects**. A series of ActiveX objects that are the preferred way to provide data access capabilities to any kind of data store, such as relational databases, message stores, etc. |
| ADS | **Active Directory Services**. A network-centric repository for all kinds of information about all the resources on the network and connected networks. New in Windows NT5. |
| ADSI | **Active Directory Service Interface**. The **API** for the Microsoft Active Directory Service. Allows programmers to read and manipulate the contents of the directory in code. |

| ANSI | **American National Standards Institute**. A standards body that provides definitions on computing topics such as programming languages and character sets. |
|---|---|
| API | **Application Programming Interface**. A series of functions exposed by an application or operating system that allow programmers to access and use the services it provides. |
| ARP | **Address Resolution Protocol**. A high-level network protocol running over **TCP/IP** that identifies network hardware addresses on a **LAN** given an **IP** address. |
| ASCII | **American Standard Code for Information Interchange**. A standard definition for character sets. Limited to 255 characters and slowly being superseded by Unicode, which uses 2 bytes per character and can store all types of foreign characters. |
| ASP | **Active Server Pages**. A Microsoft server-based scripting language that combines **HTML** and script code into a single file. Can be used create all kinds of dynamic pages. |
| ATM | **Asynchronous Transfer Mode**. A communication protocol designed to offer much higher data transmission speeds over existing networks than traditional methods such as Ethernet. |

## B

| BDC | **Backup Domain Controller**. A Windows NT Server installation that holds a read-only backup copy of security and other information for a network domain. Can authenticate users, and be promoted to a **PDC** in case of failure of the primary machine. |
|---|---|
| BSC | **Backup Site Controller**. A server within a Microsoft Message Queue Server site. It stores a backup copy of the part of the **MSMQ** Information Store database that applies to the site in case the **PSC** should fail. |

## C

| CA | **Certificate Authority**. A (usually) well known and trusted third party that issues certificates for encryption and verification use. Examples are Verisign and Thawte Consulting. |
|---|---|
| CDF | **Channel Definition Format**. A Microsoft specialized implementation of **XML**, used to define Channels in Internet Explorer 4+ and Windows 98. |
| Certificate | **A form of identification for secure communication**. Certificates are used to pass public encryption keys between applications, and to verify the certificate holder. Used for secure communication with **HTTPS** and by **MSMQ**. |
| CGI | **Common Gateway Interface**. A standardized interface exposed by most Web servers. Allows script and executable programs to access the user requests and server responses in order to create dynamic pages. |

| | |
|---|---|
| **CIFS** | **Common Internet File System**. An open and cross-platform mechanism for clients to request files over a network. Based on the **SMB** protocol widely used by PCs and workstations on a variety of operating systems. |
| **COM** | **Component Object Model**. The Microsoft open standard that defines how components communicate. Currently being extended as COM+, which adds extra features that make building component interfaces easier. |
| **CORBA** | **Common Object Request Broker Architecture**. A standard for integration and communication between components. Generally UNIX-based, and supported by Sun, Netscape, IBM, etc. |
| **Corpus** | **Index Server document collection**. The set of documents, files and other resources that are indexed by Microsoft Index Server or other indexing service. |
| **CRL** | **Certificate Revocation List**. A list of certificates that are no longer valid. Maintained and published by the **CA** that originally issued these certificates. |
| **Crossware** | **Netscape development environment**. A design methodology that defines how applications can be built so that they can run both over an internal network, and out to external partners over the Internet. |
| **CryptoAPI** | **Cryptographic Application Programming Interface**. A Microsoft **API** that provides services for authentication, encoding and encryption in Windows 32-bit applications. |
| **CSP** | **Cryptographic Service Provider**. A code module that integrates with the **CryptoAPI** to perform the authentication, encoding and encryption. Often created by **ISV**s. |
| **CSS1** | **Cascading Style Sheets (Level 1)**. The W3C-approved way to specify text formatting and layout in a Web page. Currently being expanded to **CSS2**. Several style sheets can be linked to a Web page, or the style information embedded within the page. |

## D

| | |
|---|---|
| **Daemon** | **Background network program**. A software application or service that runs continually within a network node to handle any of a range of tasks such as directing mail or routing data. |
| **DAO** | **Data Access Objects**. A Microsoft data access technology with a complex multi-level object model, introduced for use with MS Access and Office. Now superseded by **ADO**. |
| **DBMS** | **Database Management System**. A program or environment that stores, manages and retrieves data, for example SQL Server, Oracle, DB2, etc. Usually a relational database system. |

| | |
|---|---|
| **DCOM** | **Distributed Component Object Model**. The implementation of **COM** that allows components to communicate over a network connection, rather than being limited to the same machine. |
| **DES** | **Data Encryption Standard**. A standard that protects passwords from being read and then used again on the same a network to obtain unofficial access. |
| **DHCP** | **Dynamic Host Configuration Protocol**. A protocol under which a client can contact a server to obtain a valid IP network address for its own use, rather than using one hard-wired into the client. Useful on large networks to prevent **IP** address conflicts. |
| **DHTML** | **Dynamic HTML**. The overall moniker for the ability of the latest generation of browsers to change the contents of a Web page using script code, while it is loaded. |
| **DLL** | **Dynamic Link Library**. A software component or library of functions stored as a disk file in a special format. Used by other applications that require these functions. |
| **DNA** | **Distributed interNet Applications** Architecture. A methodology for three-tier application design using components that communicate via **COM** and **DCOM**. Also a broad marketing term for the combination of the different services offered by Windows NT. |
| **DNS** | **Domain Name System**. Also refers to a Domain Name Server. Translates a text **URL** (such as `http://rapid.wrox.co.uk`) into the equivalent **IP** address (`194.73.51.228`). |
| **DOM** | **Document Object Model**. A standard definition of the structure and content of a Web page when displayed in a browser or other user agent. Used in scripting to manipulate the contents of the document. |
| **DSN** | **Data Source Name**. A specification of all the information required to connect to and access a data store. Used with **ODBC**, and can also be stored a file on disk (File **DSN**) or with system-wide access (System **DSN**). |
| **DTC** | **Distributed Transaction Coordinator**. A software component that manages changes to a data source under control of a transaction manager. Allows updates to be rolled back if the transaction needs to be aborted, leaving the data store unchanged. |
| **DTD** | **Document Type Definition**. A set of rules that define how the rules of **SGML** are applied to a particular markup language. |

**E**

| | |
|---|---|
| **ECMA** | **European Computer Manufacturers Association**. A standards body that manages and ratifies proposals for computer technologies. Issues the open standard for the scripting language ECMAScript, which is based on JavaScript and JScript. |

## F

| | |
|---|---|
| **FAT** | **File Allocation Table**. The original MS-DOS format for disks. Has no built-in security, and imposes restrictions on the way files are physically stored. The limited number of allocation units it supports means that it is inefficient on large disks. |
| **FAT32** | **32-bit File Allocation Table**. An upgraded version of **FAT** introduced with the Windows 95 OSR2 update. Can handle more allocation units on large disks, with corresponding reduction in cluster size, to provide more efficient file storage. |
| **Firewall** | **Network security component**. A software component that acts as a filter restricting specific types of network packets from passing from one network to another. Often used between a **LAN** and the Internet. |
| **FTP** | **File Transfer Protocol**. A standard Internet protocol for transfering files between machines. Generally faster and more efficient than email or **HTTP**. |

## G

| | |
|---|---|
| **GIF** | **Graphics Interchange Format**. A format for graphics and images that compresses the content to provide efficient transmission over a network. Developed by CompuServe and now in common use on the Internet. |
| **GINA** | **Password filter component**. A software component that can be added to Windows NT to perform extra checking on user passwords as they are changed, ensuring they are strong enough to meet security requirements. |
| **Gopher** | **Internet search and retrieve protocol**. A protocol designed to allow clients to search for, retrieve and display documents over the Internet. Generally superseded by the Web, and no longer in common use. |
| **GUID** | **Globally Unique Identifier**. A 128-bit number that is generated automatically and used to refer to a resource, component, directory entry or any other type of object. Guaranteed to be unique. |

## H

| | |
|---|---|
| **HTML** | **Hypertext Markup Language**. The language of the Web. A way of inserting tags (elements and attributes) into a text page to add formatting, rich content, and other information. |
| **HTTP** | **Hypertext Transfer Protocol**. A protocol running over **IP** and designed for the World Wide Web. Provides packaging of information that can contain instruction headers and other data about the content. |
| **HTTPS** | **Hypertext Transfer Protocol Secure**. The secure version of **HTTP** using certificates that can uniquely identify the server and client, and encrypt all communication between them. |

*I*

| | |
|---|---|
| **ICMP** | **Internet Control Message Protocol**. An extension to **IP** that permits extra control, test and error messages to be incorporated into the packet stream. |
| **IDC** | **Internet Database Connector**. A Microsoft server-based scripting language for linking **ODBC** data sources to a Web server, so as to create dynamic pages based on a database. |
| **IE** | **Internet Explorer**. Microsoft's Web browser. What more can you say? |
| **IETF** | **Internet Engineering Task Force**. A large multi-vendor international group of engineers, operators, vendors and researchers that defines, proposes and ratifies technical standards for the Internet. |
| **IIOP** | **Internet Inter-Orb Protocol**. A standard, like **CORBA**, for communication between Java-based components such as JavaBeans. Allows components to communicate over the Internet in a Crossware application. |
| **IIS** | **Internet Information Server**. The Web server software included with Microsoft Windows NT. Supports applications that use **CGI**, **ASP**, **IDC** and **ISAPI**; and interfaces with Windows NT and other services running on the server machine. |
| **IP** | **Internet Protocol**. The low-level part of the **TCP/IP** protocol. **IP** assembles the **TCP** packets, adds address information, and despatches them over the network. |
| **IPX/SPX** | **Novell NetWare network protocol**. A network protocol developed by Novell to allow servers to provide an easily navigable network structure, and to share network resources. |
| **ISAPI** | **Internet Server Application Programming Interface**. A broadly standardized interface that allows server-side programs to create dynamic Web pages, in a similar way to **CGI**. |
| **ISDN** | **Integrated Services Digital Network**. A technology for combining voice and data in separate streams over a standard PSTN phone line to provide higher speeds, increased capacity and multiple channels. |
| **ISO** | **International Standards Organization**. A world-wide group of standards bodies that create international standards, including information technology related areas. |
| **ISP** | **Internet Service Provider**. An agency or company that provides a connection to the Internet, usually as a leased line or a dial-up link. |
| **ISV** | **Independent Software Vendor**. Term used to describe companies that produce software or components for use with other companies operating systems or technologies. |
| **ITU** | **International Telecommunications Union**. An international body that defines the standards for modems and low level transmission of data, typically over public networks like the PSTN. |

## J

| | |
|---|---|
| **JavaBean** | **Java software component**. A software component, built in Java, that implements a control or provides a series of functions for use within another application. |
| **JDBC** | **Java Database Connectivity**. A software interface layer that allows Java applications and components to access data stores via **ODBC**. |
| **JDK** | **Java Development Kit**. A set of documentation, samples and tools that provide programmers with the information required when creating Java applications and components. |
| **JIT** | **Just In Time**. An acronym applied to several technologies to indicate that a process, such as compilation of byte code, is carried out just before it is required by an application. |
| **JPEG** | **Joint Photographic Experts Group**. A body that designed and promotes the **JPEG** (**JPG**) graphics format, which combines high color depth with small file size for photographic still images by using a lossy compression scheme. |

## K

| | |
|---|---|
| **Kerberos** | **Network security protocol**. A security technology that has been under development in academic institutes for some time. Windows NT 5 uses this, replacing the existing **LAN** Manager based security methods in NT 3.5 and NT 4. |

## L

| | |
|---|---|
| **LAN** | **Local Area Network**. A series of machines in close proximity, usually in the same building, connected together. Uses any of a range of common network protocols, often referred to as Ethernet. |
| **LDAP** | **Lightweight Directory Access Protocol**. An Internet standard used to access directory information on remote servers. Uses less resources than the traditional **X.500** protocol. |
| **Locale** | **Language and locality information**. A text string such as "en-us" that accurately identifies a language and locality to allow programs to use language-specific formatting and processes. Can also be identified by a number called the LocaleID. |

## M

| | |
|---|---|
| **MAPI** | **Mail (or Message) Application Programming Interface**. The Microsoft standard application programming interface for email software. Allows programs to read, create, send and manipulate stored messages. |
| **MDA** | **Message Digest Algorithm**. A software algorithm that creates a digest for a message or other stream of data. The digest is unique, and the original data cannot be recreated from it. Generally specified as MD2, MD4, MD5, etc. |

| | |
|---|---|
| MDAC | **Microsoft Data Access Components**. A series of component objects that provide data access services such as **ADO** to Windows applications. |
| MIME | **Multipurpose (or Multimedia) Internet Mail Extension**. Defines the content type of a document, file or message attachment, for example "image/ mpeg" or "text/plain". |
| MPEG | **Motion Pictures Expert Group**. A body that designed and promotes the **MPEG** (**MPG**) moving graphics format, which combines high color depth with small file size for photographic moving images by using a lossy compression scheme. |
| MQIS | **Message Queue Information Store**. The central repository of information about an **MSMQ** enterprise, stored on the **PEC** and distributed to each site via the **PSC**s and **BSC**s. |
| MSMQ | **Microsoft Message Queue Server**. A Windows NT service that provides robust and secure transmission of messages between servers, which can be on different connected networks. |
| MTS | **Microsoft Transaction Server**. A Windows NT service that acts as both an object broker for components and as a distributed transaction manager. The basis for most **DNA** applications that require data access. |

**N**

| | |
|---|---|
| Namespace | **A name resolution area**. The bounded area within which a named object can be resolved. Examples are a subtree in a directory service, or a class within a component. |
| NDS | **Novell Directory Service**. Novell's implementation of a network-centric directory service. Has been available for some time, and is in common use on large NetWare networks. Supported by Windows NT. |
| NetBEUI | **Networking protocol**. The native protocol that forms the basis for Microsoft Networking in Windows environments. |
| NetBIOS | **Networking protocol**. A widely accepted and implemented standard for networking in a **LAN** environment. |
| NIC | **Network Interface Card**. The hardware providing the connection between a computer or peripheral and the network. Usually a plug-in card with sockets for a range of cable connector types. |
| NNTP | **Network News Transfer Protocol**. A protocol that transports news messages to special servers and client software over the Internet. Provides cross referencing, expiration, and search and retrieval facilities. |
| NOS | **Network Operating System**. A generic term for the protocol and software that provides communication services over a network. Examples are **NetBIOS, TCP/IP**, etc. |

| | |
|---|---|
| NTFS | **NT File System**. The Windows NT native disk format. Provides an efficient data storage format, and allows a range of security settings to be applied to individual files and directories. |
| NTLM | **NT LAN Manager authentication**. The protocol normally referred to as Challenge/Response that Windows NT uses to pass authentication information between the client and server when logging on. |

## O

| | |
|---|---|
| OCX | **OLE Control Extension**. A software component stored as a disk file in a special format for use by other applications. Similar to a **DLL**, but generally offers a single function to create an object or control. |
| ODBC | **Open Database Connectivity**. An open standard originally developed by Microsoft to allow transparent data access to all kinds of data stores such as relational databases. Drivers are manufactured by third parties to suit their own data store. |
| ODSI | **Open Directory Services Interface**. A set of industry-standard functions that can be implemented by a directory service, such as **LDAP** and **ADS**, to allow other applications to access the directory content. |
| OLAP | **On-line Analytical Processing**. A data store (or data warehouse) holding data in a multi-dimensional fashion. Often used for decision support and other commercial enquiry systems. |
| OLE | **Object Linking and Embedding**. The fore-runner to ActiveX. Uses COM to let components communicate, and allows applications to use the services of other applications as though they were just components. |
| OLE DB | **Object Linking and Embedding Database**. The new standard data access programming interface from Microsoft that is designed to replace **ODBC**, and provide wider coverage of different types of data stores. |
| OLTP | **On-line Transaction Processing**. The technique of performing order or information processing in real time, rather than storing the transactions for executaion as a batch at a later time. |
| OMG | **Object Management Group**. An alliance of vendors formed to define and promote the **CORBA** object spcification. Prominent members are Sun, Netscape and IBM. |
| ONE | **Open Network Environment**. A Netscape development environment based on open standards that makes it easy to build, deploy and run applications over the Internet. See also **Crossware**. |
| OSF | **Open Software Federation**. A multi-vendor body that defines and promotes open standards for Unix-based operating systems and software. |

*P*

| | |
|---|---|
| **Package** | **Group of MTS components**. A set of related components installed into **MTS** that are defined and used together in an application. The package defines the security trust boundary for the component group. |
| **PASSFILT** | **Password filter component.** An interchangeable software component within Windows NT that performs checking on user passwords as they are entered, ensuring they are strong enough to meet security requirements. |
| **PDC** | **Primary Domain Controller**. The Windows NT server installation that holds the central security and other information for the entire network domain. |
| **PEC** | **Primary Enterprise Controller**. The server that is at the root of Microsoft Message Queue Server enterprise. It stores the complete **MSMQ** Information Store database. |
| **Perl** | **Practical Extraction and Reporting Language**. A scripting language used with the first Web applications. Runs on the server and can create dynamic pages via the **CGI**. |
| **PFX** | **Personal Information Exchange**. A protocol that can safely and securely transfer the contents of a **PStore** from one location to another. |
| **PGP** | **Pretty Good Privacy**. An independently developed encryption application that uses public keys to allow secure transmission of messages. |
| **PING** | **Packet Internet Grouper**. A diagnostic utility program that uses **ICMP** to request messages from a remote server to check that it is available and can respond. |
| **PKCS** | **Public Key Cryptography Standard**. A generic term used to describe the various available types of public key encryption standards such as **DES, RSA**, etc. |
| **PNG** | **Portable Network Graphics**. A format for graphics and images that compresses the content to provide efficient transmission over a network. Developed by W3C, but not yet in commmon use. |
| **POP3** | **Post Office Protocol**. An Internet protocol designed to transmit email messages and attachments between mail servers. Offers extra features over the earlier **SMTP** protocol. |
| **PPP** | **Point-to-Point Protocol**. An industry-wide standard protocol that defines how packets are exchanged over the Internet, particularly via a modem. |
| **PPTP** | **Point-To-Point Tunneling Protocol**. A protocol that allows native network services such as **NetBEUI** and **IPX** to be used to create a secure and reliable connection over the Internet. |
| **Proxy** | **Software connection component**. A software program or service (as in proxy server) that acts as an intermediate gateway and connects two processes or users. In the case of a proxy server, it can also filter the network packets. |
| **PSC** | **Primary Site Controller**. A server that is at the root of Microsoft Message Queue Server site. It stores a copy of the part of an **MSMQ** Information Store database that applies to the site. |

| | |
|---|---|
| **PStore** | **Protected Information Store**. A Windows NT technology that provide a secure store for personal and security information about the network users. Can contain certificates, credit card details, personal information, etc. |
| **PTT** | **Private Telecommunications Technology**. A certificate-based protocol, similar to **SSL**, which can provide more robust and secure authentication and encryption over a network. |

## R

| | |
|---|---|
| **RAS** | **Remote Access Service**. A Windows technology that allows dial-up users to connect to a network (over a phone line or the Internet, for example) and access the resources on the network as though they were a local user. |
| **RDO** | **Remote Data Objects**. A Microsoft remote data access technology with a complex multi-level object model, introduced for use with programming languages like Visual Basic. Now superseded by **ADO**. |
| **RDS** | **Remote Data Service**. A Microsoft technology that provides a persistent and automatic method for caching data from a server-side data source on the client, for use in a Web page or other application. |
| **Role** | **Transaction Server security context**. Roles are used to define the user accounts that can execute a component running under **MTS**. They simplify security management in **DNA**-based applications. |
| **RPC** | **Remote Procedure Call**. A standard defined by the Open Software Foundation that allows one process to execute methods defined by another process, either on the same machine or across a network. |
| **RSA** | **Public key cryptography method**. A standard type of encryption technique designed by Rivest, Shamir and Adleman for securing data passing over a network or between components. |

## S

| | |
|---|---|
| **S/MIME** | **Secure Multipurpose Internet Mail Extension**. A version of **MIME** that allows the contents of the message and attachments to be digitally signed and encrypted, using standard public key ciphers, hash functions and certificates. |
| **SChannel** | **Secure Channel**. A security service provider module that sits on top of the Microsoft **CryptoAPI**, and implements the public key encryption between a client and the server. |
| **SDK** | **Software Development Kit**. A set of documentation, samples and tools that provide programmers with the information required to work with a technology - for example the **IE**4 **SDK** for Internet Explorer 4. |
| **SET** | **Secure Electronic Transaction**. A protocol for implementing secure electronic transactions over the Internet. Particularly aimed at financial institutions for handling credit card and related information. |

| | |
|---|---|
| SGML | **Standard Generalized Markup Language**. A root language for the formal definition of other markup languages, and not directly used for programming. Designed to provide portability and flexibility between markup languages based on it. |
| SHA | **Secure Hash Algorithm**. A software algorithm that creates a digest for a message or other stream of data. The digest is unique, and the original data cannot be recreated from it. |
| SID | **Security Identifier**. A non-volatile hidden **GUID** that identifies a user account in Windows NT. When accounts are deleted and recreated, a new **SID** is applied to them. The **SID** is passed between applications running under NT, instead of the username. |
| SMB | **Server Message Block**. A protocol used in Windows Networking to provide network-wide access to files and printers. |
| SMTP | **Simple Mail Transfer Protocol**. The first email transfer protocol for the Internet. Still used to transmit simple mail messages, but slowly being replaced by **POP3**. |
| SNA | **System Network Architecture**. A standard communication framework developed by IBM to allow communication between different models of computer, including minicomputers and mainframes. |
| SNMP | **Simple Network Management Protocol**. A standard for remote management of devices such as routers and other services over a **TCP/IP** network. Also provides monitoring services for a network. |
| SQL | **Structured Query Language**. A standard language for accessing data in relational databases. **ANSI** provide a base definition but many vendors have added extra proprietary features and extensions. |
| SSI | **Server-side Include**. An instruction within a Web page or script that causes the Web server to execute a program, or insert a file or other information into the **HTML** stream sent to the client. |
| SSL | **Secure Sockets Layer**. A technology originally developed by Netscape to provide client and server verification, and secure communication between a Web browser and server. Uses public key and secret key encryption. |
| SSP | **Security Support Provider**. A software library that manages a set of security functions. Multiple **SSP**s can be installed, each from a different vendor if required. See **SSPI**. |
| SSPI | **Security Service Provider Interface**. A standard programming interface specification that allows applications to query any SSP and use its services. Example **SSP**s are **Kerberos**, **NTLM**, and **SSL**. |
| Stub | **Software connection component**. A software component within an application that links to a corresponding proxy elsewhere, and handles the communication of data between them. May be running in a separate environment from the proxy, or just on a different execution thread. |

## T

| | |
|---|---|
| **TAPI** | **Telecommunications Application Programming Interface**. A set of standard programming functions that can be implemented by applications that interface with telecommunications equipment, i.e. telephones, exchanges, fax machines, voice mail, etc. |
| **TCO** | **Total Cost of Ownership**. The cost, generally far exceeding original purchase price, of a computer system. Includes such things as training, maintenance, support, consumables, etc. |
| **TCP** | **Transport Control Protocol**. The high-level part of the **TCP/IP** protocol. **TCP** creates the data packets and passes them to **IP** for transmission over the network. It is also responsible for marshalling and sorting received packets, and basic packet error detection. |
| **TCP/IP** | **Transport Control Protocol/Internet Protocol**. The base protocol of the Internet, also used on internal networks and Intranets. Passes data in routable packets between servers, and supports high-level protocols like **HTTP**, **FTP**, etc. |
| **TDC** | **Tabular Data Control**. An ActiveX control, part of the **MDAC** Universal Data Access components package, that provides client-side access and caching over **HTTP** for data stored in text format. |
| **TLA** | **Three Letter Acronym**. A recursive definition designed to make fun of the way the industry tends to name its products and services. |
| **TRID** | **OLE Transaction Identifier**. A unique identifier (**GUID**) for a transaction process that is executing against an **OLE** Transactions resource manager. |
| **TSQL** | **Transact SQL**. A set of extensions to **SQL** implemented in MS SQL Server, which allow (amongst other things) more complex queries to be created and compiled as stored procedures within the database. |

## U

| | |
|---|---|
| **UDA** | **Universal Data Access.** Microsoft term describing a concept of using one data access technology with all enterprise data sources. Based on **ADO** and **OLE DB**. See also **MDAC**. |
| **UNC** | **Uniform Naming Convention**. A combination of server name and resource path and name which identifies a resource on a local or wide-area network. Common **UNC**s start with the double-backslash, such as `\\sunspot\C\documents\myfile.doc`. |
| **URL** | **Universal Resource Locator**. A combination of a protocol, host name, (optional) port, path and resource name. Uniquely identifies a resource on the Internet. For example `http://www.wrox.com:8080/books/index.htm`. |

## V

| | |
|---|---|
| VB | **Visual Basic**. Microsoft's entry-level programming language and environment for Windows programming, including building components and specialist applications. |
| VBA | **Visual Basic for Applications**. Microsoft's version of Visual Basic that is designed to be used as a replacement and extension of macros in applications, rather than as a stand-alone programming language. |
| VJS | **Visual JavaScript**. A Netscape tool for rapid crossware development, providing an array of components and services together with an **HTML** page designer. |
| VRML | **Virtual Reality Modelling Language**. A strandardized programming language that allows moving 3D-style effects to be created within **HTML** applications. |

## W

| | |
|---|---|
| W3C | **World Wide Web Consortium**. The main body responsible for managing and ratifying standards for the Internet, especially the World Wide Web (WWW). |
| WAM | **Web Application Manager**. A sub-system component of **IIS** that is used to control applications that run in a separate area of memory (i.e. out of process) from the Web server. |
| WAN | **Wide Area Network**. A series of machines or networks that are outside the limits of normal network cable length limits. Usually connection is via phone lines or fibre optic cables, radio or satellite links, or the Internet. |
| WINS | **Windows Internet Name Service**. A protocol and corresponding service that maps textual addresses to the equivalent **IP** address in Windows-based networks. See also **DNS**. |
| WinSock | **Windows Sockets**. The software component that forms the connection to an **IP**-based network, and handles the transfer of data from the machine onto and off the network at the lowest level. |
| WOSA | **Windows Open System Architecture**. A range of **API**s that allow programmers to access various Windows technologies in a uniform and standard way. Includes specifications for **ODBC**, **MAPI**, and **TAPI**. |

# X

| | |
|---|---|
| **X.500** | **Directory access protocol**. The high-level specification and interface definition for directory access. Generally used in commercial mainframe environments. |
| **X.509** | **Certificate format standard.** The principal standard format definition for certificates that are used to provide encryption and authentication. |
| **XA** | **X/Open transaction interface**. The X/Open organization defined standard for communication between transaction managers and resource managers in a two-phase commit distributed transaction system. |
| **XATM** | **XA Transaction Manager**. A component included in **MTS** that allows transactions against data stores which use the **XA** interface to be integrated into **MTS** transactions. |
| **XID** | **XA Transaction Identifier**. A unique identifier for a transaction process that is executing against an **XA** resource manager. |
| **XML** | **Extensible Markup Language**. A new markup language based on **SGML**, and designed to remove the limitation imposed by **HTML**. Allows a page to contain a definition and execution plan for the elements, and well as their content. |
| **XSL** | **Extensible Stylesheet Language**. A specialist development of **XML** designed to provide flexible ways of adding style, display and layout information to a document. |

# Z

| | |
|---|---|
| **ZAW** | **Zero Administration for Windows**. A Microsoft initiative incorporated into **NT5** which provides ways to reduce the Total Cost of Ownership in networked environments by providing automatic software installation and fixes, and other features. |

# Index

# ASP Today

## www.asptoday.com

It's not easy keeping up to date with what's hot and what's not in the ever-changing world of internet development. Even if you stick to one narrow topic like ASP, trawling through the mailing lists each day and finding new and better code is still a twenty-four-seven job. Which is where we come in.

You already know Wrox Press from its series of titles on ASP and its associated technologies. We realise that we can't bring out a book everyday to keep you all up to date, so from March 1, we're starting a brand new website at www.asptoday.com which will do all the hard work for you. Every week you'll find new tips, tricks and techniques for you to try out and test in your development, covering ASP components, ADO, RDS, ADSI, CDO, Security, Site Design, BackOffice, XML and more. Look out also for bug alerts when they're found and fixes when they're available.

We hope that you won't be shy in telling us what you think of the site and the content we put on it either. If you like what you'll see, we'll carry on as we are, but if you think we're missing something, then we'll address it accordingly. If you've got something to write, then do so and we'll include it. We're hoping our site will become a global effort by and for the entire ASP community.

In anticipation,
Dan Maharry, ASPToday.com

**wrox**

PROGRAMMER TO PROGRAMMER™

Wrox writes books for you. Any suggestions, or ideas about how you want information given in your ideal book will be studied by our team. Your comments are always valued at Wrox.

Free phone in USA 800-USE-WROX
Fax (312) 397 8990

UK Tel. (0121) 687 4100      Fax (0121) 687 4101

**NB.** If you post the bounce back card below in the UK, please send it to:

Wrox Press Ltd., Arden House, 1102 Warwick Road,
Acocks Green, Birmingham B27 6BH. UK.

———— *Computer Book Publishers* ————

# Supporting you on the web
## http://www.wrox.com/

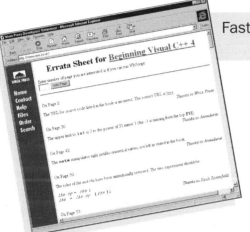

Fast download the source code to your book and collect updates on any errata

Preview forthcoming titles and test out some sample chapters

Get the full, detailed lowdown on any of our books - and read the reviews!

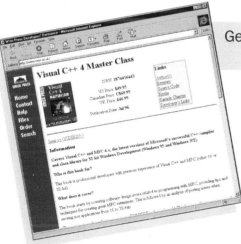

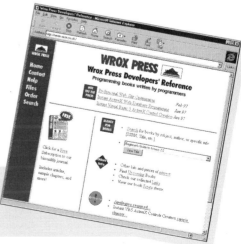

Sign-up for our free newspaper: "Developers' Journal" for Wrox activity, sample chapters and hot info on the industry

Drop into our mirror site at
## http://www.wrox.co.uk

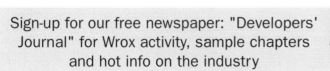